INVITATION TO THE LIFE COURSE:
Toward New Understandings of Later Life

Edited by
Richard A. Settersten, Jr.
Case Western Reserve University

Jon Hendricks, Series Editor

SOCIETY AND AGING SERIES

Baywood Publishing Company, Inc.
AMITYVILLE, NEW YORK

Library of Congress Catalog Number: 2001043577
ISBN: 0-89503-269-4 (cloth)

Library of Congress Cataloging-in-Publication Data

Invitation to the life course : toward new understandings of later life / edited by Richard A. Settersten, Jr.
    p. cm. - - (Society and aging series)
    Includes bibliographical references and index.
    ISBN 0-89503-269-4 (cloth)
    1. Gerontology. 2. Aging. 3. Life cycle, Human. I. Settersten, Richard A. II. Series.

HQ1061 .I584 2001
305.26- -dc21

                        2001043577

But at my back I alwaies hear
Times winged Chariot hurrying near:
And yonder all before us lye
Desarts of vast Eternity

Andrew Marvell (1621-1678), "To His Coy Mistress"

Table of Contents

Acknowledgments

This book grew out of a 1998 symposium at the annual meeting of the Gerontological Society of America. That symposium was titled "How Greater Attention to the Life Course Might Revolutionize Gerontology." In it, I brought together eight life-course scholars to think about the following question: If gerontologists were to take life-course concepts, principles, and methods more seriously, how might this change, and even revolutionize, scholarship on aging and later life? I asked participants to explore how greater attention to the life course might change the questions we ask, the kinds of data we collect, the ways in which we collect and analyze data, and how we interpret results and apply them to policy and practice. I asked participants to discuss the implications of life-course concerns for theories of aging—not only in terms of the potential to develop new theories, but also how existing theories might be expanded or revised. And I asked participants to speculate about the barriers that might prevent the field of gerontology from moving in these directions, and how we might overcome those barriers.

Professors Steve Cutler, Dale Dannefer, Christine Fry, Linda George, Gunhild Hagestad, Joe Hendricks, John Henretta, and I were all involved in the GSA symposium. To our surprise, over three hundred people came to hear that session. I would like to express my gratitude to everyone for their initial participation in the symposium, and for expanding and revising their papers several times in the space of time between then and now. I would also like to thank those who attended that session and participated in the discussion. Your enthusiastic response led us to develop the book you now hold before you. As the project grew, Drs. Leonard Cain, Glen Elder, Monica Johnson, and Boaz and Eva Kahana joined us. I would like to express my gratitude to them for their valuable contributions. They, like the others, were patient in developing their chapters in response to several rounds of commentary and queries.

I am very grateful for the assistance of Ms. Tanetta Andersson and Ms. Lisa Martin, two doctoral students in the Department of Sociology at Case Western Reserve University. Ms. Andersson, in particular, deserves special thanks, for she worked at my side for long hours proofreading and editing the manuscripts. Ms. Richelle Frances, Ms. Abby Gould, and Mr. Ezra Miklowski, three undergraduate students at CWRU, also helped with the final round of editions.

Professor Joe Hendricks, editor of the *Society and Aging Series* at Baywood, deserves special thanks for nurturing the project and for being tolerant of the inevitable delays that come with collaborative work. Joe oversaw the production of my previous book *Lives in Time and Place* (Baywood, 1999), and the central issues at stake in *Invitation to the Life Course* are a natural extension of that book. Throughout the process, Joe has been generous and has had great confidence in my scholarship. Thanks are also due to Mr. Stuart Cohen, Ms. Bobbi Olszewski, Ms. Julie Krempa, and others at Baywood Publishing Company for their support of the project.

Finally, I am fortunate to have an intimate circle of family and friends, and many supportive colleagues scattered across the globe. Thank you all for nourishing my mind and soul. I dedicate this book to my parents, Richard and Diann, for their love and support, and to the newest member of my family: Brandon Richard Wilson, who entered the world on August 14, 2000. Brandon is a remarkable reminder of the sheer wonder of human life. To him, I offer a passage from Victor Hugo's "By the Seaside": "Man is a point in space that flies with two great wings, Whereof the one is thought and th' other one is love." With wings of thought and love, you will always fly high.

—R.A.S.

INTRODUCTION
Invitation to the Life Course: The Promise

Richard A. Settersten, Jr.

In Michael Ondaatje's (1992, p. 261) novel *The English Patient*, the character Almásy has a profound revelation as he carries his dead lover Katherine into the desert:

> We die containing a richness of lovers and tribes, tastes we have swallowed, bodies we have plunged into and swum up as if rivers of wisdom, characters we have climbed into as if trees, fears we have hidden in as if caves. I wish for all of this to be marked on my body when I am dead. I believe in such cartography.

I, along with the other contributors to this volume, also believe in such cartography. In many ways, *Invitation to the Life Course: Toward New Understandings of Later Life* is a book aimed at the cartography of human lives, at understanding its maps. Each of the contributors to this volume has something to say about how we might come to better know the life course in contemporary societies, and how we might come to better know how that course is conditioned by time and place. Most importantly, each contributor hopes to address how these understandings carry important messages for inquiry about later life in particular, as aging (as a process) and old age (as a life period) must be accompanied by serious and systematic inquiry about the larger life course.

The foremost challenges to understanding the life course involve confronting a wide range of complexities associated with time. We must address a lived past—paths already traveled, whether chosen or forced; dreams attained, deferred, revised, or abandoned. But we must also address an anticipated future—trips expected or planned, possible routes to those places, and strategies for managing the terrain along the way. As Kierkegaard once observed, "life can only be

1

understood backwards; but it must be lived forwards," and our scientific treatments of the life course must take both retrospective and prospective views. Our treatments must take a long view of lives, mapping change and stability in individual development over many decades and explicating its causes and consequences, whether near or far away in time.

Like Shakespeare's Prospero in *The Tempest*, developmental scientists interested in midlife and beyond must confront the "dark backward and the abysm of time." This great "dark backward" relates to the fact that individuals arrive at these periods with long histories behind them, and that these pasts play critical roles in determining who they are in the second half of life and how it is experienced. Indeed, a central proposition of life-course scholarship is that development is lifelong, and that aging is a process that begins at birth, not some arbitrary point in later life. Yet these and other temporal connections are seldom taken seriously in developmental scholarship. For example, as Neugarten (1996) has argued, the field of gerontology is often "so tightly limited that you forget that a person who is 65 is a product of what he's been before. If you don't understand what he's been before, you're not going to understand him when he's old." Neugarten's comment captures the importance of tending to individuals' personal histories as we attempt to understand aging. While the same comment applies to scholarship on other periods of life, tending to the past is simultaneously more necessary and problematic for those interested in the second half of life in that they must accommodate five to as many as ten decades of lived (rather than projected) experiences. Of course, those interested in earlier life periods must instead deal with a great "dark forward"—rather than have to account for a long (but certain) past, they must instead attempt to understand how early experiences set the stage for an equally long (but uncertain) future. There is a natural, mutual attraction between scholarship on the life course and scholarship on aging.

Time is not the only dimension that poses more than its fair share of challenges for developmental scientists. Many complexities are also posed by place. Human development is intimately shaped by many social contexts both near to, and far from, individuals—including families, peer and friendship groups, schools, neighborhoods, work organizations, health care institutions, social programs and policies, historical events and periods of social change, and culture. We must understand when and how those spaces structure pathways through life and how they affect the nature and meaning of experiences along the way. And just as we must take a dynamic view of individuals' lives, we must also take a dynamic view of environments, examining when and how the characteristics and processes in those spaces change, and examining intricate connections between changing individuals and changing environments.

If gerontologists were to take life-course concerns more seriously, how might this change, and even revolutionize, scholarship on aging and later life? This book explores how greater attention to matters of time and place might change the research questions we ask, the kinds of data we collect, the ways in which we collect, analyze, and interpret data, and the implications our results hold for policy and practice. It also discusses their implications for theories of aging and later life—not only the potential for new theories, but also how existing theories might be revised or expanded in light of these concerns. It also considers the barriers that prevent the field of gerontology from moving in these directions and how these barriers might be overcome.

ON LIFE-COURSE PROPOSITIONS
AND CONTROVERSIES

Part I introduces life-course concepts, principles, and methods now emerging across academic disciplines. In Chapter 1, "Propositions and Controversies in Life-Course Scholarship," I begin by outlining the core propositions that guide developmental theory and research. Applied to the field of gerontology, these include the need to examine and explain:

- Aging as multidimensional, multispheral, and multidirectional.
- Aging as a lifelong process.
- The meanings and uses of age for individuals, groups, and societies.
- How aging-related experiences are conditioned by cohort and key demographic parameters (especially mortality, morbidity, and fertility).
- Movement through later life as a set of multiple, interdependent pathways; the proximal and distal precursors and consequences of experiences that mark those pathways; and the processes and mechanisms that drive these connections.
- How the aging-related experiences of individuals are tied to those of significant others.
- How aging-related experiences vary within individuals over time; across cohort, sex, race, and social class groups; across generations within families; across nations or cultures; and across species.
- Aging-related experiences as joint products of individual and collective action ("human agency") and the location of individuals and groups in society ("social structure").
- How aging-related experiences are shaped by proximal and distal social settings, including families, peer and friendship groups, schools, neighborhoods, work organizations, health care institutions, social policies, historical events and social change, and culture.

In the second part of Chapter 1, several emerging debates are introduced about time, age, and the rhythm of the life course in modern societies. One set of debates concerns the degree to which lives are, or have become, "chronologized" (bound to time and age), "institutionalized" (structured by social institutions and the state and its policies), and "standardized" (exhibit regularity and patterning). Another debate concerns the degree to which pathways through education, work, family, and other life spheres are, or have become, chronologized, institutionalized, and standardized. A final debate relates to differences in the degree to which men's and women's lives are, or have become, chronologized, institutionalized, and standardized.

PROMISES FOR THE GENERAL STUDY OF AGING AND LATER LIFE

Part II considers the implications of life-course concepts, principles, and methods for the general study of later life. In Chapter 2, "The Life Course and Aging: Challenges, Lessons, and New Directions," Glen Elder and Monica Johnson highlight the contributions that early longitudinal studies brought to contemporary understandings of adult development and aging, and how these advances have shaped contemporary agendas in the social and behavioral sciences. Elder and Johnson suggest that the recent growth of longitudinal studies has prompted a significant need for new theories and methods that handle time and space. They show how the emergence of life-course models offers powerful lenses for examining aging and later life. They turn our attention to how aging and later life are tied to social settings and historical time; determined by effort and planning, and by the life stages of individuals; and bound to relationships with other people. Drawing on insights from select empirical studies, Elder and Johnson illustrate how these issues might be better addressed in research on aging and later life. They close by outlining important new directions for research, particularly in incorporating personal agency and subjective perspectives, capturing the complexities of individual lives and environments (whether static or dynamic), and linking changes in individuals with changes in contexts.

PROMISES FOR UNDERSTANDING AGING AND LATER LIFE IN SPECIFIC SPHERES

Part III examines the implications of life-course concepts, principles, and methods for studying aging and later life in specific spheres: work and retirement (Chapter 3); leisure and social participation (Chapter 4); family (Chapter 5); and health and illness (Chapter 6). In Chapter 3, "The Life-Course Perspective on Work and Retirement," John Henretta begins by addressing the "institutionalization" of work and retirement because the structure of work determines much of social life in contemporary societies. Henretta's treatment of the institutionalization of work and retirement is placed within the context of debates about the "tripartition" of the life course. From this perspective, work organizes the modern life course, which is split into three distinct periods: an early segment devoted to education and training for work, a middle segment devoted to continuous work activity, and a final segment devoted to leisure. This creates an age-differentiated life course, which restricts education, work, and leisure to particular periods of life.

Henretta turns our attention to individual lives and especially the connections between institutional models and individuals' actual courses and the degree to which individual courses deviate from institutional models. Institutions set parameters on individual lives, but do not fully determine them. Henretta calls for dedicated examinations of connections between earlier and later events in individuals' work careers and of how individuals' work experiences are critically shaped by experiences outside of work. He also emphasizes the need to better integrate structural and agency-oriented perspectives because important new frontiers of scholarship on work, aging, and the life course lie at the intersection between institutional and individual levels. To reach these new frontiers, we must conceptualize and measure the degree to which, and how, institutions and careers are age-based and change in form over time. Henretta asks us to examine why educational institutions and work organizations are so rigidly age-graded, what is gained or lost in the process, and for whom. Like others in the volume, Henretta notes the demanding claims that the life-course framework makes on research—especially in terms of the types of data and analytic strategies it requires. He offers some ideas about how we might use existing data more creatively and gather new data to better meet these demands.

In Chapter 4, "Leisure in Life-Course Perspective," Joe Hendricks and Steve Cutler extend life-course concepts, principles, and methods to the topic of leisure. Like Henretta (Chapter 3), Hendricks and Cutler are concerned with the segmentation of the life course into the three boxes of education-work-leisure, as the structure and content of the leisure box are determined by the other boxes. Hendricks and Cutler consider the relevance of leisure for identities and experiences, how these relationships change over time, and how shifts in social contexts alter the nature of leisure opportunities. They highlight several trends that make it likely that leisure will play a greater role in the lives of older persons, including gains in life expectancy, improvements in health, earlier or intermittent retirement, and changes in the economy. Hendricks and Cutler persuasively argue that the topic of leisure deserves—and will take—a prominent place on the research and policy agendas of gerontologists, and they close by speculating about new directions for scholarship on leisure. Hendricks and Cutler emphasize that those who study leisure and aging must recognize the importance of individuals' decisions and shifting priorities around leisure, not just how their circumstances set parameters on their leisure activities. The nexus between leisure and aging is a critical "interpretive zone" in which individuals evaluate and express themselves, and leisure activities are a primary means for creating and sustaining meaning in later life.

In Chapter 5, "Interdependent Lives and Relationships in Changing Times: A Life-Course View of Families and Aging," Gunhild Hagestad explores how life-course concepts, principles, and methods advance our understandings of aging and the family. The life-course framework takes dynamic views of individuals and members of their families, and asks how the family setting is shaped by wider and more distal social contexts, such as history and culture. It places families at "center stage" and focuses on how families mediate between individual lives and societies, all of which change over time. It conceptualizes families as bundles of inter-connected lives, and it begs us to study those bundles as units in their own right. Hagestad explores complex relationships between individual life paths, dynamic family systems composed of interdependent relationships, and changing societies. As Hagestad considers the societal level, she highlights how family policies reinforce cultural scripts and are built on assumptions about family structures and roles, especially those related to gender. Family policies place constraints on individual family members and larger family dynamics over time, though they may also offer opportunities. Hagestad also emphasizes how individuals' family trajectories, and larger rhythms of family life, are bound to historical time and reflect the cultural, economic, political, and demographic conditions of those times. Dramatic social and demographic change in the 20th century has trans-formed the structure and experience of family life, and families of the early 21st century look and feel very different than families of the past. Hagestad closes with a discussion, prompted by life-course concerns, of important new questions that must be asked about aging and the family, new approaches to studying those questions, and new kinds of data required to answer them.

In Chapter 6, "What Life-Course Perspectives Offer the Study of Aging and Health," Linda George emphasizes the fact that while health and illness are states, and are most often studied as such, they also are processes that develop and have consequences over time. As a result, George focuses on long-term relationships between social factors and illness, on patterns that emerge over many years and span more than one period of life. George makes a strong case for why it is imperative to examine the long-ranging connections between factors and processes related to variable illness outcomes, and why the concepts, principles, and methods of life-course research are important tools with which to solve pressing questions about aging and illness. George argues that the life-course framework is best used in conjunction with existing theoretical "paradigms" in the social and behavioral sciences. She therefore anchors her discussion within the stress paradigm, which has guided much scholarship on social factors and illness. George argues that there are significant, natural links between the life-course framework and the study of social factors and illness, in that notions of time and process have long been part of this tradition. She explores how stress-related models might be revised or expanded in light of life-course concerns. To illustrate the power of a marriage between the stress paradigm and the life-course frame-work, George builds conceptual and methodological applications to several dif-ferent areas of inquiry, especially to physical disability, functional impairments, and mental health. George closes with other insights into how the life-course framework promises significant advances for the study of social factors, health, illness, and longevity. While implementing research in these directions brings obstacles, George discusses how obstacles might be overcome, what goals should be set for the future, and what steps should be taken in the interim to advance scholarship in these directions.

PROMISES FOR SOCIAL POLICY

Part IV considers the implications of life-course concepts, principles, and methods for social policy. In Chapter 7, "Rethinking Social Policy: Lessons of a Life-Course Perspective," I take up the intersection between human development and social policy, and the important role that social policies play in structuring the life course. I develop a framework with which developmental scientists, policy-makers, and policy-analysts might better address this intersection. To illustrate these connections, examples are drawn from the central policies of the American welfare state and a variety of state- and local-level policies, and those of private organizations and firms, related to education, work, family, and health. Were we to approach social policy with these questions in mind, we would alter its development, implementation, evaluation, and reform—and, in turn, improve human development and social welfare. To do so, we must also better couple the policy-making process with behavioral and social scientific research on aging and the life course. Well-crafted evaluation research will also not only shed further light on theory, but it will teach us important lessons about how to design and reform policy in the future.

PROMISES FOR UNDERSTANDING
SUCCESSFUL AGING

Part V examines the implications of life-course concepts, principles, and methods for "successful aging," one of the largest and most active strands of gerontological scholarship. In Chapter 8, "Contextualizing Successful Aging: New Directions in an Age-Old Search," Eva and Boaz Kahana point to the challenges of developing models of successful aging that address temporal and spatial contexts, yet they also show how important it is to move in these directions. To illustrate these challenges, the Kahanas extend their own model of successful aging—the model of Preventive and Corrective Proactivity (PCP)—in time and space. Their model, like much of the research that George brings to matters of health and illness (Chapter 6), is anchored in the stress paradigm.

The Kahana's revised model incorporates aspects of biography and history, on the one hand, and demographic and social contexts of successful aging, on the other. They illustrate the advantages of the expanded model by drawing upon data from their decade-long Florida Retirement Study, and by examining the relationships between gender, stress exposure, and proactivity, in particular. The Kahanas also discuss notions of successful aging within the context of alternative

models to the stress paradigm, and they consider both conceptual and methodological limitations of stress-based approaches and how these limitations might
be overcome.

FURTHER PROMISES FOR SCHOLARSHIP ON
AGING AND LATER LIFE

Part VI is composed of three final chapters by Dale Dannefer, Christine Fry,
and Leonard Cain. These chapters provide additional reflections on the power of
life-course concepts, principles, and methods for the field of gerontology. Rather
than discuss specific contributions of prior chapters in the volume, Dannefer, Fry,
and Cain use the earlier chapters as a springboard from which to launch their own
insightful discussions about the promises of a union between scholarship on the
life course and scholarship on aging and later life.

In Chapter 9, "Whose Life Course Is It, Anyway?: Diversity and 'Linked
Lives' in Global Perspectives," Dale Dannefer points to the need to more seriously
explore and explain variability in life-course experiences. He argues that many of
our descriptions and explanations of aging and life-course patterns are irrelevant to
the everyday reality of many groups of individuals worldwide. He reflects on three
"alternative" or "atypical" populations that have been ignored in life-course
scholarship: the working children of the third world, Los Angeles street gang
members, and Amazonian shamans. As Dannefer discusses the conditions of the
first two groups in particular, he develops the tantalizing hypothesis that the
oppressive life situations of these two groups are created by the desires and
lifestyles of those in the mainstream of modern Western societies. Dannefer argues
that scholarship must expand by studying the experiences of populations that have
been overlooked. What, he asks, can we expect of scholarship if it does not reflect
1) the range of life-course patterns found globally, and 2) what those patterns
mean for individuals' opportunities to develop and be valued in their societies?

In Chapter 10, "The Life Course as a Cultural Construct," anthropologist
Christine Fry explores the "deep structure" cultural assumptions upon which the
life course is based, and the assumptions about culture that underlie behavioral and
social scientific research. Fry argues that specifying and handling time and age are
central challenges to understanding variability in aging and the life course across
cultures. In particular, she discusses cultural notions of "staged," "generational,"
and "age-classed" life courses, and of time and calendars for marking time. Fry
also reflects on the many different types of time represented across the chapters of
this book, including "age/time," "health time," "work and leisure time," "family
time," and "state time."

Leonard Cain's chapter on "Age-Related Phenomena: The Interplay of
the Ameliorative and the Scientific" (Chapter 11) closes the volume. In 1964,
Cain wrote what I think is one of the most important but under-appreciated early
essays on the life course. In "Life Course and Social Structure," Cain offered many

sociological insights into why the study of aging and later life must be accompanied by the study of the life course. He linked age statuses to biological, demographic, and social determinants; to social institutions, such as the family, religion, politics, law and social policy, work and the economy; and to social change, including generational phenomena and youth and old age movements.

In Chapter 11, Cain now reflects on some of the central themes of his work, covering nearly four decades of scholarship since that early chapter. He discusses age status as an institution, generational phenomena and birth cohort analysis, aging and the law, and, to a lesser degree, aging and the family. A central tension throughout his chapter is that between "ameliorative" gerontology (which explicitly advocates on behalf of older people, and which focuses on what "ought to be") and "scientific" gerontology (which does not inherently seek to advocate on behalf of older people, and which focuses more on what "is"). He concludes by reiterating some "intemperate remarks" from the past, and by speculating about the prospects for integrating the endeavors of social gerontologists with those of sociologists of age and the life course.

FINAL THOUGHTS

Invitation to the Life Course: Toward New Understandings of Later Life is a natural extension of *Lives in Time and Place: The Problems and Promises of Developmental Science* (Settersten, 1999), which discusses the challenges of handling matters of time and place in developmental scholarship. Together with Giele and Elder's (1999) *Methods of Life-Course Research: Qualitative and Quantitative Approaches, Lives in Time and Place* is a good reference for those who want to learn about and conduct life-course research. There is much talk about "life-course" and "life-span" theory and research, yet few scholars actually *do* it. Instead, the terms "life course" and "life span" are most often general references to time and not to a common set of concepts, principles, and methods. A central premise of this volume is that if scholars who focus on specific age groups were to seriously incorporate (and not just pay lip service to) life-course concepts, principles, and methods, the face of developmental science would be revolutionized. It would largely change the theory we generate, the questions we ask, the data we collect, and the ways in which we analyze, interpret, and apply our data. Yet the contributors to this volume also suggest that we will never (and should not try to) create an all-encompassing "theory" of the life course. Instead, we must make it our mission to transform substantive areas of disciplinary and interdisciplinary scholarship by infusing them with life-course concepts, principles, and methods. Nowhere is this more important than in the field of gerontology, and each of the contributors to this volume hopes to move scholarship on aging in these directions. They illustrate why aging (as a process) and old age (as a period) must be accompanied by systematic attention to the life course as a whole.

Some scholars have even expressed the hope that the study of specific life periods will vanish altogether. For example, Neugarten recently made what became a controversial statement among gerontologists: "When I am asked about the future of gerontology, I am greatly tempted to predict that the field of gerontology is going to disappear over the next couple of decades" (Neugarten, 1996 [1994], p. 402). Why? From an intellectual or academic standpoint, aging is a lifelong process that begins at birth, not at an arbitrary point in the latter third of life. Age-based academic specialties belittle the idea of lifelong development; an individual cannot be understood at a particular point in time by ignoring her or his past. From a policy standpoint, age-related entitlements are being called into question. And on the "front lines," service providers are also recognizing that it is hard to design and provide services for clients based on age alone. However, age-based specialties continue to "justify professional specialization and the preoccupations of professionals with particular ages, as well as the organization of professionalized services around the age of the population served" (Schroots, 1995, p. 48). The compartmentalization of scholarship on specific life phases seems entrenched in the organization of developmental science (Magnusson & Stattin, 1998; Settersten, 1999).

It is time for change. It is not enough to simply note that age-specific research must be placed within a lifelong framework. We must actively generate substantive theory, ask questions, collect data, and choose methods with the whole of life in mind. Of course, this is not to imply these can be managed well in a single study. The life-course framework, like other more "metatheoretical frameworks" (Winegar, 1997), is a broad heuristic device, and it makes strong demands of our theoretical and empirical work. Yet the intention of such frameworks has never been that the entire universe ought to be examined in a single study. Bergman and Magnusson (1997), in discussing holistic, interactionist models of human development, draw a parallel to the natural sciences: The "fact that specific studies in, for example, nuclear physics or astrophysics are planned and interpreted with reference to the same general model of nature does not imply that each study includes the whole universe. A common general framework does, however, facilitate communication between different researchers and the accumulation of knowledge" (p. 291). Admittedly, individual scientists will inevitably have to direct their work at specific aspects of the framework or incorporate limited parts of it. But having a common framework permits scholars to communicate more effectively and better coordinate and integrate the results of a cumulative body of scientific work (see also Magnusson, 1995). This also requires scholars to take an active interest in the theories and concepts of other disciplines, and to embrace different epistemological-ontological assumptions and their associated methodological implications. At the same time, it is clear that the organization of science makes it difficult for this to happen, particularly with respect to overcoming obstacles to conducting interdisciplinary scholarship (see Settersten, 1999).

As the contributors to this volume clearly show, scholarship on aging and later life has much to gain by taking life-course matters seriously, despite the many challenges these matters bring to our work. These are exciting times for developmental science, for the theoretical and methodological advances of the last few decades have changed the face of our scholarship. There is a growing sense that a bright new dawn looms on the horizon—something akin to Kuhn's (1962) "scientific revolution" or to Merton's (1968) time of great "anticipations and adumbrations." This excitement is fostered as we develop and integrate an emerging set of concepts, principles, and methods related to the study of lives, and as we generate theory and conduct research in line with them.

To close this chapter, I offer a vision from Norman Maclean's (1976, p. 104) *A River Runs Through It:*

> As the heat mirages on the river in front of me danced with and through each other, I could feel patterns from my own life joining with them . . . stories of life are often more like rivers than books. . . . Eventually, all things merge into one, and a river runs through it. The river was cut by the world's great flood and runs over rocks from the basement of time. On some of the rocks are timeless raindrops. Under the rocks are the words, and some of the words are theirs. I am haunted by waters.

Developmental scientists, too, are haunted by stories of life. Like Maclean's raging river, the words on which we rely are found within those we study: they are stories of life as composed by those who have lived them. Yet many of the words are also ours: they are stories we tell about lives, whether individual or collective, that are based on research we have conducted and theories we have generated. In the end, they are also stories built upon the lives of those who have come before us: on the individuals and families formally documented in the historical record or informally preserved in the tales passed down from one generation to the next, and on prior scholars on whose shoulders we stand.

Unlike Maclean's raging river, however, these stories rarely merge into one. Despite our dedicated search for patterns, we are haunted by the complex and variable nature of lives in contemporary societies. And we are haunted by the questions that these complexities pose for our work: Questions about how human development is conditioned by time and place. Questions about knowing and about ways of knowing. Questions about maps.

REFERENCES

Bergman, L. R., & Magnusson, D. (1997). A person-oriented approach in research on developmental psychopathology. *Development and Psychopathology, 9,* 291-319.

Cain, L. D., Jr. (1964). Life course and social structure. In R. Faris (Ed.), *Handbook of modern sociology* (pp. 272-309). Chicago: Rand-McNally.

Giele, J., & Elder, G. H., Jr. (Eds.) (1999). *Methods of life-course research: Qualitative and quantitative approaches.* Newbury Park, CA: Sage.

Kuhn, T. S. (1962). *The structure of scientific revolutions.* Chicago: University of Chicago Press.

Maclean, N. (1976). *A river runs through it and other stories.* Chicago: University of Chicago Press.

Magnusson, D. (1995). Individual development: A holistic integrated model. In P. Moen, G. H. Elder, Jr., & K. Lüscher (Eds.), *Examining lives in context: Perspectives on the ecology of human development* (pp. 19-60). Washington, DC: American Psychological Association.

Magnusson, D., & Stattin, H. (1998). Person-context interaction theories. In R. M. Lerner (Ed.), *Handbook of child psychology: Vol. 1. Theoretical models of human development* (5th ed., pp. 685-759). New York: John Wiley & Sons.

Merton, R. K. (1968). *Social theory and social structure.* New York: The Free Press.

Neugarten, B. L. (1996 [1994]). The end of gerontology? In D. Neugarten (Ed.), *The meanings of age: Selected papers of Bernice L. Neugarten* (pp. 402-403). Chicago, IL: University of Chicago Press.

Neugarten, B. L. (1996). *Nothing as rich as human life: A conversation with Bernice Neugarten, PhD* [videorecording]. Chicago, IL: Buehler Center on Aging, Northwestern University.

Ondaatje, M. (1992). *The English patient.* New York: Vintage Books International.

Schroots, J. J. F. (1995). Psychological models of aging. *Canadian Journal on Aging, 14*(1), 44-66.

Settersten, R. A., Jr. (1999). *Lives in time and place: The problems and promises of developmental science.* Amityville, NY: Baywood.

Winegar, L. T. (1997). Developmental research and comparative perspectives: Applications to developmental science. In J. Tudge, M. J. Shanahan, & J. Valsiner (Eds.), *Comparisons in human development* (pp. 13-33). New York: Cambridge University Press.

PART I

On Life-Course Propositions and Controversies

CHAPTER 1

Propositions and Controversies in Life-Course Scholarship*

Richard A. Settersten, Jr.

Through the first half of the 20th century, the study of human development was largely devoted to child development. It was not until the latter half of the 20th century that developmental scientists more seriously turned their attention to adult development and aging. As they did, several important challenges surfaced (see Elder, 1998; Settersten, 1999). The concepts and issues at stake with respect to children could not simply be extended to adults. And new and difficult questions were raised about continuity and change in adult lives over time, about social settings that structure movement through those years, about connections between lives, time, and place, and how to handle these complexities in theory and research. These remain the most important challenges for developmental scholarship in the 21st century. In addition, early models were developed under very different demographic conditions, and dramatic demographic change in the past century has set new and unknown parameters on human life.

Earlier notions of the "life course," "life span," and "life cycle" were in principle based on holistic conceptions of human lives. Yet the dominant theme was one borrowed from biology: maturation and growth, followed by decline and regression. Only as a subtopic did the idea of *lifelong* growth, whether actual or potential, begin to surface (Baltes, Lindenberger, & Staudinger, 1998). While the terms "life course," "life span," and "life cycle" are often used interchangeably, they have different intellectual origins and concerns (for a review, see O'Rand & Krecker, 1990). Yet as these terms are commonly used, they do not carry strong assumptions but instead denote temporality in a general sense.

---

*This chapter draws some material from Chapter 1 of *Lives in Time and Place: The Problems and Promises of Developmental Science* (Settersten, 1999).

Most developmental scientists view the term "life cycle" as problematic. Strictly defined, "life cycle" refers to "maturational and generational processes driven by mechanisms of reproduction in natural populations" (O'Rand & Krecker, 1990, p. 242). That is, these models posit the life movement through a fixed sequence of irreversible stages, some part of which is tied to sexual reproduction. These are cyclical in that they assume that phenomena repeat themselves from one generation to the next, that the organism regularly returns to certain states or circumstances throughout life, or that the organism ends life in the same state or circumstance in which it began life. Many early "stage" theories in psychology exemplify this spirit (e.g., Erikson, 1980; Freud, 1923). Similarly, "family life cycle" models, popular from the post-war years through the early 1960s, construed family life as a fixed sequence of discrete stages. These stages were marked by "courtship, engagement, marriage, birth of the first and last child, children's transition in school, departure of the eldest and youngest child from the home, and marital dissolution through the death of one spouse" (Elder, 1998, p. 945).

"Life cycle" models seem largely inappropriate in contemporary times. Marriage and parenting are often independent of one another; family size has shrunk; a period of cohabitation may occur before marriage; "non-traditional" family forms are prevalent; divorce occurs in record numbers; children return to the nest; and the joint survival time of spouses has lengthened. In the modern world, these models seem too deterministic and leave little or no room for deviation. Indeed, few developmental scientists today value models proposed as fixed and universal. These models ignore the ways in which lives are self-regulated and variable. In addition, models that explicitly tie human development to reproduction cannot be applied to individuals who do not, or cannot, parent.

This chapter introduces propositions and controversies about human development and the life course that are emerging across academic disciplines. The first part of the chapter outlines some central principles that underlie and guide developmental theory and research, drawing especially on advances in life-course sociology and life-span developmental psychology. The life-span orientation in psychology emphasizes "intra-psychic" (or interior) phenomena and changes in these phenomena over the span of individual lives. In contrast, the life-course perspective in sociology emphasizes external social forces, changes in those forces over time and, ultimately, how they shape the development of individuals and larger groups. Though the term "life course" is associated with the discipline of sociology, this chapter does not equate life-course scholarship as the exclusive terrain of sociology. Instead, this chapter and others equate life-course scholarship with "developmental science" (Carolina Consortium on Human Development, 1996; Settersten, 1999)—a synthesis of central concepts, propositions, and methods pertaining to human development that cuts across disciplines and life periods. Table 1, which appears at the conclusion of the chapter, outlines the most central of these propositions and controversies at-a-glance.

EMERGING PROPOSITIONS IN LIFE-COURSE SCHOLARSHIP

Development as Multidimensional and Multispheral

Individual development is *multidimensional,* occurring along biological, psychological, and social dimensions. It is also *multispheral,* occurring in family, work, education, leisure, and other spheres. Life-course scholarship seeks not only to address multiple dimensions and spheres, but also to *link dimensions together and to link spheres together*—experiences in one dimension or sphere carry significant implications for experiences along other dimensions or spheres. For example, psychological or social well-being are tied to physical well-being (and vice versa), just as educational or work-related experiences are conditioned by family matters (and vice versa).

Life-Course Scholarship as Multidisciplinary or Interdisciplinary

Given the orientation just described, life-course scholarship is inherently *multidisciplinary.* At the very least, it requires contributions from anthropology, biology, economics, history, psychology, sociology, and other disciplines. Ideally, life-course scholarship also aspires to be *interdisciplinary,* moving in directions that transcend disciplinary boundaries and actively integrate disciplinary perspectives.

Development as Multidirectional

Individual development is also *multidirectional,* characterized by differing levels and rates of change across dimensions of functioning. In fact, development involves the *simultaneous occurrence of both gains (growth) and losses (declines)* within and between areas of functioning. Indeed, in life-span developmental psychology, one of the most common approaches to defining "successful" development is to view it in terms of maximizing or promoting gains and minimizing or managing losses (Baltes, 1997). Gains and losses may be permanent (irreversible) or impermanent (reversible), and they may be more or less beneficial or costly depending on when they are experienced (Uttal & Perlmutter, 1989).

Development as Lifelong

A fundamental premise of life-course scholarship is that individual development is *lifelong* (Baltes et al., 1998). Development does not stop in adulthood, but extends from birth to death. Even in later life, development need not only be about decline, but may also involve psychological, social, and biological gains.

All life periods are understood to involve unique and important developmental experiences, and *no single age period is taken as more important than any other.* Few would contest the former point, though the latter may be questionable, given that gains during the later years surely pale in comparison to those early in life, just as losses in the early years surely pale in comparison to those later in life. In advanced old age, the balance between gains and losses becomes less positive, if not negative (Baltes, 1997). In addition, the "plasticity" (or malleability) of human potential decreases with age, and the optimization of development becomes increasingly difficult as life extends to its maximum biological limits (Baltes & Smith, 1999).

Given the lifelong nature of development, specific life periods (e.g., adolescence, adulthood, old age) cannot be adequately understood in isolation from other periods. While development during a specific life period may be unique, it is experienced within the context of the past, present, and anticipated future. As a result, the life course becomes "an endogenous causal system" (Mayer & Tuma, 1990). However, experiences early in childhood are no longer viewed as determining subsequent pathways through adolescence and adulthood. While early experiences set the stage for later experiences, these experiences need not be viewed as so constraining that individuals cannot move beyond them. Of course, even early conditions and experiences that are positive may carry unintended or unforeseen consequences.

Life-course scholarship takes a long view of development, one that incorporates the whole of life into theory and research. From this standpoint, it is important to consider how specific developmental sequelae play out over time. Developmental scientists who concentrate on different life periods must not only work together, but they must *integrate* theory and research on multiple life periods. As Baltes and colleagues (1998) have noted, there is significant need to generate theory and conduct research that "has as its *primary* substantive focus the structure, sequence, and dynamics of the *entire* life course" (p. 1034, emphasis added). Ultimately, these points emphasize the need to *take time and change seriously in research designs and sampling, data collection and organization, and analytic strategies* (for an overview, see Giele & Elder, 1999; Settersten, 1999).

Continuity and Discontinuity

The theme of *continuity and discontinuity* throughout adult life is one of the great themes of developmental scholarship. Some developmental processes are continuous and extend across life, while others are unique to certain periods and discontinuous over time. ("Discontinuity" may refer to a notable shift in *levels* of functioning or the emergence of qualitatively distinct *forms* of functioning.) However, explicit theoretical or empirical models for understanding continuity and discontinuity are seldom offered in the literature. In fact, Chiriboga (1996,

p. 174) notes that developmental scientists "have long decried the lack of theoretical guidelines for investigating continuity and change over time."

However, Gergen's (1977) three underlying models of adult development are a useful way to frame questions about continuity and discontinuity. These are the developmental stability model, the orderly change model, and the random change model. (For a classic introduction to models and theories of human development, see Reese and Overton, 1970). The *stability template* emphasizes the stability of "behavioral patterns" (and presumably traits, attitudes, and the like) over time. In the stability framework, "whatever exists tends to endure" (Gergen, 1977, p. 141). The template of *ordered change* emphasizes change over time, but change that is patterned, fixed, and forward-moving. In contrast, the *aleatory change* template takes little about development to be "preprogrammed." Our biological and psychological makeup establishes the *limits or range* of our activities, but *not* the precise character of the activities themselves" (p. 148, emphasis added). Of course, *social* systems do this as well. At the same time, some *dis*advantages may also be transcended. This makes the course of development contingent on many factors in both the individual and the environment, and therefore highly variable.

Twenty years ago, Gergen argued that the aleatory template was significantly less developed than the stability or ordered change templates. Nearly 25 years later, most developmental scholarship advocates a position in line with the aleatory template, though more in principle than practice. Many theoretical and methodological challenges come with identifying "continuity" and "discontinuity." But once continuities and discontinuities have been identified, we can explore their short- and long-term effects and the processes and mechanisms that bring them about.

The Salience of Age in the Life Course

Age is important from the perspectives of individuals, groups, and society. In fact, every society has unique ways of approaching the meanings and uses of age. Sociologists, historians, and anthropologists have long asked questions about the ways in which age functions in social structure: as a dimension organizing families, educational institutions, work organizations, and other spheres. Similarly, social psychologists and anthropologists have suggested that age functions as a convenient dimension with which to map social and cultural expectations about experiences and roles. Individuals use age-linked "mental maps" to organize their own lives, the lives of others, and their general expectations about the life course (Settersten & Hagestad, 1996a, 1996b). These maps, in turn, serve important human needs for order and predictability. Of course, lives as they are actually lived may deviate from cultural models of the life course (Rindfuss, Swicegood, & Rosenfeld, 1987). Indeed, age-related expectations and goals may differ by gender and other social dimensions (especially cohort, race, and social class), life sphere (family, education, work, or leisure), and culture. Individuals' perceptions, and the degree to which age is tied to these perceptions, may be powerful determinants of how the life course is actively negotiated and experienced (Fry, 1996).

Age also enters into and shapes everyday social interaction, affecting the expectations and evaluations of individuals involved in those exchanges. For example, age has been described as a "diffuse status characteristic," in that individuals may use cues about others' ages to make more general assumptions about their attributes and abilities (Boyd & Dowd, 1988). This practice seems especially likely when little else is known about a person besides visible "master status" characteristics such as race or sex. As Boyd and Dowd (1988, p. 87) point out, the "diffusiveness" of age probably has its origin in its "portability"—age always accompanies the individual.

Personality psychologists have also debated about whether and how age is linked to personality attributes and behavioral dispositions (e.g., Costa & McCrae, 1994), conceptions of the self (e.g., Markus & Herzog, 1991), and self-regulation and goal-setting (e.g., Heckhausen & Schulz, 1995).

Chronological age serves as a *rough indicator of biological, psychological, and social statuses.* Age itself is rarely assumed to cause something; instead, it is whatever age presumably indexes that is important. For example, age may index an individual's physical and emotional maturity, readiness to assume responsibilities, or the probability of experiencing medical or social problems (Chudacoff, 1989; Fry, 1986). In addition, most researchers do not use age as an index for a single underlying dimension or process, but instead for a host of dimensions and processes (Birren & Schroots, 1996).

However, the life-course framework emphasizes the need to *identify the processes and mechanisms that underlie age-related effects.* When researchers use age as a causal variable, they must consider why it is important, what exactly it indexes, and the processes and mechanisms through which it plays itself out over time. Similarly, researchers must not mistake the *age differences* that result from cross-sectional research designs (in which age, period, and cohort effects are confounded) for *age changes* that can only be demonstrated with longitudinal designs. *Cohorts* are generally defined as groups of people born at the same point in historical time, and *cohort effects* are the result of the unique historical times in which these groups are born and live their lives. (These will be discussed shortly.) *Age effects* come naturally with aging—they are due to maturation and transcend cohort. *Period* or *time-of-measurement* effects have relatively uniform effects across cohorts. For further discussion of these effects, and of the complexities of disentangling them in research, see Settersten (1999).

The Life Course as Age Stratified

The link between social structures and human lives has been a central concern to sociologists of the life course, and the "age-stratification" framework of Riley and her colleagues has been especially important in this regard (e.g., Riley, Foner, & Waring, 1988). This framework emphasizes the movement of individuals, as they grow up and older, through successive age "strata" (groups) in society. An age stratum is a position in the population structure, but it is constantly replenished as old members move out of it and new members move into it. Larger cohorts of individuals, born at specific points in historical time, therefore move together through age strata in the population as their lives unfold.

As individuals move through these strata, they move through sequences of roles and statuses. Many of the social settings in which these roles and statuses are located are *age-homogeneous.* For example, high schools and senior centers are age-homogeneous environments, with the former largely composed of young people and the latter largely composed of old people. However, some contexts are also *age-heterogeneous.* For example, the larger family matrix, and even the immediate family environment, is composed of individuals of varied ages. Regardless of whether particular settings are age-homogeneous or age-heterogeneous, *age strata are interdependent.* What happens in one stratum often has consequences for others, as the lives of members of different age strata are intertwined. They interact with, and are reciprocally socialized by, each other. Nonetheless, chasms or conflicts may emerge between age strata. For example, shared experiences or interests within a stratum may foster its solidarity as an age group and its tensions with other age groups.

More recent work in this tradition references the "dynamic interplay" between individuals and society (e.g., Riley, Kahn, & Foner, 1994). This work emphasizes that the *life patterns of successive cohorts are different because the social world changes and new life patterns, in turn, prompt change in the social world.* This reciprocity, in which people are both shaped by and actively shape their environments, is a key element in frameworks that emphasize the ecology of human development.

Riley and her colleagues argue that while lives change rapidly, social struc-tures fail to keep pace with these changes, thereby creating *structural lag.* They tie the problem of structural lag to society's inability to provide "meaningful opportunities" for people of all ages in the realms of education, work, family, and leisure. The problem of structural lag is taken to be the result of the heavily "age-differentiated" life course that is common in most modern societies (Keith, Fry, Glascock, Ikels, Dickerson-Putnam, Harpending, & Draper, 1994). In an age-differentiated life course, social roles and activities are restricted to, and allocated on the basis of, age or life stage. This brings us to what has been described as the "tripartition" of the life course (Kohli, 1986a).

The tripartition of the life course. From this perspective, *work is the central activity that organizes the modern life course,* which is split into three distinct periods. The early segment is devoted to *education and training* for work; the middle segment is devoted to continuous *work* activity; and the final segment is devoted to *leisure* and the absence of work activity. (Segments of this partition are discussed further in Chapters 3, 4, and 7.) Life-course scholarship is concerned with the *structure and content of these three periods,* and how this structure and content has *changed historically.* For example, the boundaries between the three "boxes" have shifted: The trend toward early retirement at the upper end of work life, coupled with an extension of schooling at the lower end of work life, has made the period of gainful work shorter. In addition, early retirement, coupled with increased longevity, has lengthened the period of retirement.

This tripartition is convenient in that it creates "orderliness" in the entry to, and exit from, social roles and activities; at the same time, it is "ageist" in that it restricts opportunities for various types of activities to specific periods of life (Riley, Kahn, & Foner, 1994). This tripartition is also reinforced by work and educational policies (see Chapter 7). There is growing interest in how to build an age-integrated life course, one in which opportunities for participation in all spheres of life are open to people of all ages (see a recent collection of papers edited by Uhlenberg & Riley, 2000).

The sphere of *family* is often de-emphasized in, or is absent from, discussions about age-differentiation and the life course, yet it is clear that family roles and responsibilities are also an important part of this equation. Indeed, family demands often explicitly condition participation in education, work, and leisure. However, the family sphere seems more naturally age-integrated than other spheres. It assembles together and connects individuals of different ages and from different cohorts, and family roles and activities also extend across the entire life course, though they clearly change as individuals grow up and older. At the same time, families are also differentiated by age, generation, and cohort, and demographic change has dramatically altered the structure of the extended family matrix. Increases in longevity and decreases in fertility have created "bean pole" families in which more generations are alive at once, fewer members exist within each generation, and generations are significantly different from one another in age (Bengtson, Rosenthal, & Burton, 1990). These shifts have, in turn, altered that nature and experience of family life (e.g., Hagestad, 1988; Riley, 1985; Uhlenberg, 1980). For example, children now come to know grandparents, great-grandparents, and even great-great-grandparents; and spouses, parents and children, and siblings survive jointly for long periods of time. Besides age integration, other forms of integration seem equally important, such as the need to provide more meaningful opportunities in education, work, family, and leisure for women and men, and across races, social classes, and other important social divisions.

The Life Course as Embedded in Historical Time and Bound to Cohort

Human lives are *framed by historical time and shaped by the unique social and cultural conditions* that exist during those times. This applies both to the course of individual lives and to the collective lives of larger cohorts of people born at similar points in historical time. Life-course scholarship emphasizes the likelihood that cohorts do not age alike, and that what is typical for one cohort may not apply to other cohorts. Many experiences related to aging are conditioned by cohort and the ways in which social, cultural, and environmental changes leave a unique imprint on members of a cohort.

Indeed, the field of gerontology is relatively "young," and most of what is known about aging has been based on cohorts born early in the 20th century. The lives of members of these cohorts have been much different from those of later cohorts. This raises a critical question about *generalizability:* To what degree have the effects of specific historical conditions on aging been mistaken for general aging patterns and processes? To what degree is knowledge about aging historically specific? This is what Caspi (1998) calls the problem of *historical specificity,* and it is a problem to which scholarship on aging and the life course must be especially sensitive. We must make a dedicated attempt to understand these questions and not simply dismiss cohort as a "nuisance" or as "noise" in our search for larger developmental patterns. This also serves as a reminder that developmental scholarship is plagued by difficulties associated with *separating the unique effects of cohort from those of age and period,* as noted earlier.

Where cohort effects are concerned, life-course scholarship emphasizes the fact that historical time, like age, is an "empty" variable. The life-course framework demands that when aspects of historical time are used as causal variables in developmental models, researchers must *identify the processes and mechanisms that underlie cohort effects.* Researchers must be attentive to why and precisely how large-scale historical events and periods of social change affect the development of individuals and cohorts.

The concept of cohort is based on the idea that cohorts have unique historical experiences. In demonstrating cohort effects, life-course researchers must demonstrate both *distinctive experiences* within cohorts and *differential effects* between them (Rosow, 1978). They must show not only that the members of specific cohorts share unique historical experiences, but that each cohort, relative to those adjacent to it, responds in its own way to a set of phenomena. For example, the impact of an event or change should generally depend on the age at which an individual or cohort experiences it. This is what Elder (1995) describes as the *life-stage principle.* As a specific birth cohort grows up and older, its members encounter an historical event or change at roughly the same point in their lives; and as successive birth cohorts encounter those same events or changes, they experience them at different points in life. As a result, the impact of the event or change is contingent on the age or "life stage" of a cohort when the event or change occurs. This is an example of *inter-cohort differentiation,* which emphasizes variability between cohorts in "size, composition, patterns of aging, characteristics of its members, or experiences associated with the differing historical eras spanning their respective lives" (Uhlenberg & Riley, 1996, p. 299).

With respect to the problem of distinctive experience, can or should we ever assume that members of a cohort have uniform experiences? While the same historical event or change may impinge on members of a cohort, the nature of individual experiences with it, and the meanings that result, may vary significantly as a function of personal characteristics and resources. This is an example of *intra-cohort differentiation,* which emphasizes variability within a cohort and denotes sub-cohorts with shared life-course patterns and experiences. Sub-cohorts may be defined by characteristics such as "gender, race, or class, or by exposure to particular historical trends or events" (Uhlenberg & Riley, 1996, p. 299).

Cohort size and composition are especially important in determining the opportunities and constraints that its members face and the implications it has for social institutions that must assimilate it as it ages. In addition to the fact that the characteristics of a cohort set parameters on the lives of its *own* members, these characteristics also carry implications for adjacent and distal cohorts. Cohorts do not stand in isolation from one another, and the lives of members of multiple cohorts are inextricably linked within social settings of everyday life, such as schools, work places, social groups and organizations, and communities. And just as cohorts change in size and composition, so, too, does society and its organization. As each new cohort encounters social institutions, its experiences are often different from those of previous cohorts because social institutions are themselves different.

The Life Course as Conditioned by Other Demographic Parameters

In addition to cohort, life-course scholarship emphasizes the need to be sensitive to other population-level issues. In fact, the field of demography has a natural and "mutual attraction" with life-course analysis, given that the life course "begins and ends with demographic events—birth and death" and is shaped by events such as migration, marriage, and childbearing (Uhlenberg & Miner, 1996, p. 226). In addition, key demographic parameters, and changes in these parameters, also condition the nature of the life course. In particular, the demography of an aging society, especially decreases in mortality, morbidity, and fertility, have transformed the nature of individual lives, family life, social institutions, and society at large (e.g., Hagestad, 1988; Riley 1985; Uhlenberg, 1980).

Understanding the Life Course as a Set of Trajectories

The concept of a life *trajectory,* or pathway, is similar to that of a career (Elder, 1998; see also Chapter 2). A trajectory is long in scope, charting the course of an individual's experiences in specific life spheres over time. The individual *life course is composed of multiple, interdependent trajectories* (for example, work, family, and educational trajectories). What happens along one trajectory often has an effect on what happens along other trajectories, and roles held along each trajectory are often coordinated with roles along other trajectories. Labor force patterns are a good example of the interlocked nature of trajectories, as work-related decisions are often a function of family demands and responsibilities. Asynchronous trajectories likely create strain for individuals, as when demands in one sphere are incompatible with those in another.

Events, Transitions, and Turning Points

Trajectories are marked by life *events, transitions, and turning points,* which are central concepts in life-course scholarship (Elder, 1998; see also Chapter 2). Events and transitions are brief in scope, and refer to changes in an individual's state. However, an *event* is usually conceptualized as a relatively abrupt change, while a *transition* is usually conceptualized as a more gradual change, and one that is generally tied to acquiring or relinquishing roles. The concept of a *turning point* is used to refer to the points at which a trajectory shifts significantly in direction or is "discontinuous" in form. This discontinuity may be "objectively" defined as such by an researcher who has examined the shape of the trajectory, or it may be "subjectively" defined as such by the person who has experienced it.

Timing, Sequencing, Spacing, Density, and Duration

Timing, sequencing, spacing, density, and duration are central parameters for describing experiences along trajectories. *Timing,* the most frequently explored of these concepts, refers to the age at which experiences occur. The powerful nature of timing is exemplified in Elder's pioneering work on the differential impact of the Great Depression and World War II across cohorts of individuals born early in the 20th century (see Chapter 2). It is also exemplified in classic and contemporary research on age norms for life-course transitions, which examines the effects of "early," "on-time," or "late" transitions such as leaving home, finishing school, securing full-time work, getting married, having children, or retiring (e.g., Neugarten, Moore, & Lowe, 1965; Settersten & Hagestad, 1996a, 1996b).

Other important parameters for describing and analyzing life experiences and trajectories include *sequencing,* which refers to the order in which experiences occur; *spacing,* which refers to the amount of time between two or more ordered experiences; *density,* which refers to the compression of transitions within a bounded period of time; and *duration,* which refers to the length of time spent in any particular role or "state."

The timing, sequencing, spacing, density, and duration of earlier experiences may have important "domino" effects that shape the nature of later experiences. Attention to these parameters illustrates the fact that *a single event, transition, or turning point cannot be understood in isolation from others that surround it.*

Proximal and Distal Precursors and Consequences

Attention to trajectories naturally emphasizes the connections between earlier and later experiences—to the *distal and proximal precursors of an outcome,* and to the *proximal and distal outcomes of an earlier experience.* (Distal precursors and outcomes are far away in time, while proximal precursors and outcomes are close in time.) Elder and Caspi's (1990) two models for studying the effects of historical events and changes on the life course are good examples of these connections. These models, the *outcome-oriented model* and the *event-oriented model,* are presented in Figure 1.

In Model A, the outcome-oriented model, a specific life "outcome" is the focus, and we move backward through time, building into the model past events that may be directly linked to our outcome. These experiences may be proximal or distal to the outcome in time. For example, if we are interested in understanding the timing of fatherhood as an outcome, we might link it to more proximal events, such as immediate career demands (X) or financial status (Z); and we might link it to more distal events, such as the timing of marriage (Y), which may be linked to events still further back in time, such as the timing of school completion (Y_1) or military service (Y_2). In this case, we capture an event in which we are particularly interested, such as military service, as one of many events that ultimately affect the timing of fatherhood.

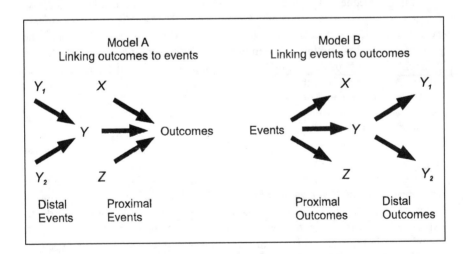

Figure 1. Studying social change in the life course: Two models.
Source: Elder G. H., Jr., & Caspi, A. (1990). Studying lives in a changing society: Sociological and personological explorations. In A. I. Rabin (Ed.), *Studying persons and lives: The Henry A. Murray lectures in personality.* New York: Springer, p. 212.

In Model B, the event-oriented model, a specific event earlier in life is the focal point. Here, we examine how that particular experience plays itself out over time, tracing its short- and long-term effects (both proximal and distal outcomes). For example, if we are interested in understanding the effects military service, we begin with that experience and link it to proximal outcomes, such as a disruption to work history (X) or psycho-social adjustment (Z); and we link it to more distal outcomes, such as a delay in marriage (Y), which may lead to late fatherhood (Y_1) or affect marital satisfaction (Y_2).

Model B is clearly preferable if we are interested in studying the full range of consequences brought about by an experience, and if we are interested in understanding the processes and mechanisms that drive these temporal connections. Of course, as the span of time to be analyzed increases, the number of experiences to be handled, the possible connections between, and the mechanisms that link them together, become infinitely complicated.

The Interdependence of Lives

The principle of "interdependent" or "linked" lives is that *individual lives are intimately connected to the lives of others,* and individual development is bound to and shaped by these ties (Elder, 1998; see also Chapter 2). Of course, it is also important to remember that the quantity and quality of intimate ties also change as individuals move through life.

Interdependence may create unexpected changes and circumstances. What happens in the life of one individual has implications for the lives of others, and this interdependence creates the need to actively coordinate and synchronize lives to reduce the potential friction. When lives are "out of synch," or asynchronous, relationships are often strained in significant ways. For example, couples generally plan retirement jointly; the timing of retirement for one partner is often contingent on when the other plans to retire, and vice versa. Interdependence may constrain and foreclose the options open to individuals. For example, women at midlife, who often simultaneously care for both older parents and dependent children, may do so at the expense of their careers. At the same time, these ties may enable individuals and provide them with important resources. For example, during times of hardship, family members may serve as important sources of emotional or economic support.

The Importance of Comparisons in Life-Course Scholarship

Life-course scholarship emphasizes the need to make *multiple, systematic comparisons.* The comparative method is basic to all sciences, natural and social alike, and is the primary means for generating knowledge; its success hinges on whether the units and features of the comparison are explicitly selected and defined on sound scientific bases (Fry, 1990; Tudge, Shanahan, & Valsiner, 1997). *Within-person* comparisons over time stand at the foundation of the study of developmental phenomena. It is also common for developmental scientists to make other group comparisons in their analyses. Besides *age and cohort* comparisons, comparisons across *sex, race, and social class* groups are commonplace (e.g., Mekos & Clubb, 1997). Because individual lives are embedded in historical time, *cross-historical* comparisons are also essential (e.g., Shanahan & Elder, 1997). Important comparisons are also made across *generations within families* (e.g., Attias-Donfut, 1992), *nations, cultures, or subcultures* (e.g., Hantrais & Mangen, 1996; van de Vijver & Leung, 1997), and *species* (e.g., Sameroff & Suomi, 1996). The *life course itself* must also become a comparative unit, accompanied by a search for variation in its structure and nature (Fry, 1990). When the life course is compared across nation-states, it is particularly important to explicate how the state and institutional structures specific to each setting shape the life course.

Coordinated comparisons along each of these dimensions will reveal the degree to which knowledge about human development can be generalized. Of course, comparisons *per se* tell us little about how or why the attribute that defines the group is tied to different developmental patterns. In making group comparisons, the relevant *processes and mechanisms* through which differences are created must also be identified. Of course, it is also important to gather and compare evidence based on a *wide range of methods,* whether objective or subjective, primary or secondary, or quantitative or qualitative in nature.

Variability in Life-Course Experiences

Systematic comparisons reveal *variability* in development, and contemporary scholarship emphasizes the need to examine the *range* of variability in human experiences, its *shape* over time, and its *sources and consequences.* A multi-faceted set of social, biological, and psychological factors and experiences interact to shape the pathways of individuals and groups in unique ways. The "principle of behavioral individuality" stresses the uniqueness of each individual, part of which is due to the unique experiences between the individual and her or his environments (Alwin, 1995). At the same time, the "principle of common experience" stresses the fact that individuals are nonetheless similar to others— part of which is the result of common or shared experiences between individuals and their environments (Alwin, 1995). There is a clear tension between these principles.

Recent research in the field of gerontology has led the emphasis on variability. Older people may be especially different from one another, given that "the longer people live, the more different they become . . . Lives fan out with time as people develop their own patterns of interests and commitments, their own sequences of life choices, their own psychological turning points, and their own patterns of relations with the few significant other people whose development impinges most directly on their own" (Neugarten, 1996, p. 48).

Sociologists now use a similar concept, the "Matthew effect," to explain "aged heterogeneity" (Dannefer, 1987; Dannefer & Sell, 1988). This principle is based on a passage in the Gospel of Matthew: "For unto every one that hath shall be given and he shall have abundance, but from him that hath not, shall be taken away even that which he hath." Sociologist Merton (1968) first described the "Matthew effect" as a general principle of social life: The effects of early *advantage and disadvantage often cumulate over time.* In this scenario, "divergent" pathways unfold over time, as early experiences set the stage for later ones, either limiting or promoting future life chances along the way. As a cohort grows up and older its members therefore become increasingly different from each other. (In addition to the divergence trajectory, several other trajectory patterns are also possible, including "constancy," "u-shaped," "trigger-event," and "convergence" patterns; see Dannefer & Sell, 1988.)

When considerable heterogeneity exists within a group, it becomes difficult to discuss that group as a clear social category, or to discuss general or universal patterns of development, without stereotyping and oversimplifying (Fry, 1990). Serious attention to heterogeneity requires us to abandon *a priori* assumptions about the existence of general or universal developmental "laws" (Lerner, 1995). At the same time, one might argue that doing the reverse—making *a priori* assumptions about the *non-existence* of larger developmental laws—may be equally problematic. From this standpoint, greater attention to heterogeneity should not lead us to abandon the search for commonalties in developmental experiences within or between groups, or the ways in which developmental experiences are patterned by the characteristics of, and processes occurring within, social settings. Similarly, the challenges posed by heterogeneity should not prevent us from attempting to understand and actively incorporate heterogeneity into our "scientific imagination" (Fry, 1990, p. 129). Variability is a natural part of the social world, and it cannot simply be dismissed as "scientifically uninteresting" or as "error variance" (Valsiner, 1984, p. 450). We must document and attempt to fully understand heterogeneity—to consider the explanatory factors and causal processes that produce it, and to consider its full range of consequences. Theories related to the "Matthew effect" are an important development along these lines.

These issues are also tied to another central proposition about human development: that *human lives are significantly malleable or "plastic."* Lifecourse scholarship emphasizes the "plasticity" of the human organism and the need to "test the limits" of human potential, its conditions, and its ranges (Baltes et al., 1998). In part, the emphasis on plasticity in developmental thought seems a counter-response to prevalent assumptions that the course of human life takes the shape of an inverted-U: significant growth during the early years, stability through the middle years, and significant decline in later life. Of course, plasticity can be a "double-edged sword" in that a system open to improvement is also open to decline (Lerner, 1985, p. 182).

The Life Course as a Product of Human Agency and Social Structure

Life-course scholarship seeks to *integrate action-oriented* and *structure-oriented* perspectives, and to examine the *reciprocal interaction* between personal action and social structures. On the one hand, one can find perspectives in the literature that place a strong, and even exclusive, emphasis on the role of individual agency in determining development; these are models of agency without structure. On the other hand, one can find perspectives in the literature that place a strong, and even exclusive, emphasis on the role of social structures in determining or constraining development; these are models of structure without agency. Instead, an emerging emphasis in developmental science is to conceptualize the life course *as actively created by individuals and groups, but within the confines of the social worlds in which they exist;* these are models of *agency within structure.*

A good example of this is what has been described as the "cultural canalization" of development (Valsiner & Lawrence, 1997). The metaphor of "canalization" is set within a "co-constructivist" framework, which emphasizes the joint and active roles that people and their contexts play in shaping human development. Within this framework, the person and the social world are taken to be "co-constructing agents" that set mutual constraints on each other. These constraints limit present and future possibilities for development. They may operate on multiple levels, and may constrain development in synchronic ways (at a specific point in time) and diachronic ways (at a future point in time by pushing individuals forward in specific directions). These constraints "reduce the unmanageable excesses of uncertainty" and specify possible developmental routes to be followed (Valsiner & Lawrence, 1997, p. 84). An actual course is then chosen from this set of possibilities. The canalization of development by social structures is not viewed as deterministic; while these forces do limit future activity, they provide an acceptable arena within which an individual may develop and perform. The dialectic between social and personal constraints produces new syntheses in the development of both the person and the context. Another good example is the parallel Heinz (1998) draws between the modern life course and a self-service cafeteria, in which individuals make selections from a menu of possible options available to them. Of course, while social structures are often assumed to constrain individuals, they need not be conceptualized in this way. Social structures also serve to enable individuals, and much remains to be learned about both their enabling and constraining aspects.

The idea that individuals are producers of their own development is not new. This notion has been emphasized in interactionist, contextualist, and organismic-structuralist approaches (e.g., Ford, 1987; Magnusson, 1996). Each of these approaches emphasizes the fact that individuals are not simply passive products of larger environmental forces. It is also reflected in other recent work that stresses the importance of "planful competence" (Clausen 1995), "mindfulness" (Langer, 1989), self-efficacy (Bandura, 1992), personal control (Brandtstädter, 1998), primary and secondary control processes (Heckhausen & Schultz, 1995), and proactive adaptation (Kahana & Kahana, Chapter 8, this volume).

Levels of Analysis and Context

The last section emphasized the importance of viewing individuals as active agents of their own development, but within the confines of the "social structures" in which they exist. *Macro-sociological* approaches, in particular, focus on the latter—on social forces that structure the life course. These forces are viewed as guiding, and even dictating, the movement of individuals through social roles, positions, and statuses over time, and as providing the life course with a standard shape and set of meanings, expectations, and aspirations. In addition, macro-sociological approaches focus on the collective life patterns of birth cohorts, and on differences within and between cohorts, as discussed earlier. However, in macro-sociological frameworks, the life course is often portrayed as being shaped exclusively by social structures and forces. Whether individuals are aware of larger structural influences, and how individuals evaluate, live out, and give meaning to their lives, are largely irrelevant. As a result, subjective concerns are generally of little or no importance in these frameworks.

In contrast, *micro-sociological* approaches take subjective concerns to be of central interest: They focus on the meanings that "actors" create, and the plans they make and experiences they have as they move through life. In some micro-sociological approaches, individuals may even be aware of, and react to, macro-level social forces. These approaches may also contrast the ways in which individual life courses actually unfold relative to "official" institutionalized versions of the life course (Marshall, 1995). However, most micro-sociological frameworks neglect larger social structures and forces. While sociological approaches to the life course are often found at purely macro- or micro-sociological levels, it is the intersection between these levels that represents the most exciting juncture for the study of lives.

Human lives must be understood in light of the *many social spaces and inter-related systems* in which they are embedded. Life-course scholarship must therefore be conducted at *multiple levels of analysis* and aimed at understanding lives in place. It must link individual development to *proximal environments,* such as families, peer and friendship groups, schools, workplaces, and neighborhoods; and to more *distal environments,* such as the state and its policies, culture and nation, and history. (For a discussion of the difficulties of conceptualizing and measuring social environments, see Settersten, 1999.)

Bronfenbrenner's (1979) ecological framework is an excellent example of the need to link levels of analysis. Bronfenbrenner considers the structures and processes in the "microsystem" (the immediate setting containing the developing person), the "mesosystem" (two or more immediate settings in which the individual is present), the "exosystem" (two or more settings, at least one of which does *not* contain the person but nonetheless has important effects on the individual), and finally the "macrosystem" (an overarching system in which all lower levels of the ecological environment contained). These systems point to the need to consider not only the proximal processes and mechanisms through which features of the immediate setting affect the individual, but also the processes and mechanisms through which features of more distal settings influence the individual both directly and indirectly. Indeed, one of the most difficult challenges we face is to adequately examine the ways in which higher-order settings play themselves out in lives, and the ways in which *changes* in these settings create *changes* in individuals.

Bronfenbrenner initially labeled his model a "process-person-context" (PPC) approach to studying human lives. As such, any research design in line with this model must gather data in three separate areas: the *contexts* in which development occurs; the *personal characteristics* of the individuals in those contexts; and the *processes* that bring about development. More recently, Bronfenbrenner (1995) renamed this a "bio-ecological model," and added an additional dimension—*time,* which resulted in a "process-person-context-time" (PPCT) approach. With this addition, Bronfenbrenner emphasizes the fact that processes, people, and contexts change over time. This is consistent with an emerging emphasis on time and place in life-course theory and research. It serves as a reminder that single social contexts cannot be studied as isolated entities. Instead multiple contexts must be studied as interdependent, interactive, and dynamic entities. In addition, it serves as a reminder that distal environments and processes are no less significant than proximal ones, though they do pose bigger theoretical and analytic challenges.

Life-course scholarship takes social contexts to be a set of systematically organized processes that have significant effects on development outcomes (see Dannefer, 1992). It emphasizes the need for theory and research to offer an *explicit formulation of the structural characteristics of contexts, and of the processes operating within those contexts, that shape development.* Of course, the ways in which contexts are conceptualized and believed to affect development will depend on which aspects of development are being examined. It is important to consider whether (1) "target phenomena" are especially open to the influence of the environment at particular points in time, (2) certain contexts are particularly influential at certain points in life, and (3) the strength of their effects on target phenomena changes over time. If possible, a *developmental frame* should be identified, within which particular types of environments and environmental factors play clear roles in shaping development (Kindermann & Skinner, 1992, p. 160). Once identified, the points of measurement in a study should be timed to best capture those influences. However, for many phenomena, these windows may not be known or clear, or they may vary across individuals.

It is also important to note that individuals may be *systematically sorted into or excluded from specific contexts,* just as individuals may *self-select* themselves into specific contexts. As such, this leads to another principle: Life-course scholarship emphasizes the need to better examine the *unique, reciprocal,* and *dynamic nature of relationships between individuals and their environments over time* (see also Kindermann & Skinner, 1992). Ultimately, these points emphasize the importance of taking matters of place seriously in research designs and sampling, data collection and organization, and analytic strategies (for an overview of these methods, see Giele & Elder, 1999; Settersten, 1999). Recent advances in multi-level modeling have been particularly helpful in this regard (see DiPrete & Forristal, 1994).

EMERGING CONTROVERSIES ON THE RHYTHM OF THE LIFE COURSE IN MODERN SOCIETIES

Several recent scholarly and policy debates relate time and age to the nature of the life course in modern societies (for a complete discussion, see Settersten, 1999). One set of debates concerns the degree to which the lives are, or have become, more or less "chronologized," "institutionalized," and "standardized." Another debate concerns the degree to which trajectories though different life spheres are, or have become, more or less chronologized, institutionalized, and standardized. A final debate relates to differences in the degree to which men's and women's lives are, or have become, more or less chronologized, institutionalized, and standardized.

The Chronologization of Lives

The debate about the *chronologization,* to use Kohli's (1986a) term, concerns the degree to which time and age are, or have become, salient dimensions of human life. Along these lines, Chudacoff (1989) argues that an important turning point occurred in the early part of the 20th century. It was at this point in history that an increased awareness of age presumably emerged as part of a larger process of "social segmentation" in America: Organizations became more bureaucratic; landmark developments occurred in science, industry, and communication; concerns about efficiency and productivity grew; and society became more dependent on the clock and on being "on time." Similarly, Graff (1995) suggests that these and other large-scale developments in the first two decades of the 20th century (e.g., major shifts in immigration and urbanization, social policies aimed at women and the young) transformed pathways to adulthood, culminating in patterns now considered "modern." New emphases on age and time have accompanied these historical trends. This evidence contradicts common assumptions that contemporary societies have successfully combated ageism (Kertzer, 1989), and that achievement matters more than age, sex, or other forms of ascription in determining life chances (Kohli, 1986b).

The Institutionalization of Lives

The debate about *institutionalization* concerns the degree to which the life course is, or has become, structured by social institutions and the state and its policies. (The intersection between human development and social policy is the topic of Chapter 7.) Indeed, for many sociologists, the life course is understood to be a unit of social structure and an institution of socialization in its own right. There is evidence that individuals have been freed from traditional forms of informal social control (e.g., status, locality, family; Kohli, 1986a), and that, with these freedoms, the state began to regulate individuals more formally, thereby "institutionalizing" lives. This authority evolved as the rights and duties of citizenship were established and, as the welfare state emerged. As the state began to target individuals through policies, age became a central dimension of concern (Mayer & Schöpflin, 1989). Chronological age is a convenient and practical administrative gauge; it is easily-measured, objective, and universal.

The emergence of an age-bound life course as an institution of socialization—as a system of rules and regulations that order life—resulted from and solved several structural problems (Kohli, 1986a, 1986b). These included the need (a) to organize public services and transfers in a rational manner, (b) for new forms of social control, (c) to find ways to allocate positions and roles in different social domains, and (d) to better integrate and synchronize aspects of family and work. While institutionalization occurs through state intervention and regulation, it also occurs through formal pathways through educational institutions and work organizations. Its effects trickle down to the "life-worlds" of individuals as they "orient themselves and plan their actions" (Kohli & Meyer, 1986, p. 147). Thus, institutionalization creates both constraints and new "potentialities" for individuals, actively organizes the life course and links life stages, and enhances individual development by integrating experiences and fostering a sense of continuity over time (Kohli & Meyer, 1986).

The Standardization of Lives

The debate about *standardization* concerns the degree to which life patterns exhibit regularity, and the degree to which regularity in life patterns has changed historically. There are multiple ways to think about the standardization of the life course. An event may be standard in that it simply occurs, or it may be standard with respect to its timing, which has been the primary focus of most inquiry (Henretta, 1992). It may also hold a standard place within sequence of experiences, have standard spacing with respect to another experience or set of experiences, or be of standard duration. Clearly, trends toward standardization are also tied to trends toward chronologization and institutionalization.

The De-Chronologization, De-Institutionalization, and De-Standardization of Lives

There is also evidence that runs counter to the theses just described. This evidence suggests that lives are, or have become, *de-chronologized, de-institutionalized, and de-standardized.* Together, these trends point to new hopes that the life course is now, or has the potential to become, more flexible. Several factors bring the potential for greater flexibility in the life course and new opportunities to simultaneously manage work, family, education, and leisure experiences (for a more complete discussion, see Settersten, 1999; see also Chapters 3, 4, and 5). These factors include new "time budgets" for adulthood as the result of historical shifts in key demographic parameters, particularly longevity, fertility, and morbidity; new possibilities for work in the last third of life (again the partial result of reduced morbidity, along with several work and pension-related policy changes); new routes to retirement; the erosion of "lifetime" models of work; flextime work policies; and growth in adult enrollment in higher education and in educational programs aimed at adults. In addition, several individual-level characteristics may promote or constrain life-course flexibility depending on their direction. These factors include an individual's level of "planful competence"; motivation and coping skills; comfort with "risk-taking"; time and financial resources; family responsibilities and support; and employment status and occupational position.

The Nature of Trajectories Through Different Life Spheres

Another debate concerns the degree to which trajectories *though different life spheres* are, or have become, chronologized, institutionalized, and standardized. Here, most research has suggested that work and educational trajectories are more rigid than trajectories in the family domain, which instead seem characterized by greater flexibility. However, there is also evidence of increased flexibility in the work and educational spheres, particularly as age-structured lifetime models of employment erode and as educational experiences occur more regularly throughout adult life.

Another factor that may prompt flexibility, at least within American culture, is the strong ideology of individualism, which emphasizes personal growth and choice. This ideology may also be a reaction to the trends noted above, and particularly to institutionalization. When the life course becomes too institutionalized, cultural traditions and customs may become less important and new "biographical options" may be sought and tested, especially in life spheres that are not, or cannot be, well regulated, such as the family sphere (e.g., Buchmann, 1989). These factors, coupled with evidence of increased variability in life experiences (especially in the family sphere), suggest that the life course has become partially de-standardized. It is also possible that the *informal* regulation of lives may be stronger in spheres that are not, or cannot be, formally regulated by the state.

The Nature of Men's Versus Women's Lives

A final debate concerns the degree to which *men's versus women's lives* are, or have become, chronologized, institutionalized, and standardized. Scholars have suggested that the social meanings of age and time differ for men and women, that men and women use different guidelines to measure the progress of their lives, that they have different needs for predictability and order, and that their lives run on different kinds of time (e.g., Hagestad, 1991; Hernes, 1987; Moen, 1996). These differences may be linked to the fact that, traditionally, the lives of women have been more firmly bound to the family sphere, which seems to operate on non-linear time, while the lives of men have been more firmly bound to spheres outside the family, which instead seem to operate on linear time. The result is that men's lives are (or are perceived as) more rigid, while women's lives are (or are perceived as) more flexible, with the exception of biological clocks around reproduction. At the same time, men and women alike are simultaneously tied to multiple spheres in multiple ways. Much of the inflexibility that individuals may feel likely results from clashes between family, work, and educational spheres as they are negotiated over time.

CONCLUSION

The first part of the chapter introduced some of the central principles that underlie and guide developmental theory and research across several disciplines, especially life-course sociology and life-span developmental psychology. The latter part of the chapter introduced several emerging debates about the rhythm of the life course in modern societies, and how the life course has changed historically. Table 1 outlines these propositions and controversies. Readers will find this table helpful as they approach the remaining chapters in this volume.

Table 1. Emerging Propositions and Controversies in
Life-Course Scholarship

Emerging Propositions in Life-Course Scholarship

Development as Multidimensional and Multispheral

1A. Individual development is multidimensional, occurring along biological, psychological, and social dimensions.

1B. Individual development is multispheral, occurring in family, work, education, leisure, and other life spheres.

1C. Life-course scholarship seeks to link these dimensions and spheres together.

Life-Course Scholarship as Multidisciplinary or Interdisciplinary

2A. Life-course scholarship is multidisciplinary, combining the contributions of many disciplines.

2B. Ideally, life-course scholarship is interdisciplinary, moving in directions that transcend disciplinary boundaries and actively integrate the perspectives of different disciplines.

Development as Multidirectional

3A. Individual development is multidirectional, chacterized by differing levels and rates of change across dimensions of functioning.

3B. Development involves the simultaneous occurrence of both gains (growth) and losses (declines) within and between dimensions and domains of functioning.

Development as Lifelong

4A. Individual development does not stop in adulthood but continues throughout life and into advanced old age.

4B. All life periods involve important developmental experiences.

4C. Specific life periods must be understood within the context of a lived past and anticipated future.

4D. Development is characterized by both continuity (experiences that extend across life) and discontinuity (experiences unique to certain periods).

4E. Time and change must therefore be taken seriously in research designs and sampling, data collection and organization, and analytic strategies.

The Salience of Age in the Life Course

5A. Age is important from the standpoints of individuals, groups, and society.

5B. Chronological age is a rough proxy for biological, psychological, and social statuses.

5C. Developmental scientists must identify the processes and mechanisms that bring about age-related effects.

Table 1. (Cont'd.)

5D. Age differences cannot be mistaken for age changes.

5E. The life course is age stratified. Roles and statuses are often allocated on the basis of age, and social settings are often age-homogeneous.

5F. Work is a central activity that organizes modern life courses, which are partitioned into three periods of training, work, and retirement.

The Life Course as Embedded in Historical Time and Bound to Cohort

6A. Lives are framed by historical time and shaped by the unique social and cultural conditions of those times.

6B. Cohort effects are critical to understand, both in terms of distinctive experiences and differential effects. This requires full exploration of intra- and inter-cohort differences. It also requires developmental scientists to separate the unique effects of cohort from those of age and period.

6C. Developmental scientists must identify the processes and mechanisms that bring about cohort-related effects.

The Life Course as Conditioned by Other Demographic Parameters

7. The life course is conditioned by central demographic parameters (especially mortality, morbidity, and fertility) and changes in these parameters over time.

Understanding the Life Course as a Set of Trajectories

8A. The life course is composed of multiple, interdependent trajectories.

8B. Trajectories are punctuated by life events, transitions, and turning points.

8C. Timing, sequencing, spacing, density, and duration are central parameters for describing these experiences.

8D. A specific experience cannot be understood in isolation of the other experiences around it.

8E. Attention to trajectories naturally emphasizes the distal and proximal precursors of an outcome, and the proximal and distal outcomes of an earlier experience.

8F. Developmental scientists must identify the processes and mechanisms that bring about these temporal connections.

The Interdependence of Lives

9A. Individual lives are intimately connected to the lives of others, and individual development is bound to and shaped by these ties.

9B. The quantity and quality of intimate ties change as individuals move through life.

9C. Interdependence creates unexpected changes and circumstances, and it creates the need to actively coordinate and synchronize lives.

9D. These attachments may constrain and foreclose the options open to individuals, but they may also be enabling and provide important resources.

Table 1. (Cont'd.)

The Importance of Comparisons in Life-Course Scholarship

10A. Life-course scholarship emphasizes the need to make multiple, systematic comparisons within individuals, and within and between groups. The life course itself must also become a comparative unit.

10B. Life-course scholarship must gather and compare evidence based on a wide range of methods.

10C. Developmental scientists must identify the processes and mechanisms that produce the differences that result when comparisons are made.

Variability in Life-Course Experiences

11A. Developmental scientists must examine the range of variability in human experiences, its shape over time, and its sources and consequences.

11B. Life-course scholarship emphasizes the malleability or "plasticitiy" of the human organism.

The Life Course as a Product of Human Agency and Social Structure

12. The life course is a partial product of human action. It is actively created within the confines of the social worlds in which individuals exist. Life-course scholarship therefore promotes models of human agency within structure.

Levels of Analysis and Context

13A. Human lives must be understood in light of the many social spaces and inter-related systems in which they are embedded. Life-course scholarship must therefore be conducted at multiple levels of analysis.

13B. Life-course scholarship must link individual development to proximal environments, such as families, peer and friendship groups, schools, work-places, and neighborhoods; and to more distal environments, such as the state and its policies, culture and nation, and history.

13C. Social contexts are taken to be a set of systematically organized processes.

13D. Life-course scholarship requires an explicit formulation of the structural characteristics of contexts and the social processes within them that shape individual development.

13E. Developmental scientists must consider whether "target phenomena" are especially open to the influence of the environment at particular points in life, whether certain contexts are particularly influential at certain points in life, and whether the strength of their effects on target phenomena changes over time.

13F. Individuals may be systematically sorted into or excluded from specific contexts, just as individuals may self-select themselves into specific contexts.

13G. Matters of "place" must therefore be taken seriously in research designs and sampling, data collection and organization, and analytic strategies.

Table 1. (Cont'd.)

**Emerging Controversies on the Rhythm of the Life Course
in Modern Societies**

1. The debate about the *chronologization* of lives concerns the degree to which time and age are, or have become, salient dimensions of human life.

2. The debate about the *institutionalization* of lives concerns the degree to which the life course is, or has become, structured by social institutions and the state and its policies.

3. The debate about the *standardization* of lives concerns the degree to which life patterns exhibit regularity, and the degree to which regularity in life patterns has changed historically.

4. The debate about the nature of *trajectories though different life spheres* concerns the degree to which the spheres of education, work, family, and leisure are, or have become, chronologized, institutionalized, and standardized.

5. The debate about the nature of *men's versus women's lives* concerns the degree to which men's and women's lives are, or have become, chronologized, institutionalized, and standardized.

REFERENCES

Alwin, D. (1995). Taking time seriously: Studying social change, social structure, and human lives. In P. Moen, G. H. Elder, Jr., & K. Lüscher (Eds.), *Examining lives in context: Perspectives on the ecology of human development* (pp. 211-262). Washington, DC: American Psychological Association.

Attias-Donfut, C. (1992). Transmissions between generations and the life course. In W. J. A. van den Heuvel, R. Illsley, A. Jamieson, & C. P. M. Knipscheer (Eds.), *Opportunities and challenges in an ageing society* (pp. 53-60). Amsterdam: Koninklijke Nederlandse Akademie van Wetenschappen.

Baltes, P. B. (1997). On the incomplete architecture of human ontogeny: Selection, optimization, and compensation as foundation of developmental theory. *American Psychologist, 52*(4), 366-380.

Baltes, P. B., Lindenberger, U., & Staudinger, U. (1998). Life-span theory in developmental psychology. In R. M. Lerner (Ed.), *Handbook of child psychology: Vol. 1. Theoretical models of human development* (5th ed., pp. 1029-1143). New York: John Wiley & Sons.

Baltes, P. B., & Smith, J. (1999). Multilevel and systemic analyses of old age: Theoretical and empirical evidence for a fourth age. In V. L. Bengtson & K. W. Schaie (Eds.), *Handbook of theories of aging* (pp. 153-173). New York: Springer.

Bandura, A. (1992). Exercise of personal agency through the self-efficacy mechanism. In R. Schwarzer (Ed.), *Self-efficacy: Thought control of action* (pp. 3-38). Washington, DC: Hemisphere.

Bengtson, V. L., Rosenthal, C., & Burton, L. (1990). Families and aging. In R. Binstock & L. George (Eds.), *Handbook on aging and the social sciences* (pp. 263-287). San Diego, CA: Academic Press.

Birren, J., & Schroots, J. F. (1996). History, concepts, and theory in the psychology of aging. In J. Birren & K. W. Schaie (Eds.), *Handbook of the psychology of aging* (pp. 3-23). San Diego, CA: Academic Press.

Boyd, J. W., & Dowd, J. J. (1988). The diffusiveness of age. *Social Behaviour, 3,* 85-103.

Brandtstädter, J. (1998). Action perspectives on human development. In R. M. Lerner (Ed.), *Handbook of child psychology: Vol. 1. Theoretical models of human development* (5th ed., pp. 807-863). New York: John Wiley & Sons.

Bronfenbrenner, U. (1979). *The ecology of human development: Experiments by nature and design.* Cambridge, MA: Harvard University Press.

Bronfenbrenner, U. (1995). Developmental ecology through space and time: A future perspective. In P. Moen, G. H. Elder, Jr., & K. Lüscher (Eds.), *Examining lives in context: Perspectives on the ecology of human development* (pp. 619-647). New York: American Psychological Association.

Buchmann, M. (1989). *The script of life in modern society: Entry into adulthood in a changing world.* Chicago, Illinois: University of Chicago Press.

Carolina Consortium on Human Development. (1996). Developmental science: A collaborative statement. In R. B. Cairns, G. H. Elder, Jr., & E. J. Costello (Eds.), *Developmental science* (pp. 1-6). New York: Cambridge University Press.

Caspi, A. (1998). Personality development across the life course. In N. Eisenberg (Ed.), *Handbook of child psychology: Vol. 3. Social, emotional, and personality development* (5th ed.). New York: John Wiley & Sons.

Chiriboga, D. A. (1996). In search of continuities and discontinuities across time and culture. In V. Bengtson (Ed.), *Adulthood and aging: Research on continuities and discontinuities* (pp. 173-199). New York: Springer.

Chudacoff, H. P. (1989). *How old are you? Age consciousness in American culture.* Princeton, NJ: Princeton University Press.

Clausen, J. A. (1995). Gender, contexts, and turning points in adults' lives. In P. Moen, G. H. Elder, Jr., & K. Lüscher (Eds.), *Examining lives in context: Perspectives on the ecology of human development* (pp. 365-389). New York: American Psychological Association.

Costa, P. T., & McCrae, R. R. (1994). Set like plaster? Evidence for the stability of adult personality. In T. F. Heatherton & J. L. Weinberger (Eds.), *Can personality change?* (pp. 21-40). Washington, DC: APA Press.

Dannefer, D. (1987). Aging as intracohort differentiation: Accentuation, the Matthew effect, and the life course. *Sociological Forum, 2,* 211-236.

Dannefer, D. (1992). On the conceptualization of context in developmental discourse: Four meanings of context and their implications. In D. L. Featherman, R. M. Lerner, & M. Perlmutter (Eds.), *Life-span development and behavior* (Vol. 11, pp. 83-110). Hillsdale, NJ: Lawrence Erlbaum Associates.

Dannefer, D., & Sell, R. (1988). Age structure, the life course, and "aged heterogeneity": Prospects for research and theory. *Comprehensive Gerontology, 2,* 1-10.

DiPrete, T. A., & Forristal, J. D. (1994). Multi-level models: Methods and substance. *Annual Review of Sociology, 20,* 331-357.

Elder, G. H., Jr. (1995). The life course paradigm: Social change and individual develop-ment. In P. Moen, G. H. Elder, Jr., & K. Lüscher (Eds.), *Examining lives in context: Perspectives on the ecology of human development* (pp. 101-139). Washington, DC: American Psychological Association.

Elder, G. H., Jr. (1998). The life course and human development. In R. M. Lerner (Ed.), *Handbook of child psychology: Vol. 1. Theoretical models of human development* (5th ed., pp. 939-991). New York: John Wiley & Sons.

Elder, G. H., Jr., & Caspi, A. (1990). Studying lives in a changing society: Socio-logical and personological explorations. In A. I. Rabin (Ed.), *Studying persons and lives: The Henry A. Murray lectures in personality* (pp. 201-247). New York: Springer.

Erikson, E. (1980). *Identity and the life cycle.* New York: W. W. Norton Press.

Ford, D. H. (1987). *Humans as self-constructing living systems: A developmental perspective on behavior and personality.* Hillsdale, NJ: Lawrence Erlbaum Associates.

Freud, S. (1923/1974). *The ego and the id.* London: Hogarth.

Fry, C. L. (1986). Emics and age: Age differentiation and cognitive anthropological strategies. In C. L. Fry & J. Keith (Eds.), *New methods for old age research: Strategies for studying diversity* (pp. 105-131). Massachusetts: Bergin and Garvey.

Fry, C. L. (1990). Comparative research in aging. In K. Ferraro (Ed.), *Gerontology: Perspectives and issues* (129-146). New York: Springer.

Fry, C. L. (1996). Age, aging, and culture. In R. Binstock & L. George (Eds.), *Handbook of aging and the social sciences* (4th ed., pp. 117-136). San Diego: Academic Press.

Gergen, K. (1977). Stability, change, and chance in human development. In N. Datan & H. Reese (Eds.), *Life-span developmental psychology: Dialectical perspectives on experimental research* (pp. 136-158). New York: Academic Press.

Giele, J., & Elder, G. H., Jr. (Eds.) (1999). *Methods of life-course research: Qualitative and quantitative approaches.* Newbury Park, CA: Sage.

Graff, H. (1995). *Conflicting paths: Growing up in America.* Cambridge, MA: Harvard University Press.

Hagestad, G. O. (1988). Demographic change and the life course: Some emerging trends in the family realm. *Family Relations, 37,* 405-410.

Hagestad, G. O. (1991). Trends and dilemmas in life course research: An international perspective. In W. R. Heinz (Ed.), *Theoretical advances in life course research* (pp. 23-57). Weinheim, Germany: Deutscher Studien Verlag.

Hantrais, L., & Mangen, S. (Eds.) (1996). *Cross-national research methods in the social sciences.* New York: Pinter.

Heckhausen, J., & Schulz, R. (1995). A life-span theory of control. *Psychological Review, 102,* 284-304.

Heinz, W. R. (1998, May). Work and the life course: Cross-cultural research perspectives. Paper presented at "Restructuring Work and the Life Course: An International Symposium," University of Toronto, Toronto, Ontario.

Henretta, J. (1992). Uniformity and diversity: Life course institutionalization and late-life work exit. *Sociological Quarterly, 33*(2), 265-279.

Hernes, H. M. (1987). *Welfare state and woman power: Essays in state feminism.* Oslo, Norway: The Norwegian University Press.

Keith, J., Fry, C. L., Glascock, A. P., Ikels, C., Dickerson-Putnam, J., Harpending, H. C., & Draper, P. (1994). *The aging experience: Diversity and commonality across cultures.* Newbury Park, CA: Sage.

Kertzer, D. I. (1989). Age structuring in comparative and historical perspective. In D. I. Kertzer & K. Warner Schaie (Eds.), *Age structuring in comparative and historical perspective* (pp. 3-21). Hillsdale, New Jersey: Lawrence Erlbaum Associates.

Kindermann, T. A., & Skinner, E. A. (1992). Modeling environmental development: Individual and contextual trajectories. In J. B. Asendorpf & J. Valsiner (Eds.), *Stability and change in development: A study of methodological reasoning* (pp. 155-190). Newbury Park, CA: Sage.

Kohli, M. (1986a). The world we forgot: A historical review of the life course. In V. Marshall (Ed.), *Later life* (pp. 271-303). Beverly Hills, California: Sage.

Kohli, M. (1986b). Social organization and subjective construction of the life course. In A. B. Sørensen, F. E. Weinert & L. R. Sherrod (Eds.), *Human development and the life course: Multidisciplinary perspectives* (pp. 271-292). Hillsdale, NJ: Lawrence Erlbaum Associates.

Kohli, M., & Meyer, J. W. (1986). Social structure and the social construction of life stages. *Human Development, 29,* 145-149.

Langer, E. J. (1989). *Mindfulness.* Reading, MA: Addison-Wesley.

Lerner, R. M. (1985). Individual and context in developmental psychology: Conceptual and theoretical issues. In J. R. Nesselroade & A. von Eye (Eds.), *Individual development and social change: Explanatory analysis* (pp. 155-187). San Diego, CA: Academic Press.

Lerner, R. M. (1995). Developing individuals within changing contexts: Implications of developmental contextualism for human development research, policy, and programs. In T. A. Kindermann & J. Valsiner (Eds.), *Development of person-context relations* (pp. 13-37). Hillsdale, NJ: Lawrence Erlbaum Associates.

Magnusson, D. (Ed.). (1996). *The life-span development of individuals: Behavioural, neurobiological, and psychosocial perspectives.* New York: Cambridge University Press.

Markus, H., & Herzog, A. R. (1991). The role of the self-concept in aging. *Annual Review of Gerontology and Geriatrics, 11,* 111-143.

Marshall, V. W. (1995). Social models of aging. *Canadian Journal on Aging, 14*(1), 12-34.

Mayer, K. U., & Schöpflin, U. (1989). The state and the life course. *Annual Review of Sociology, 15,* 187-209.

Mayer, K. U., & Tuma, N. B. (1990). Life course research and event history analysis: An overview. In K. U. Mayer & N. B. Tuma (Eds.), *Event history analysis in life course research* (pp. 3-20). Madison, WI: University of Wisconsin Press.

Mekos, D., & Clubb, P. A. (1997). The value of comparisons in developmental psychology. In J. Tudge, M. J. Shanahan, & J. Valsiner (Eds.), *Comparisons in human development: Understanding time and context* (pp. 137-161). New York: Cambridge University Press.

Merton, R. (1968). The Matthew effect in science: The reward and communications systems of science. *Science, 199,* 55-63.

Moen, P. (1996). Gender and the life course. In R. Binstock & L. George (Eds.), *Handbook of aging and the social sciences* (4th ed., pp. 171-187). San Diego: Academic Press.

Neugarten, B. L., Moore, J. W., & Lowe, J. C. (1965). Age norms, age constraints, and adult socialization. *American Journal of Sociology, 70,* 710-717.

Neugarten, D. A. (Ed.) (1996). *The meanings of age: Selected papers of Bernice L. Neugarten.* Chicago, IL: University of Chicago Press.

O'Rand, M., & Krecker, M. L. (1990). Concepts of the life cycle: Their history, meanings and issues in the social sciences. *Annual Review of Sociology, 16,* 241-262.

Reese, H. W., & Overton, W. F. (1970). Models of development and theories of development. In L. R. Goulet & P. B. Baltes (Eds.), *Life-span developmental psychology: Research and theory* (pp. 115-145). New York: Academic Press.

Riley, M. W. (1985). Men, women, and the lengthening of the life course. In A. Rossi (Ed.), *Gender and the life course* (pp. 333-347). New York: Aldine.

Riley, M. W., Foner, A., & Waring, J. (1988). Sociology of age. In N. Smelser (Ed.), *Handbook of sociology* (pp. 243-290). Newbury Park, CA: Sage.

Riley, M. W., Kahn, R. L., & Foner, A. (Eds.). (1994). *Age and structural lag: Society's failure to provide meaningful opportunities in work, family, and leisure.* New York: John Wiley & Sons.

Rindfuss, R., Swicegood, C., & Rosenfeld, R. (1987). Disorder in the life course: How common and does it matter? *American Sociological Review, 52,* 785-801.

Rosow, I. (1978). What is a cohort and why? *Human Development, 21,* 65-75.

Sameroff, A. J., Suomi, S. J. (1996). Primates and persons: A comparative developmental understanding of social organization. In R. B. Cairns, G. H. Elder, Jr., & E. J. Costello (Eds.), *Developmental science* (pp. 97-120). New York: Cambridge University Press.

Settersten, R. A., Jr. (1999). *Lives in time and place: The problems and promises of developmental science.* Amityville, NY: Baywood.

Settersten, R. A., Jr., & Hagestad, G. O. (1996a). What's the latest? Cultural age deadlines for family transitions. *The Gerontologist, 36*(2), 178-188.

Settersten, R. A., Jr., & Hagestad, G. O. (1996b). What's the latest? II. Cultural age deadlines for educational and work transitions. *The Gerontologist, 36*(5), 602-613.

Shanahan, M. J., & Elder, G. H., Jr. (1997). Nested comparisons in the study of historical change and individual adaptation. In J. Tudge, M. J. Shanahan, & J. Valsiner (Eds.), *Comparisons in human development: Understanding time and context* (pp. 109-136). New York: Cambridge University Press.

Tudge, J., Shanahan, M. J., & Valsiner, J. (1997). *Comparisons in human development: Understanding time and context.* New York: Cambridge University Press.

Uhlenberg, P. (1980). Death and the family. *Journal of Family History, 5,* 313-320.

Uhlenberg, P., & Miner, S. (1996). Life course and aging: A cohort perspective. In R. Binstock & L. George (Eds.), *Handbook of aging and the social sciences* (4th ed., pp. 208-228). San Diego, CA: Academic Press.

Uhlenberg, P., & Riley, M. W. (1996). Cohort studies. In J. Birren (Ed.), *Encyclopedia of Gerontology: age, aging, and the aged* (Vol. 1, pp. 299-309). San Diego, CA: Academic Press.

Uhlenberg, P., & Riley, M. W. (Ed.) (2000). Essays on age integration. *The Gerontologist, 40*(3), 261-307.

Uttal, D. H., & Perlmutter, M. (1989). Toward a broader conceptualization of development: The role of gains and losses across the life span. *Developmental Review, 9,* 101-132.

Valsiner, J. (1984). Two espistemological frameworks in psychology: The typological and variational modes of thinking. *Journal of Mind and Behavior, 5,* 449-470.

Valsiner, J., & Lawrence, J. A. (1997). Human development in culture across the life span. In J. W. Berry, P. R. Dasen, & T. S. Saraswathi (Eds.), *Handbook of cross-cultural psychology: Vol. 2. Basic processes and human development* (pp. 69-106). Boston, MA: Allyn & Bacon.

van de Vijver, F., & Leung, K. (1997). *Methods and data analysis for cross-cultural research.* Thousand Oaks, CA: Sage.

PART II

Promises for the General Study of Aging and Later Life

CHAPTER 2

The Life Course and Aging: Challenges, Lessons, and New Directions*

Glen H. Elder, Jr. and Monica Kirkpatrick Johnson

Theoretical advances of some note often evolve from modest beginnings and unplanned circumstances. This observation applies to ways of thinking about the social pathways of people's lives and their historical times. Perspectives of this kind owe much to a band of American psychologists in the 1920s who launched a series of longitudinal studies of child development (see Elder, 1998). They broke new ground with support from colleagues in other disciplines. Sociologist W. I. Thomas claimed in the mid-1920s that priority should be given to the "longitudinal approach to life history" and that studies should investigate "many types of individuals with regard to their experiences and various past periods of life in different situations" (in Volkart, 1951, p. 593). Thomas had in mind a study that followed children from their earliest years to young adulthood. The first half of life, he assumed, would set in motion the pathways of later life.

These pioneering investigators intended to establish longitudinal studies of children, yet before long the studies had evolved into very different projects as the children moved through adolescence to adulthood. The study members married, had children, and pursued careers, sometimes interrupted by military service. By the 1970s, the study children had launched their own careers and families. Retirement and grandchildren became key events for them in the 1980s and 1990s.

*We acknowledge support by the National Institute of Mental Health (MH 00567, MH 57549), the U.S. Army Research Institute, the MacArthur Foundation Research Network on Successful Adolescent Development Among Youth in High-Risk Settings, a grant from the National Institute of Child Health and Human Development to the Carolina Population Center at the University of North Carolina at Chapel Hill (PO1-HD31921A), a Spencer Foundation Senior Scholar Award to Elder, and a NICHD-NRSA postdoctoral fellowship (HD07168-21) to Johnson.

The projects helped shape a new field of study on adult development and aging, with emphases on individual lives and intergenerational relationships.

Left out of the picture is the tumultuous history of the times and its influence on lives, a neglected topic up to the 1960s. But from recent analyses of the study members in historical context (Elder, 1999), we see them amidst the hardships of the Great Depression and, later, the dramatic changes of World War II. The war's end brought prosperity to many parts of the United States, as well as new questions to the project investigators. Why did some men and women overcome difficult childhoods and achieve rewarding lives in adulthood? And how did the historical times influence who they became? Fortunately, the investigators managed to follow the study members into the middle years and others have continued this remarkable effort into late life and a new century. Questions posed by these studies have challenged new investigators up to the present.

We begin this chapter by noting the critical role of early longitudinal studies in placing adult development and relevant approaches on the agenda of the social and behavioral sciences. This includes the explanatory potential of these studies in linking childhood and the later years (Rutter, 1988). Since this early research, the growth of prospective longitudinal studies has fostered theoretical and methodological models for research on human development and aging as lifelong processes in changing contexts (Cairns, Elder, & Costello, 1996; Magnusson & Bergman, 1990). This work spawned two lines of inquiry on life-course and life-span development in the disciplines of sociology and psychology, respectively.

The emergence of life-course models, in particular, addressed the neglected behavioral contexts of individual lives—their social pathways and settings in historical time and place. Both types of context can be described and assessed by key principles of the life course. Underlying the emerging study of the whole life course is a principle on human development and aging as lifelong processes. The other principles stress the agency and life stage of the individual in making choices among alternatives, as well as the embeddedness of lives in relationships with other people and in historical time and place. We apply these principles to empirical studies for conceptual and methodological insights, and conclude with promising new directions for research.

MAKING SENSE OF LIVES IN CHANGING TIMES

The early longitudinal studies were launched into an unknown future, and subsequent events invariably altered the expected life course. Lewis Terman, an eminent psychologist at Stanford University, began his longitudinal study of "talented or gifted" children seven years before the economy collapsed in the Great Depression, and two decades away from the greatest war of the century, the Second World War (Holahan & Sears, 1995). Terman's sample of Californians, born between 1900 and 1920, looked ahead to a seemingly golden future, unimpaired by hard times and the perils of war. But the 20th century had another life course in mind.

About 40 percent of the Terman men served in the armed forces over three to five years and another 25 percent were recruited for work in war industries. These experiences became "hidden influences" as they moved into the later years. Hasty marriages, unplanned births, and divorces were all part of wartime experience. Demobilization required two years or more, and related job changes placed men in different lines of work. Women frequently assumed volunteer roles in the war effort or worked in critical industries and offices. At war's end, most of these women returned to domestic circumstances. However, through their wartime activities women often revised their initial goals and ambitions. The implications of these changing times for aging were not addressed by the investigators as they shifted their study to the middle years and old age. Only in the past decade have studies begun to assess the impact of wartime activities for later life.

The same unknown future played havoc with a longitudinal study of Berkeley children, born 1928-29. Macfarlane (1938) established experimental-control groups of couples and their newborn children, but soon found that her well-conceived design was undermined by the hardships of the Great Depression. Parents from both groups sought help from her staff. Hard times persisted across the 1930s and even into the Second World War among working class families. By the end of the Depression and World War II, the parents' lives had been recast by the times.

Many children were adversely influenced by this change, particularly sons. Some 15 years after the war, Macfarlane (1963) reported developmental gains that seemed most unexpected, especially among men who once lacked self-confidence, stamina, and ambition. She speculated about the sources of this turnaround in psychological well-being, but had little to say about the potential role of men's differing pathways to young adulthood—through higher education, military service, and new families.

Dramatic social change posed new issues for this research group, as did the diverse lives of the study members. But the investigators did not address a more general question: What is the most useful way to assess the developmental relevance of changing times in lives? This question was also ignored by a team of investigators (Kagan & Moss, 1962) who were following children from birth (mid-1930s) to their early 20s in Ohio. A large percentage of the children's fathers were mobilized into the military or war industries during World War II, and their mothers assumed important work and volunteer roles. These circumstances were not explored and neither were the study members' routes to adulthood. Instead, the children were studied from "birth to maturity" by using correlation coefficients to depict behavioral stability and change across the years. As studies now indicate, life-course variations in childhood to the adult years have enduring consequences for health in later life (Keating & Hertzman, 1999).

Despite the flaws of these studies, they expanded our appreciation of longitudinal research designs and challenged us to think in new ways about whole lives. In part, we understand aging in late life by linking it to the early life course. By extending the duration of study, these projects generated questions about the diversity of lives and their connections to late-life adaptations and the larger world, including the behavioral consequences of social change. Starting in the 1960s, these questions and challenges began to prompt: (1) more innovative thinking about how lives are socially organized and evolve over time; and (2) greater recognition of the linkages between social pathways, developmental trajectories, and changes in society (Elder, 1998). Investigators also had to face the obvious limits of child-based, growth-oriented accounts of development.

In response to these challenges, two contrasting lines of work emerged during the 1970s: (1) a life-span approach in developmental psychology, and (2) a sociological perspective on the life course of social roles and events in changing environments. Both sought intellectual breadth across disciplinary boundaries, though neither fully achieved this objective in practice. The life-span movement addressed the description and explanation of age-related biological and behavioral changes from birth to death, with emphasis on the adult years (e.g., Baltes & Reese, 1984). Variations in age-related change across successive birth cohorts were investigated initially (Nesselroade & Baltes, 1974), but research soon shifted away from the differential effects of changing environments. Instead, questions about invariant behavioral changes across cohorts became more compelling. These questions focused on the generalizability of behavior patterns across contexts defined by historical time and place. Changes of this kind began to characterize approaches in life-span developmental psychology.

In contrast, the life-course approach emerged as part of a trend toward a contextual understanding of developmental processes and outcomes (Elder, 1975, 1998; Settersten, 1999). Life-course studies sought to develop a conceptual framework of social pathways and their relation to social-historical conditions, with emphasis on their implications for human development and aging. Some life changes stem from large-scale social transformations, as when regimes fall, economies flourish or collapse, and wars call for the military mobilization of young people. Other changes occur through conventional life transitions. We turn now to the life-course and life-span perspectives, and the contrasting paths they have followed.

LIFE-COURSE AND LIFE-SPAN STUDIES

Life-course ideas focus on the changing contexts of lives and their consequences for human development and aging. The "individual life course" is structured by social influences and the life choices people make in constrained situations. Any change in the way people live their lives affects their development and both are subject to change in established pathways—for example, in workplaces and communities. These pathways are interrelated across the life span. As Bronfenbrenner (1996, p. xi) notes, the life course "encompasses the continuities and changes in the biopsychological characteristics of particular individuals or groups as they proceed along a given environmental pathway through time." Large-scale social forces can alter these pathways through planned intervention (e.g., social policies and programs) and unplanned process of change (e.g., economic cycles and population movements).

Varied pathways to adulthood through military service, post-secondary studies, and early work experience are likely to produce developmental variations. The same can be said about successive birth cohorts. People in historically different cohorts tend to age differently (Elder, 1999; Shanahan & Elder, in press). However, not all members of a birth cohort are exposed in the same way to historical changes. A case in point is the variable experience of Chinese youth in the Cultural Revolution of the late 1960s to the mid-1970s (Zhou & Hou, 1999), a time when millions of urban youth were "sent down" to rural villages. Other young people of similar ages remained in school and followed different pathways to adulthood. These differences in the early life course bear upon subsequent options and personal choices that differentiate the experience of aging in later life.

By comparison, life-span models focus on individual development in a "typical life course." Hetherington and Baltes (1988, p. 9) observe that "child psychologists are likely to postulate a 'typical' course of ontogeny and to view non-normative and history-graded factors as modifiers, not as fundamental constituents, of development." Dannefer (1984, p. 847) affirms this by noting that standard definitions in developmental psychology do not ensure that "research will be designed, nor findings be interpreted, in a way that apprehends social structure as a constituent force in development, and that views the social environment as more than a setting that facilitates maturational unfolding." A typical life course might take the form of the conventional pathway in retirement. Life course variation is not recognized as a potential source of behavioral and psychological change.

Typical environments could also take the form of an assumed "historical continuity" across successive birth cohorts. In life-span studies, cohort-sequential designs are ways of testing the boundaries of generalization in multiple samples (Cairns & Cairns, 1994). The purpose is not to understand the developmental implications of historical context. Indeed, any variation between adjacent birth cohorts is likely to be viewed more as statistical error than as a plausible source of historical effects with developmental implications (Baltes, Cornelius, & Nesselroade, 1979). The task is to determine whether patterns of development and aging generalize across cohorts, yet studies are often hard pressed to explain cohort differences (Nesselroade & Baltes, 1974).

Has the life-span movement become more contextual over the years? In the mid-80s, Schaie (1984) reached this conclusion by pointing to a shift in focus, "from the search for purely developmental patterns of a normative nature to the context in which development occurs." Fifteen years later, Cairns and Rodkin

(1998, p. 248) assert that developmentalists believe that the discipline should describe "the pathways of individual adaptations over time in the concrete context of each life." If so, we should be able to find compelling evidence of this design among empirical studies of child and adult development. We have yet to find substantial evidence of this kind.

Even Heckhausen (1999), who views the age-graded life course in the adult years as a major source of developmental regulation, along with biological constraints, includes only minimal reference to the lives people have actually lived or to issues of historical time and place. Heckhausen notes (Schulz & Heckhausen, 1996, p. 703) that a "comprehensive theory of development should be able to explain developmental phenomena from infancy to old age," but explanatory efforts to date *seldom* take the life course of individuals into account or its ecological and historical circumstances.

When life-span models view contexts of development, they tend to neglect both history and the life course as constituents of human development and aging. The approach does not investigate questions concerning the process by which environmental changes make a difference (Elder & Caspi, 1990). However, life-span models often consider the processes by which people are *selected* into particular social roles and situations (Caspi & Bem, 1990). This process has much in common with the life-course approach and its view of the individual actor as capable of making deliberate choices in life.

The life-span movement has focused on developmental trajectories across the life span, giving little attention to the age-graded life course, its developmental effects, and especially its historical context. By contrast, life-course models address contextual issues, including life patterns and their variation by historical time and place. But what is meant by the life course? For one answer to this question, we turn to life-course concepts and principles that bring contexts to lives.

THE LIFE COURSE THEORETICAL ORIENTATION AND ITS CONCEPTS

We consider the life course a theoretical orientation with great relevance to scholarship on human development and aging. According to Merton (1968), theoretical orientations establish a common framework to guide descriptive and explanatory research. They do so in the identification and formulation of research problems, the selection of variables and rationales for them, and strategies for designing research and analyzing data. In this regard, the life course refers to age-graded life patterns that are embedded in social structures and historical change. It is rooted in a contextualist perspective.

The organizing concepts of the life course, as a theoretical orientation, include *trajectories* and *transitions*. A long view of the life course takes the perspective of trajectories with sequences of family and work roles, among others. A shorter view focuses on life transitions that represent a change in state(s), such as when children leave home. Some transitions involve multiple changes in a multi-phasic process. Disillusionment in marriage may lead to separation and then divorce. The transition to teenage motherhood that begins with sexual experimentation may lead to pregnancy and child-birth; or birth control may be used to prevent unwanted pregnancies. At each phase of the process, the selection of certain options over others results in a different course. Transitions are embedded within larger trajectories.

A substantial change in direction represents a potential *turning point* (Rutter, 1996). Whether planned or not, this change may be worked out in the lives of individuals, or it may be institutionalized in an established social pathway. An institutionalized re-direction of the life course is reflected in corresponding life changes among people, including the possibility of change in the course of aging. For example, in a low-income Boston sample, Sampson and Laub (1993) found that young men were often able to turn away from an early history of crime through the decision to marry and take a stable job. These decisions placed the men in a world that rewarded conventional achievement. Men who followed an institutionalized route to military service after high school were also often able to escape the clutches of a deviant past. Entry into military service became a turning point by placing former delinquents on the road to a stable family life and work role.

These changes are best understood by noting how life trajectories are formed: by linking states across successive years, such as the states of employment in a job or of a residential location. The resulting life record includes the biographical dates of each state, the duration of each state, and linking transitions. Both transitions and *durations* (the time spent in state) have developmental implications. Life transitions may place people in new environments that alter behavior, whereas the forces of habituation and obligation cumulate when people occupy the same residence, job, or marital relationship over many years. The greater the duration of status or social role, the more occupants are committed by others to remain in place (Becker, 1961). They become more embedded in the social environment. Long durations thus increase the likelihood of behavioral continuity over the life course.

Early models generally centered on a single role sequence, as in the notion of a family cycle (Elder, 1978; Hareven, 1978). Children mature, marry, and have children who then grow up and start a family as the cycle continues into another generation. Yet these changes occur in different sequences, and people also move into roles beyond the family, including education, work, leisure, and citizenship. The life-course approach provides a framework within which to view these multiple role sequences and their interactions over time. It has done so in part with the familiar concept of "career," which has much in common with the concept of a social trajectory. Role histories become careers, and multiple roles become multiple careers. However, neither concept, family cycle or career, locate people in historical context and identify their temporal location within the life span.

Age and its meanings provide an essential dimension in life-course study (Neugarten, 1996; Riley, Johnson, & Foner, 1972; Ryder, 1965). It does so by linking age to time, context, and process. An appreciation for *variability in life experiences* emerged from this pioneering work, including an awareness of social and historical context. The social meanings of age structure the life course through age expectations and informal sanctions, social timetables, and generalized age grades (such as childhood or adolescence) (Neugarten, 1996; Settersten & Hagestad, 1996a, 1996b). A normative concept of social time specifies an appropriate age for transitions such as entry into school, marriage, and retirement, leading to relatively "early" and "late" transitions, though little still is known about variability across social class and racial-ethnic cultures. Nevertheless, empirical findings are beginning to cumulate on variations in the age boundaries of particular phases in the life course, such as the transition to adulthood (Shanahan, 2000). These studies also demonstrate the historical significance of age by locating people in age cohorts according to birth year.

When historical change differentiates the lives of successive birth cohorts, it constitutes a *cohort effect*. Older and younger children, for example, were differentially vulnerable to the economic stresses of the Great Depression (Elder, 1999). History also takes the form of a *period effect* when the impact of a social change is relatively uniform across successive birth cohorts. Secular trends in the scheduling of marriages and first births in the 20th century represent a massive period effect. Both period and cohort effects constitute evidence of historical influences. Efforts to disentangle these effects from aging itself have not significantly advanced knowledge of social change in human development. Greater advances have been achieved by measuring the exposure of people to changing environments and by studying the actual process by which the change has consequences (Elder & Pellerin, 1998). Members of a birth cohort are not uniformly exposed to change, suggesting that cohort subgroups should be identified in terms of similar exposure.

Three concepts make unique distinctions in life-course study—life span, life history, and life cycle. *Life span* indicates the temporal scope of inquiry and specialization. A life-span study extends across a substantial period of life and typically links behavior in two or more life stages. This scope moves beyond age-specific research. Life-span questions require longitudinal studies, and thus it is not surprising to note a strong correlation between the increasing popularity of both.

Life history refers to a chronology of events and activities across life domains, such as residence, household composition, education, worklife, and family events. These records may be generated by obtaining prospective information from archival materials or from interviews with a respondent, as in the use of a retrospective life calendar or age-event matrix (Brückner & Mayer, 1998; Caspi, Moffitt, Thornton, Freedman, Amell, Harrington, Smeijers, & Silva, 1996; Freedman, Thornton, Camburn, Alwin, & Young-DeMarco, 1988). Life calendars record the age (year and month) at which a transition occurs in each domain, and thus depict an unfolding life course in ways ideally suited to event-history analyses (Mayer & Tuma, 1990). Retrospective life histories record past events and experiences in terms of the present, and thus entail potential distortion or misrepresentation, especially in relation to emotion-laden events and their meaning. Life history also refers to self-reported narrations of life which may be recorded in this form. They may also be synthesized through the mind of an interviewer. Clausen (1993), for example, interviewed members of the Berkeley studies in later life, and then used the narrations to assemble a set of life histories.

The *life cycle* describes a sequence of events, though it has distinct meaning in population studies where it refers to the reproductive process from one generation to the next. In human populations, the life cycle represents the sequence of parenthood stages, from the birth of children through their departure from home and their own childbearing. Within a framework of generational succession, the cycle is repeated at the population level. At the level of individuals, some people do not have children, for example, and thus are not part of an intergenerational life cycle.

All of these concepts have a place in life-course studies. The scope of work extends across the life span and draws upon the life records and life cycles of generations. The concepts discussed up to this point also have relevance to core principles of the life course.

Life Course Principles and Developmental Contexts

Five principles of the life course make contributions to the contextual study of human development and aging. They are: (1) the principle of human development and aging as lifelong processes; (2) the principle of human agency in situations that vary in constraints and options; (3) the principle of historical time and place; (4) the principle of timing in lives; and (5) the principle of linked lives.

The Principle of Lifelong Development and Aging: Human Development and Aging are Lifelong Processes

This principle reflects the shift from "age-specific" studies to research that extends across long segments of life (Baltes & Baltes, 1990; Riley, Johnson, & Foner, 1972). Behavior cannot be fully explained by restricting analysis to a specific life stage in question. From this perspective, childhood is relevant to understanding adaptations in later life, not only in adolescence and young adulthood.

Longevity is itself a selection process involving many elements, including genetic endowment and health. For satisfactory answers, any question concerning sources of health and longevity requires long-term longitudinal studies of people who have survived from childhood to later life (Kuh, Power, Blane, & Bartley, 1997). Examples include the three national longitudinal studies in Great Britain with birth dates of 1946, 1958, and 1970 (on the 1946 cohort, see Wadsworth, 1991). Consider also the Terman study which followed a sample of Californians from their births in the first decade of the 20th century up to their deaths. The survivors were last followed up in 1992. The study's archival records have contributed to greater understanding of differential morbidity and mortality, including the adverse health effect of exposure to combat during the Second World War (Elder, Shanahan, & Clipp, 1997) and the disruptive impact of late mobilization (after the age of 32) (Elder, Shanahan, & Clipp, 1994).

Research that follows children into adulthood can link childhood influences to adult outcomes through events, relationships, and experiences. An example comes from McAdam's (1989, 1992) study of the enduring consequences of Civil Rights involvement among young people in the Southern region of the United States. Activism during the late 1960s was predictive of activism some years later (the early 1980s), as well as unstable work and marriages. Social ties that led to Civil Rights activity played an important role in sustaining activism, especially among women.

But what about the potential interplay of social change and individual functioning over the years? Unfortunately, longitudinal studies rarely provide the necessary data on contexts, and on changes in context, that this question requires—of residential and socioeconomic changes, as well as changes in culture, population, and social institutions. However, the availability of Geo codes with coordinates that map households for users of large data sets now enable investigators to assess contextual changes and their effects. Of course, in the study of old age, even midlife experiences are relatively "distal" influences. Linking very early experiences to old age outcomes therefore presents major analytic challenges.

Expansion of the temporal span of study is correlated with the increasing significance of aging as a scientific field of study and a social problem, and with the recognized value of life-course models for studying aging. Yet life-course projects inevitably pose challenges around: (1) the continuous interplay of changing lives and changing times; (2) greater sensitivity to continuity and change across life; and (3) the increasing relevance of a multi-generational perspective that links phases of the life course. Consistent with the first issue, the longer a life is studied, the greater its risk of exposure to social change. Long lives are thus most likely to reflect the particular contours of a changing society. Lives and times are interwoven and represent an ever-changing dynamic across the years. One of the most dramatic examples comes from the reunification of Germany in the lives of men and women who grew up in communist East Germany and now find themselves in a new country with little appreciation for their work skills as they enter the later years (Noack, Hofer, & Youniss, 1995).

Second, the problematics of social and behavioral continuity and change are heightened by an extension of the span of study to longer segments of the life course. Why do some behavioral patterns persist while others fade? What influences play a role in this change? We are just beginning to identify mechanisms that drive patterns of continuity and change. For example, Caspi and Bem (1990) identify three types of interaction between person and situation that have relevance to individual continuity and change: reactive, evocative, and proactive interactions. *Reactive interaction* refers to people who encounter the same situation but interpret and respond to it differently. Examples include divorce which has different meaning to family members and possibly to people at different life stages. *Evocative interactions* refer to the process by which an individual's behavior, appearance, or personality elicits distinctive responses from others. Consider the process of caregiving where the physical decline of an older person leads to changes in children's support and interaction with the parent. *Proactive interactions* are expressed in the selection of social environments, such as friendships and residential areas.

Third, age-specific studies lose significance as people are followed across stages of life. A sequence of age specific studies cannot replace prospective longitudinal studies and their contribution for understanding the interplay of changing lives and trajectories of aging. The young, middle-aged, and old are interwoven in the lives of individuals. This applies, most notably, to the developmental trajectories of parents and children (Cowan & Cowan, 1992), as intergenerational models have particular relevance to lifelong development and aging. Social relationships influence the course of aging, as through the presence or absence of companionship and emotional support. The trajectory of aging also affects the continued vitality of these relationships.

Work is an important source of personal continuity and change for most men and women. Kohn and Schooler's (1983) research on a national sample of American men shows that substantively complex work promotes intellectual flexibility, and that such men also tend to select work of this kind. This reciprocal process no doubt occurs across life. Indeed, studies are beginning to ask whether the developmental effects of work diminish over time, are constant or even increase with age.

With multiple data points in a national study, Schooler (with Mulatu & Oates, 1999) finds that substantively complex work continues to influence men's intellectual functioning well into the later years, and that the effect is greatest among the oldest workers. Although they do not fully explain this differential effect, it may be that men who have complex jobs are more likely to invest in them, and that this investment may continue into later life through second careers or consulting. Other types of jobs are likely to be more alienating over time. We have much to learn about the workplace as a central context for adults and how the organization of some workplaces and jobs may undermine the meaning of work for older people, as through job discrimination on wage increases and promotions.

The health of women in the middle to later years also appears to benefit from productive labor, although the mechanisms remain a matter of speculation. Pavalko and Smith (1999) use panel data between 1982 and 1989 from the National Longitudinal Survey of Mature Women to investigate the link between worklife dynamics and both emotional and physical health. Physical health limitations play an increasingly important role in shaping women's work experience as they move across the middle and later years, though historical change may be at work as well. Consistent with a thesis of multiple roles benefiting women's health and longevity (see Moen, Dempster-McClain, & Williams, 1989), this study indicates that healthier women are more likely to be employed at this time of life, and that the more time they spend at work, the better their health. The payoffs are both physical and emotional. Employed women are less likely to have physical limitations and to feel emotionally depressed. However, selection processes must be considered, as they play an important role in structuring women's lives, especially with respect to work roles.

Frequently the designs of longitudinal projects rule out studies of trajectories that extend from childhood to the later years. These include the mature cohorts of American adults in the National Longitudinal Surveys (Pavalko & Smith, 1999) and the Health and Retirement Surveys. Another example is the Berlin Aging Study of people over the age of 75 (Baltes & Mayer, 1999), which addresses resourcefulness among the very old. Studies of aging that begin with adults in their 50s or 60s lack a developmental history of prior years on health, nutrition, and physical change, and a life record of environmental change, as when people change societies or communities, schools, work roles, and marriages. These records are essential for identifying the explanatory mechanisms of diverse life pathways. With their heavy attrition, late-life samples also rule out studies of wartime trauma in old age, despite the prevalence of such experiences among older men. Nevertheless, major longitudinal studies of aging continue to launch their data collections in later life.

Questions that motivate studies of later life are often prompted by the political need for "quick answers" to such matters as disability and long-term care. In addition to time pressures, matters of cost are also important. Long-lived studies far exceed their original budgets, and many have been threatened with termination during periods of economic retrenchment. The Panel Study of Income Dynamics, for example, launched in 1968 nearly died from lack of funds during the early 1980s (Duncan & Morgan, 1985). However, the study continues to serve as a model for comparable studies in other countries, including Canada and members of the European community.

The Principle of Human Agency: Individuals Construct Their Own Life Course Through the Choices and Actions They Take Within the Opportunities and Constraints of History and Social Circumstances

Transitions across the life course involve individual initiatives, situational constraints and opportunities, influence from others, and the dispositions and prior experiences that individuals bring to new situations. Elements of agency have been prominent in life history studies (see Haidt & Rodin, 1999; Thomas & Znaniecki,

1918-20) and are central to life-course studies that relate individuals to broader social contexts. Within the particular limitations of their worlds, people are planful and make choices that allow them to control their lives (Clausen, 1993).

Social structures vary in the extent to which they enable expressions of agency. Work units in Communist China made most decisions for urban youth during the Cultural Revolution (Zhou & Hou, 1999), but even in this constrained world young people had some choices that made a difference in the quality of their lives. Real world constraints and opportunities are under-represented in most psychological accounts of agency, including that based on action theory, genetic influences and selection processes, and self-efficacy. However, the role of agency has become a vital element in theoretical accounts of the life course and human development.

The incorporation of people and social structures in life-course models establishes the potential for "loose coupling" between the age-graded life course and lives as lived by individuals. Whatever the influence of age norms, people of the same age do not move in concert through life. They vary on age at leaving school and entering a job or advanced education, on age at marriage and first child. Thus, "age grades and loose coupling exemplify two sides of the life course—its social regulation and the actor's behavior within conventional boundaries, and even outside of them" (Elder & O'Rand, 1995, p. 457).

Choice-making processes are vividly revealed in Hagan's (2001) account of American war resisters during the Vietnam War, and their anguished decision to take the "northern passage" to Toronto, Canada, a legal sanctuary from the Selective Service System. Nearly 10,000 men chose to defy the military draft and the counsel of their families. Some went with female friends, and most carried on their protest of the war. Though many years removed from the Vietnam crisis, former war resisters (most of whom still live in Canada) recalled the emotional complexity and discord of their decision process. The motivating force behind the "northern passage" made this experience a wrenching psychological act for many. War resisters made their decision to live in Canada after countless appeals and protests, recognizing the moral stigma of their action in the American public. Hagan's interviews recall this traumatic time and the process by which "each decision against service in the war" constructed a deviant path from the perspective of American society.

Resisters resembled their siblings in family patterns, but differed in line of work and total earnings. They were likely to be employed in human service and artistic professions, and their lower earnings were partly due to this occupational difference. However, the more important source of income inequality involved the socioeconomic costs of prolonged involvement in war protests and the world of activism, which also recast their sense of self, social identity, and relationships with family and friends.

Social constraints restrict and direct the expression of agency. Consider, for example, a planful view of one's future in the 1930s to 1940s (Shanahan & Elder, in press). Events beyond one's control were prominent in these decades, and an uncontrollable environment was characteristic of the lives of older men in the Stanford-Terman study, born between 1903 and 1911. Most had completed college before the Stock Market Crash, and consequently entered a labor market that soon became stagnant in the financial crisis of the 1930s. Their dismal chances in the labor market kept them in school, acquiring advanced degrees. By contrast, younger men (born between 1911 and 1920) remained in some form of schooling throughout the 1930s, long enough to acquire attractive jobs as the economy improved through wartime. Nearly 70 percent either served in the military or war industry during World War II.

Contrary to Clausen's (1993) initial concept, the effects of planfulness in adolescence depend on historical context and social support. The teenage planfulness of the younger men predicted a relatively stable and successful life course. Apart from family background and IQ, more planful men did better in life than other men of similar age—in education, marriage, and civic involvement—and they were especially satisfied with their lives. By contrast, planfulness in adolescence revealed little about the lives of the older men. Planful older men were not more successful in education, and their marriages were not more stable. Disrupted times undermined the usefulness of their planful orientation. In all of these ways, the next principle speaks to the constraints and options in peoples' lives.

The Principle of Historical Time and Place: The Life Course of Individuals is Embedded in and Shaped by the Historical Times and Places They Experience Over Their Lifetime

The ecologies of historical time and place are expressed in Bronfenbrenner's (1979) pioneering book, *The Ecology of Human Development*, which viewed children's environments as multi-level contexts. These ecologies range from the macro and meso levels to the microenvironment. In *Children of the Great Depression* (Elder, 1999), for example, changes in the economy at the macro level were traced to the micro family experiences of children.

For many years, we merely described such levels. We could not do more until methods for hierarchical linear modeling were introduced by Bryk and Raudenbusch (1992) and others to investigate developmental influences at multiple levels (for a review, see DiPrete & Forristal, 1994), since then, hierarchical linear models have been usefully employed in many studies of school and neighborhood influences, though largely limited to the development of children and adolescents. Multi-level models tend to under-represent the "complexity" of changing social structures and their influence on the life course. Causal mechanisms are frequently left to speculation.

The same historical event or epoch may differ in substance and meaning across different regions or nations. For example, the immediate postwar years were deprivational in many parts of Europe, unlike the prosperity experience in the

United States, and war experiences entailed widespread suffering among veterans and civilians. Using a retrospective life history method (Brückner & Mayer, 1998), Mayer (1988) found that German men, born between 1915 and 1925, were almost universally involved in military service—about 97 percent of these cohorts. These men lost as many as nine years of their occupational careers, and many could not find employment afterward. They suffered high rates of imprisonment, both during and after the war, and only 75 percent survived the war. The cohort of 1931 also suffered widespread and profound hardship in the war. It disrupted their families and schooling, and the devastated economy made stable employment illusory for many. Work experiences were poor and mixed with spells of jobless-ness. Opportunities for advancement were unlikely in the late 1940s. Even the economic boom of the 1950s and 1960s did not fully compensate this younger cohort for its war-related losses in occupational advancement.

One of the most dramatic examples of different pathways of change in a birth cohort comes from a longitudinal study following 12th-grade students (1983-85) from fifteen regions of the former Soviet Union up to 1999 and beyond (Titma & Tuma, 1995). Called "Paths of a Generation," the study assessed the life expectations, achievements, and backgrounds of young people before the Soviet Union disintegrated circa 1990, and then traced their lives into a period of extraordinary change and instability. One region retained the command economy of the old Soviet Union (Belarus), while others adopted a market economy (e.g., Estonia) or returned to a more primitive rural exchange system (e.g., Tajikistan). The socioeconomic lives of men and women resembled the changes of their respective regions of the old Soviet Union. The Estonian cohort is most prosperous, whereas downward trajectories are common among youth from Belarus and the Ukraine.

Despite such regional differences and profound social instability, the future of this generation to date was written in large part by their personal accom-plishments, self-assessments, and goals when they were in high school. Periods of transition and instability tend to accentuate individual differences (Caspi & Moffitt, 1993), and the Paths of Generation study finds academic success and high aspirations to be more predictive of subsequent occupational status and income than family background. Interestingly, young men who had become entrepreneurs with hired personnel were most distinguished in high school by their ambition and high self-appraisal of personal skills in managing people.

A number of "mechanisms" link these sorts of social changes to lives. When people enter a new situation, they encounter its *behavior imperatives*—the rules, expectations, and sanctions that ensure compliance with the demands of the new setting. Consider a setting with many tasks and few people—in Barker's terminology (1968, p. 190), an "undermanned environment." The Baltic states' economy most closely represent this setting in the former Soviet Union—a flourishing economy with a strong demand for skilled workers. Small com-munities and schools create "undermanned" expectations in which even the least skilled participants are expected to contribute. According to Barker, the older and younger residents of undermanned settings tend to be involved in more challenging and consequential actions when compared to the occupants of overmanned environments. They are "busier, more versatile, and more orientated vis-a-vis the settings they inhabit, and more independent" (Barker, 1968, p. 198). Small rural communities, with their relatively large older population, are typically undermanned environments and must draw upon people of all ages to ensure that basic tasks are done.

Entry into a new situation and social role entails some loss of control, a change that initiates a *control cycle* involving efforts to regain control. The new situation might entail an elderly woman's transition to her child's home or to a program of "assisted care." Loss of control sets in motion efforts to regain it, though both settings signify a decline in personal autonomy. Entry into a new job following retirement, such as part-time consulting, illustrates a selection process in which the new environment may have been chosen for its manageability (Brim, 1993).

The way lives are influenced by social change depends in part on what the individual brings to the new situation. These experiences are frequently accentuated by the new environment. We refer to this process as an *accentuation dynamic*. Prominent attributes brought to the new situation are likely to be amplified, a process that is common in circumstances where people are selected into new environments. An example comes from migration. The more resourceful members are most likely to migrate to other regions and countries, and the transition itself tends to accentuate such qualities in adaptations to the new environment.

The Principle of Timing: The Developmental Antecedents and Consequences of Life Transitions, Events, and Behavior Patterns Vary According to Their Timing in a Person's Life

Life-long human development, its historical and spatial context, and human agency underscore ways of thinking about timing and life contexts. Historical changes have different implications for people of different ages– that is, for people who differ in *life stage* (Ryder, 1965). One rationale for this variation involves the developmental meaning of different life stages. People of different ages bring different experiences and resources to situations and consequently adapt in different ways to new conditions. Adaptations of this kind structure the life course through a selective process of decision-making.

The developmental and social implications of life stage help to explain why two birth cohorts from the 1920s were affected so differently by the Great Depression (Elder, 1999). For members of the Oakland Growth Study, childhood occurred during the prosperous 1920s, whereas for members of the Berkeley Guidance Study, childhood occurred during the 1930s. Born at the beginning of the 1920s, the Oakland children were not as susceptible to the effects of family disruption and hardship as their younger Berkeley counterparts, with birth dates in the late 1920s, and the Oakland children were also too young to be exposed to the harsh labor conditions of a depressed economy. If we think in terms of a developmental match between person and environment (Eccles, Midgley, Wigfield, Buchanan, Reuman, Flanagan, & MacIver, 1993), this "goodness of fit" best applies to the Oakland children. The timing of prosperity, depression, and war placed the two birth cohorts on different developmental pathways.

One might expect the Depression experiences of children and their families to affect their subsequent work, family, and financial decisions. Indeed, financial security became an important concern for men who were children with below average IQ skills in economically deprived homes. These men may have been especially vulnerable to subsequent events in later life, such as downsizing and the closure of plants (Newman, 1992). Did such events accelerate the retirement of some Depression men and "bring back" long suppressed emotions?

The worklives of Depression men were described in follow-ups into the 1980s, but no follow-up included information on their firms and economic health. One might imagine that some men had entered new technology firms, while others ended up in the declining manufacturing sector. In view of their insecure 1930s background, how might they approach retirement? This is a question that requires life history information in order to link childhood with later life.

A study of retirement decisions among autoworkers in the 1980s (Hardy & Hazelrigg, 1999) enables us to place this decision process in the context of an uncertain future, with plant closings likely. During the late 1980s, approximately one-fifth of the autoworkers for General Motors (USA) who were eligible for early retirement chose this option. The percentage was significantly higher among the workers in plants that were scheduled to close. Traditional worker characteristics might explain this result, such as physical health and pension wealth. The study shows, however, that both levels of analysis (worker and plant) are needed for a complete explanation. Workers in poorer health but with good pensions were most likely to choose early retirement, and this was especially likely in plants characterized by worker solidarity and/or scheduled to be shut down. Most retirees were satisfied with their new status. Dissatisfaction was concentrated among workers who felt they had retired "too early," owing to circumstances.

Other macrosocial changes can differentially influence the lives of persons of different ages, as in time of war. Early transition to military service, before the establishment of families and careers, tends to minimize life disruption and even enhance life chances through early skill training and leadership experience, the formation of life goals, and post-service education through the GI Bill. From this vantage point, early entry provides a good fit between the recruit and the social environment, notwithstanding the risk of combat and injuries or death. Evidence of this "life-course fit" comes from longitudinal studies of American men who served in World War II or the Korean conflict. For two cohorts from the 1920s, early entry into military duty established a pathway of personal growth, greater opportunity, and life achievement (Elder, 1986, 1987). When mobilized at later ages, men experienced greater disruption by being pulled away from well-established patterns of family life, work, and civic roles (Elder & Chan, 1999).

A valuable assessment of the "early entry hypothesis" in World War II is provided by a longitudinal study of approximately 1000 boys, mostly born between 1925 and 1935, from low-income areas of Boston (Sampson & Laub, 1996). More than 70 percent served in World War II. The matched control design, 500 delinquents and 500 controls, was established by Sheldon and Eleanor Glueck (1968) for a longitudinal study of criminal careers. Men in both subsamples tended to enter the service at 18 or 19, and most served overseas and for at least two years. Consistent with prior studies, men mobilized into active duty at an early age tended to do better in their work careers, avoidance of problem behavior, and family life after demobilization.

As expected, men with a delinquent history experienced higher rates of dishonorable discharge and other forms of official misconduct, but they also were more apt to benefit from the service over their lives. This benefit was especially true of men who entered the service early in life. These men were young enough to take advantage of what the military had to offer, such as the broadening perspectives gained from overseas duty, the skills developed through in-service schooling, and educational benefits from the GI Bill. These benefits were particularly great for men with delinquent pasts. Because very few of these men had the background for college, all benefits were typically associated with training for the trades. This training enhanced men's occupational statuses, job stability, and economic well-being up to midlife, apart from childhood differences and socioeconomic origins.

Two kinds of change across the life course suggest a pattern of time-varying historical influences. One involves a change in social roles, tasks, and settings; the other involves the aging of the individual. Initial thinking on the relation between SES and health (Adler, Boyce, Chesney, Cohen, Folkman, Kahn, & Syme, 1994) ignored life-course variability, but studies are beginning to examine this variation and its implications. For example, emotional depression follows a socioeconomic gradient; as socioeconomic status declines, depression generally increases in prevalence. However, the mechanisms may vary for different age groups. For example, before midlife, depression may be linked to socioeconomic status through low education and mastery, whereas in late life, depression may be related to socioeconomic status through impaired physical health (Miech & Shanahan, 2000).

Similarly, the timing of exposure to poverty in childhood and adolescence may have differential effects on cognitive ability and achievement, as well as health. Guo (1998) found that long-term poverty has substantial influences on both ability and achievement, but that the time patterns of these influences differ. Ability represents a more stable trait than achievement and is influenced by both environmental and genetic factors early in life. The years of childhood proved to be more crucial for the development of cognitive ability than early adolescence. By comparison, exposure to poverty in adolescence was more consequential for achievement than exposure early in childhood.

An ill-timed event may set in motion cumulative disadvantages. For young girls, an early teenage birth may be followed by other births in the absence of a partner's support. With prolonged hardship and stress, this accelerated life course may also accelerate the pace of aging, including a sense of being old. A case in point is the initial transition to the grandparent role (Kaufman & Elder, under review). When mothers enter the grandparent role at an early age, they define themselves as "older" than their agemates.

The connection between an early birth and an older self-definition also appears in a study of African-American generations in Los Angeles (Burton & Bengtson, 1985). The early timing of a young daughter's giving birth had repercussions for the roles, responsibilities, and social identities of grandparents. A birth in early adolescence increased deprivations and strains, reflecting the violation of deep-seated expectations about how life should be lived. The new mothers still thought about themselves as children and expected their mothers to help care for their child. This expectation seldom materialized because the new grandmothers felt too young for the grandmother role. As one new grandmother put it, "I can't be a young momma and a grandmomma at the same time."

Physical maturation provides another example of "an accelerated life course." In Sweden, Stättin and Magnusson (1990) found that girls who reached menarche very early (before age 12) were at risk of greater alcohol consumption, school cheating, and rates of sexual activity at age 14. Early maturation increased the developmental gap between the sexes in early adolescence, motivating early maturers to associate with more mature, older boys who are typically out of school and working. Early maturing girls chose older friends who in turn encouraged their sexual activity. Selection and social causation are evident in this developmental trajectory. Both the sexual and social behaviors of these girls deviated from age norms over a 15-month period. However, maturational differences beyond this period proved insignificant, although the behavioral consequences of health-risk behaviors are likely to have long-term consequences. The larger community context might also perpetuate problem behavior. For example, Caspi (1995) found developmental patterns among early maturing girls that were similar to Stättin and Magnusson (1990), though only for girls *in coeducational schools,* not single-sex schools. Little is known about the long-term implications of off-time maturation for girls or boys.

Across a range of deviant and health-risk behaviors, relatively early onset (before age 13 or 14) tends to predict continuity in negative behaviors and cumulative disadvantages over time (Moffitt, 1993), though few studies of high-risk children have extended to midlife and beyond. For example, early arrest and incarceration are predictive of subsequent involvement in deviant activities; and early onset of heavy drinking and drug use are predictive of future problem behavior of this kind (Schulenberg, Maggs, & Hurrelmann, 1997). Early onset of problem behavior has been linked to neurological, behavioral, and family deficits, though it is unclear how these influences play out over time. Selection processes are noteworthy, more so than environmental deprivation, though interaction effects seem likely. Later onset of problem behavior is less predictive of problem continuity, but little is known about longer-term sequelae that extend into later life.

The behavioral effects of life changes, whether linked to large-scale events or not, are contingent on when they occur (George, 1993). Thus, the differential timing of the first grade transition can place children on different trajectories of success and failure (Alexander & Entwisle, 1988). Within the framework of human agency, timing becomes one element in strategies of behavioral adaptation, to the extent that timing can be controlled. Delayed transitions may enhance the ability to prepare for the change and synchronize change with others, as when husband and wife coordinate exits from full-time careers (Han & Moen, 1999). The extent of synchronization can be thought of in terms of a general normative expectation or according to the multiple trajectories of an individual and those of significant others. From this perspective, timing is expressed in the synchrony and asynchrony of lives.

The Principle of Linked Lives: Lives are Lived Interdependently and Social-Historical Influences are Expressed Through this Network of Shared Relationships

Social relationships can be thought of as a "developmental context" (Hartup & Laursen, 1991) and as a "convoy" of significant others (Antonucci & Aikyama, 1995). Consider mate selection and the mutual regulatory influence of each partner. Caspi and Herbener (1990) investigated the influence of marital relations on the developmental trajectory of husbands and wives. In "choosing situations that are compatible with their dispositions and by affiliating with similar others, individuals may set in motion processes of social interchange that sustain their dispositions across time and circumstance" (p. 250). Among couples with strong marriages, they found evidence of a trajectory of parallel development over 20 years. Husbands and wives did not become more like each other, but they did show a strikingly parallel course of psychological development. When marriages dissolved, the former partners tended to follow different trajectories. A late-life follow-up of Bennington College graduates from the 1930s came to similar conclusions (Alwin, Cohen, & Newcomb, 1991). Women tended to select a college environment that matched their political beliefs, and they married men with similar beliefs, which sustained their own beliefs into the later years.

Family changes are especially relevant to the principle of linked lives and its effects. Hernandez (1993) refers to a number of revolutionary family changes in the lives of children and adults, including migration off the land, decline in family size, the growth of maternal employment, and divorce and single parenting.

Migration off the land deserves mention because it has been largely ignored, despite the scope of the change from rural to urban society. The stunning growth of maternal employment also raises questions about linked lives and the vocational development of children, especially daughters (Parcel & Menaghan, 1994). Divorce and remarriage alter the matrix of social relationships for adults and children. Multiple transitions of this kind produce unstable family lives for young and old alike (Wu & Martinson, 1993).

Farm families are characterized by strong community and intergenerational ties, and migration off the land has weakened the family and community support of young people. A longitudinal study of families in the rural Midwest documents this loss and the greater social resources of young people with families on the land (Elder & Conger, 2000), despite economically difficult times. Youth with ties to the land ranked among the more competent and successful adolescents, and their accomplishments had much to do with their social capital—with the greater community ties of parents and children, and with strong ties across the generations. Young people with ties to the land were more involved in joint activities with their parents and had stronger relationships with grandparents and teachers. Their social responsibilities fostered a sense of "mattering" to others, a feeling of significance because other people counted on them. The transition from rural to urban has many correlates, but the decline in social capital is dramatic. Linked lives regulate personal development and the aging experience.

Intergenerational ties link the experiences of one generation to the development of the next. The work values of parents are a case in point. Shaped in part by job conditions, they are passed on to their children through family relations. Using data from longitudinal study based in St. Paul, Minnesota, Ryu and Mortimer (1996) show that parental work experiences and values are correlated with the work values of children. Mothers' extrinsic work values (e.g., money, security) fostered similar values among daughters; and mothers with strong intrinsic values (e.g., work autonomy, interest in job) were least likely to have daughters who valued extrinsic rewards such as high income and status. For sons, the supportiveness of parents mattered more than parents' actual work values and occupational experience. The more supportive the father and mother, the stronger the son's intrinsic values. Supportive fathers with self-directed jobs were most likely to have sons with intrinsic values. Clearly, the experiences of one family member may influence the work values of others.

Linked lives extend beyond the family to friends, teachers, and neighbors. Theories of resilience commonly assume that positive influences can offset negative influences. A positive school environment of classmates and teachers might make up for a child's punitive family environment or a drug-infested neighborhood. A second perspective stresses individual differences and the differential impact of environments on young people. For example, less able students might benefit more from a small school or classroom than more able students. A third perspective asserts that the effects of social contexts on development may be cumulative rather than interactive. Support for this perspective comes from a recent study of adolescents in Prince George's County in the Washington D.C. area (Cook, Herman, Phillips, & Settersten, under review). The joint role of nuclear families, friendship groups, schools and neighborhoods were assessed on healthy adolescent development (7th and 8th grades) during the early 1990s. The quality of all four contexts had independent and additive influences on adolescent "success," defined by a composite of school performance, social behavior, and mental health indicators. No interactions among the four contexts were observed. Though the effects of any one context were not large, the total contextual effect was substantial. Each context can operate as a risk factor when it is negative, and as a protective factor when it is positive.

Conventional approaches to the study of peers and friends, as linked lives, have viewed the relationship only from the perspective of the child or adolescent. The perspective of others has not been considered. Studies have also ignored the developmental history of friendship and peer experiences. Bearman and Brückner (1999) address both of these deficiencies in their investigation of girls' friendships and peer groups as contributing factors to sexual intercourse and pregnancy in adolescence. Their study, based on the National Longitudinal Study of Adolescent Health, provides evidence of the positive influence of peers at multiple levels. Both adolescent girls and their friends were classified as "high risk" or "low risk" by school orientation and success as well as evidence of health-risk behavior, such as drinking, skipping school, and fighting. A girl's own risk status was less important for her first sexual intercourse and pregnancy than the risk status of her male and female friends. Moreover, the age of a girl's friends tended to be more important than her own. Girls with older friends were more likely to themselves engage in sexual intercourse. A girl's circle of close friends and her wider peer network also mattered more than her best friends, and the effects were predominantly protective. Girls who had low-risk friends among their close circle of friends or in their peer group were less likely to have sex or experience a pregnancy.

Although less is known about friends and peers after childhood and adolescence, the transition to marriage produces a major turnover in the friends of the husband (Wellman, Wong, Tindall, & Nazer, 1997), and this is one factor that enables delinquent youth to steer away from crime (Sampson & Laub, 1993). Among older American males, military service establishes networks of long-term friendships involving visits, letters, and phone calls (Elder & Clipp, 1988). Reunions of military units draw upon these networks and participation strengthens social ties. Shared memories of comrades who did not survive represents another key source of the veteran social bond. In view of the prevalence of veterans among retirees, it is unfortunate that we know little about their service experience and its lifelong impact on health and social well being.

The influence of multi-level contexts on the life course and human development is informed by each of the paradigmatic principles. Lifelong development

THE LIFE COURSE AND AGING / 71

underscores the challenge for assessing the impact of changing environments. The impact of social change in childhood interacts with subsequent forms of social change. Variable times and places of lives can be better understood by investigating the timing of lives and their relation to significant others. Historical contexts, the timing of events, and linked lives enable us to understand the contexts in which life choices are made.

Life-course study has flourished over the past 30 years, and we see this in terms of theory and method, empirical projects, new questions, and new sources of data. Colby (1998, p. x) describes the life-course movement as one of "the most important achievements of social science in the second half of the 20th century." However, we have much unfinished work to do.

NEW DIRECTIONS FOR STUDYING
LIVES IN CONTEXT

We began by describing the different paths that life span and life-course studies have taken in relation to the social contexts of human development and aging. We need models in which both traditions inform research. One way to think of a productive convergence is to consider the multiple points of entry in a study. As a rule, large complex studies have multiple levels and entry points. For example, social change and individual development may be linked through community structure to family-level processes and the individual. The objective for a study that is framed in terms of social change is to nest developmental analyses within these contexts. The most important decision involves the entry point that frames the study; it spans multiple levels from proximal to distal social contexts of the individual. Work by Cairns and Cairns (1994, p. 250) illustrates this strategy. These investigators identified multiple points of entry and levels of analysis relevant to a study of aggression, extending from the individual and inter-individual levels to social networks that link people, connections between networks, and the larger cultural-ecological system. Change in the latter system might be traced through social networks to the individual parent, grandparent, or child. The causal sequence depends in part on the relation between family and school or family and peers. The complexity of tending to all levels might seem impractical, yet recognition of this conceptual map constitutes a first step toward informed research decisions.

Contemporary life-course studies suggest a number of promising methods for future studies of human development and aging in context. For example, as noted earlier, analytic techniques now enable us to assess the multi-level effects of people's environments, as with hierarchical linear models. This research often draws upon multiple generations and uses qualitative and quantitative data in mixed-method designs. The creative integration of ethnographic and other qualitative data is an important step forward. The study of change processes has been advanced by latent trajectory analysis (Muthén & Khoo, 1998). Repeated measures of a phenomena (trait, ability, or behavior) represent the observable products of an underlying trajectory of development or change. Both initial levels of the phenomenon and its rates of change can be treated as outcomes and as influences on other outcomes. Early events or transitions can be modeled as influences on subsequent trajectories, which in turn are linked to other factors. The technique is flexible and enables the simultaneous modeling of interrelated trajectories.

Three other issues deserve consideration. These are (1) personal agency and subjective perspectives on the life course, (2) challenges in linking individual and contextual change, and (3) ways of capturing the complexity of individual lives and environments.

Human Agency and Subjective Understanding of Lives

The social environment creates opportunities for and constraints on individual action, and it shapes personal preferences and perceptions of opportunities and constraints. A contextual understanding of agency needs further development along these lines. What do people want, plan, and intend for their lives, and how do these change over the life course? How do desires and intentions vary across time, place, and individual experience? By what process do the social norms and values of a cultural environment influence decisions and subsequent reactions to life transitions? These choices involve a constructionist perspective, which is most vividly expressed in subjective accounts of life experience.

A subjective perspective is one of the oldest approaches to the study of lives, and yet it is undeveloped relative to its potential (Settersten, 1999). Consider normative dimensions of the life course, such as age expectations and sanctions, beliefs about the appropriate time for certain events, and popular concepts about the stages of life. Normative explanations of life events are common in the research literature, yet we have little empirical knowledge of such norms and how they are experienced. This observation was made over 25 years ago (Elder, 1975), and remains valid today. What are the milestones in life, the events that tell us where we are? What are the best and worst times in life, and how do such assessments affect feelings of contentment and personal gratification? When does the subjective experience of time begin to move faster or slower? What life transitions and events account for this change, if any? Bernice Neugarten (1996) first asked such questions in the 1950s. We have much unfinished work to do in addressing them, and in relating social pathways to their subjective representations.

Changing Lives in Dynamic Environments

One of the new frontiers of life-course study is the direct measurement of changing contexts and modeling the interplay of lives and environments over long periods of time (i.e., longitudinal multi-level analysis). Data on social contexts too often describe only a single point in time. Family structure during childhood is not adequately represented by a single time-point measure, as children may experience a sequence of family structures that vary in duration (Wu & Martinson, 1993). Peer networks change over time, as do neighborhoods and workplaces. Economic conditions also change, both for individuals and families. These changes continue over the life course, though some at a diminished frequency.

Dynamic relationships with other people constitute an important changing context for development. New projects have been launched to study relationships over time and will improve our understanding of linked lives. The National Longitudinal Study of Adolescent Health is a case in point. Relationship data will be collected on friends and romantic partners in the transition from school to adult roles. This procedure offers the potential to assess relationships that hold back and place young people at risk, or offer support and sustain them, as they enter adulthood.

The Carolina Longitudinal Study has examined young people's peer relationships over time. By charting youth's friendship groups over time, Cairns and Cairns (1994) have documented the fluidity of friendships at this stage. Despite this, they found continuity in the characteristics of persons who became friends. This means that friendship groups can have a continuing and influential effect on the behavior of young people, despite the fleeting nature of specific friendship ties. Similar designs and research foci are needed for studies of friendships from midlife to the later years.

Understanding the Complexity of Lives and Times

An important step in life-course thinking occurred in the 1960s through the recognition of variability and complexity in individuals and their environments. The life course of an individual is comprised of multiple, interlocking trajectories that vary according to the synchronization of those trajectories. Trajectories in one life domain affect those in other domains, as observed in families and work careers. Life stages and transitions are linked over time, as when early events and processes are related to later ones. Dealing with the complexity of whole lives in context remains very challenging

As we have seen, "context" has many faces, and each can be studied at ever greater levels of specificity. Do we then end up with knowledge of more about less? Are generalizations out of reach? Clearly, an ongoing challenge in life-course studies is to attend simultaneously to the contextual specificity of development and aging while identifying generalizable patterns toward more useful theory. The objective is to understand contextual variations that make a difference in human lives, development, and aging.

CONCLUSION

The earliest longitudinal studies in the United States focused on child development, but they contributed in notable ways to a contemporary view of aging as a lifelong process embedded in social pathways and structures, geographic settings, and historical time. The post-1970 growth of longitudinal studies and the emergence of the life-course framework are key elements of this contribution. This chapter tells the story of such change in thinking and research, with emphasis on the life course and its distinctive contribution to empirical and theoretical studies of aging.

The original longitudinal studies were few in number, and yet they set in motion forces that currently underlie the stunning growth of life-course research. Such growth is especially evident in the United States but it appears throughout the Western world and even in some developing societies. In particular, the studies helped to make a compelling case for understanding how people develop and age; and for charting the explanatory process by which early and later development and aging are linked. These studies advanced a design for studying aging that is gaining favor, despite heavy costs and time requirements. In Great Britain, for example, the case for a new national longitudinal study of children has been made in terms of its contribution to knowledge of the whole life course, with emphasis on adult health and competence (Bynner, 2000, personal communication). And increasingly the extension of adolescent studies has become more attractive and even deemed necessary for adequate studies of trajectories of adult development and aging. The National Longitudinal Survey of Youth is now a study of young adults; and the National Longitudinal Study of Adolescent Health includes plans for extension to the 30s and beyond.

When early studies of child development were extended up to and across stages of adulthood, new ways of thinking about how lives are organized and change emerged. Because changing lives often reflect changing times, this greater span of study called for theories that would place lives in context. Life-span psychologists have increasingly focused only on typical trajectories of development and aging, with little interest in the developmental implications of historical variation, whereas life-course sociologists produced a theoretical orientation that emphasized age-graded social pathways. This orientation to the life course calls attention to human development and aging as lifelong processes, the role of human agency and choice-making, timing and the interdependence of lives, and their historical time and place.

Each of these principles orients research on human development and aging in context. By extending the field of study across life stages, we see that individuals' own life histories form a context with behavioral implications. The timing of events and transitions in lives brings life stage and past experience together. Individuals select social environments and thereby construct their own life course. Linked lives specify the behavioral influence of interpersonal contexts. The principle of historical time and place relates life changes and aging to specific historical times and places.

Life-course concepts are well suited to research on aging that follows children into and through adulthood and the later years. They locate the individual along diverse social pathways and link their life course to changes in society. But we know little about social-structural effects and historical changes across the *entire life course,* though statistical and methodological innovations may enable their study over long segments of life. Progress in this direction will flourish with cross-disciplinary exchange and collaboration.

Life-span knowledge of individual development has much to offer life-course studies; and the life-course research of historians, sociologists, geographers, and anthropologists bring potential contextual variation and influence to life-span models of individual aging. Most importantly, life-course studies persuasively demonstrate that social contexts are more than simply behavioral settings. The social forces of particular times and places shape individual pathways and together become constituents of human development and aging. Where we have been in our lives tells a story of who we are.

REFERENCES

Adler, N. E., Boyce, T., Chesney, M. A., Cohen, S., Folkman, S., Kahn, R. L., & Syme, S. L. (1994). Socioeconomic status and health: The challenge and the gradient. *American Psychologist, 49*(1), 15-24.

Alexander, K. L., & Entwisle, D. R. (1988). Achievement in the first two years of school: Patterns and processes. *Monographs of the Society for Research in Child Development, 53*(2, Serial No. 218).

Alwin, D. F., Cohen, R. L., & Newcomb, T. M. (1991). *Political attitudes over the life span: The Bennington women after fifty years.* Madison: University of Wisconsin Press.

Antonucci, T. C., & Akiyama, H. (1995). Convoys of social relations: Family and friendships within a life span context. In R. Blieszner & V. H. Bedford (Eds.), *Handbook of aging and the family* (pp. 355-371). Westport, CT: Greenwood Press.

Baltes, P. B., & Baltes, M. M. (Eds.). (1990). *Successful aging: Perspectives from the behavioral sciences.* New York: Cambridge University Press.

Baltes, P. B., Cornelius, S. W., & Nesselroade, J. R. (1979). Cohort effects in developmental psychology. In J. R. Nesselroade, & P. B. Baltes (Eds.), *Longitudinal research in the study of behavior and development* (pp. 61-87). New York: Academic Press.

Baltes, P. B., & Mayer, K. U. (Eds.). (1999). *The Berlin aging study: Aging from 70 to 100.* Cambridge, UK: Cambridge University Press.

Baltes, P. B., & Reese, H. W. (1984). The life-span perspective in developmental psychology. In M. H. Bornstein & M. E. Lamb (Eds.), *Developmental psychology: An advanced textbook* (pp. 493-531). Hillsdale, NJ: Erlbaum

Barker, R. G. (1968). *Ecological psychology: Concepts and methods for studying the environment of human behavior.* Stanford, CA: Stanford University Press.

Bearman, P., & Brückner, H. (1999). *Power in numbers: Peer effects on adolescent girls' sexual debut and pregnancy.* Washington, DC.: National Campaign to Prevent Teen Pregnancy.

Becker, H. S. (1961). Notes on the concept of commitment. *American Journal of Sociology, 66,* 32-40.

Brim, G. (1993). *Ambition: How we manage success and failure throughout our lives.* New York: Basic Books.

Bronfenbrenner, U. (1979). *The ecology of human development: Experiments by nature and design.* Cambridge, MA: Harvard University Press.

Bronfenbrenner, U. (1996). Foreword. In R. B. Cairns, G. H. Elder, Jr., & E. J. Costello (Eds.), *Developmental science* (pp. ix-xvii). New York: Cambridge University Press.

Brückner, E., & Mayer, K. U. (1998). Collecting life history data: Experiences from the German life history study. In J. Z. Giele & G. H. Elder, Jr. (Eds.), *Methods of life course research: Qualitative and quantitative approaches* (pp. 152-181). Thousand Oaks, CA: Sage

Bryk, A. S., & Raudenbush, S. W. (1992). *Hierarchical linear models: Applications and data analysis methods.* Newbury Park, CA: Sage.

Burton, L. M., & Bengtson, V. L. (1985). Black grandmothers: Issues of timing and continuity of roles. In V. L. Bengtson, & J. F. Robertson (Eds.), *Grandparenthood* (pp. 61-77). Beverly Hills: Sage.

Bynner, J. (2000). Personal communication.

Cairns, R. B., & Cairns, B. (1994). *Lifelines and risks: Pathways of youth in our time.* Cambridge: Cambridge University Press.

Cairns, R. B., Elder, G. H., Jr., & Costello, E. J. (Eds.). (1996). *Developmental science.* New York: Cambridge University Press. Cambridge studies in social and emotional development.

Cairns, R. B., & Rodkin, P. C. (1998). Phenomena regained: From configurations to pathways. In R. B. Cairns, L. R. Bergman, & J. Kagan (Eds.), *Methods and models for studying the individual* (pp. 245-265). Thousand Oaks, CA: Sage.

Caspi, A. (1995). Puberty and the gender organization of schools: How biology and social context shape the adolescent experience. In L. J. Crockett & A. C. Crouter (Eds.), *Pathways through adolescence: Individual development in relation to social context* (pp. 57-74). Mahwah, NJ: Erlbaum. The Penn State series on child and adolescent development.

Caspi, A., & Bem, D. J. (1990). Personality continuity and change across the life course. In L. A. Pervin (Ed.), *Handbook of personality: Theory and research* (pp. 549-575). New York: Guilford Press.

Caspi, A., & Herbener, E. (1990). Continuity and change: Assortative marriage and the consistency of personality in adulthood. *Journal of Personality and Social Psychology, 58*(2), 250-258.

Caspi, A., & Moffitt, T. E. (1993). When do individual differences matter? A paradoxical theory of personality coherence. *Psychological Inquiry, 4,* 247-271.

Caspi, A., Moffitt, T. E., Thornton, A., Freedman, D., Amell, J. W., Harrington, H., Smeijers, J., & Silva, P. A. (1996). The life history calendar: A research and clinical assessment method for collecting retrospective event-history data. *International Journal of Methods in Psychiatric Research, 6,* 101-114.

Clausen, J. A. (1993). *American lives: Looking back at the children of the Great Depression*. New York: Free Press.

Colby, A. (1998). Foreword: Crafting life course studies. In J. Z. Giele & G. H. Elder, Jr. (Eds.), *Methods of life course research: Qualitative and quantitative approaches* (pp. viii-xii). Thousand Oaks, CA: Sage.

Cook, T. D., Herman, M. R., Phillips, M., & Settersten, R. A., Jr. (Under review). How neighborhoods, families, peer groups, and schools jointly affect changes in early adolescent development.

Cowan, C. P., & Cowan, P. G. (1992). *When partners become parents: The big life change for couples*. New York: Basic Books.

Dannefer, D. (1984). The role of the social in life-span developmental psychology, past and future: Rejoinder to Baltes and Nesselroade. *American Sociological Review, 49*, 847-850.

DiPrete, T., & Forristal, J. D. (1994). Multilevel models: Methods and substance. *Annual Review of Sociology, 20*, 331-357.

Duncan, G. J., & Morgan, J. N. (1985). The panel study of income dynamics. In G. H. Elder, Jr. (Ed.), *Life course dynamics: Trajectories and transitions: 1968-1980* (pp. 50-71). Ithaca, NY: Cornell University Press.

Eccles, J. S., Midgley, C., Wigfield, A., Buchanan, C. M., Reuman, D., Flanagan, C., & MacIver, D. (1993). Development during adolescence: The impact of stage-environment fit on young adolescents' experiences in schools and in families. *American Psychologist, 48*(2), 90-101.

Elder, G. H., Jr. (1975). Age differentiation and the life course. *Annual Review of Sociology, 1*, 165-190.

Elder, G. H., Jr. (1978). Family history and the life course. In T. K. Hareven (Ed.), *Transitions* (pp. 17-64). New York: Academic Press.

Elder, G. H., Jr. (1986). Military times and turning points in men's lives. *Developmental Psychology, 22*(2), 233-245.

Elder, G. H., Jr. (1987). War mobilization and the life course: A cohort of World War II veterans. *Sociological Forum, 2*(3), 449-472.

Elder, G. H., Jr. (1998). The life course and human development. In R. M. Lerner (Ed.), *Handbook of child psychology, Vol. 1: Theoretical models of human development* (5th ed., pp. 939-991). New York: Wiley.

Elder, G. H., Jr. (1999). *Children of the Great Depression: Social change in life experience*. 25th Anniversary Edition. Boulder, CO: Westview Press.

Elder, G. H., Jr., & Caspi, A. (1990). Studying lives in a changing society: Sociological and personological explorations. In A. I. Rabin, R. A. Zucker, R. A. Emmons, & S. Frank (Eds.), *Studying persons and lives* (pp. 201-247). New York: Springer. Henry A. Murray Lecture Series.

Elder, G. H., Jr., & Chan, C. (1999). War's legacy in men's lives. In P. Moen, D. Dempster-McClain, & H. A. Walker (Eds.), *A nation divided: Diversity, inequality, and community in American society* (pp. 209-227). Ithaca, NY: Cornell University Press.

Elder, G. H., Jr., & Clipp, E. C. (1988, May). Wartime losses and social bonding: Influences across 40 years in men's lives. *Psychiatry, 51*, 177-198.

Elder, G. H., Jr., & Conger, R. D. (2000). *Children of the land: Adversity and success in rural America*. Chicago: University of Chicago Press.

Elder, G. H., Jr., & O'Rand, A. M. (1995). Adult lives in a changing society. In K. S. Cook, G. A. Fine, & J. S. House (Eds.), *Sociological perspectives on social psychology* (pp. 452-475). Boston: Allyn & Bacon.

Elder, G. H., Jr., & Pellerin, L. A. (1998). Linking history and human lives. In J. Z. Giele & G. H. Elder, Jr. (Eds.), *Methods of life course research: Quantitative and Qualitative Approaches* (pp. 264-294). Thousand Oaks, CA: Sage

Elder, G. H., Jr., Shanahan, M. J., & Clipp, E. C. (1994). When war comes to men's lives: Life course patterns in family, work, and health. *Psychology and Aging, Special Issue* 9(1), 5-16.

Elder, G. H., Jr., Shanahan, M. J., & Clipp, E. C. (1997). Linking combat and physical health: The legacy of World War II in men's lives. *American Journal of Psychiatry, 154*(3), 330-336.

Freedman, D., Thornton, A., Camburn, D., Alwin, D., & Young-DeMarco, L. (1988). The life history calendar: A technique for collecting retrospective data. *Sociological Methodology, 18*, 37-68.

George, L. K. (1993). Sociological perspectives on life transitions. *Annual Review of Sociology, 19*, 353-373.

Glueck, S., & Glueck, E. (1968). *Delinquents and nondelinquents in perspective.* Cambridge, MA: Harvard University Press.

Guo, G. (1998). The timing of the influences of cumulative poverty on children's ability and achievement. *Social Forces, 77*(1), 257-288.

Hagan, J. (2001). *Northern passage: American Vietnam War resisters in Canada.* Chicago: University of Chicago Press.

Haidt, J., & Rodin, J. (1999). Control and efficacy as interdisciplinary bridges. *Review of General Psychology, 3*(4), 317-337.

Han, S. K., & Moen, P. (1999). Work and family over time: A life course approach. *Annals of the American Academy of Political and Social Science, 562*, 98-110.

Hardy, M. A., & Hazelrigg, L. (1999). A multilevel model of early retirement decisions among autoworkers in plants with different futures. *Research on Aging, 21*(2), 275-303.

Hareven, T. K. (1978). *Transitions: The family and the life course in historical perspective.* New York: Academic Press.

Hartup, W. W., & Laursen, B. (1991). Relationships as developmental contexts. In R. Cohen & A. Siegel (Eds.), *Context and development* (pp. 253-279). Hillsdale, NJ: Erlbaum.

Heckhausen, J. (1999). *Developmental regulation in adulthood: Age-normative and socio-structural constraints as adaptive challenges.* Cambridge, UK; New York: Cambridge University Press.

Hernandez, D. J. (1993). *America's children: Resources from family, government, and the economy.* New York: Russell Sage.

Hetherington, E. M., & Baltes, P. B. (1988). Child psychology and life-span development. In E. M. Hetherington, R. M. Lerner, & M. Perlmutter (Eds.), *Child development in life-span perspective* (pp. 1-19). Hillsdale, NJ: Erlbaum.

Holahan, C. K., & Sears, R. R. (1995). *The gifted group in later maturity.* Stanford, CA: Stanford University Press.

Kagan, J., & Moss, H. A. (1962). *Birth to maturity, a study in psychological development.* New York: Wiley.

Kaufman, G., & Elder, G. H., Jr. (Under review). Aging fast and aging slow: Life experiences and age identity.

Keating, D. P., & Hertzman, C. (Eds.). (1999). *Developmental health and the wealth of nations: Social, biological, and educational dynamics.* New York: Guildford Press.

Kohn, M. L., & Schooler, C. (1983). *Work and personality: An inquiry into the impact of social stratification.* Norwood, NJ: Ablex.

Kuh, D., Power, C., Blane, D., & Bartley, M. (1997). Social pathways between childhood and adult health. In D. Kuh & Y. Ben-Shlomo (Eds.), *A life course approach to chronic disease epidemiology* (pp. 169-198). Oxford; New York: Oxford University Press.

Macfarlane, J. W. (1938). Studies in child guidance, I: Methodology of data collection and organization. *Monographs of the Society for Research in Child Development, 3*(6, Serial No. 19).

Macfarlane, J. W. (1963). From infancy to adulthood. *Childhood Education, 39*(7), 336-342.

Magnusson, D., & Bergman, L. R. (1990). *Data quality in longitudinal research.* New York: Cambridge University Press.

Mayer, K. U. (1988). German survivors of World War II: The impact on the life course of the collective experience of birth cohorts. In M. W. Riley, & (in association with Bettina J. Huber and Beth B. Hess) (Ed.), *Social change and the life course, Vol. I: Social structures and human lives* (pp. 229-246). Newbury Park, CA: Sage. American Sociological Association Presidential Series.

Mayer, K. U., & Tuma, N. B. (Eds.). (1990). *Event history analysis in life course research.* Madison, WI: University of Wisconsin Press.

McAdam, D. (1989). The biographical consequences of activism. *American Sociological Review, 54,* 744-760.

McAdam, D. (1992). Gender as a mediator of the activist experience: The case of Freedom Summer. *American Journal of Sociology, 97*(5), 1211-1240.

Merton, R. K. (1968). *Social theory and social structure.* New York: Free Press.

Miech, R. A., & Shanahan, M. J. (2000). Socioeconomic status and depression over the life course. *Journal of Health and Social Behavior, 41*(2), 162-176.

Moen, P., Dempster-McClain, D., & Williams, R. M., Jr. (1989, August). Social integration and longevity: An event history analysis of women's roles and resilience. *American Sociological Review, 54,* 635-647.

Moffitt, T. E. (1993). Adolescence-limited and life-course-persistent antisocial behavior: A developmental taxonomy. *Psychological Review, 100*(4), 674-701.

Muthén, B. O., & Khoo, S.-T. (1998). Longitudinal studies of achievement growth using latent variable modeling. *Learning and Individual Differences, 10*(2), 73-101.

Nesselroade, J. R., & Baltes, P. B. (1974). Adolescent personality development and historical change: 1970-1972. *Monographs of the Society for Research in Child Development, 30* (1, Serial No. 154).

Neugarten, B. L., with a foreword by Dail A. Neugarten (Ed.). (1996). *The meanings of age: Selected papers of Bernice L Neugarten.* Chicago: University of Chicago Press.

Newman, K. S. (1992). Culture and structure in the truly disadvantaged. *City and Society, 14*(1), 3-25.

Noack, P., Hofer, M., & Youniss, J. (Eds.). (1995). *Psychological responses to social change: Human development in changing environments.* New York: Walter de Gruyter.

Parcel, T. L., & Menaghan, E. G. (1994). *Parents' jobs and children's lives.* New York: Aldine deGruyter

Pavalko, E. K., & Smith, B. (1999). The rhythm of work: Health effects of women's work dynamics. *Social Forces, 77*(3), 1141-1162.

Riley, M. W., Johnson, M. E., & Foner, A. (Eds.). (1972). *Aging and society, Vol. 3: A sociology of age stratification.* New York: Russell Sage.

Rutter, M. (Ed.). (1988). *Studies of psychosocial risk: The power of longitudinal data* (pp. 184-199). Cambridge, UK: Cambridge University Press.

Rutter, M. (1996). Transitions and turning points in developmental psychopathology: As applied to the age span between childhood and mid-adulthood. *International Journal of Behavioral Development, 19*(3), 603-626.

Ryder, N. B. (1965). The cohort as a concept in the study of social change. *American Sociological Review, 30*(6), 843-861.

Ryu, S., & Mortimer, J. T. (1996). The "occupational linkage hypothesis" applied to occupational value formation in adolescence. In J. T. Mortimer & M. D. Finch (Eds.), *Adolescents, work, and family: An intergenerational developmental analysis* (pp. 167-190). Thousand Oaks, CA: Sage.

Sampson, R. J., & Laub, J. H. (1993). *Crime in the making: Pathways and turning points through life.* Cambridge, MA: Harvard University Press.

Sampson, R. J., & Laub, J. H. (1996). Socioeconomic achievement in the life course of disadvantaged men: Military service as a turning point, Circa 1940-1965. *American Sociological Review, 61*(3), 347-367.

Schaie, K.Warner. (1984). Historical time and cohort effects. In K. A. McCluskey & H. W. Reese (Eds.), *Life-span developmental psychology: Historical and generational effects* (pp. 1-15). Orlando, FL: Academic Press.

Schooler, C., Mulatu, M. S., & Oates, G. (1999). The continuing effects of substantively complex work on the intellectual functioning of older workers. *Psychology and Aging, 14*(3), 483-506.

Schulenberg, J., Maggs, J. L., & Hurrelmann, K. (Eds). (1997). *Health risks and developmental transitions during adolescence.* New York: Cambridge University Press.

Schulz, R., & Heckhausen, J. (1996). A life span model of successful aging. *American Psychologist, 51*(7), 702-714.

Settersten, R. A., Jr. (1999). *Lives in time and place: The problems and promises of developmental science.* Amityville, NY: Baywood.

Settersten, R. A., & Hagestad, G. O. (1996a). What's the latest? Cultural age deadlines for family transitions. *Gerontologist, 36*(2), 178-188.

Settersten, R. A., & Hagestad, G. O. (1996b). What's the latest? Cultural age deadlines for educational and work transitions. *Gerontologist, 36*(5), 602-613.

Shanahan, M. J. (2000). Pathways to adulthood in changing societies: Variability and mechanisms in life course perspective. *Annual Review of Sociology, 26*, 667-692.

Shanahan, M. J., & Elder, G. H., Jr. (in press). History, human agency, and the life course. *Nebraska symposium on motivation.* Lincoln, NE: University of Nebraska Press.

Stättin, H., & Magnusson, D. (1990). *Pubertal maturation in female development.* Hillsdale, NJ: Erlbaum.

Thomas, W. I., & Znaniecki, F. (1918). *The Polish peasant in Europe and America, Volumes 1-2*. Boston: Badger.

Titma, M., & Tuma, N. (1995). Paths of a Generation: A Comparative Longitudinal Study of Young Adults in the Former Soviet Union. Stanford, CA: Center for Social Research in Eastern Europe, Tallinn, Estonia.

Volkart, E. H. (1951). *Social behavior and personality: Contributions of W.I. Thomas to theory and social research*. New York: Social Science Research Council.

Wadsworth, M. E. J. (1991). *The imprint of time: Childhood, history, and adult life*. Oxford, UK: Clarendon Press.

Wellman, B., Wong, R. Y., Tindall, D., & Nazer, N. (1997, January). A decade of network change: turnover, persistence and stability in personal communities. *Social Networks, 19*, 27-50.

Wu, L. L., & Martinson, B. C. (1993). Family structure and the risk of a premarital birth. *American Sociological Review, 58*(2), 210-232.

Zhou, X., & Hou, L. (1999). Children of the Cultural Revolution: The state and the life course in the People's Republic of China. *American Sociological Review, 64*(1), 12-36.

PART III

Promises for Understanding Aging and Later Life in Specific Spheres

CHAPTER 3

The Life-Course Perspective on Work and Retirement

John C. Henretta

This chapter considers three themes as they relate to a life-course perspective on work and retirement: the significance of institutional structure in forming an age-based life course; the way that the individual life course is rooted in the institutional life course but departs from it in important ways, and the relationship between inference about life-course processes and existence of life-course data. Employment institutions are the starting point for consideration of these themes because such institutions are so important in structuring the multiple dimensions of social life in industrial societies. Indeed, one influential view takes work to be the central organizing principle of life. According to this view, the standard life course is divided into three distinct periods of (1) preparation for work, (2) work, and (3) retirement. This division is reinforced by technological and institutional factors that generate employment structures (Kohli, 1988), such as the demand for higher level job skills that have led to lengthening of the preparation phase of the life course. These three life-course phases occur in distinct, age-differentiated institutional contexts (Riley, 1993, 1998). For example, though the U.S. school system provides general preparation for work, schools normally exist and operate quite independently of employment institutions. Yet, there are important linkages across the three phases, giving them coherence despite the shift in institutional context. Kohli (1988) points out that Western societies may be viewed as "work societies" in that the three phases are linked together through their relationship to paid employment, with education serving as preparation for work and retirement being structured by career lines in employment. This "tripartition" is central to any discussion of the place of work and retirement in the life course.

In addition to institutions, concern about individuals and the connections between individuals and institutions are central to a life-course approach to work and retirement. The *institutional* context of employment creates the social structure in which individuals live a major segment of their lives. The technology and organization of employment generates pressures that influence the nature and length of the preparation phase and the retirement phase as well as the characteristics of the career lines within the work phase. At the institutional level, the most important issues relevant to the life-course perspective relate to the social structure of employment and state institutions that produce age-based life-course structuring. This employment structure may be highly heterogeneous or highly uniform in its effects on age-based behavior. It may create either strong or weak age structuring. Moreover, this social structure may change over time; hence historical time serves as a marker for the institutional structures in effect at any one period (Riley, 1987).

While the *individual* life course is partly derivative of employment institutions, individual trajectories are not the same as institutional career lines. Individual time in the context of work and retirement focuses on the relation of early- and late-life events in the work career (including the preparation and retirement phases). Individual life-course trajectories differ from social structures in existence at any one time for two reasons. Individual careers may span different institutional contexts because of job changes. In addition, individual careers cross-cut different historical periods, so that—unless employment structures are unchanging—each cohort faces a unique sequence of different institutional structures as they age (Riley & Riley, 1994). Finally, individual choice differentiates the institutional and individual life course.

As noted earlier, taking life-course concepts seriously in the study of work and retirement requires careful attention to the institutional level of analysis, the individual life course, and the relationship between them. At the institutional level, we must consider how to conceptualize and measure the extent to which social structure is age based and how to carefully measure change in institutional age structuring. These issues are particularly compelling because there is so much heterogeneity in institutional structures governing work. For example, different employer pension plans have quite different incentives to retire at particular ages. Second, it is equally important to consider why life-course institutions are age differentiated, so that periods of education, work, and retirement generally occur sequentially instead of simultaneously. A third issue is examining how the institutional life course and individual trajectories are linked? Is there a "loose" or "tight" connection between the individual life course to the institutionalized life course? Should analysis of trajectories give primary weight to individual agency, as is typically done by economists, or to exogenous factors, as is typical among sociologists? Finally, at the individual level, it is important to consider how factors external to the institutionalized life course, such as family events or health, modify the institutional life course. Taken together, these issues define an important agenda that will allow a fuller articulation of the life-course perspective on work and retirement.

THE INSTITUTIONAL LEVEL OF ANALYSIS

The basic conceptual tools required for understanding institutional aspects of life-course institutionalization have been well developed. The basic conceptualization is that employment and state institutions create an institutionalized life course so that the rules of these institutions determine the tempo of individual lives, governing transitions from education to work to retirement. At a finer level of detail, institutional rules also govern movement within the education, work, and retirement phases of the life course. For example, institutional rules help define the possibilities for partial retirement and part-time employment after retirement from the primary job. Age and time play central roles as modulators of this institutional life course. The following two sections consider how and why age and time are important markers that govern the institutional life course and define the three phases of the life course.

IS LIFE COURSE INSTITUTIONALIZATION DECLINING?

The standard account of the significance of age in the structuring of individual lives is that the life course became increasingly age structured during the twentieth century with standardized sequence and timing of events created by welfare state and employment institutions (Anderson, 1985; Kohli, 1986, 1987; Mayer & Schoepflin, 1989). The historical literature on retirement provides good examples of the highly individualized life course that preceded development of institutionalized retirement. Recent historical research has focused on the role of savings (Gratton, 1996) and earlier career moves into self-employment (Carter & Sutch, 1996) that allowed later retirement. These individual pathways to retirement developed within a social structure in which there were virtually no state and workplace institutions supporting retirement so that there was little institutional age structuring. The emphasis in the historical literature on savings and self-employment emphasizes this point. One exception is the case of Civil War veterans' pensions (Costa, 1998), which affected a particular set of cohorts.

The decline in the role of traditional institutions, such as the family, in determining the pattern of individual lives, the growth of the welfare state, and the growing bureaucratization of the workplace created an "institutionalized" life course with rules based on age or its correlate, time. In the institutionalized life course, the age at which events occur becomes more predictable because their timing is strongly influenced by institutional rules.

The state has played an important role in life course institutionalization at both ends of the life course. Laws concerning child labor and the long-term increase in minimum schooling levels (reflecting a decline in the demand for unskilled labor) have created the education phase of the life course. The creation of public retirement systems with benefits based on age (instead of illness, for example) has helped define the retirement phase. Within work institutions, conceptualization of the institutionalized life course focuses on the extent to which job sequences are age-based—that is, the extent to which seniority within a firm brings additional benefits such as higher wages, pension entitlements or job security (Spilerman, 1977). Age-based career lines developed, according to one view, because of labor shortages during the first and second world wars plus development of the ideology of personnel management (Jacoby, 1985). Alternatively, age-based career lines have been conceptualized by economists as a choice of the best available employment strategy (Bulow & Summers, 1986; Yellen, 1984) or as reflecting firm-specific skills (Hurd, 1996).

The age-based career line is generally conceptualized as one in which the rewards of a long-term relationship with an employer are concentrated at the end of the work career. For example, compensation at the beginning of the career may be below average lifetime productivity while late career compensation may be above this level. Compensation reflects both wages and fringe benefits, and the latter are an increasingly significant proportion of compensation at older ages (Hurd, 1996). This age-based career is consistent with higher loyalty by employees and greater investment by the employer in training the worker. Moreover, such a system may attract workers who are viewed as more desirable employees—for example, those who value a long-term relationship and will sacrifice some benefits at the beginning of the career for later rewards.

Traditionally, mandatory retirement was seen as defining an end point to the age-structured career (Lazear, 1979). Because age-based careers concentrated rewards at the end of the career in the form of high wages and increasing job security that may exceed productivity increases, employers would want to declare an end to the relationship at some point (Hurd, 1996), through mandatory retirement. Since the abolition of mandatory retirement in the United States in 1986, employers have used pension incentives in defined benefit pensions to accomplish the same task.

Age-based career lines did not characterize all institutional work structures. While many large firms utilized this technique, small firms and self-employment were unlikely to be affected. The existence of age-structured careers coexisted and even required that some jobs be outside age-structured careers in order to offer flexibility to employers. Many of these jobs have been held by women (Osterman, 1988).

More recently, some analysts have suggested that the trend toward the age-structured institutionalized life course has either halted (Henretta, 1994a) or perhaps reversed (Guillemard, 1989; Kohli, 1986). At older ages, declining institutionalization is sometimes attributed to the reduced importance of traditional state retirement institutions. As these uniform, age-based institutions have declined in relative importance, the predictability of retirement timing has declined and has become more variable. For example, in the continental countries of Europe, the role of the uniform state pension as a determinant of retirement timing has declined to be replaced by other pathways to retirement, including disability benefits or unemployment benefits (Guillemard & Rein, 1993; Henretta, 1994b) which fall with uneven force and at different ages across the population. Though disability has played a role in declining retirement age in the United States and Britain (Henretta, 1994b; Henretta & Lee, 1996), a very important trend in the United States and Britain has been the growing importance of workplace factors in producing retirement before the age of eligibility for state retirement pensions. Firm pensions have become an increasingly important determinant of retirement timing relative to Social Security, and variability in these arrangements induces variability in retirement timing (Henretta, 1992, 1994a, 1994b; Wise, 1997). Employers have utilized the mechanisms of age-structured employment to bring an earlier end to career employment in some cases. Many firm pensions allow early retirement as early as age 55 (Wise, 1997) and average regular retirement age hovers around 61 or 62 (Gustman, Mitchell, & Steinmeier, 1995). In addition, a number of firms have used early retirement incentives to encourage even earlier retirement among some segments of their workforce (Brown, 1997; Mutschler, 1996).

A more controversial deinstitutionalization argument is that a number of changes in employment structures have reduced age structuring of the life course at both younger and older ages. For example, the use of contingent employment arrangements (Belous, 1989), the increasing importance of defined contribution pensions, and the relative shift from highly age-structured manufacturing employment to typically less age-structured service employment (Henretta, 1994a) have meant that the life course is less organized by age than in the past. One difficulty with these ideas is that we have no standard way of measuring the degree to which the life course is organized by age. While each of these trends will have the effect of reducing age structuring of employment for the individuals affected, it is far from clear whether these changes mean that, overall, the life course is less organized by age.

The introduction of less age-structured employment mechanisms means that there is more variation in the institutional contexts in which employment occurs. Hence the growing heterogeneity of work contexts is an institutional force creating greater variation in the individual life course. In the United States, this process is also related to the declining retirement age. As the mean age of retirement has declined, those who retire earlier than average are primarily influenced in their retirement behavior by the highly variable structure of the workplace and less influenced by the relatively uniform structure of the Social Security retirement systems. As a result, variability has increased in retirement timing among the earlier-retiring half of successive cohorts (Henretta, 1992).

While important work has been done on the topics of life-course institutionalization and deinstitutionalization, much remains unexplored. For example, we still lack a compelling analysis of whether the life course as a whole has, in recent years, become less organized in recent years by age. The discussion of increases or decreases in life-course institutionalization typically focuses on changes in one or two aspects of employment organization—for example, a change in type of pensions. In some cases, such as changes in state retirement institutions in Europe, one factor analyses may be highly informative since those institutions have traditionally dominated the retirement process. But in the context of the United States or Britain in which highly diverse workplace factors play a very important part in retirement, any discussion of a decline in the degree of institutionalization of the life course should simultaneously consider the possibility of increasing heterogeneity of institutional career paths. Future analyses should give explicit attention to the task of characterizing the overall level of life-course institutionalization in societies in which there are highly diverse workplace institutions that influence age patterning of behavior.

THE TRIPARTITE DIVISION OF THE
LIFE COURSE

A second key conceptual idea is that the life course is divided into three segments of preparation for education, work, and retirement. The highly age-differentiated nature of the institutions related to the three segments is an important topic for research. It is important to understand why employment institutions produce this structure instead of one in which periods of education, work, and non-market pursuits are interspersed throughout the life course. In the contemporary United States, not only are institutions age differentiated, there is relatively little inter-penetration between the three segments. While it is true that many students are also employed and many retirees work part-time, such work is usually not performed on a career job. As a result, it is not so much employment as it is the main career line of employment that is segregated from preparation and retirement phases of the life course.

Work in economics provides insight into the ways that the technological and organizational basis of society produce age differentiated employment and retirement institutions. For example, Hurd (1996) poses the issue of why most career jobs do not allow workers to vary their hours or weeks of work, even though many older workers would like to reduce work gradually. Hurd attributes the rigidity in jobs to aspects of the technology of team production. Coordination among workers is implied by the technology being used (e.g., an assembly line), and organizational factors create fixed costs of employment (e.g., training costs and health insurance, primarily). Employers would prefer to spread these fixed costs across more hours per worker to reduce their total labor cost per hour worked.

The implication of this rigidity is that workers must work full-time or stop work completely. To continue part-time work, it is usually necessary to switch to a new (and usually lower-paying) job. Given the analysis of why career job employers do not allow gradual retirement, the new part-time job must be one that involves low training costs and low levels of other fixed costs, such as pensions and health insurance. It is therefore likely to be in a different occupation from the career job and current skills will not be highly valued by the new employer. Taken together, these restrictions imply that part-time jobs will pay less per hour than the individual's previous full-time job.

While explanations such as these provide insight into why life-course institutions are age differentiated, they involve hypotheses about employers' behavior under a particular set of circumstances. In the past, older workers constituted a relatively small proportion of the trained workforce and they tended to have lower levels of schooling relative to the younger population. In the near future, however, both these factors will change. The entry of large numbers of the post-war baby boom cohorts into the category of older workers, coupled with the stability of educational distributions over the last quarter century, create the possibility that employers will be more anxious to retain trained older workers in the future than they were in the past (Henretta, 2000). Moreover, the larger number of older workers desiring part-time work may influence government to foster employment flexibility. If these things happen, employers and government may be more innovative in overcoming technological and organizational rigidities, with the result that there will be less age differentiation of work institutions and increasing inter-penetration of work and retirement as more workers engage in part-time work on a career job.

THE MICRO-LEVEL LINK BETWEEN INSTITUTIONAL STRUCTURE AND AGE STRUCTURING

Examining the extent to which social structure is age based involves more than the discovery of empirical regularities in behavior. There is an important conceptual element in understanding how particular institutional rules produce age-based behavior. The best work on this topic combines a conceptual understanding of the built-in incentives found in social institutions that create certain age-structured behavior with empirical analyses that confirm this conceptual understanding.

For example, economists have done excellent work on the way in which specific characteristics of firm pensions encourage or discourage retirement at particular ages (e.g., Gustman & Steinmeier, 1995; Wise, 1997). While defined benefit pensions (that is, pensions that calculate benefits based on a formula that typically includes final salary and number of years with the firm) differ in the particular construction of their incentives, many provide a strong incentive to remain with the firm until a particular time and then retire. As a result, defined benefit pensions are highly age-structured and particularly benefit those workers who remain with an employer until retirement. Their pattern of incentives mark the boundary of work and retirement and define the end of the age structured work career. The specific age pattern of incentives can be derived from pension rules (Wise, 1997).

Conversely, defined contribution pensions (that is, plans in which employers contribute a certain amount each year and in which employees typically bear the investment risk) lack such incentives to retire at a particular age or time. However, the increasing value of such plans will increase the probability of retirement by increasing total wealth. Defined benefit pensions, in contrast to defined contribution plans, therefore, play an important part in defining the end of career lines by encouraging exit from the firm at a particular age. Research on the structure of pension plans provides an excellent example of how the rules that underlie work-related policies may create or reinforce behavior.

The effects of institutional age structuring are mediated in their effects on the individual life course by choices at key branching points. For example, the shift from defined benefit to defined contribution pensions has been cited as one aspect of declining age structuring (Henretta, 1994a). Yet even among those workers who remain in the highly age structured defined benefit pension plans, age structuring may decline because of early retirement pension incentives. The effects of such plans are particularly complex because they involve a significant element of individual choice. Workers may decline an early pension offer, and about half do indeed decline them (Brown, 1997). Workers who accept these offers have more pessimistic evaluations of their wage prospects at the current firm (Brown, 1997).

The state provides a second element of age structuring, primarily through the Social Security retirement and disability programs. Social Security retirement benefits became a more important influence on retirement timing during the 1970s because of large increases in Social Security benefits (e.g., Ippolito, 1990). The tendency of retirement ages to cluster around ages 62 and 65 (Hurd, 1996)—ages at which workers become eligible for reduced and non-reduced Social Security benefits—provides an indication of the significance of state programs in defining the work to retirement transition. In addition, though its effect has varied with shifts in administrative rules, the Social Security disability system also influences age at exit from the labor force (Henretta, 1994a; Henretta & Lee, 1996). While uniform ages for Social Security retirement benefits are likely to reduce variance in retirement and foster an age-based life course, the individual nature of disability benefits that require that each recipient qualify on the basis of health considerations is likely to decrease age structuring.

There are two important principles underlying the linkage between institutional rules and individual behavior. First, there are important differences in the extent that one set of rules applies to the entire population—primarily between employment and state institutions, with the latter generally being more universal in their effects. Workplace institutions tend to be variable across industry, firm size, and specific characteristics of the individual firm. To the degree that workplace institutions are more important than state institutions in shaping the life course, as they are in the United States and Britain because the state retirement pension does not overwhelm workplace sources of retirement income, the result will be great heterogeneity and less age structuring. (Heterogeneity implies a low level of age structuring because it means the ages at which events occur are less predictable.) Second, institutional rules differ in the degree to which they provide strong or weak incentives to conform to age-based structures. For example, though defined benefit pension plans vary (Mitchell, 1999), they provide more incentives to retire at a particular time than do defined contribution plans as we have already seen. Defined contribution plans have a less distinct incentive to retire with increasing age because wealth does not increase in a uniform or predictable way with age.

UNDERSTANDING WORK AND RETIREMENT AT THE INDIVIDUAL LEVEL OF ANALYSIS

While institutional and individual employment trajectories are used most naturally to analyze events such as job changes or retirement, their effects are broadly important in shaping the individual life course. For example, Dannefer (1984) proposed the provocative hypothesis that the mid-life crisis—that is, dissatisfaction with one's job and other aspects of one's life—is at least partially created by the nature of age-graded movement through bureaucratic hierarchies. The hierarchical nature of many organizations creates inequality as members of the same entering cohort either are promoted or reach the limits of their career. Such events may lead to acceptance of an early retirement offer (e.g., Brown, 1997) or may produce dissatisfaction and a renewed search for meaning in life. Expanding this idea further, not all members of the entering cohort will stay with the same firm; some will leave early to enter a non-hierarchical career structure such as self-employment. Moreover, the blocking of further occupational mobility may have effects that are conditional on events in other domains. For example, blocked mobility at age 45 may lead to more dissatisfaction in an individual whose children have already completed college than in one with preschool children. An individual whose spouse has serious health problems may be more concerned with retaining employer-provided health insurance than a renewed search for meaning. While the institutional hierarchical structure creates the blocked mobility problem, individual reactions to it are likely to depend on their earlier career trajectories and events in other life-course domains.

These examples illustrate the broad potential significance of individual work trajectories as well as the differences between individual and institutional trajectories. While the hypothesized source of the midlife crisis flows from institutional structure, a number of individual contingencies condition the effects of institutional career structures. Individual trajectories depart from institutional career lines for a number of reasons: Individual careers cross-cut institutions, span historical periods, are affected by individual choice at key points, and involve coordination with non-institutional domains such as the family. Though individual work and retirement trajectories are strongly rooted in institutional rules and structures, they are also uniquely affected by events that occur within, across, and outside of institutional contexts.

This section will consider three issues that differentiate institutional and individual careers: Shifts between institutional employment contexts in the late career, the coordination of events in the lives of different family members, and the relation of work to other life spheres. While these three issues do not exhaust life-course research on work and retirement, they do illustrate the range and complexity of effects in the individual life course that differentiate it from the institutional life course.

CROSSING INSTITUTIONAL CONTEXTS:
LATE CAREER JOB CHANGES

Individual careers may span multiple institutional contexts, either because of job displacement, job availability, or individual choice. These changes may occur at any age, though late career changes are particularly interesting. They have received extensive research attention in recent years and characterize the late career trajectory of about one quarter of workers (Quinn, Burkhauser, & Myers, 1990). These shifts are particularly interesting because they illustrate two other life-course principles: change over historical time and individual agency.

In the past several years, increasing attention has been paid to the complexity of the work-to-retirement transition. Rather than experiencing a simple transition from full-time work to full-time retirement, a significant minority of workers experiences complex patterns of work exits and reentries into and through old age (Elder & Pavalko, 1993; Gustman & Steinmeier, 1984; Hayward, Crimmins, & Wray, 1994; Honig, 1985; Quinn, Burkhauser, & Myers, 1990; Ruhm, 1990). These proportions may have increased in recent years. For example, Hayward, Crimmins, & Wray (1994) find increasing rates of labor force exit and reentry among older workers between the 1970s and the 1980s. Using two cohorts born in the early part of the twentieth century, Elder and Pavalko (1993) find that the more recent cohort exhibited more complex retirement patterns, including both labor force reentry and partial retirement.

These late-career work exits, reentries, and job changes imply that this subset of individuals experience shifts across institutions (that is, they move between employers). For some workers, such shifts are simply the continuation of a lifetime of changes between jobs that are not age-graded. However, for those in age-structured career lines, there are likely significant consequences when age-structured career lines are abandoned for new late-career jobs. A new employer is not likely to honor the entitlements from seniority, such as higher wages, that long-term employees on career jobs often enjoy. The prior firm-specific skills of the worker are not likely to be valued by the new employer (Hurd, 1996), and the nature of age-structured careers outlined earlier implies that late-career compensation is greater than the current productivity of the employee because it is part of a long-term "implicit contract" or reflects other employer-specific effects. In addition, because those who make late-career job shifts will remain at the new job for a relatively short period of time, jobs taken late in life are often jobs that do not require large investments in training. (Hutchens, 1988). Many of those who either accept an early retirement offer (Brown, 1997) or are pension recipients under age 65 (Herz, 1995) take new jobs. For these workers, as well as for most workers who make late-career job shifts, wages usually decline (Brown, 1997; Herz, 1995; Hurd, 1996).

Late career shifts are not a new phenomenon. The data from which most of our knowledge of this pattern is derived were collected during the 1970s. However, if it is true that the pattern has become more common as some of the research discussed above indicates, these shifts between employers may result from historical changes in employment arrangements. As workers have become more exposed to the vagaries of changing markets (Cappelli, Bassi, Katz, Knoke, Osterman, & Useem, 1997), the age-structured career may end earlier through involuntary job loss or early acceptance of a pension. The rate at which such transitions occur is rooted in institutional structures.

Yet late career shifts definitely characterize the individual life-course. First, late-career job shifts involve shifts across institutional structures. Therefore, there are differences in conditions of work on the new job, which serves we a source of individual variation. While most of those who change jobs late in life move to positions of lower status, some workers do take or find jobs of higher status. The new job may or may not have benefits such as health insurance. Individuals may end up in different jobs because of variation in available job opportunities, variation in individual skills, and individual agency (e. g., willingness to move long distances, energy expended in a job search). Willingness to move may depend on spouse's employment and other aspects of the family domain. Second, there is variation, even within one firm, in whether these job shifts occur as a result of job loss (Kohli, Rosenow, & Wolf, 1983). Individual work-related characteristics, such as seniority with the firm and current pension eligibility may influence whether a job is lost or a new job sought. Third, individual agency is inextricably tied to the pattern, as noted earlier. For example, Brown (1997) points out that approximately half of early retirement pension incentives offers are declined by workers. Brown's work suggests that there is an important process of selection among a segment of workers taking new, late-career jobs so that the benefits of an early pension plus a new job exceed the expected benefit of remaining at the previous job.

A great deal of research remains to be done on this topic. For example, prevalence estimates of bridge jobs (jobs that span the time between a long-term career job and final retirement) are dependent on the specific definition used (Hurd, 1996). Further analyses and conceptualization are therefore required to develop a consensus on this issue. Two substantive issues are worth noting: the links between late-career job shifts and employment trajectories, and the complex interaction between institutional rules and individual life-course events in producing these shifts. First, it is important to view late-career jobs shifts within the context of the individual's lifetime job trajectory. For some workers, late-career job shifts suggest an earlier-than-desired end to an age-structured career. But for other workers, late shifts simply represent the continuation of an earlier pattern of shifts between jobs that have little age structuring. The meaning and significance of a late-career job shift is tied very closely to the nature of the larger employment trajectory. While this issue is widely noted and recognized (Quinn & Kozy, 1996), the real need is to incorporate the insight into research and differentiate the two types of late career shifts—those in which a worker has had many employer changes over the career, and those in which there have been very few employer changes. The significance of a late-career job change is likely to be different, both for the worker and the analyst in these two cases. Restated, the meaning of the late career trajectory is at least partly determined by the earlier lifetime trajectory.

A second critical issue that must be explored is the relationship between institutional rules and individual life events. The issue of late-career job changes is a particularly interesting example of this relationship because it illustrates the complexity of the relationship between the two levels of analysis. It is possible to trace a number of late-career job shifts to characteristics of institutional age structuring, such as early pension offers. The standard way to combine an institutional or structural analysis with an individual analysis is to view social structural characteristics as characteristics of the individual. For example, the characteristics of the firm's pension are treated as the individual's characteristics. With this approach, institutional characteristics are only one of several elements affecting behavior. While analysts use this technique to combine the two levels of analysis, it is equally important to retain a parallel institutional analysis so that elements of institutional age structuring do not become indistinguishable from individual level processes such as agency or the interrelationship among domains.

RELATION OF EVENTS IN DIFFERENT DOMAINS AND ACROSS FAMILY MEMBERS

The individual life course is differentiated from the institutional life course by the highly individualized relationship among events in different domains. Variability in the range of life-course domains will affect employment and retirement trajectories. For example, there is great variation in marital and fertility histories. Some individuals have no events—that is, they remain never married and childless—while others have multiple events occurring in different orders. Patterns vary by cohort. Women born in the 1930s had the most uniform family life course of any U.S. cohort born in the twentieth century. Both earlier and later cohorts experienced more variability in proportion ever married, proportion childless, and age at which children were born (O'Rand & Henretta, 1999).

These family events—many of them distal to the timing of retirement—have been shown to produce important effects on retirement timing. Pensions are an obvious mechanism for transmitting the effect of early events on later events since pension rights are based on long-term relationships with an employer. While such relationships reflect the institutional structure of work, they also reflect individual life-course events. For example, women with more extensive early and mid-life employment are more likely to be eligible for a pension (O'Rand & Henretta, 1982b) and retire earlier (Henretta, O'Rand, & Chan, 1993; O'Rand & Henretta, 1982b; O'Rand, Krecker, & Henretta, 1992). Among women, childbearing and late entry into the labor force result in being in an industry with a low probability of pension coverage (O'Rand & Henretta, 1982b).

This pension literature establishes important links between the institutional structure of pensions and early events in the family domain. Women with an employment career that starts early and is uninterrupted—a pattern that characterized women with few or no children in earlier cohorts—retired earlier because this work pattern led to greater pension coverage and earlier eligibility. More proximal family events also affect retirement patterns in important ways. Research indicates extensive coordination between retirement timing of husbands and wives (Clark, Johnson, & McDermed, 1980; Henretta & O'Rand, 1983), suggesting that institutional constraints on one spouse may affect the behavior of the other. Restated, family relationships create interdependent lives. These patterns of joint retirement are also affected by family history such that there is a stronger pattern of mutual influence when husbands and wives have had similar work careers—similarity in lifetime work and family investments by husbands and wives produces more similar behavior late in the life course (Henretta, O'Rand, & Chan, 1993).

More complex ties to the family domain exist in the relationships between family members. Events in the life of one family member can have important effects on other family members—indeed, one might define the boundary of "family" by the distance that such effects run. A standard topic of research in gerontology has been the effect of caregiving to elderly parents on adult children. Certain children are "selected" to provide care through complex life-course family processes (e.g., Henretta, Hill, Li, Soldo, & Wolf, 1997), and care provision may affect the child's employment career and eventual retirement. In the gerontological literature, caregiving has been examined primarily as a proximal factor affecting the child's behavior.

Less attention has been given to the proximal effect of relationships with children on the retirement of parents. The findings discussed earlier on women's employment history, pensions, and retirement focused on the distal effect of relationships with children. We know relatively little about the proximal effect of children on the retirement of parents, other than having young children may slow retirement (Henretta, O'Rand, & Chan, 1993). Unexplored issues include relationships with adult children, and especially the effects of the financial transfers to children that are fairly common around the time of parents' retirement (McGarry & Schoeni, 1995). Yet, there has been no research on the effects of the volume of transfers on retirement timing—do large transfers to children delay retirement? Or, alternatively, does early retirement reduce transfers to children? Since payment of post-secondary schooling expenses is the source of the largest transfer between parents and children, examination of these expenses seems a natural choice. The long-term effects of such expenditures have not been examined since there are no appropriate data.

In sum, the family domain has both proximal and distal effects on the late career. While institutional factors may affect marriage and fertility (e.g., school leaving ages which determine when young people can be economically independent, employment opportunities for women, tax treatment of married couples vs. singles, child benefits in European countries), the family domain is less constrained by institutional age structuring than employment. Yet, over the entire life course there is a close interaction between the two, with events in each domain affecting the other in both the short and long term. Much of the detail of these relationships remains unexplored, but existing research indicates their importance in differentiating the individual life course from the institutional life course.

COORDINATING WORK AND OTHER
LIFE SPHERES

The family is not the only life-course domain that influences employment trajectories. Individuals also have health trajectories that have been the focus of some research. For example, current health is a well-established predictor of retirement (Bound, Schoenbaum, & Waidmann, 1995, 1996; Quinn, Burkhauser, & Myers, 1990), and other closely related research examines the relationship between health and socioeconomic status over the life course (e.g., Feinstein, 1993; Kaplan & Keil, 1993; Mare, 1990; Menchik, 1993; Smith, 1998; Smith & Kington, 1997; Wolfson, Rowe, Gentleman, & Tomiak, 1993). Modeling the relation between health and employment (or health and socioeconomic status) over the life course is very complex. As with family and work, causation runs in both directions—early health problems can affect work careers and economic status and vice versa (Elo & Preston, 1992; Kaplan & Keil, 1993). Disentangling this relationship is an important frontier for retirement research and one that fits very naturally in the life-course framework. Examining the issue, however, requires data on early events—early health events, and early socioeconomic status. These data also are difficult, though not impossible, to collect retrospectively.

IMPLEMENTING A LIFE COURSE APPROACH:
DATA AND CONCEPTUAL ISSUES

The discussion of the individual life course makes clear that a complete analysis of the individual life course requires extensive data. For example, exploring the significance of late-career job changes requires data on the pattern of job shifts throughout the life course. The examination of the relationship between family or health trajectories and employment requires data on both distal and proximal events in their respective domains. Because of these data demands, research has not specified in very much detail most of the links between early and later retirement-related events. In principle, an analyst could estimate the probability path through events across the entire life course, but in practical terms the data demands of such an enterprise make it impossible. When aspects of the earlier life course have been measured, analysts have typically chosen a fixed characteristic, such as years of schooling, or have exploited data originally collected with a somewhat different purpose in mind—for example, inclusion of an employment history and current age of children allow construction of a variable measuring early coordination of work and family events (e.g., Henretta, O'Rand, & Chan, 1993; O'Rand & Henretta, 1982b). As a result, the limited attention to earlier events is dictated primarily by the characteristics of data collection.

Gathering histories of events is time consuming and likely to result in a great deal of missing data and measurement error (Clogg, 1986). Moreover, collecting data on the history of events across several domains—such as work and family—for more than one family member increases the respondent burden greatly. It is difficult to imagine a comprehensive data collection that would allow an analyst to measure the complexity of time paths in the relevant domains that are conceptual parts of the life-course perspective. In addition, there would be great difficulty in estimating the full complexity of such a model. For both these reasons, researchers normally settle for examining a small part of the model. Therefore, the life-course perspective is likely to remain an overarching, guiding framework and not an account of the strength of all or most of the links between events over the life course.

ADVANTAGES OF A LIFE-COURSE PERSPECTIVE

Given the high data demands for a full account of the links within and across domains in the individual life course, it is important to consider the circumstances under which the life-course perspective adds analytic leverage, and the circumstances under which incorporating the life-course perspective actually requires full life-course data. The conceptual advantages of incorporating the life-course perspective in studies of individual work and retirement behavior turn primarily on two factors: the importance of history (i.e., the trajectory of previous events in the individual's life) for understanding current behavior and whether the analyst simply wishes to predict current behavior or understand its development.

The effects of the earlier trajectory might be considered at the institutional level, the individual level, or both. Attention to the history of previous events might add additional explanatory power for two reasons. First, it may include critical information not captured by current state. In the context of retirement, for example, one might argue that current job characteristics do not capture all the relevant elements of occupational history that affect retirement. Take the example of "disorderly" career endings (multiple exits and re-entries into the labor force around retirement age) that was discussed earlier. Disorderly endings may reflect a larger work career that is also disorderly, and this factor will not likely be captured by current occupation. Information on the earlier career pattern is critical to interpret the meaning of the late-career pattern. Does the late-career pattern represent continuity or change in the individual's life course?

Alternatively, the analyst might wish to understand the distribution of pre-retirement states. Pension eligibility may contain all the information required to understand when and why retirement occurs, but the analyst might ask about the distribution of pension eligibility. Why and how do workers reach retirement age with different levels of pension eligibility? Using an earlier example, how does the level and timing of early fertility affect pension eligibility at age 60? Examining this issue combines individual history, cohort patterns of fertility, and historical changes in pension systems.

Assets at the time of retirement present a similar issue. One might argue that proximal level of assets contains all the required information about retirement preparation that is required to understand retirement timing. However, understanding the process that produces level of assets near retirement may be useful because it indicates the trade-offs parents make between investments in children and their own retirement—trade-offs made over a lifetime that reflect individual agency. Moreover, understanding the process may help to explain differences in asset accumulation among those with equal lifetime income.

In sum, knowing history is important in some situations because it is critical to addressing the meaning and significance of current life-course transitions. In other cases, it is important so that we may understand how individuals reach mid- or late-life with the characteristics they have. Yet actual measurement of individual history is not always necessary to achieve some more limited research goals, even within a life-course perspective, because current state may capture some relevant historical information. Using an example presented earlier, eligibility for a defined benefit pension in a particular firm implies that a series of earlier events on the current job have occurred. The institutional structure of pensions makes earlier events (e.g., years of uninterrupted service) important to pension determination. Knowing pension eligibility, and therefore tenure on the current job, may not exhaust career information, but it may be sufficient to predict retirement timing. This example uses an *implicit* life-course perspective, as there is a clear conceptual significance to earlier events, even though those earlier events are not measured directly. This type of research therefore does not assume that history is unimportant. It only assumes that for more limited research goals, the relevant aspects of history may be adequately captured by current state. When considered in this way, the amount of research on retirement that has been done in the general tradition of the life-course perspective, including both direct measurement of pathways and measurement of proximal states that include relevant information about the past, is quite large.

AN AGENDA FOR FUTURE RESEARCH ON
WORK AND RETIREMENT

This chapter has considered three themes: the significance of institutional structure in forming an age-based life course; the way in which the individual life course is rooted in institutional structures but departs from these structures in important ways; and the relationship between inference about life-course processes and the concomitant life-course data needed to capture and analyze these processes. Earlier sections of this chapter have addressed specific directions for advancing research on these topics. This section will therefore provide an overview of the relationships between the three topics.

For the most part, the institutional life course has provided a conceptual, interpretive framework for understanding individual behavior while most research has focused on the individual life course. The reason for this is that the great heterogeneity of social structure defies easy description except by reference to the variation in individual behavior. For example, employment-related social structure varies between employers and across time; it is usually easier to characterize the behavior of a particular birth cohort rather than to describe all the social structures that have affected their lives. While there are important studies of particular institutions that focus on their age-based rules, we still lack a systematic approach to understanding whether work trajectories and the life course as a whole are becoming more or less structured by age. One important agenda for research is the greater specification of the overall institutional basis for the age structuring of work and the larger life course.

Research on retirement has generally used a framework that is consistent with a life-course framework. While some research examines proximal factors only, such factors sometimes imply earlier events. In addition, there is extensive research that actually utilizes data on earlier events or events in other domains. There is clearly an important agenda in both specifying life-course processes in greater detail and in recognizing the implicit life-course perspective in much existing research.

The most interesting and challenging issues lie in two other areas. There are two levels of analysis in life-course research that have been outlined in this chapter—the institutional and individual levels. New and critical frontiers of research lie at the intersection between the two levels. In particular, explicit attention should be paid to measuring change at the institutional level and assessing its significance at the individual level. Has the life course become less structured by age, and has that change made the individual life course more variable? There are excellent examples of research that simultaneously considers these two levels of analysis empirically (e.g., Kohli, Rein, Guillemard, &

van Gunsteren, 1991) or conceptually (e.g., Dannefer, 1984), and this approach should become the norm. Second, life-course research makes demanding requests of data—both in the types of data it asks us to gather and how it asks us to analyze those data. Hence, analysts need to be very creative in their use of existing data (e.g., Elder & Pavalko, 1993) and creative in their implicit life-course analyses (e.g., Wise, 1997) that utilize life-course concepts but don't demand data measuring events over the entire life course.

REFERENCES

Anderson, M. (1985). The emergence of the modern life cycle in Britain. *Social History, 10*, 69-87.

Belous, R. (1989). Flexible employment: The employer's point of view. In P. B. Doeringer (Ed.), *Bridges to retirement* (pp. 111-129). Ithaca, NY: ILR Press.

Bound, J., Schoenbaum, S., & Waidmann, T. (1995). Race and education differences in disability status and labor force attachment. *Journal of Human Resources, 30*(supplement), S227-S267.

Bound, J., Schoenbaum, S., & Waidmann, T. (1996). Race differences in labor force attachment and disability status. *The Gerontologist, 36*, 311-321.

Brown, C. (1997). *Early retirement windows: Evidence from the Health and Retirement Study.* Unpublished manuscript, University of Michigan, Ann Arbor, Michigan.

Bulow, J. I., & Summers, L. H. (1986). A theory of dual labor markets with application to industrial policy, discrimination, and Kenysian unemployment. *Journal of Labor Economics, 4*, 376-414.

Cappelli, P., Bassi, L., Katz, H., Knoke, D., Osterman, P., & Useem, M. (1997). *Change at work.* New York: Oxford.

Carter, S. B., & Sutch, R. (1996). Myth of the industrial scrap heap: A revisionist view of turn of the century American retirement. *Journal of Economic History, 56*, 5-38.

Clark, R. L., Johnson, T., & McDermed, A. (1980). Allocation of time and resources by married couples approaching retirement. *Social Security Bulletin, 43*, 3-16.

Clogg, C. C. (1986). Invoked by RATE. *American Journal of Sociology, 92*, 696-706.

Costa, D. L. (1998). The evolution of retirement: Summary of a research project. *American Economic Review, 88*, 232-236.

Dannefer, D. (1984). Adult development and social theory: A paradigmatic reappraisal. *American Sociological Review, 49*, 100-116.

Elder, G. H., Jr., & Pavalko, E. K. (1993). Work careers in men's later years: transitions, trajectories, and historical change. *Journals of Gerontology: Social Sciences, 48*, S180-191.

Elo, I. T., & Preston, S. H. (1992). Effects of early life conditions on adult mortality: A review. *Population Index, 58*, 186-212.

Feinstein, J. S. (1993). The relationship between socioeconomic status and health: A review of the literature. *Milbank Quarterly, 71*, 279-323.

Gratton, B. (1996). The poverty of impoverishment theory: The economic well-being of the elderly 1890-1950. *Journal of Economic History, 56*, 39-61.

Guillemard, A. M. (1989). The trend towards early labour force withdrawal and the reorganization of the life course: A cross-national analysis. In P. Johnson, C. Conrad, &

D. Thomson (Eds.), *Workers versus pensioners: Intergenerational justice in an ageing world* (pp. 163-180). Manchester, UK: Manchester University.

Guillemard, A. M., & Rein, M. (1993). Comparative patterns in retirement. *Annual Review of Sociology, 19,* 469-503.

Gustman, A. L., Mitchell, O. S., & Steinmeier, T. L. (1995). retirement measures in the health and retirement study. *The Journal of Human Resources, 30,* S57-S83.

Gustman, A. L., & Steinmeier, T. L. (1984). Partial retirement and the analysis of retirement behavior. *Industrial and Labor Relations Review, 37,* 403-415.

Gustman, A. L., & Steinmeier, T. L. (1995). *Pension incentives and job mobility.* Kalamazoo, MI: W. E. Upjohn Institute for Employment Research.

Hayward, M. D., Crimmins, E. M., & Wray, L. A. (1994). The relationship between retirement life cycle changes and older men's labor force participation rates. *Journals of Gerontology: Social Sciences, 49,* S219-230.

Henretta, J. C. (1992). Uniformity and diversity: Life course institutionalization and late-life work exit. *The Sociological Quarterly, 33,* 265-279.

Henretta, J. C. (1994a). Social structure and age-based careers. In M. W. Riley, R. L. Kahn, & A. Foner (Eds.), *Age and structural lag* (pp. 57-79). New York: Wiley.

Henretta, J. C. (1994b) Recent trends in retirement. *Reviews in Clinical Gerontology, 4,* 71-81.

Henretta, J. C. (2000). The future of age integration in employment. *The Gerontologist, 40,* 286-292.

Henretta, J. C., Hill, M. S., Li, W., Soldo, B. J., & Wolf, D. A. (1997). Selection of children to provide care: The effect of earlier parental transfers. *Journals of Gerontology: Social Sciences, 52B*(Special Issue), 110-119.

Henretta, J. C., & Lee, H. (1996). Cohort differences in men's late-life labor force participation. *Work and Occupations, 23,* 214-235.

Henretta, J. C., & O'Rand, A. M. (1983). Joint retirement in the dual worker family. *Social Forces, 62,* 504-519.

Henretta J. C., O'Rand, A. M., & Chan, C. G. (1993). Joint role investments and synchronization of retirement: A sequential approach to couples' retirement timing. *Social Forces, 71,* 981-1000.

Herz, D. E. (1995). Work after early retirement: An increasing trend among men. *Monthly Labor Review, 118*(4), 13-20.

Honig, M. (1985). Partial retirement among women. *Journal of Human Resources, 20,* 613-621.

Hurd, M. D. (1996). The effect of labor market rigidities on the labor force behavior of older workers. In D. A. Wise (Ed.), *Advances in the economics of aging* (pp. 11-60). Chicago: University of Chicago.

Hutchens, R. M. (1988). Do job opportunities decline with age? *Industrial and Labor Relations Review, 42,* 89-99.

Ippolito, R. A. (1990). Toward explaining earlier retirement after 1970. *Industrial and Labor Relations Review, 43,* 556-569.

Jacoby, S. M. (1985). *Employing bureaucracy.* New York: Columbia University Press.

Kaplan, G. A., & Keil, J. E. (1993). Socioeconomic factors and cardiovascular disease: A review of the literature. *Circulation, 88,* 1973-1998.

Kohli, M. (1986). The world we forgot: A historical review of the life course. In V. W. Marshall (Ed.), *Later life: The social psychology of aging* (pp. 271-303). Beverly Hills, CA: Sage.

Kohli, M. (1987). Retirement and the moral economy: An historical interpretation of the German case. *Journal of Aging Studies, 1,* 125-144.

Kohli, M. (1988). Aging as a challenge to sociological theory. *Aging and Society, 8,* 367-394.

Kohli, M., Rein, M., Guillemard, A. M., & van Gunsteren, H. (Eds.) (1991). *Time for retirement: Comparative studies of early exit from the labor force.* Cambridge, UK: Cambridge University Press.

Kohli, M., Rosenow, J., & Wolf, J. (1983). The social construction of aging through work: Economic structure and life-world. *Aging and Society, 3,* 23-42.

Lazear, E. (1979). Why is there mandatory retirement? *Journal of Political Economy, 87,* 1261-1284.

Mare, R. D. (1990). Socioeconomic careers and differential mortality among older men in the united states. In J. Vallin, S. D'Souza, & A. Palloni (Eds.), *Measurement and analysis of mortality: New approaches* (pp. 362-387). Oxford: Clarendon.

Mayer, K. U., & Schoepflin, U. (1989). The state and the life course. *Annual Review of Sociology, 15,* 187-209.

McGarry, K., & Schoeni, R. F. (1995). Transfer behavior in the Health and Retirement Study: Measurement and the redistribution of resources within the family. *Journal of Human Resources, 30,* S184-S226.

Menchik, P. L. (1993). Economic status as a determinant of mortality among black and white older men: Does poverty kill? *Population Studies, 47,* 427-436.

Mitchell, O. S. (1999). *New trends in pension benefit and retirement provisions* (Working Paper 7381). Cambridge, MA: National Bureau of Economic Research.

Mutschler, P. H. (1996). Early retirement incentive programs (ERIPS): Mechanisms for encouraging early retirement. In W. H. Crown (Ed.), *Handbook on employment and the elderly* (pp. 182-193). Westport, CT: Greenwood.

O'Rand, A. M., & Henretta, J. C. (1982a). Midlife work history and the retirement income of older single and married women. In M. Szinovacz (Ed.), *Women's retirement: Policy implications of recent research* (pp. 25-44). Beverly Hills, CA: Sage.

O'Rand, A. M., & Henretta, J. C. (1982b). Delayed career entry, industrial pension structure, and early retirement in a cohort of unmarried women. *American Sociological Review, 47,* 365-373.

O'Rand, A. M., & Henretta, J. C. (1999). *Age and inequality: Diverse pathways through later life.* Boulder, CO: Westview.

O'Rand A. M., Krecker, M. L., & Henretta, J. C. (1992). Family pathways to retirement: Early and late life family effects on couples' work exit patterns. In M. Szinovacz, D. J. Ekerdt, & B. H. Vinick (Eds.), *Families and retirement: Conceptual and methodological issues* (pp. 81-98). Beverly Hills, CA: Sage.

Osterman, P. (1988). *Employment futures.* New York: Oxford.

Quinn, J. F., Burkhauser, R. V., & Myers, D. A. (1990). *Passing the torch: The influence of economic incentives on work and retirement.* Kalamazoo, MI: W. E. Upjohn Institute for Employment Research.

Quinn, J. F., & Kozy, M. (1996). The role of bridge jobs in the retirement transition: Gender, race, and ethnicity. *The Gerontologist, 36,* 363-372.

Riley, M. W. (1987). On the significance of age in sociology. *American Sociological Review, 52,* 1-14.

Riley, M. W. (1993). *The coming revolution in age structure.* Pepper Lecture on Aging and Public Policy, Florida State University, Tallahassee.

Riley, M. W. (1998). *The hidden age revolution: Emergent integration of all ages.* (Policy Brief No. 12/1988). Syracuse, NY: Syracuse University, Center for Policy Research.

Riley, M. W., & Riley, J. W. (1994). Structural lag: Past and future. In M. W. Riley, R. L. Kahn, & A. Foner (Eds.), *Age and structural lag* (pp. 15-36). New York: Wiley.

Ruhm, C. J. (1990). Career jobs, bridge employment, and retirement. In P. B. Doeringer (Ed.), *Bridges to retirement* (pp. 92-110). Ithaca, NY: ILR Press.

Smith, J. P. (1998). Socioeconomic status and health. *American Economic Review, 88,* 192-196.

Smith, J. P., & Kington, R. (1997). Demographic and economic correlates of health in old age. *Demography, 34,* 159-170.

Spilerman, S. (1977). Careers, labor market structure, and socioeconomic attainment. *American Journal of Sociology, 83,* 551-593.

Wise, D. A. (1997). Retirement against the demographic trend: More older people living longer, working less, and saving less. *Demography, 34,* 83-95.

Wolfson, M., Rowe, G., Gentleman, J. F., & Tomiak, M. (1993). Career earnings and death: A longitudinal analysis of older Canadian men. *Journals of Gerontology: Social Sciences, 48,* S167-179.

Yellen, J. L. (1984). Efficiency wage models of unemployment. *American Economic Review, 74,* 200-205.

CHAPTER 4

Leisure in Life-Course Perspective*

Jon Hendricks and Stephen J. Cutler

Interest in the life course has been growing and the value of life-course analyses is increasingly recognized. By concentrating on the "intersection of social and historical factors with personal biography" (George, 1996, p. 249), the life-course perspective emphasizes such issues as duration, timing, and sequencing of life events; roles and status transitions; and other factors contouring the pathways of a person's life. It also weighs their relative influence in different contexts and evaluates the heterogeneity these contexts exhibit. The life-course paradigm recognizes that life is a confluence of dynamic aligning and realigning factors that shift over a lifetime, allowing an individual to build on accumulated experience at each turn. When an examination of the life course is based on this precept, it can shed light on aging and on "how society gives social and personal meanings to the passage of time" (Hagestad, 1990, p. 151). In its broadest sense, life-course analysis attends to the intricate web of social, cultural, and historical influences patterning beliefs, behavior, and events.

Although the explanatory value of life-course analyses is generally acknowledged, it is no exaggeration to say the perspective has yet to realize its full potential. Notable contributions have been made (Baltes, 1987; Baltes, Reese, & Lipsett, 1980; Elder, 1974, 1985; Neugarten & Hagestad, 1976; Riegel, 1975; Settersten, 1997, 1999; Sørensen, Weinert, & Sherrod, 1986), but life-course analyses have been hampered by the need for conceptual development, by limitations in the availability of suitable data, and until recently by the absence of analytical tools appropriate for longitudinal analysis of circumstances unfolding

*We would like to express our appreciation to Nicole Kafer and Ann Donahue for their many contributions to the preparation of this chapter.

over several decades. Moreover, life-course models as they apply to later life are in the early stages, and the substantive foci have been limited, in that the predominant point of convergence has been on age grading of family, work, and retirement roles, and the importance of health status (George, 1996).

Our objective is to sketch the outlines of a life-course perspective on the topic of leisure. With increasing life expectancy, improvements in health status, earlier or intermittent retirement, not to mention sweeping changes in the economy, it is likely that leisure will occupy an even more significant place in the lives of older persons than it has to date. The interaction with and relevance of work roles also needs to be specified as the import of leisure is considered. First, there is no doubt that the structure of work furnishes symbolic markers of life-course transitions, especially for middle- and upper-management workers who customarily anticipate a progression of opportunities. We recognize there are a host of built-in biases to such a view. What, for example, of that cadre of workers who move from one entry-level position to another or those for whom work is not a source of rewards or significant milestones? What of those workers, or others for that matter, confined to subordinate positions, who do not experience many options in their lives? For this latter group, a discussion of meaningful leisure opportunities may sound like fodder for the parvenu but not for the rest.

Second, technology and the times are marching on, altering the nature of work. Work, as it was known throughout the twentieth century, may be in for some fairly sweeping reorganization. As Henretta (1994) reported, long familiar entitlements and emoluments are disappearing with the shift away from patterns of lifetime employment in firms marked by internal labor markets and age-structured hierarchies. Instead, new modal categories of work, sometimes termed contingent employment, are taking root. In that the new patterns are not characterized by comparable continuities and are not particularly age-structured, they are similar to "spot markets" that do not incorporate comparable internal labor markets, fringe benefits as recompense, or retirement benefits. It may be that for a growing segment of the work force the intrinsic meanings of work will dwindle as service economies expand, contingent employment replaces lifetime career transitions, upward mobility is flattened, downsizing occurs, or work is altered in ways that affect rewards or alter opportunities for personal agency. Even with traditional lifetime employment, the evidence suggests that with advancing age, the relative meaning that an employee extracts from work roles declines, provided financial security is assured (Crimmins & Easterlin, 2000). If this shift takes hold, there is every probability that leisure will become a more prominent aspect of an individual's identity. In the event that significant shifts occur in these patterns, explaining life-course trajectories or alterations in hierarchical concerns, continuities, or discontinuities will become problematic.

Not to be forgotten is that the size of a cohort affects the life chances of its members. As larger numbers of people live into the second half of life, their prospects will be different from those of their predecessors. Might it be that for the elderly of tomorrow, regardless of cohort size, other realms of endeavor will become relatively more important insofar as self-concept and life-course transitions are concerned? If modal structures derived from labor force participation decline, so too will modal transitions and sources of meaning. These complexities are exacerbated still further once age, stage, duration, or previous experiences are factored into the equation (Dannefer & Perlmutter, 1990; Hendricks, 1984; Riley, Kahn, & Foner, 1994).

How life-course studies might better illuminate the importance of leisure and the forms it takes is at the core of our discussion. Although it is quite likely that age is a useful index to various forms of leisure engagement (Kelly, 1992), that is not at the heart of our discussion; neither are we concerned with looking at leisure as an indicator of incipient disengagement from other valued roles, as was the case with the Kansas City Studies of Adult Life (Havighurst, 1961). Our concern is somewhat broader than these considerations. To make sense of what constitutes leisure, its relevance for personal identities, and its self-referential value, analysts must consider individual-level changes over time and societal-level shifts in the structure and allocation of opportunities. On the one hand, casting patterns of leisure in a life-course perspective and interpreting them in terms of movement from one membership category to another will provide insights into long-term trends and the relevance of leisure as a type of social behavior. On the other hand, leisure is more than just an activity in which individuals participate. Leisure is an expressive domain within industrial and postindustrial societies and, as such, is part of a larger set of social, cultural, economic, and political institutions. Changes in any of these, either in their entirety or in the way they are structured, will affect leisure participation through shifts in values, role opportunities, the distribution of resources, or the enabling characteristics of those who participate or are barred from participation for whatever reason (Cheek & Burch, 1976; Kelly, 1992).

Be that as it may, leisure is not merely a derivative outgrowth of economic roles. It has always had profound meaning for those who do not ground their self-concept in the world of paid work. For example, older black women, who volunteer at rates in excess of others their age, may view and then utilize their free time as a way to "give back" to their communities (Allen & Chin-Sang, 1990; Harootyan & Vorek, 1994). We are of the opinion that leisure will gain significance as a generative transaction zone, providing both an action space for interpretative activity and anchoring the tacitly accepted conventions that make up personal meaning systems (Dittmann-Kohli & Westerhof, 1999). Leisure deserves greater attention if only because it represents an option compatible with what Coser (1991) described as the "plurality of life worlds" that has myriad ameliorative effects during adulthood.

To underscore the portent of leisure, we begin by examining customary perspectives on its relevance for successful aging, and then briefly summarize what is known about leisure over the life course. Next we consider selected applications of a life-course perspective on leisure and the life-course implications of leisure and what is considered age-appropriate recreation. We conclude by speculating on the place of leisure in the lives of older persons in the twenty-first century and about directions for research. A theme running throughout our discussion is that leisure researchers must recognize the importance of personal agency and the shifting priorities a person manifests over time, in order to understand how the broader social currents affect the quality of life and the nature of experience. We contend that because they provide a social space, an interpretive zone wherein actors not only ground their self-appraisals (Felson, 1992; Kelly, 1987) but express themselves, leisure opportunities are more central to the generation of meaning than has previously been acknowledged. We eschew efforts that would define leisure as one thing or another, for all people. Rather, we assert that leisure is discretionary, provides intrinsic rewards, and is self-defined by participants. Certainly leisure is not merely a listing of activities that do not involve wages or cross-cutting obligations (Kelly, 1992), but has meaning that is inordinately more phenomenological than any binary definition can convey.

TRADITIONAL PERSPECTIVES ON THE RELEVANCE OF LEISURE FOR SUCCESSFUL AGING

According to Kelly (1992), leisure studies have passed through at least three phases. Initially, leisure was seen as part of other forms of community studies and examined along organizational lines. Next, as implied above, analysts looked at leisure as a consequence of work and economic roles. The third focus viewed leisure as a distinct place where important meaningfulness is created, but as Kelly noted, its potential is far from realized or linked to other areas of inquiry. As attention turned to the place of leisure in adulthood, research on the link between leisure and successful aging has typically taken the approach of examining the relationship between leisure participation rates and various dimensions of the psychological and physical well-being of older persons (Osgood, 1995). For example, Kelly, Steinkamp, and Kelly (1987), Stebbins (1992), and others, report a direct link between expressions of well-being and leisure participation. Underlying their contentions is an assumption that leisure provides a "social life space" wherein interpersonal bonding as well as personal discovery can be accomplished. Interestingly, Stebbins (1992) spoke of "serious leisure" and Kelly (1992) referred to "high-investment" leisure, defined in terms of time, effort, commitment, and so on, as providing proportionately greater salutatory effects. Although an explicit life-course framework did not guide these studies, the findings are sufficiently robust and consistent to demonstrate the salience of meaningful leisure participation (Lawton, Moss, & Fulcomer, 1986–87). Higher levels of self-esteem and morale; lower levels of depression; and elevated feelings of self-worth, control, and solidarity have all been shown to be associated with leisure participation (Baltes, Wahl, & Schmid-Furstoss, 1990; Herzog, Franks, Markus, & Holmberg, 1998; Huyck, 1991; Reitzes, Mutran, & Verrill, 1995). There is some evidence that cognitive functioning is also related to leisure activities (Cockburn & Smith, 1991; Fabrigoule, 1995). Some studies suggest that lower fracture risk (Sorock, Bush, Golden, Fried, Breuer, & Hale, 1988), greater knowledge and use of health and social services (West, Delisle, Simard, & Drouin, 1996), and lower mortality (Andersen, Schnohr, Schroll, & Hein, 2000; Glass, Mendes de Leon, Marottoli, & Berkman, 1999; Musick, Herzog, & House, 1999) are also linked to various aspects of leisure engagement.

To the extent voluntary activity is considered a dimension of leisure involvement, there is all the more reason for closer scrutiny. Previous research among the elderly has included volunteerism as leisure, since it is undertaken for non-remunerative reasons (Osgood, 1995). Certainly for some segments of the population, older black females for example, this is quite likely the case, in that "giving back" is an important aspect of their identity separate from paid work (Allen & Chin-Sang, 1990; Chin-Sang & Allen, 1991).

There should be little doubt that leisure is a valuable albeit marginalized pursuit. For one thing, leisure is big business. Estimates vary from a low of more than $431 billion in personal expenditures for recreation in 1996 (U. S. Bureau of the Census, 1997, Table 425) to the $1-trillion expenditure reported by Kammen (1999). Once the approximately $20 billion spent by various governmental agencies for recreational opportunities is added (U.S. Bureau of the Census, 1997, Tables 501, 506), the size of the leisure market begins to loom large—it is greater than the health care or housing market in terms of personal expenditures. In light of its significance as a source of personal gratification, it may not be surprising that the amounts spent on leisure are as great as they are. Certainly leisure is a domain in which structural latitude is greater than in many other realms that not only have more rigid conventional boundaries but hold sway over individual priorities and affective meaning.

If a rationale were to be needed, in the face of structurally fettered age-grading, leisure engagements: (1) help compensate for normatively constrained passage; (2) provide opportunities for experimentation and integration of identity in the face of other institutionalized or involuntary role transitions; (3) create emotionally meaningful bonds among consociates through informal interaction; (4) provide ideational flexibility giving rise to definitions of meaningful experience and mechanisms for maintaining integration of self-concept; (5) permit mediation between individual readiness and structurally imposed processes to provide a kind of ipsative stability to life (Elder & O'Rand, 1995); and (6) provide arenas in which adaptive competencies can be honed through expressive outlets permitting maximal personal agency. In a nutshell, socially constructed meaning making occurs through leisure engagements when other aspects of life are perceived as rigid or enduring. If social structures are nonresponsive or lag behind personal competencies and capabilities, an intrinsic tension develops that restrains developmental potential (Riley et al., 1994; Settersten, 1999).

Most leisure researchers see leisure as restorative, spontaneous, and as a compensatory or congruous reflection of other aspects of life (Kelly, 1992; Osgood, 1995). As has been noted, it is frequently seen as a "bulk quality" accruing along institutionalized age boundaries on either end of the life cycle. In the traditional view of work as all-consuming, it may have made sense to think of leisure in this way, insofar as leisure clustered in the extensive blocks of time available following diminution of work roles (Kaplan, 1979). Seen thus, leisure has been analyzed in terms of age-appropriate forms of engagement, as a way to fill time and as compensation for lost work roles. It has also been analyzed as a vehicle for promoting interaction and retaining social support (Gordon, Gaitz, & Scott, 1976; Kelly, 1992). Frequently, leisure in later life has been analyzed from the standpoint of the environments or institutions within which it occurs— organized and informal settings ranging from nursing homes and retirement facilities to pick-up leagues, reading clubs, and travel groups, among others. Sometimes the focus is attention to active versus passive leisure activities deemed appropriate, based on skill or aptitude levels, and involves attention to what changing physical capabilities imply for the provision of appropriate leisure (Leitner & Leitner, 1996; Osgood, 1995).

Many leisure researchers have taken their lead from the landmark edited volume *Aging and Leisure* (Kleemeier, 1961) and the groundbreaking work of Kaplan (1979). Perhaps the overriding focus has been in terms of the implications of leisure as a compensatory mechanism facilitating adjustment to retirement, with work and leisure juxtaposed as meaning-making pursuits and as ways to bolster morale and life satisfaction. The agenda has largely revolved around Burgess's (1960) characterization of retirement as "the roleless role." Intentionally or unintentionally, such a portrayal circumscribed the relevance and denigrated the importance of what people do when they are no longer working. We maintain that this work-leisure dichotomy is counterproductive and masks the significance of leisure as a transactional zone wherein developmental objectives may be effected (Baltes, Lindenberger, & Staudinger, 1998; Cutler & Hendricks, 1990). It is also inopportune in that it ill fits the experience of those who have not had extensive labor force involvement. Many sweeping changes are afoot, and they will likely mean alterations in the way we think of leisure as an arena where societal and individual opportunities intersect.

In a comprehensive overview of conceptual approaches to leisure, Kelly (1987) noted that with a complex and fluid phenomenon, the tendency is to divide it into as many small pieces as possible to make analysis manageable. This certainly seems to have happened in scholarship on leisure. Kelly (1987, 1992) stands out as one of the few leisure researchers who have endeavored to meld a substantive focus with a conceptually based developmental perspective. As he pointed out, virtually every social, cultural or psychological influence an individual faces factors into their leisure pursuits. Although Kelly's (1987) focus was restricted to three broadly defined phases of the life course, and to the relationship of learned behavior and socialization to expectations, he attempted to fuse conceptual perspectives from a generalized developmental model to the substantive analysis of leisure. Building on existing literature, he pointed out that the developmental agenda is ongoing, that intrinsic rewards are important, and that leisure is "more central to the working out of a number of developmental tasks than had usually been recognized" (Kelly, 1987, p. 69). At the time Kelly was assembling his synopsis, few researchers were focused on a life-course perspective on leisure. Rapoport and Rapoport (1975) incorporated the family life cycle in a prominent publication of the mid-1970s, and Gordon et al. (1976) put a life span spin on their chapter in the *Handbook of Aging and the Social Sciences*. The general conclusion was that leisure is extensively grounded in the family; therefore, its evolution reflects family life cycles. Even with such auspicious beginnings, we have been unable to discover significant contributions beyond those initial forays—leisure research appears to have been insulated from a dynamic life-course perspective or developmental template.

LEISURE OVER THE LIFE-COURSE PERSPECTIVE

Importance of Conceptual Integration

Despite agreement that age is integral to many forms of social organization, the assumption of a dynamic life course has been incorporated into gerontology in only the past few decades (Baltes et al., 1980; Riegel, 1975; Settersten, 1999). In that period, the notion of ongoing and emergent development has had an incisive impact and furnished an integrative template for interpreting age changes. Many insights have been generated under the rubric of a life-course perspective, and this perspective, broadly conceived, has lent order to inquiries that previously yielded considerable data without necessarily contributing comparable insight. It should come as no surprise that a principal finding has been that the relative importance of different domains shifts over time, depending on previous engagements and emergent opportunities for corroborative feedback. Not only have the combined points of view moved psychology away from ontogenetic explanations of development, they have prompted other social scientists to recognize that actors are not passive in the face of what goes on about them. It has also brought recognition that because individuals inhabit a world at the intersection of biographies and social structure, to understand aging, analysts must examine the two dimensions simultaneously (Dannefer & Uhlenberg, 1999; Moen, Dempster-McClain, & Williams, 1992).

One major repercussion has been to nudge analytic frameworks away from facile characterizations of antecedents or independent and dependent factors or imputation of simple cause and effect relationships. Among the more obvious alloys that accompany a life-course perspective is increasing attention to how constitutive elements of meaningfulness align, metamorphose, and then realign with age. One of the reasons this is so is that life-course development is conceived as transactional, with individuals being active agents in the process. In other words, one's view of the world, of time, and of what is important, is indexed to transitions implicit in diverse domains of aging, and the effects of these are mediated by individual-level considerations. It is the relative balancing of alignment and transformative change that undergirds a sense either of continuity or of change in adult life. A concomitant benefit of such a life-course perspective is that not only is context important, but the relevance of diverse facets of context change as perceptual priorities evolve. How a person is affected by a given assemblage of environmental components also evolves with time, as do personal prerogatives, such that over the long term, noticeably different factors make a difference (Lawton, 1983). Bronfenbrenner (1979, 1995) used the phrase "ecology of human development" as a means of conveying the inviolate but dynamic interconnections between self, sense of well-being, and contextual factors.

Life-course developmental change and environmental adaptability build on a compilation of two types of resources. First, there are personal attributes, traits, and skills customarily categorized as forms of human capital. These are acquired characteristics associated with personal competencies and personalities. At the same time, people rely on an array of social or situational resources that exist independently of individual actors but are available to them by virtue of their being embedded in socially relevant membership categories (Bourdieu, 1986). The latter, collectively termed social capital, are irreducible to human capital but cannot be said to be entirely exterior to individuals. In other words, one's location in the social landscape channels (variously facilitates or constrains) the distribution of certain types of resources. Included among the dimensions of social capital are such accouterments of membership as language, social networks, peer communities, and world views used by individuals in negotiating their path. Both forms of capital constitute resources available to actors that mold the meaning of all activity, including leisure.

Another factor influencing an individual's process of negotiation is that as populations themselves age, interactions between age strata, opportunity structures, and social policies also change. These, too, may be considered forms of social capital. Finally, non-normative life events may enter the picture and deflect the best-laid plans. As with other environmental ingredients of the life course, the interrelationships are complex and dynamic (Settersten, 1999). In fact, it may be the complexity of those interrelationships that accounts for the disparities of experience and diversity of characteristics among the elderly (Dannefer, 1996). The same admixture of resources operating on many different levels likely explains the difference between usual and successful aging (Rowe & Kahn, 1998). By attempting to disentangle these sundry dimensions of aging, leisure analysts can provide a more holistic, integrative template that will yield more accurate data and better insight.

In terms of leisure, the merit of a life-course perspective rests with its potential for providing an analytic template that fosters greater conceptual integration than has heretofore been the case. To anticipate some of what we will assert, leisure is invaluable in helping actors create sense as they move through life, as a milieu for experimentation that helps define or reinforce personal identity, especially when meaningful work roles are unavailable or diminished. Seen in this light, leisure is not the marginal, ancillary activity it is sometimes thought to be. It is a forum, though certainly not the only forum, wherein important agency takes place and possible selves are tried out as actors adapt to the ongoing flow of events in their lives (Kelly, 1992; Rapoport & Rapoport, 1975).

Gerontologists may be missing an opportunity if they continue to view leisure as a by-product or derivative outcome of work. It is likely that leisure pursuits are provenance of, or at least integral to, evolving identities. Seen in this way, leisure is returned to its roots as *play* (Huizinga, 1955), wherein anticipatory socialization takes places, discovery is possible, and identity is maintained as meaningfulness is created. Leisure embodies the contention that it is through play, in one form or another, that all of us, and not just children, find relatively low-risk opportunities to try out alternative self-concepts, modes or styles of interaction, personas, capabilities, and competencies. It is in this same realm where actors explore alternative selves in activities requiring no justification. In the event of failure, the only response required is that one was merely playing, fooling around, trying things out, or goofing off. In the face of success, new experiences are sorted and assimilated into a person's identity and presentation. Considered thus, play is not trivial but an important venue for self-discovery. As the portent of role transitions is realized and identity shifts, leisure permits generative trials related to the reformulation of "personal meaning systems"—interpretative and directional aspects of meaning (Dittmann-Kohli & Westerhof, 1999) that can provide an organizing template incorporating principal life themes and identity projects into interpretations of daily life. Whether or not it is explicitly acknowledged, self-referential meaning is central to interpretative practice (Brandtstädter, 1990; Hendricks, 1999).

The above does not imply leisure is somehow insulated from the distribution of power, access, and prestige that accrues in so many other endeavors. To illustrate the point, consider some of the subtle aspects of family leisure that reflect the gendered distribution of roles, internal hierarchies, and obligations. In the case of family leisure, there is little doubt that preparation is necessary and to the extent it falls to women to ensure that "leisure" happens, the term may be tantamount to an oxymoron—leisure for one part of the family but a continuation of responsibilities for another part. What is played out in family contexts is mirrored in other subgroups of the population; gendered roles, the division of responsibilities, and perquisites persevere. The pattern is probably a reflection of existing inequities and the distribution of advantage characteristic of many groups, including the elderly (Kelly, 1992; Wearing, 1998).

Leisure in the Course of Adulthood

Drawing on Weber, Marshall (1998) recently termed the exposition and abstractions gerontologists employ "ideal types," helpful for heuristic purposes, existing as mental constructions not literal reproductions of what can be found in reality. Relying on a comparable approach, a fresh interpretative template for making sense of leisure can be formulated. Life-course constructions have not only challenged the notion that childhood is the only malleable period of life but incorporated attention to adaptation and organizing principles individuals utilize to interpret experience and the "developmental effects of changing circumstances" (Elder, 1998, p. 942). In a thoroughgoing synopsis, Elder focused on a number of relevant dimensions, including one having to do with his contention that lives are systematized by roles, cycles, and age-grading, which pertains to the present topic.

In reference to roles, life-course theorists attend to how social circumstances imply diverse normative definitions within the aging process. They look not only for the presence, absence, or alteration of roles that shape life chances but ask how particularities structure the ways roles play out. Similarly, rhythms of family life, for example, child rearing and cycles of parenting, independence, as well as dependence and overlapping obligations, affect both the individual and the family group's trajectories. Roles themselves are seldom static; they evolve as incumbents, role partners, and circumstances change. This is just as true for the sphere of work as it is for families or other social spheres. As opportunities and autonomy within the workaday world ebb and flow due to structural or population changes or shifts in the relative congruence between individuals' skills and job demands, a desire for immersion in alternative venues for affirmation of self-concept may emerge. If identity is not affirmed at work or within the context of family life, the centrality of either realm will decline and alternative domains will be considered desirable. Presumably, fulfilling jobs will suffice for many workers, but absent that positive valence, nonwork domains can provide alternative sources of affirmation. As members of work groups, families, or social groups, individuals move into and out of multiple roles, each of which builds on those that have gone before, including those defined by previous generations and by structural circumstances. Socialization is essential to the acquisition of successive roles, for it is through anticipatory socialization and experimentation that individuals try out a role prior to having to assume it for real. Age-grading enters the picture insofar as access to many roles is contingent on broader societal currents as well as on human capital characteristics of individual incumbents. Leisure pursuits may provide an optimal forum for exactly these goals (Csikszentmihalyi, 1981).

Elder (1998) captured the dynamic quality of life-course contingencies when he noted that people do not march in perfect cadence past life's turning points but demonstrate varied pacing and sequencing of transitions depending on the peculiarities and timing of their personal engagements. The point is that people partake of a wide array of experiences over time, experiences from which they derive personally meaningful referential significance. Some of these leave tracings and presage what follows, while others pass away, virtually unnoticed and without effect. Though not singled out by Elder, gender, ethnicity, social class background, and other social circumstances make up the social resources upon which actors draw and which are brought into play in successive adjustments. That they are not uniformly distributed or valued implies other social differentiation and contributes to the expression of diversity and differential life chances. As noted, incumbents bring to roles not only their own competencies and skills but also a panoply of social capital characteristics that are reflected in how roles are enacted. As they perform, actors add resources to their personal resource inventory that can be brought to bear in subsequent situations.

The latter contention underscores a major facet of life-course perspectives deserving of further consideration: The relevance of social relationships and the availability of types of social resources that derive from membership in social class categories. It is through the resources and constraints that accompany these categories that pacing and sequencing of age grades are scheduled. These categories constrain and channel, thereby circumscribing future options. Dannefer (1996) hypothesized that some of the diversity distinguishing members of age-linked cohorts is a consequence of differential experiences along the way. Kohn and Slomezynski (1993), in their cross-national analysis of work for establishing personal identities, asserted that work roles permitting maximal opportunity for self-direction have a profound impact on how self-concepts evolve over time. In that such roles customarily provide benchmarks affirming that either change or continuity is occurring, they account for why individuals from disparate backgrounds with dissimilar work roles can each manifest a highly differentiated sense of self. In short, the social resources available through role performance, in this case work, are incorporated into self-concepts and many related facets of an actor's symbolic universe. Giddens (1984) apprehended the importance of social resources in his concept of "structuration"—wherein structures mediate individual agency and vice versa. An important element of the correlative process of structuration and agency is the necessity for affirmation of self-concepts in the processing of experience (Dannefer & Perlmutter, 1990, p. 115).

Experience is the term used to describe a succession of events, but experience also has a long tradition of referring to transactional, or personally meaningful, activity, not merely occurrences per se. Dewey (1934) highlighted the notion of "meaningful experience" as distinct from simple experience. To accentuate the two uses of the term, we define primary experience as comprising those meaning-making activities associated with valued role engagements that are embraced by intentional consciousness. Absent the potential for meaningfulness, creative synthesis, or simply stimulation, events or activities either may be unnoticed or may be perceived as boring. Because it is through this conceptual processing that personal agency is expressed, it is likely that people seek out personally mediated self-relevant implications of experience. In those instances in which meaning cannot be extracted, attention may shift to alternative venues or other opportunities that lie within reach (Dannefer & Perlmutter, 1990; Hendricks, 1999).

LEISURE IN LIFE-COURSE PERSPECTIVE

Riley and colleagues (Riley & Riley, 1994; Riley et al., 1994) called attention to how the age patterning of roles can lag behind the changing characteristics and capabilities of the older population. A prime example of "structural lag" is seen in an age-differentiated society where the younger years are devoted to education, middle years to work, and later years to leisure. Whatever sense this sequencing may once have made, it does not describe current circumstances. Still, the pattern perseveres notwithstanding ample rationale for reallocations. Leisure provides another case in point. Leisure pursuits are certainly not the exclusive province of any particular age group, no matter how broadly defined. To the extent leisure is concentrated at the nether reaches of the life course, and in the absence of shifts toward a more fully age-integrated role structure, increases in life expectancy are lengthening the period in which leisure may potentially serve as a primary activity—provided retirement circumstances permit options. Because of their inherent flexibility, leisure engagements may provide a context in which inter-pretative practice (Holstein & Gubrium, 1994) is more accepted than in a rigidly organized work environment, for example, and thus provide a forum for personal discovery.

In 1900, life expectancy in the United States averaged 47.3 years (46.3 years for males and 48.3 for females) (Treas, 1995, Table 4). By 1998, life expectancy had risen to 76.7 years overall (73.9 years for males and 79.4 years for females) (Martin, Smith, Mathews, & Ventura, 1999, Table 16). It is generally assumed that slow but progressive increases are to be expected in the decades ahead and that the period of well-being will increase accordingly. Although there is considerable variation in the averages when gender, racial, or socioeconomic differences are considered, it can safely be assumed that leisure will acquire greater consequence as a primary experience as life expectancy lengthens. And, the potential goods and services to be both contributed and consumed as part of the leisure market of a growing and healthy older population are also likely to expand considerably. Both factors justify a better understanding of what leisure is all about.

There is considerable evidence suggesting the prospect for improvements in the quality of life of future cohorts of older persons, the result being that individuals will be better situated to take advantage of leisure opportunities. For example, studies have consistently demonstrated that both the extent and the forms of leisure participation are associated with health and with socioeconomic status (e.g., Kaplan, 1979; Lawton et al., 1986–87). Recent work by Manton and others (e.g., Manton, Stallard, & Corder, 1998) highlighted declining disability rates among the elderly, with an increase in active life expectancy. The socioeconomic status of future cohorts of older persons will also likely be relatively higher than is currently the case. The consensus among leisure researchers is that higher levels of the three traditional components of socioeconomic status result in greater leisure involvement (Lawton, 1985; Osgood, 1995). Economic deprivation, with the resulting lack of discretionary income, power, and access to opportunity, affects leisure. Less obvious effects, but equally germane, are educational attainment and occupational background. The former has been shown conclusively to color preferences for activities, opportunities for participation, and types of leisure activities (Cheek & Burch, 1976). As the population over age 65 becomes progressively better educated through cohort succession, possibly more affluent, and certainly healthier, their orientation toward leisure will reflect that progression.

Still another factor to be considered is the migratory patterns of older persons. Although older persons are less prone to make long-distance moves than their younger counterparts, recent decades have witnessed a growing propensity among the elderly to move to retirement communities, to migrate from "frost-belt" and "rust-belt" regions to "sun belt" and "new sun belt" states, and to engage in seasonal migration (Flynn, Longino, Wiseman, & Biggar, 1985; Frey, 1999). Such trends are significant for two reasons. First, such migration streams tend to be disproportionately composed of younger, healthier, and economically secure segments of the older population (Litwak & Longino, 1987; Serow, 1988). Because the proportion of older persons with these characteristics will grow, it can be anticipated that steadily increasing numbers of elders will make such amenity moves. Second, if these moves lead to growing concentrations of older persons in retirement areas and retirement communities that place a high value on leisure, recreation, and activity, this should facilitate the process Riley and Riley (1986) refer to as "cohort norm formation": "as members of the same age cohort respond to shared experiences, they gradually and subtly develop common patterns of response, common definitions, and common beliefs, all of which crystallize into shared norms about what is appropriate, proper, or true" (p. 58). Along similar lines, the expansion of time spent in retirement and the puzzles it poses as a life stage in a society heretofore dominated by the "work ethic" led one observer (Ekerdt, 1986) to suggest that a new complex of norms and values has emerged—the "busy ethic." Promoted by a variety of interested parties, it "legitimates the leisure of retirement, it defends retired people against judgments of senescence, and it gives definition to the retirement role" (Ekerdt, 1986, p. 243).

A host of other facets of social change may contribute to a growing prominence of leisure in later life. Just as time spent in work and retirement has changed, so too have other aspects of employment. The average number of hours worked per week has declined among some categories of workers (U.S. Bureau of the Census, 1997, Table 634), especially among older workers and older men in particular. One result is that they may have more aggregate time available for leisure pursuits. To the extent that flex time or four-day programs are adopted by industry and chosen by employees, they too should produce larger blocks of time for participation in leisure activities. Clearly, some of the time made available will likely be redirected to other obligatory functions but some of it will be used for leisure activities (Gordon et al., 1976; Zuzanek, 1974). Then, too, major industries have chosen locations not only on the basis of tax advantages and other economic factors but where amenities attractive to workers are plentiful, including those associated with leisure and recreation. If persons at mid-life have more opportunity to participate in leisure, they may carry these long established patterns into the later years, when they will serve as important cynosures for assessing relative status (Atchley, 1999).

There have been other important structural changes in the economy. It is too soon to say what the long-term effects may be, but the shift in the composition of the labor force away from blue-collar manufacturing and production jobs toward white-collar occupations, and the ongoing changes in workplace expectations as jobs requiring intensive physical labor are replaced by work involving automated technology, may leave workers with more energy to engage in leisure. The next shift, already under way, to a service economy heavily coupled with automation will have as yet unknown effects on leisure participation. The picture may not be entirely rosy if enforced idleness results; such an outcome will not constitute leisure, for it will lack the optional quality that is key to meaningful leisure.

As Estes, Swan, and Gerard (1982, p. 155) pointed out, "the structural view of aging starts with the proposition that the status and resources of the elderly, and even the trajectory of the aging process itself, are conditioned by one's location in the social structure and the economic and political forces that affect it." One implication is that the way work is structured affects many other aspects of the way life is lived. For those for whom work is a primary focus, its organization has broad implications. Besides imposing linearity to the perception of time and the structure of activities, work has been the bedrock of anticipated scripts. As some have argued (Estes, Swan, & Gerard, 1982; Hendricks & Leedham, 1987), the organization of the economy portends qualitatively distinct social realities for aging actors. To the extent that it does, the question of leisure becomes a structural concern. How does the organization of work and the temporal structuring of work transitions condition involvement in leisure? It is possible leisure engagements will be structured to include consumption or as a means of creating consensus among the populace. Not only would this represent a corruption of leisure per se, it would carry other unfortunate results as it would put leisure in the service of other ends. The daily lives of older persons are a result of their systematic location during their working lives. To speak of factors circumscribing the activities of elders, researchers need to consider macrolevel patterns evident in the economic realm—its influence extends well beyond the mere economic sphere.

As has been noted, the service sector of the economy has tangibly expanded. Between 1970 and 1996, in the United States, growth in the contingent employment pool in the service sector, and in entertainment and recreation services in particular, was substantially higher than that for the total economy (U. S. Bureau of the Census, 1997, Table 649). Bureau of Labor Statistics projections suggest a continuation of this trend through the first decade of the twenty-first century (U. S. Bureau of the Census, 1997, Table 650). Whether the past and projected growth in the service economy represents a response to the demand for leisure and recreation, stimulates that demand, or both is a relevant question, but perhaps less important for present purposes than the existence of these markedly different rates of growth. It is our contention that economies with large investments in service industries will evince qualitatively distinct patterns of leisure as workers seek alternative venues for self-ratification.

Governmental bodies have been active participants in providing leisure opportunities and in facilitating the leisure involvement of older persons. State and local expenditures on parks and recreation, for example, amounted to $17.9 billion in 1995 (U.S. Bureau of the Census, 1997, Table 506). Several benefit programs designed to reduce financial barriers to recreation and leisure are available and special provisions for "senior citizens" are the norm. As Chambré (1993) noted, perhaps the major consequence of governmental involvement in leisure time activities of older persons has been in the area of voluntarism. Due in part to limitations in expenditures for direct services to frail and needy populations, and in part to a conviction that voluntary service benefits both recipients and providers, governmental programs in the United States have been expanded to promote voluntarism as an optional form of engagement among the older population. Although some involve reimbursement and modest stipends, the bulk do not. Programs such as the Retired Senior Volunteer Program, the Foster Grandparent Program, and the Senior Companion Program, to name but a few, provide vehicles for older persons to contribute to the delivery of desirable services and to "give back" to their communities. Ongoing programs and demonstration projects initially funded by the Administration on Aging, under the Older Americans Act, and some of the larger voluntary aging organizations (e.g., the American Association of Retired Persons, the National Council on the Aging) have played important roles in recognizing and supporting contributions of the voluntary sector. Given that voluntarism tends to be associated with viable health and socioeconomic status, the prospect of changing characteristics of future cohorts of older persons suggests that voluntary participation may become an even more significant aspect of leisure activities (Cutler & Hendricks, 2000).

To this point, we have been treating leisure largely in generic terms; little attention has been paid to the contexts in which leisure activities occur or to sources of heterogeneity in patterns of leisure participation, and leisure has not really been looked at in terms of primary meaning. When we move from consideration of how the broader currents of change discussed above affect patterns of leisure participation, the value of a life-course perspective becomes even more apparent.

Researchers know relatively little about long-term consequences of leisure participation and the forces that shape their trajectories. Even though there is some evidence that early formative experiences exert an influence over leisure in later life, the picture is far from clear. A life-course approach suggests that cumulative experiences accreting over a lifetime have profound effects on leisure. To illustrate, Elder (1974) found that persons who grew up in economically deprived families during the Great Depression placed a lower value on the whole concept of leisure than those who faced less deprived circumstances. Similarly, belonging to birth cohorts that, by virtue of age, were eligible to serve in the military during major conflicts accounted for much of the continued and pronounced age differences in patterns of participation in veterans' organizations (Cutler, 1976). Then, too, coming of age during the 1960s will undoubtedly shape the kind of old age a person will likely desire and the types of activities they will likely select (Chambré, 1993). Finally, the familiarity hypothesis, that people will engage in behavior that is already familiar to them, may not only influence the types of leisure preferred in the later years but dramatically alter the preferences of future cohorts (Kelly, 1974, 1977; Yoesting & Christensen, 1978).

An examination of the timing and duration of leisure roles and the factors that account for transitions between one type of leisure participation and another will enrich our understanding. We know from cross-sectional analysis that active forms of leisure participation are negatively associated with age, but it is unclear to what extent this reflects cohort differences in values, health, income, experience, or some combination of these factors (Bijnen, Feskens, Caspersen, Mosterd, & Kromhout, 1998; Horgas, Wilms, & Baltes, 1998). We also know that gender and stage in the family life cycle account for some of the discretionary activities in which people participate. But the differences may be more profound than bivariate differences imply. Gender differences may influence the ways tasks are defined and the kinds of interactions that take place around nonpaid assignments, and the resulting relationship differences will factor into distinct uses of leisure. In her cross-national compendium dealing with women's leisure participation, Samuel (1996) and her colleagues found that nearly all forms of participation in which women engage were associated with family life stage and cultural values. Similarly, Robinson (1977) and Kelly (1983) have shown that the amount of leisure activity, the types of outdoor recreational activities in which one participates, and the persons with whom one participates are all contingent on stage of the family life cycle. Participation in certain types of voluntary associations is also closely linked with family life cycle (Cutler, 1976), with peak membership rates in organizations such as youth groups and school service groups occurring when children are most likely to be present in the home and steadily declining thereafter. Despite these clear patterns, much needs to be learned about the sequencing and duration of leisure pursuits, about the timing of transitions and what accounts for them, and about how *changes* in the contexts of one's life—from work to retirement, from being married to being widowed, from child rearing to the empty nest—bring changes in the type and level of involvement in leisure. And, finally, while we know that such factors as gender, health, income, and type or areas of residence are all associated with leisure participation, variability in life-course patterning of leisure along these and other dimensions remains a puzzle. An important aspect of the latter is the relative meaning of leisure for men and women at various stages of life.

LEISURE IN THE TWENTY-FIRST CENTURY

As the preceding discussion makes clear, the topic of leisure is one that deserves a prominent place on the gerontological agenda. Regardless of other prospects, demographic changes lying ahead portend a more consequential role for leisure. Perhaps even more important, however, is our contention that leisure is a domain where personal choice and agency are more prominently on display than in other domains in which autonomy and volition are scarce commodities or structural constraints are more rigid. At the dawn of the twenty-first century, older persons in the United States will number approximately 35 million and make up about 13 percent of the population. When the baby boom generation begins to reach retirement age, the older population will increase dramatically. By the year 2030, persons 65 years of age or older will number some 70 million and account for about 20 percent of the population (U.S. Bureau of the Census, 1996). But they will also likely enjoy better health and viability relative to cohorts past. The health and sociodemographic characteristics of future cohorts of older persons will be conducive to extensive and diverse forms of leisure involvement. As Roszak (1998) recently noted, the nearly 80 million babies born between 1946 and 1964 transformed many aspects of society as they aged and will continue to do so. Marketers have been taking note of these trends for some time now; those who attend to the life course should as well.

Longer Lives, Longer Leisure

As Han and Moen (1999) argued, to the extent that the organization of the life course has been ordained by the organization of work, these patterns may go away as the labor market shifts from manufacturing to the provision of services, as it responds to "spot market" exigencies of the moment, profit margins, and shifting loyalties brought on by new economic realities. That is, the stability that life-long employment patterns and career ladders have provided is likely to be diminished in the early decades of the twenty-first century. As Han and Moen (1999) put it, in addition to demographic changes, the landscape of constraint and opportunity associated with the world of work may be radically altered in the coming decades. We would assert that it also means that much of what we think we know about the contours of the life course is likely to require reformulation.

It is not that everything is going to fall into chaos or that all previous sources of satisfaction are going to dry up suddenly. But upwardly mobile or intrinsically rewarding career trajectories may become far less normative. It is also likely that other domains will emerge as sources of affirmation, continuity, or change as far as the generation of meaning is concerned. So what is it that is going to help people adapt to change, and what realm may be particularly germane in adapting to shifting priorities implicit in life-course possibilities? As one might anticipate, our answer is leisure. If shifting patterns of labor force participation imply that previous directional influences are attenuated, then alternative forms of engagement become more significant. If work no longer definitively influences the sequencing of the life course or sense of self to the extent it has in the past, that, too, suggests alternatives are likely to emerge. As Marshall (1998) observed, it also means that new venues promoting social cohesion must surface lest social solidarity be compromised.

New Forms of Leisure Involvement

By now it should be clear that there is more to leisure than meets the eye and that leisure comes in many guises, some of which are difficult to define in any universalistic way. An activity that appears to be leisure can be work and activities that are not immediately apparent as leisure may be exactly that. It is up to the actors involved to determine the meaning of a phenomenon. For example, the meaning of education varies a great deal by age. For young adults, education is seldom considered leisure. For adults engaged in life-long learning, leisure may be the most apt connotation of education. Adult education, life-long education, and so on appear to be neither fish nor fowl—not education in the sense of preparation for a career, yet characterized by more structure and temporal order than most nonwork activities. As others have noted, a substantial portion of the adult population is involved in some form of educational experience on an ongoing basis (U.S. Bureau of the Census, 1999). They are also heavily involved in voluntary memberships that are an aspect of leisure participation (Cutler & Hendricks, 2000). The question is, why? What is the motivation among those who seek out continuing education, volunteer, or engage in other activities for which no remuneration is forthcoming?

Implications for Research on Leisure

As with much research on aging, gerontological research on leisure has generally been descriptive and cross-sectional. As noted, much of it has focused on the relationship between age and various forms of leisure participation. Although notable exceptions have used longitudinal designs to good advantage (e.g., Bijnen et al., 1998; Singleton, Forbes, & Agwani, 1993; Verbrugge, Gruber-Baldini, & Fozard, 1996), investigators have tended to look primarily at how the extent and nature of leisure involvement differ among persons of various ages. When temporal differences and changes are examined, they are often based on retrospective accounts despite known biases in recall accuracy. That leisure has been considered subordinate, as a by-product, may explain why it has not been a central topic of inquiry in longitudinal studies.

The descriptive focus of much of the work on leisure has also meant that little attention has been paid to *explaining* age differences. While it is important to know to what extent and in what ways patterns of leisure participation vary by age, somewhat less effort has been directed at identifying factors responsible for the differences observed. Again, with some notable exceptions (e.g., Horgas et al., 1998), investigators have been content to note the presence of age differences without examining within appropriate multivariate frameworks whether important variables associated with age account for the observed age differences. Are age-based patterns of leisure involvement due to known age-linked changes in health, in socioeconomic status (income, education, occupation), in marital status, in living arrangements, to name just a few? Do they reflect gender, racial, or ethnic differences? Less easily identifiable, of course, but nevertheless of considerable importance, is whether age-based patterns reflect cohort differences.

A principal contention of this chapter is that what constitutes leisure is in part a subjective issue, making measurement a critical consideration in its analysis. The most exemplary work (e.g., Baltes et al., 1990; Horgas et al., 1998) has examined whether persons are involved in a variety of types of activities predefined as leisure by the investigators, the extent of their involvement in each, where the activity takes place, and with whom it occurs. The use of time budgets or diaries may yield reasonably reliable data provided the analytic model is well conceived (Robinson, 1991). As we have suggested, however, participation in a particular activity may be leisure for one person but an obligation for another. For example, shopping may be considered a pleasant, leisure pastime (Graham, Graham, & MacLean, 1991) or an activity of last resort; cooking may be an enriching hobby or little more than a necessity; and tending a lawn or garden may be a source of pride and great satisfaction or a burden. In other words, there is an essential subjective dimension to the measurement of leisure that remains to be examined closely. How leisure is defined, not by the investigator but by the leisure participant, as well as how and for what reasons those definitions change over time are among the important questions prompted by taking a life-course perspective.

What do these considerations add up to for the study of leisure from a life-course perspective? First, leisure must be accorded more than residual status in gerontological research. At several points, we have averred that leisure is a fundamental, social psychological mechanism capable of contributing to self-identity. The relationships between work, education, and other institutional sectors point to the structural significance of leisure (Frey & Dickens, 1990). Changing patterns of leisure over time suggest its salience as a barometer of social and cultural change. And life-course patterns of leisure support its relevance from a developmental perspective. For these and other conceptual and substantive reasons, the study of leisure deserves to occupy a far more central place on the agenda of gerontological research in general and life-course research in particular than has previously been the case.

Second, leisure research must be approached from both quantitative and qualitative perspectives. Quantitative approaches can yield valuable information about the nature of leisure participation—its extent, its forms, its locations, its embeddedness in social networks, and so on. Quantitative designs can help researchers understand the correlates and consequences of involvement in leisure activities. Where quantitative approaches fall short, however, is in identifying deeper personal meanings of leisure to the participants and even the more fundamental question of what constitutes leisure per se? Moreover, we know very little about how these subjective dimensions change over the life course (Allen & Chin-Sang, 1990; Chin-Sang & Allen, 1991).

Third, a life-course approach prompts us to examine closely inter- and intragenerational trajectories of leisure participation over time. To what extent and under what conditions are patterns of leisure characterized by inter- and intragenerational continuity and discontinuity (Kelly, Steinkamp, & Kelly, 1986)? A life-course perspective on leisure prompts researchers to be concerned with the intersection between biography and history, with links between individuals and social settings, and with the ways interdependence among persons influences leisure participation. At the aggregate or societal level, we must examine the roles played by social and cultural change, by changes in employment patterns, by the commodification of leisure, by changes in the availability of leisure opportunities, and by changes in public policy that may have implications for leisure. At the individual level, we must examine whether the patterns established earlier in the life course carry over to later stages, and at what points and for what reasons transitions in leisure participation occur (Cousin & Keating, 1995). We must examine how shifts in preferences and forms of engagement are linked to age-related changes in personal agendas and priorities, and how individual patterns and transitions are related to family circumstances. Where the latter are concerned, it is certainly to be expected that the presence of children in the household, and the ages of those children, will have an effect on leisure activities. We need to look at how preferences or opportunities for and engagement in different types of leisure vary by area of residence (i.e., rural vs. urban) or by type of community and housing (i.e., retirement communities, congregate housing), or by living arrangements (Brown & Tedrich, 1993; Cutler & Hendricks, 1990; Sherman, 1974). It would be of interest to determine whether social networks and friendship groups facilitate leisure, follow from leisure, or both. We need to learn more about the extent to which and the ways in which resources (i.e., income, health) and changes in resource levels facilitate or constrain leisure participation (Heinemann, Colorez, Frank, & Taylor, 1988; Zimmer, Hickey, & Searle, 1997). And we need to consider how gender, race, and ethnicity interpose themselves on all these issues.

Finally, research on leisure has been seriously hampered by the absence of longitudinal data. Cross-sectional studies can provide many clues about the trajectories and pathways experienced by individuals as they engage in leisure pursuits. Yet, the temporal dimension can only be inferred from patterns of age differences. It cannot be examined directly. Further, researchers should not make the mistake that patterns observed in cross-sectional data are historically invariant. Changing norms about age-appropriate activities, changing capabilities of individuals to engage in certain activities, and changing levels of personal resources (Jones, 1986) will likely mean that patterns of leisure observed now are different from those observed two or three decades ago. The life-course perspective's emphasis on temporality underscores the importance of employing appropriate research designs that allow us to learn about how lives change at different times.

Developing a Life-Course Appreciation for Leisure

Viewed within a life-course perspective, leisure provides both a linking mechanism and a domain wherein social transitions and personal priorities find voice throughout life (Cutler & Hendricks, 1990; Gordon et al., 1976; Kelly, 1992). In the years ahead, it is reasonable to expect that the organization of work will shift to a contingent model that is not highly age-structured (Henretta, 1994). If the nature of work is altered by technological innovation, abetted by movement to a service economy affecting the meaning derived from labor force participation, it is likely leisure will emerge even more clearly as a pursuit in which actors try out, affirm, and express their identities (Brandtstädter, 1984; Hendricks & Cutler, 1990; Kelly, 1992). Ponder for a moment the possibility that work-related transitions may lose some of their sway, either because of the shift to a contingent labor market or because people make greater investments in leisure pursuits. Might certain normative transitions with which we have long been familiar have relatively less consequence as turning points? Perhaps it is time to consider whether the role of leisure today is akin to the role of work throughout most of the twentieth century. Whether age becomes less relevant or whether work roles are altered and not perceived as a principal source of identity, leisure engagements will mirror both and reflect the ways in which people explore, maintain, and create a sense of identity. As we have written elsewhere (Cutler & Hendricks, 1990), the symbolic value of leisure exceeds its being viewed as an outcome of other aspects of life's involvements.

During the modern period of industrial societies, the social construction of the life course has permitted little time for leisure, except during the beginning and end of the continuum, perhaps a third of a lifetime altogether. As we move into a post-industrial period, during which many of the pursuits and patterns of the twentieth century will likely be recast, there is reason to expect that leisure opportunities will be distributed more equitably across the life course and will loom large as a source of personal gratification. If our assumptions are reasonable, leisure pursuits and activities will become increasingly congruent with Elder's (1998) description of realms that can benefit from an appropriate life-course perspective. In short, leisure is a "construction zone"—perhaps a kaleidoscope is a more apt analogy—in which individuals exercise agency, make choices, and take actions that define self, other, and interpersonal relationships. As life expectancy increases and the suzerainty of the workaday world is reconfigured, leisure is likely to be an increasingly important domain in which both continuity and change take shape and individuals "invest" themselves in activities and pursuits that are not subject to the same constraints as the workplace. When recognized as profoundly meaningful, leisure is a form of engagement, a source of affirmation protective of selfhood (George, 2000). Leisure is also a kind of consumerism capable of bridging the separation between person-object and actor-context, acting as a kind of loom for the "intricate interweaving of biological, sociocultural and psychological processes" that is life-course development (Diehl, 1999, p. 159; Cutler & Hendricks, 1990).

As Diehl (1999) emphasized, people become authors of their own development as they age (c.f. Baltes et al., 1980; Riegel, 1975). Their subjective reading and editing of life's script and their perceptions of the setting will influence the way they live and the meaning they construct. When leisure provides an opportunity for personal agency, when other roles become tenuous or too ambiguous, or when structural conditions are such that flexibility and thereby meaningful reinforcement are rare, it furnishes an opportunity to create meaning, formulate identity, and, ultimately, sustain development. After all, these lie at the core of what the life-course perspective maintains is the motivating force behind life-course development. On the one hand, to the extent that human and social capital resources comparable to those operating in other realms influence leisure pursuits, it can be expected that leisure will manifest normative patterns related to developmental priorities. On the other hand, leisure is also a provenencial factor in the generation of meaning. In short, leisure provides the kind of real world setting Riegel (1975) posited as necessary to understanding how the life course is shaped in a relatively less constraining context. There is formality, to be sure, but there is also emergent creativity that provides maximum latitude to experiment with new identities.

Brandtstädter (1984, p. 15) called for an analysis of the life course that acknowledges the "important boundary conditions of personal action potentials at a respective age level or developmental stage." The realm of leisure may permit exactly this kind of optimal exploration. Diehl (1999) was unmistakable: Much of the research on life-course development has focused on "reactive" as opposed to "proactive" origins of meaning. As he further noted, understanding the constraints of and influences on self-appraisals and other self-related processes is crucial to understanding the experience of changing identities with age. As should be clear, we believe that leisure pursuits provide a clarion call to embrace the opportunities it offers for assessing self-competencies and associated self-related perceptions. As Diehl and other developmentalists have reminded us, redefining self-environmental fit is as important for the developmental agenda as adapting to time and temporality. It is also a natural aspect of leisure engagements. Perhaps leisure is even more natural than the vast majority of other domains where social roles play out, since opportunities for assimilative or accommodative action and proactive self-enhancements may be at their apogee during leisure. To the extent that discretion and choice are central, the world of leisure permits individuals to exercise various forms of *primary control* revolving around changing interactions with their world, to align evolving needs and self-referential motivations with minimal repercussions.

REFERENCES

Allen, K. R., & Chin-Sang, V. (1990). A lifetime of work: The context and meanings of leisure for aging black women. *The Gerontologist, 30,* 734–740.

Andersen, L. B., Schnohr, P., Schroll, M., & Hein, H. O. (2000). All-cause mortality associated with physical activity during leisure time, work, sports, and cycling to work. *Archives of Internal Medicine, 160,* 1621–1628.

Atchley, R. C. (1999). Continuity theory, self, and social structure. In C. D. Ryff & V. W. Marshall (Eds.), *The self and society in aging processes* (pp. 94–121). New York: Springer.

Baltes, M. M., Wahl, H. W., & Schmid-Furstoss, U. (1990). The daily life of elderly Germans: Activity patterns, personal control, and functional health. *Journal of Gerontology: Psychological Sciences, 45,* P173–P179.

Baltes, P. B. (1987). Theoretical propositions of life-span developmental psychology: On the dynamics of growth and decline. *Developmental Psychology, 23,* 611–626.

Baltes, P. B., Lindenberger, U., & Staudinger, U. (1998). Life-span theory in developmental psychology. In R. M. Lerner (Ed.), *Handbook of child psychology: Vol 1. Theoretical models of human development* (pp. 1029–1043). New York: John Wiley & Sons.

Baltes, P. B., Reese, H. W., & Lipsitt, L. P. (1980). Life-span development in psychology. *Annual Review of Psychology, 31,* 65–110.

Bijnen, F. C. H., Feskens, E. J. M., Caspersen, C. J., Mosterd, W. L., & Kromhout, D. (1998). Age, period, and cohort effects on physical activity among elderly men during 10 years of follow-up: The Zutphen elderly study. *Journal of Gerontology: Medical Sciences, 53A,* M235–M241.

Bourdieu, P. (1986). The forms of capital. In J. Richardson (Ed.), *Handbook of theory and research for the sociology of education* (pp. 241–258). New York: Greenwood Press.

Brandtstädter, J. (1984). Personal and social control over development: Some implications of an action perspective in life-span developmental psychology. In P. B. Baltes & O. G. Brim, Jr. (Eds.), *Life-span development and behavior* (Vol. 6, pp. 1–32). New York: Academic Press.

Brandtstädter, J. (1990). Development as a personal and cultural construction. In G. R. Semin & K. J. Gergen (Eds.), *Everyday understanding: Social and scientific implications* (pp. 83–107). London: Sage.

Bronfenbrenner, U. (1979). *The ecology of human development.* Cambridge: Harvard University Press.

Bronfenbrenner, U. (1995). Developmental ecology through space and time: A future perspective. In P. Moen, G. H. Elder, Jr., & K. Lüscher (Eds.), *Examining lives in* context: Perspectives on the ecology of human development (pp. 619–647). New York: American Psychological Association.

Brown, M. B., & Tedrick, T. (1993). Outdoor leisure involvements of black older Americans: An exploration of ethnicity and marginality. Activities, Adaptation, and Aging, 17, 55–65.

Burgess, E. W. (1960). Aging in western societies. Chicago: University of Chicago Press.

Chambré, S. M. (1993). Volunteerism by elders: Past trends and future prospects. The Gerontologist, 33, 221–228.

Cheek, N., & Burch, W. (1976). The social organization of leisure in human society. New York: Harper and Row.

Chin-Sang, V., & Allen, K. R. (1991). Leisure and the older black woman. Journal of Gerontological Nursing, 17, 30–34.

Cockburn, J., & Smith, P. T. (1991). The relative influence of intelligence and age on everyday memory. Journal of Gerontology: Psychological Sciences, 46, P31–P36.

Coser, R. L. (1991). In defense of modernity: Role complexity and individual autonomy. Stanford, CA: Stanford University Press.

Cousins, S. O., & Keating, N. (1995). Life cycle patterns of physical activity among sedentary and active older women. Journal of Aging and Physical Activity, 3, 340–359.

Crimmins, E. M., & Easterlin, R. A. (2000). What really matters: A comment. In K. W. Schaie & J. Hendricks (Eds.), Societal impact on the aging self (pp. 159-168). New York: Springer.

Csikszentmihalyi, M. (1981). Leisure and socialization. Social Forces, 60, 332–340.

Cutler, S. J. (1976). Age profiles of membership in sixteen types of voluntary associations. Journal of Gerontology, 31, 462–470.

Cutler, S. J., & Hendricks, J. (1990). Leisure and time use across the life course. In R. H. Binstock & L. K. George (Eds.), Handbook of aging and the social sciences (3rd ed., pp. 169–186). San Diego, CA: Academic Press.

Cutler, S. J., & Hendricks, J. (2000). Age differences in voluntary association memberships: Fact or artifact. Journal of Gerontology: Social Sciences, 55B, S98–S107.

Dannefer, D. (1996). The social organization of diversity and the normative organization of age. The Gerontologist, 36, 174–177.

Dannefer, D., & Perlmutter, M. (1990). Development as a multidimensional process: Individual and social constituents. Human Development, 33, 108–137.

Dannefer, D., & Uhlenberg, P. (1999). Paths of the life course: A typology. In V. L. Bengtson & K. W. Schaie (Eds.), Handbook of theories of aging (pp. 306–326). New York: Springer.

Dewey. J. (1934). Art as experience. New York: Minton, Balch Press.

Diehl, M. (1999). Self-development in adulthood and aging: The role of critical life events. In C. D. Ryff & V. W. Marshall (Eds.), The self and society in aging processes (pp. 150–183). New York: Springer.

Dittmann-Kohli, F., & Westerhof, G. (1999). The personal meaning system in a life span perspective. In G. Reker & K. Chamberlain (Eds.), Exploring existential meaning (pp. 107-122). Newbury Park, CA: Sage.

Ekerdt, D. J. (1986). The busy ethic: Moral continuity between work and retirement. The Gerontologist, 26, 239–244.

Elder, G. H., Jr. (1974). Children of the great depression. Chicago: University of Chicago Press.

Elder, G. H., Jr. (1985). Perspectives on the life course. In G. H. Elder, Jr. (Ed.), *Life course dynamics* (pp. 23–49). Ithaca, NY: Cornell University Press.

Elder, G. H., Jr. (1998). The life course and human development. In R. M Lerner (Ed.), *Handbook of child psychology: Vol. 1. Theoretical models of human development* (pp. 939–991). New York: Wiley.

Elder, G. H., Jr., & O'Rand, A. M. (1995). Adult lives in a changing society. In K. Cook, G. Fine, & J. House (Eds.), *Sociological perspectives on social psychology* (pp. 452–475). Needham Heights, MA: Allyn and Bacon.

Estes, C. L., Swan, J. H., & Gerard, L. E. (1982). Dominant and competing paradigms in gerontology: Towards a political economy of ageing. *Ageing and Society, 2*, 151–164.

Fabrigoule, C. (1995). Social and leisure activities and risk of dementia: A prospective longitudinal study. *Journal of the American Geriatrics Society, 43*, 485–490.

Felson, R. (1992). Self-concept. In E. Borgatta & M. Borgatta (Eds.), *Encyclopedia of sociology* (pp. 1743–1749). New York: Macmillan.

Flynn, C. B., Longino, C. F., Jr., Wiseman, R. F., & Biggar, J. C. (1985). The redistribution of America's older population: Major national migration patterns of three census decades. *The Gerontologist, 25*, 292–296.

Frey, J. H., & Dickens, D. R. (1990). Leisure as a primary institution. *Sociological Inquiry, 60*, 264–273.

Frey, W. H. (1999). "New sun belt" metros and suburbs are magnets for retirees. *Population Today, 27* (9), 1–3.

George, L. K. (1996). Missing links: The case for a social psychology of the life course. *The Gerontologist, 36*, 248–255.

George, L. K. (2000). Well-being and sense of self: What we know and what we need to know. In K. W. Schaie & J. Hendricks (Eds.), *Social impact on the aging self* (pp. 1-35). New York: Springer.

Giddens, A. (1984). *The constitution of society.* Berkeley: University of California Press.

Glass, T. A., Mendes de Leon, C., Marottoli, R. A., & Berkman, L. F. (1999). Population based study of social and productive activities as predictors of survival among elderly Americans. *British Medical Journal, 319*, 478–483.

Gordon, C., Gaitz, C., & Scott, J. (1976). Leisure and lives: Personal expressivity across the life span. In R. Binstock & E. Shanas (Eds.), *Handbook of aging and the social sciences* (pp. 310–341). New York: Van Nostrand Reinhold.

Graham, D. F., Graham, I., & MacLean, M. J. (1991). Going to the mall: A leisure activity of urban elderly people. *Canadian Journal on Aging, 10*, 345–358.

Hagestad, G. O. (1990). Social perspectives on the life course. In R. H. Binstock & L. K. George (Eds.), *Handbook of aging and the social sciences* (pp. 151–168). San Diego, CA: Academic Press.

Han, S-K., & Moen, P. (1999). Clocking out: Temporal patterning of retirement. *American Journal of Sociology, 105*, 191–236.

Harootyan, R. A., & Vorek, R. E. (1994). Volunteering, helping, and gift giving in families and communities. In V. L. Bengtson & R. A. Harootyan (Eds.), *Intergenerational linkages: Hidden connections in American society* (pp. 77–111). New York: Springer.

Havighurst, R. (1961). The nature and values of meaningful free-time activity. In R. Kleemeier (Ed.), *Aging and leisure* (pp. 309–344). New York: Oxford University Press.

Heinemann, A. W., Colorez, A., Frank S., & Taylor, D. (1988). Leisure activity participation of elderly individuals with low vision. *The Gerontologist, 28,* 181–184.

Hendricks, J. (1984). Impact of technological change on middle-aged and older workers: Parallels drawn from a structural perspective. In P. K. Robinson, J. Livingston, & J. E. Birren (Eds.), *Aging and technological advances* (pp. 113–124). New York: Plenum Press.

Hendricks, J. (1999). Practical consciousness, social class, and self-concept: A view from sociology. In C. D. Ryff & V. W. Marshall (Eds.), *The self and society in aging processes* (pp. 187–222). New York: Springer.

Hendricks, J., & Leedham, C. A. (1987). Making sense of literary aging: Relevance of recent gerontological theory. *Journal of Aging Studies, 1,* 187–208.

Hendricks, J., & Cutler, S. J. (1990). Leisure and the structure of our life worlds. *Ageing and Society, 10,* 85–94.

Henretta, J. C. (1994). Social structure and age-based careers. In M. W. Riley, R. L. Kahn, & A. Foner (Eds.), *Age and structural lag* (pp. 57–79). New York: Wiley-Interscience.

Herzog, R. A., Franks, M. M., Markus, H. R., & Holmberg, D. (1998). Activities and well-being in older age: Effects of self-concept and educational attainment. *Psychology and Aging, 13,* 179–185.

Holstein, J. A., & Gubrium, J. F. (1994). Phenomenology, ethnomethodology, and interpretative practice. In N. K. Denzin & Y. S. Lincoln (Eds.), *Handbook of qualitative research* (pp. 262–272). Thousand Oaks, CA: Sage.

Horgas, A. L., Wilms, H., & Baltes, M. M. (1998). Daily life in very old age: Everyday activities as expression of successful living. *The Gerontologist, 38,* 556–568.

Huizinga, J. (1955). *Homo ludens: A study of the play element in culture.* Boston: Beacon Press.

Huyck, M. H. (1991). Predictors of personal control among middle-aged and young-old men and women in middle America. *International Journal of Aging and Human Development, 32,* 261–275.

Jones, S. (1986). The elders: A new generation. *Ageing and Society, 6,* 313–331.

Kammen, M. (1999). *American culture, American tastes: Social change and the 20th century.* New York: Knopf.

Kaplan, M. (1979). *Leisure lifestyle and lifespan.* Philadelphia: W. B. Saunders.

Kelly, J. R. (1974). Socialization toward leisure: A developmental approach. *Journal of Leisure Research, 9,* 181–193.

Kelly, J. R. (1977). Leisure socialization: Replication and extension. *Journal of Leisure Research, 9,* 121–132.

Kelly, J. R. (1983). *Leisure identities and interactions.* London: Allen and Unwin.

Kelly, J. R. (1987). *Freedom to be: A new sociology of leisure.* New York: Macmillan.

Kelly, J. R. (1992). Leisure. In E. Borgatta & M. Borgatta (Eds.), *Encyclopedia of sociology* (pp. 1099–1107). New York: Macmillan.

Kelly, J. R., Steinkamp, M. W., & Kelly, J. R. (1986). Later life leisure: How they play in Peoria. *The Gerontologist, 26,* 531–537.

Kelly, J. R., Steinkamp, M. W., & Kelly, J. R. (1987). Later-life satisfaction: Does leisure contribute? *Leisure Sciences, 9,* 189–200.

Kleemeier, R. W. (Ed.). (1961). *Aging and leisure.* New York: Oxford University Press.

Kohn, M. L., & Slomezynski, K. M. (1993). *Social structure and self-direction: A comparative analysis of the United States and Poland.* Cambridge, UK: Basil Blackwell.

Lawton, M. P. (1983). Environment and other determinants of well being in older people. *The Gerontologist, 23,* 349–357.

Lawton, M. P. (1985). Activities and leisure. In M. P. Lawton & G. L. Maddox (Eds.), *Annual review of gerontology and geriatrics* (pp. 127–164). New York: Springer.

Lawton, M. P., Moss, M., & Fulcomer, M. (1986–87). Objective and subjective uses of time by older people. *International Journal of Aging and Human Development, 24,* 171–188.

Leitner, M. J., & Leitner, S. F. (1996). *Leisure in later life* (2nd ed.). Binghamton, NY: Haworth Press.

Litwak, E., & Longino, C. F., Jr. (1987). Migration patterns among the elderly: A developmental perspective. *The Gerontologist, 27,* 266–272.

Manton, K. G., Stallard, E., & Corder, L. S. (1998). The dynamics of dimensions of age-related disability 1982 to 1994 in the U.S. elderly population. *Journal of Gerontology: Biological Sciences, 53A:* B59–B70.

Marshall, V. W. (1998, August). *Restructuring the life course: Linking biography and emerging patterns of work.* Paper presented at the annual meeting of the American Sociological Association, San Francisco.

Martin, J. A., Smith, B. L., Mathews, T. J., & Ventura, S. J. (1999). *Births and deaths: Preliminary data for 1998* (National Vital Statistics Report Vol. 47, No. 25). Hyattsville, MD: National Center for Health Statistics.

Moen, P. E., Dempster-McClain, D., & Williams, R. M. (1992). Successful aging: A life course perspective on women's roles and health. *American Journal of Sociology, 97,* 1612–1638.

Musick, M. A., Herzog, A. R., & House, J. S. (1999). Volunteering and mortality among older adults: Findings from a national sample. *Journal of Gerontology: Social Sciences, 54B,* S173–S180.

Neugarten, B. N., & Hagestad, G. O. (1976). Age and the life course. In R. Binstock & E. Shanas (Eds.), *Handbook of aging and the social sciences* (pp. 35–55). New York: Van Nostrand Reinhold.

Osgood, N. J. (1995). Leisure. In G. L. Maddox (Ed.), *Encyclopedia of aging.* New York: Springer.

Rapoport, R., & Rapoport, R. (1975). *Leisure and the family life cycle.* London: Routledge and Kegan Paul.

Reitzes, D. C., Mutran, E.J., & Verrill, L. A. (1995). Activities and self-esteem: Continuing the development of activity theory. *Research on Aging, 17,* 260–277.

Riegel, K. F. (1975). Toward a dialectical theory of development. *Human Development, 18,* 50–64.

Riley, M. W., & Riley, J. W., Jr. (1986). Longevity and social structure: The potential of the added years. In A. Pifer & L. Bronte (Eds.), *Our aging society: Paradox and promise* (pp. 53–77), New York: Norton.

Riley, M. W., & Riley, J. W., Jr. (1994). Age integration and the lives of older people. *The Gerontologist, 34,* 110–115.

Riley, M. W., Kahn, R., & Foner, A. (1994). *Age and structural lag.* New York: Wiley.

Robinson, J. P. (1977). *How Americans use time: A social-psychological analysis of everyday behavior.* New York: Praeger.

134 / INVITATION TO THE LIFE COURSE

Robinson, J. P. (1991). Quitting time. *American Demographics, 13,* 34–36.

Roszak, T. (1998). *America the wise: The longevity revolution and the true wealth of nations.* Boston: Houghton Mifflin.

Rowe, J. W., & Kahn, R. L. (1998). *Successful aging.* New York: Pantheon Books.

Samuel, N. (Ed.) (1996). *Women, leisure, and the family in contemporary society: A multinational perspective.* Wallingford, England: CAB International.

Serow, W. J. (1988). Why the elderly move: Cross-national comparisons. *Research on Aging, 9,* 582–597.

Settersten, R. A., Jr. (1997). The salience of age in the life course. *Human Development, 40,* 257–280.

Settersten, R. A., Jr. (1999). *Lives in time and place: The problems and promises of developmental science.* Amityville, NY: Baywood.

Sherman, S. R. (1974). Leisure activities in retirement housing. *Journal of Gerontology, 29,* 325–335.

Singleton, J. F., Forbes, W. F., & Agwani, N. (1993). Stability of activity across the lifespan. *Activities, Adaptation, and Aging, 18,* 19–27.

Sørensen, A., Weinert, F., & Sherrod, L. (Eds.) (1986). *Human development and the life course: Multidisciplinary perspectives.* Hillsdale, NJ: Erlbaum.

Sorock, G. S., Bush, T. L., Golden, A. L., Fried, L. P., Breuer, B., & Hale, W. E. (1988). Physical activity and fracture risk in a free-living elderly cohort. *Journal of Gerontology: Medical Sciences, 43,* M134–M139.

Stebbins, R. A. (1992). *Amateurs, professionals, and serious leisure.* Montreal: McGill-Queen's University Press.

Treas, J. (1995). Older Americans in the 1990s and beyond. *Population Bulletin, 50* (2), 1–48.

U. S. Bureau of the Census. (1996). Population projections of the United States by age, sex, race, and Hispanic origin: 1995 to 2050. *Current Population Reports* (series P25-1130). Washington, DC: U. S. Government Printing Office.

U. S. Bureau of the Census. (1997). *Statistical abstract of the United States: 1997* (117th ed.). Washington, DC: U. S. Government Printing Office.

U.S. Bureau of the Census. (1999). *Statistical abstract of the United States: 1999* (119th ed.). Washington, DC: U.S. Government Printing Office.

Verbrugge, L. M., Gruber-Baldini, A. L., & Fozard, J. L. (1996). Age differences and age changes in activities: Baltimore Longitudinal Study of Aging. *Journal of Gerontology: Social Sciences, 51B,* S30–S41.

Wearing, B. (1998). *Leisure and feminist theory.* Thousand Oaks, CA: Sage.

West, G. E., Delisle, M. A., Simard, C., & Drouin, D. (1996). Leisure activities and service knowledge and use among the rural elderly. *Journal of Aging and Health, 8,* 254–279.

Yoesting, D. R., & Christensen, J. E. (1978). Reexamining the significance of childhood recreation patterns on adult leisure behavior. *Leisure Sciences, 1,* 219–229.

Zuzanek, J. (1974). Society of leisure or the harried leisure class? Leisure trends in industrial societies. *Journal of Leisure Research, 6,* 293–304.

Zimmer, Z., Hickey, T., & Searle, M. S. (1997). The pattern of change in leisure activity behavior among older adults with arthritis. *The Gerontologist, 37,* 384–392.

CHAPTER 5

Interdependent Lives and Relationships in Changing Times: A Life-Course View of Families and Aging

Gunhild O. Hagestad

Increasingly, the attention of aging researchers has been centered on aging individuals in their *current proximal environments* (Hagestad & Dannefer, 2001). Two aspects of this trend are particularly worrisome. First, we "freeze" lives in motion and seemingly forget that old age is part of a long life journey. Second, we take a static and myopic view of social contexts. Taking core principles of the life course perspective seriously would help us overcome the individualistic bias of much current work and challenge us to consider multiple temporal dimensions. The perspective puts families at center stage, conceptualizing them as bundles of interconnected lives; as critical mediators between developing individuals and societies in flux; and as units that also need to be studied in their own right.

In this chapter, my goal is to explore rich interdependencies between three levels: a changing society, dynamic family systems with complex webs of relationships, and individual life paths. A life-course perspective encourages us to consider three types of temporal locations: life phase and chronological age, with associated roles, rights, and duties; family membership, especially generational position; and historical time, often expressed as cohort membership.

On the level of biographical time, the life-course perspective traces individuals along an age-differentiated, socially-marked sequence of *transitions*— points at which new states or roles are entered. Across the span of life, individuals are seen as following a pathway of transitions and states, a socially shaped *trajectory* (Bengtson & Allen, 1993; Elder, 1985; Hagestad, 1990) Three core concepts help us describe transitions and trajectories: *timing, sequencing,* and *duration.* Timing refers to the age at which transitions occur; sequencing means the relative timing of two or more transitions; duration describes the length of time individuals spend in given states. Much North American scholarship has focused on how cultural forces shape life's timetables and create "normal, expectable lives"—scripts that become part of culturally-shared cognitive maps (Settersten & Hagestad, 1996). European scholars have put more emphasis on how institutions and policies of the modern welfare state structure the life course and create a "normal biography" by marking turning points, delineating life phases, and creating safety nets to guard against life disruption (Kohli, 1986; Leisering & Leibfried, 1999; Mayer & Müller, 1986). Regardless of whether our main focus is on cultural or structural forces that shape the life course, gender needs to be considered. The social structuring of age is very often paired with constructions of gender, resulting in distinct contrasts between *his and her life.*

Family units also have trajectories. Nuclear units go through a sequence of stages, starting with early family building and childrearing and ending with the empty nest and widowhood. Furthermore, family lineages have their own rhythms of change, a sequence of generational structures, which evolve through generational turnover. At one point, family structures may contain five "tiers"; at another point, they may include only two. As individuals, we typically begin life in an *Alpha generation,* a position of having only ascendant kin. Most of us typically end our lives in an *Omega position,* where we have only descendants. In between, we may spend decades in *Janus positions,* where we relate to generations both above and below us, and where we simultaneously occupy the roles of parent and child, and even grandparent and grandchild.

Cultural images of normal expectable lives include a sense of the timing of generational turnover and the duration of generational structures. For the first two decades of adulthood, we count on some undisturbed duration in the parent-child relationship. This is the time to add a generation, not to lose one. Movement into the Omega generation too early leads to a sense of adult orphanhood, a pronounced feeling of vulnerability. There are indications that generational turnover can also be too late. Mature adults who are not yet grandparents and suffer from "grandparent anxiety" (Christian, 1984) have formed support groups in which they discuss how to let their children know that "it is time." When families have two generations of pensioners, or two tiers of individuals with health problems, conflict might arise as to who has the right to be needy, and whose duty it is to make sure the needs are met. Such situations emerged in a German study of five-generation families (Lehr & Schneider, 1983). A Norwegian study of the oldest-old (Romøren, 1999) found that among care providers who experienced burnout or overload, many could be described as "vertically overextended" because they faced strong care needs from parents and grandchildren at a time when their spouses were also experiencing health problems.

Social policy is often built on cultural assumptions about normal, expectable generational structures and individual family roles, especially those related to gender (Walker, 1993, 2000). Policies may also deliberately be designed to *alter* the family involvement of men or women in certain life phases. An example would be recent legislation in Norway and Sweden requiring fathers to take parental leaves in order to obtain the maximum duration of paid leave for the couple.

Finally, the course of individual life trajectories, as well as rhythms of family development and generational turnover, are embedded in historical time and reflect cultural, economic, political, and demographic conditions and events (Hareven, 1977). In societies characterized by rapid social change, we recognize that the social meanings of age and age-related experiences are closely linked to historical location—that different cohorts age in different ways and may have quite contrasting family patterns. As we attempt to understand aging individuals and their families, we need to pay close attention to the historical landscapes that they have traversed.

On both individual and societal levels, we recognize that calendar years are not created equal. There are times of reasonable stability and times of rapid change. In describing individual development, we use such terms as "critical periods" or growth spurts." In life-course studies, we recognize that some phases are "transition dense," that life changes often come in bundles. Historians struggle with this issue in discussions of "periodicity," the uneven ebb and flow of historical time. In the flow of cohorts, there are watersheds: times when social conditions change so drastically that we speak of a divide, a "before" and "after" line. When we tentatively identify such historical divides among cohorts, it becomes important to ask how they play themselves out in intergenerational family ties. Do "cohort gaps" translate into "generation gaps," making intra-family negotiations of understandings and expectations difficult?

It is easy to find examples of how family structural patterns show the footprints of history. In many societies, the Depression led to unusually high rates of childlessness among the 1900-1910 cohorts, whose members were over-represented in institutions for the aged toward the end of the 20th century. The recent Berlin Aging Study showed the additional impact of two world wars. Among the oldest old, 40 percent had no surviving children (Maas, Borchelt, & Mayer, 1999). In my own work, I found that Norwegian families started in 1946 had an unusually high proportion of only children. Most of them had quite old parents, couples who, during the Depression, waited for better times and then further postponed childbearing because of World War II. Post-war housing shortages affected co-residence patterns in many European countries. When I contacted a sample of Norwegian first-borns from the 1946 cohort when they were in their 40s, nearly 40 percent spoke of living with grandparents for part of childhood. Such co-residence is an example of how history takes on personal meanings in the family. The family level mediates between the macro-level of history and the micro-level of individual biographies.

Elder's (1974, 1998) work on the Depression has provided classic illustrations of how focusing on family relationships helps us understand individual effects of macro-level change. For example, he showed that a national economy in crisis left lasting marks in individual lives because it lead to dramatically reduced household resources and family disorganization. In his attempt to connect the micro-level of individual lives and the macro-level of a society undergoing upheaval, Elder introduces a set of what he labels *linking mechanisms*. One such mechanism is of central importance here: *interdependence among lives*, or linked lives. Below, I explore how this concept of interdependence can be expanded if we approach interwoven lives on several levels of analysis. First, we need to briefly review historical changes in patterns of duration, timing, and interconnections on the family level. In many ways, families of late 20th century look markedly different from families at the previous fin-de-siècle.

LIVES AND RELATIONSHIPS IN CHANGING TIMES

Duration

Living beyond the age of 80 has now become part of the normal, expectable life for women in a number of countries. Mass longevity means new co-longevity in families (Hareven, 1977; Plath, 1980) What is referred to as the *rectangularization of survival curves* has had profound consequences in the family realm because deaths are more predictable and bonds more durable. Members of different generations are "fellow life travelers" (Plath, 1980) for unprecedented durations, sharing decades of co-biography. For the first time in history, it is expectable that our family of origin and the role of child remain available to us well into middle age or early old age. In today's families, it is not uncommon to find retired children and menopausal grandchildren. Parents and children commonly share half a century of life, and grandparent-grandchild relationships last three to four decades. In contrast, it has been estimated that around 1800, only 3 percent of American women over the age of 60 had at least one living parent. By 1980, the corresponding figure was 60 percent (Watkins, Menken, & Bongaarts, 1987). Uhlenberg (1996) estimates that based on 1980 parameters, 68 percent of 30-year-olds would have at least one living grandparent. The corresponding figure under 1900 conditions was 20 percent.

In today's life course, we spend more time as children of surviving parents than we do as parents of minor children (Gee, 1986, 1987; Menken, 1985). In the case of Canada, Gee estimates that under demographic conditions of the 1830s, 90 percent of women's remaining years after marriage were spent rearing dependent children. By 1950, the figure had declined to 40 percent. Menken suggests that reduced fertility may in part reflect an awareness of shifts in the "time budgets" of adulthood and the number of years when parents may need support. What Attias-Donfut (2000) calls "changing family calendars" was also the focus of attention in the earlier work of Glick, a pioneer in family demography. Examining historical trends in the timing and duration of periods of the family "life cycle," Glick (1977) pointed out that the empty nest phase did not emerge until well into the 20th century.

Timing

Of course, increased durations reflect a story of altered timing in family deaths and generational turnover. Increasingly, the death of one's parents and the entry into an Omega generation come in late-middle or young-old age, while the death of one's grandparents occurs at a time in adulthood when many grand-children have already become parents.

The recent Norwegian study of the oldest-old followed a population of people over 80, nearly 450 individuals, longitudinally through the last phase of their lives (Romøren, 1999). At the time of their deaths (the median age at death being between ages 87 and 88), the median age of the oldest surviving child was 63, while the median age of the oldest grandchild was about 35. At least in the case of parental death, new mortality trends have therefore created clearer patterns of timing. Winsborough (1980) argues that as a result, loss of parents has become a more significant life-course transition, shared by a majority of people within a limited age band. He also suggests that off-time early parental death is more likely to become a personal crisis because it catches the individual unprepared and without the empathetic support from peers.

Altered Vertical Mosaics

Reduced fertility and mortality produce increasing *top-heaviness* in family lineages and result in a *verticalization* of family ties. Such verticalization has two aspects: a trend toward fewer horizontal kin ties (within generations), and an increase in relationships across generational lines (as multi-generation units are more common). Some authors refer to this vertical extension as "the beanpole family" (Bengtson, Rosenthal, & Burton, 1996). The critical nexus in inter-generational vertical webs is the parent-child tie, both in individuals' sense of closeness, responsibility and obligation, (Rossi & Rossi, 1990) and in the actual flow of support. The mother-daughter connection is particularly pivotal for intergenerational cohesion and exchange. Women function as "kin-keepers" (Rosenthal, 1985) and develop complex ties with the longest average duration of any parent-child relationship.

Once we realize the centrality of parent-child dyads, we must acknowledge the fact that for a major part of adulthood, individuals belong to two sets of parent-child relationships. In their recent study of Great Britain, Grundy, Murphy, and Shelton (1999) found that 70 to 80 percent of individuals between the ages of 30 and 50 have both parents and children. At the age of 42, more than 80 percent the Norwegian firstborns from the 1946 cohort were in a Janus position.

When multiple parent-child connections are considered, the discussions often have a pessimistic tone. Much has been written about the stresses and strains of being in a middle generation, often under the headlines "women in the middle" or "the sandwich generation" (Brody, 1982). Such discussions assume that members of middle generations, particularly women, find themselves pulled between parents and children who both are in need of care. I believe that such reports are exaggerated. Data from Canada (Rosenthal, Matthews, & Marshall, 1986), the European Union (Dykstra, 1997), and my own work in Norway all indicate that such cases of coinciding responsibilities are less common than is often assumed. In her overview of 12 European Union countries, Dykstra (1997) reports that overall, 4 percent of the men and 10 percent of the women between 45 and 54 have overlapping responsibilities for children and old parents who require care. Typically, by the time parents are so old that they have serious illness and impairments, the children are grown. If competing needs arise in a web of intergenerational interdependence, it is more likely to be between grandchildren and parents, or, in the case of women, between an ailing spouse and an old mother.

How individuals in Janus positions prioritize the needs of parents and children depends, in part, on cultural context. As is well known, Asian cultures have traditionally emphasized "filial piety," while Nordic countries have a strong focus on ties to children, what we may call "parental piety." The European Value Study attempted to measure such orientations (van den Akker, Halman, & de Moor, 1993) and revealed striking national contrasts. Norwegians were the most child-centered, with nearly 30 percent more respondents agreeing that parents must do their best than agreed that children must respect parents (73 versus 45 percent). In contrast, Italy and Spain had a slightly higher agreement with the importance of respecting parents (in the case of Italy, 84 versus 79 percent). Even more striking is how the two Mediterranean countries strongly emphasized ties in both directions. Both Italian and Spanish cultures have been labeled "familistic." As I discuss in the section on interdependence, several authors have argued that such cultural values are reinforced through social policy. The point here is that the experience of being in a generational squeeze is created by a combination of demographic, cultural, and political forces.

Of course, the likelihood of ending up in a "sandwich generation" reflects the timing of parenthood in two or three generations. When the 1946 cohort of Norwegian first-borns were contacted at the age of 42, 38 percent were experiencing a generational "squeeze" with at least one child under 16 and a parent with health problems. As I already mentioned, quite a few of these first-borns came relatively late in their mothers' lives as a result of the Depression and World War II. In other words, historical forces that shaped the parents' trajectories had ripple effects for their children's adulthood. A recent comparison of Dutch and Hungarian families (Knipscheer, Dykstra, Utasi, & Cxeh-Szombathy, 2000) found that although old people in Hungary had lower life expectancy and fewer grandchildren than their counterparts in the Netherlands, many more of them were great-grandparents. A substantial difference in timing of first births created accelerated generational turnover among the Hungarians. In a recent study of families in Great Britain and the United States, Henretta, Grundy, and Harris (1999) illustrate the importance of considering a range of social factors that influence family timing and generational structures. Among middle-aged individuals between 55 and 63, those with higher SES were more likely to have both parents and children, but lower SES groups had a higher average number of children (that is, they were in more "bottom-heavy" structures).

Families as Agoras

As the above examples illustrate, families are unique *meeting grounds,* creating their own age/generation/cohort combinations and offering quite varying sets of "windows" on life phases and cohorts. Some may have members whose ages span nearly a century between the oldest and the youngest; others span only a third of that. Some have six generations; others have only two. We have quite limited knowledge of existing generational structures. Even less is known about the significance of generational structure for the quality of relationships, family cohesion, patterns of support, and what some authors call "intergenerational ambivalence" (Lüscher & Pillemer, 1998).

Our common-day "folk psychology" includes ideas of how age and cohort might make a difference. Young people are still told by parents that, with time and age, they will understand. On the other hand, the young frequently also listen to stories of "when I was a child," or "when I was a student," which implicitly acknowledge that history makes a difference.

Among social scientists, we find continuous discussion of issues related to "the Arab proverb question" cited in Ryder's (1965) classic article on the cohort as a unit in the study of social change: "A man resembles his times more than his father." The question is: In what ways do our values, choices, and behavior reflect our time (period and cohort) or our parents (family generation)? Furthermore, we can ask: Do long durations of shared relationships reduce the significance of contrasts created by cohort and age differences? Are there instances in which dramatic historical change makes it extraordinarily difficult to build understanding and consensus across family generations?

A number of authors have suggested that social change, and the conditions associated with late modernity and population aging, profoundly affect family members' abilities to develop a common platform and shared set of expectations. Such abilities, in turn, affect family ties. Not only do vertically extended families embed their members in a complex web of roles, but some of these relationships have little or no definition and normative structuring through culture. Examples would be that between a young-old child and an old-old parent, or a between a grandchild and a grandparent's cohabiting partner. Some scholars have argued that many of today's intergenerational relationships are "anomic" (Hess & Waring, 1978), and that modern families consequently find themselves in a "negotiation crunch." In some cases, the lack of cultural guidelines is handled with humor. The oldest person in my province in Norway is a retired military officer of 107. He lives on a farm with his son and daughter-in-law, but teaches an exercise class at the local senior center once a week. In an interview, the journalist asked the lively old man if his children attend the class. "Only the oldest, my 80-year-old daughter," was the answer. With a smile, he added: "But you know how it is. When kids grow up, isn't cool to do what Dad does!"

Since the tumultuous 1960s and early 1970s, researchers have pondered the effects of social change on generational ties in families. Much such work has explored possible watersheds, asking if cohort chasms translate into irreconcilable differences that constitute family generation gaps.

Societies with new patterns of co-longevity have already moved through the "demographic transition" and now have aging populations. They are also, typically, post-industrial and in late modernity. European demographers have recently presented thought-provoking discussions of *the second demographic transition*. They identify a set of changes that occurred with a striking simul-taneity: sharply declining fertility, decreasing and delayed nuptiality, and increas-ing divorce and cohabitation (Lestheaghe, 1983; van den Kaa, 1994). Scholars from a variety of disciplines agree that the 1960s mark a watershed in contexts for the transition to adulthood, particularly among women. The individualism that grew steadily in the 20th century emphasized individuals as the architects of their own lives (Beck, 1995, 2000). Access to modern contraceptives, often accompanied by liberalized abortion laws, gave women who came of age in the late 1960s and early 1970s unprecedented control over their fertility. At the same time, new educational and occupational opportunities opened. This period therefore created a new *psychology of choice*.

There is fairly strong agreement that we observe clear cohort contrasts in values and orientations across a number of societies as a result of these changes, but authors differ in their views on how these macro-level patterns will play themselves out in the microcosms of family lineages. Two Scandinavian researchers (Gullestad, 1996; Waerness, 1999) suggest that stark contrasts in values, orientations, and "symbolic dialects" (Newman, 1986) may make negotia-tions and the forging of shared perspectives difficult, especially among women. Gullestad portrays a grandmother, born around 1920 and who grew up and lived her life with the guiding principle of "doing her duty," as accepting her station in life. This woman faces her granddaughter, whose key life project is self-actualization and who emphasizes "what it's good to be, rather than what it's right to do," as Taylor (1989) puts it. Authors speculate about the consequences of such differences for the development of affective bonds, sense of obligation, and readiness to provide support.

Rosenmayr and Majce (1998) discuss a survey from Switzerland in which individuals over the age of 60 (that is, cohorts born before World War II) indicate that they feel responsible for family members, even if they do not like them. On the other side of a cohort divide (that is, in post-war cohorts), the sense of responsibility was instead linked to having positive relationship histories with family members. These authors conclude that cultural change has made it increasingly difficult to build and sustain intergenerational continuity in "the choice society," in which kin ties are voluntary and "a la carte," and in which the family is "a matrix of latent relationships" (Riley & Riley, 1993). Similarly, in Giddens' (1991) discussion of intimacy in late modernity, he speaks of "pure relationships"—ties that are maintained because they are gratifying to their members, not because of external normative pressures. While Giddens emphasizes marriage, he suggests that relationships between adults and their parents may follow suit. Several recent publications from the Longitudinal Study of Generations at the University of Southern California report that conflict does not seem to impede the exchange of support between adults and their parents (Parrott & Bengtson, 1999). The same study illustrates the central importance of gender, as affect and obligation appear to operate quite differently for men and women. This finding is confirmed in a study of a national sample of adults (Lawton, Silverstein, & Bengtson, 1994; see also Silverstein & Bengtson, 1997). While duty appears central for men, long-term affinity and affection shape support patterns for women.

Relationship histories are strongly emphasized in Finch and Mason's (1993) study of how families negotiate obligations. In such a perspective, *duration* seems central: with the passage of time, ties grow stronger (Attias-Donfut, 2000). Turner (1970) speaks of *crescive bonds:* "As two or more persons have a succession of shared experiences, they develop a wider and more firmly rooted common conception of reality, setting them apart from others, who have not been part of the same experience circle" (p. 82). Does a long trail of shared history—with its memories, inside jokes, and rituals for how to mark special occasions—create particular relationship bonds that override contrasts in age and cohort location? If so, it would seem reasonable that women, as kin-keepers, are central in the creation of crescive bonds and may be more influenced by affinity than by normatively defined obligations and duties. It would also seem that families without an active "matriarch" would have a more difficult time maintaining a sense of continuity and belonging. Before we can begin to explore the relative significance of gender, age, cohort, generation, and duration constellations in family units, we must find good ways to describe intergenerational structures.

Mapping Intergenerational Structures

As I have emphasized in previous work, it is of utmost importance to specify *whose* structures we are focusing on, what I call naming the *anchor*. Attias-Donfut (1995) uses the term *pivot*. Researchers need to keep in mind that in our kinship system, families look different from the "top" than what they do from the "bottom." Most past research on intergenerational structures has been anchored in middle-aged and old individuals—views from the top. We know much less about the kin structures surrounding children and youth—views from the bottom. For example, we have estimates of how many older adults are great-grandparents, but little information on how many young people are great-grandchildren.

In order to better describe structures, we need the following core information: 1) the number of generations (degree of verticalization), 2) the relative balance between old and young (top- versus bottom-heaviness), 3) sex ratios ("family population pyramids"), 4) the age span between the youngest and the oldest across the entire structure and within each generation, and 5) the age distance between the generations. The latter two variables allow us to characterize lineages as *age compressed* versus *age dispersed*. For many purposes, we also want to collect data on marital disruption through divorce and death, remarriage and cohabitation. In addition, it is also important to gather information on individuals with health problems. With the above information, we can identify and examine "generational squeezes" and "family bundles," such as multiple members with care needs, "divorce-proneness," "non-married families," and complex blended families. We can also identify "solo individuals" with neither direct ascendant nor descendant kin. When anchors are not in the top (Omega) generation, we need to get data on both maternal and paternal lines. For anchors who are part of a couple, information must be obtained on the lineage of both partners.

Consequences of Intergenerational Constellations: Unexplored Issues

Once we are able to describe generational structures, we can begin to explore how different combinations of temporal locations affect family units and inter-generational relationships. Let me give some examples of questions that have seldom been raised about the significance of age composition. Here again, issues may look quite different depending on where we anchor them. Over the last few decades, a great deal of concern has focused on teenage childbearing, generating reams of publications. Virtually no research exists on how one-time teenage mothers fare in old age, when they are close to being age-peers of their children and may attend senior centers with them.[1] To complicate matters, such lineages may also be more vertically extended (that is, more generations may be alive at once). It is not that uncommon to see pictures of five-generational families in which it is difficult to sort members into correct generational location. Do age-compressed families have an easier time building cohesion and consensus than is the case for age-dispersed units? Do age-compressed families more often go through times when care needs pile up? Burton's (1996) unique work on family patterns of timing has alerted us to the possibility that lineages have their own "kinscripts" for distributing care and resources.

---

[1] A course paper by Marla McDaniel alerted me to this issue.

Does the meaning of age compression/dispersion change over the duration of relationships? Attias-Donfut (2000) argues that as individuals live longer, age differences between parents and children "symbolically contract." While most of us agree that the difference between a 10-year-old and a 35-year old feels greater than that between individuals aged 35 and 60, there might be less consensus that the subjective experience of age difference is reduced similarly between persons aged 60 and 85. If experiences of being different prevail, is it because of contrasting life phases and length of experience, or do historical experiences create the strongest feelings of commonalties as well as differences?

And what happens when families have "fuzzy sets," to use Ragin's (2000) term, in their generational structures, and there is a lack of correspondence between generational position, age, and cohort location? Do we share more with family members who are our age peers even if they are in a generation above or below us? Is an aunt who is roughly the same age as nieces and nephews still regarded as an aunt? Can cohort contrasts make us feel closer to members of generations other than our own because they are on "our" side of a divide? In Norwegian society, cohorts born during World War II and in the immediate post war-era grew up with rationing of food and clothing because supplies were extremely limited. Many of these individuals have siblings born in the 1950s, when material resources were more readily available. These cohorts have been labeled "the dessert generation" because they not only had adequate food, they had dessert! Among sisters, such contrasts are amplified by sharp differences in their social contexts for the transition to adulthood, as pointed out by students of the second demographic transition. In some ways, women whose childhoods were marked by the closeness to war may have lifestyles and symbolic dialects more like their mothers than their younger sisters. A current study of Norwegian women born in 1946 (Gautun, in progress) shows that although these women represent a "tipping cohort," they tend to be more traditional than later cohorts of women. For example, in contrast to women less than 10 years their junior, women born in 1946 have had fairly low rates of divorce and cohabitation, and few of them have had steady full-time attachment to the labor force. Do the older sisters in such cohort-divided sibling sets end up with stronger ties and intensified exchanges with their parents?

By now, the returns are beginning to come in on the long-term consequences of divorce and remarriage for intergenerational ties. Again, gender appears to be a central part of this story. Relationships to fathers and paternal grandparents show more negative impact of marital disruption than is the case for ties in the maternal line (Cooney & Uhlenberg, 1990; Dykstra, 1998; Johnson, 1993; Lawton et al., 1994). However, we know very little about families that for several generations have been "divorce-prone" or units that have experienced "divorce bundles," such as marital disruption among all the children. What happens to the well-being of older members in such lineages? How are crescive bonds and long relationship histories affected by marital dissolution and remarriages in the lineage? Not infrequently, individuals who for decades were part of family celebrations, and who were included in jokes, stories, and pictorial records of shared history, suddenly become "non-persons." In extreme cases, they are cut out of all pictures in family albums!

Many questions remain unanswered about how recent societal change has affected intergenerational relationships in the family. It is my firm conviction, however, that in order to understand how such ties are sustained in the face of pronounced social shifts, we must examine complex patterns of interdependence among family members. Again, it is essential that we think across levels.

INTERDEPENDENCE AMONG LIVES: FROM MICRO TO MACRO VIEWS

Interdependence and Individual Experience

As mentioned earlier, a central concept in the life-course perspective is the interdependence of lives. Much discussion of this principle has taken a micro view, focusing on the intra-individual or inter-individual level. For example, a great deal of attention has been given to interdependence of role trajectories within the individual life course, such as between work and family careers among women (Moen, 1996; O'Rand & Henretta, 1999) or the interplay of military engagement and family careers in men's lives (Elder & Bailey, 1988). There is also strong recognition that our personal experience of the life course is closely interconnected with those of fellow life travelers, what Schutz (1971) called *consociates*.

Family members provide essential material for the writing of autobiographies and for the subjective marking of time. The past is often measured against the transitions of others: "It was the year Pete graduated, so it must have been. . . ." Similarly, especially in the later phases of the life course, the future gets structured through the anticipated lives of younger members: "I want to see my grandchild graduate. . . ." A recent study of unemployed, non-custodial fathers, many of whom had a troubled past, found that focusing on their children allowed these men a new start, a form of "life-course extension" (Roy, 1999). As most parents will testify, accomplishments of children and grandchildren are often experienced as personal triumphs. The flip side, of course, is that their failures and crises also leave their marks on parents. Children who are "off course" leave parents with a sense of work undone. Tobin (1996) provides moving accounts of old parents whose developmentally disabled adult children keep them from tending to issues related to their own aging.

Anthropology provides rich illustrations of societies with clear regulation of interwoven life careers. Prins (1953) and Whiting (1981) describe the Kikuy of Kenya, a group in which the highest status for a man, that of ritual elder, could not be reached until their youngest sons were circumcised and their wives had gone through menopause. In several European countries, for example Ireland, a system of primogeniture created villages of old bachelors, places where women gave up waiting for first-born men who could not start their own families until their fathers relinquished the farm or died. Historian Hareven (1982) argues that in 19th century families, the crucial aspect of marital or parental timing was not the individual's age, but other family members needs and resources. Our urban, post-industrial societies have few cultural norms that state such life-course contingencies, but we nevertheless recognize that our life progress hinges on the progress of others. Let me give four examples of such life interweaving: the coordination of constraints and resources, countertransitions, Janus-interdependencies, and implicit contracts.

Shared Constraints and Resources

Elder's (1974) work on the Depression is a prime example of how the lives of parents and children are interdependent with regard to resources and stresses, illustrated in cases of unemployment or illness. Writer Terry Tempest Williams (1991) captures the point well: "A person does not get cancer—a family does." Oppenheimer (1981) has discussed how the timing of parenthood and work careers in two or more generations shapes the likelihood that family units will experience generational squeezes, situations in which resources are overloaded. Several authors have argued that we need to examine "couple trajectories," as partners attempt to negotiate and synchronize timetables in family and work (Moen, 1996; O'Rand & Henretta, 1999; Roth, 1983). We know very little about how decisions regarding the timing of retirement, and where to live during retirement years, are shaped by considerations of needs and resources in younger generations.

Countertransitions

Several authors have described life changes created by other people's transitions, what Riley and Waring (1976) originally called "counterpoint-transitions, and which I have shortened to *countertransitions* (Hagestad & Neugarten, 1985). Examples would be the entry into grandparenthood or the creation of "ex"-relationships by divorce. Anthropologist Mead (1972) writes of grandparenthood: "the extraordinary sense of having been transformed not by an act of one's own but by the act of one's child" (p. 302). The complexities of family interdependence surrounding grandparenthood are clearly illustrated in societies where it is a necessary status in becoming recognized as an elder. In our type of society, many grandparents, particularly in the paternal line, struggle not to become an "ex" as a ripple effect of a son's divorce.

Janus-Interdependencies

The fact that any parent-child relationship is typically part of a longer intergenerational chain is often neglected in discussions of interdependence. All too often, research focuses on one relationship in isolation, tearing it out as a separate piece from a dense weave of lives. The meanings of modern parenthood, in part, are shaped by the meanings of being an adult child. Of course, ties to children and grandchildren also influence relationships to aging parents. The development of what Blenkner (1965) labeled *filial maturity*, a new readiness to accept dependence in parents, builds on *parental maturity*, a new type of relationship with adult children (Nydegger, 1991).

Work on intergenerational relations needs to include what I call *indirect relationships*. One generation may help a second, in order that the second can help a third. A good deal of support from grandparents is given to the middle generation, but earmarked for the third generation, the grandchildren. My own work suggests that an important part of being a modern grandparent is to continue being a good parent, what Gutmann (1987) calls being "an emeritus parent," and supporting your children's parenting. Such support can be emotional, through encouragement and advice, or it can be practical and material, for instance helping with major purchases. Attias-Donfut and Wolff (2000) find that the employment status of the child generation is more important predictor of help with grandchildren than is the employment status of grandparents. Such help, they argue, is about the "social promotion" of children, especially daughters. In new patterns of co-longevity, inheritance from parents often comes at a time when the children do not need it and consequently pass it on to the third generation, their children.

Times of generational turnover, points at which links are added or lost, often lead to changes in the quality of existing or remaining relationships. Children's entry into parenthood, making their own parents grandparents, appears to create new closeness, especially between mothers and daughters (Fischer, 1982). On the other hand, the loss of a generation and movement into the Omega generation may create a new sense of vulnerability. In a study of divorce in middle age, we found that individuals who were in an Omega position (that is, they had no surviving parent) reported less use of their children as emotional supports following the marital breakup than individuals who still had parents living (Hagestad, Smyer, & Stierman, 1984). The Omegas seemed to have a sense of vulnerability, and of not wanting to overload their family networks. This trend was particularly clear for men.

Hogan and his colleagues found that adults facing the transition into the Omega position, with very old and frail parents, are less likely to provide assistance to younger generations because they experience increased rates of depression, reduced social integration, and financial stress (Hogan, Eggebeen, & Snaith, 1996). However, these authors do not consider structures "below" the persons who are "moving up" a notch. Future research might examine the potential mediating effects of having grandchildren at the time of the transition into the Omega generation.

Implicit Contracts

There is another type of support offered by mature adults to their children and grandchildren that is often neglected in family scholarship, perhaps because it is not an easy type of support to measure. Often, the mere presence of an older generation provides security, a sense that should crises occur, the older generation would step in to help. Older parents serve as a "reserve army" of support. Parental resources and health statuses are surely important factors in many young adults' housing and fertility choices. Such potential back up is often part of unstated, implicit contracts. When caregivers in the study of the Norwegian oldest-old were asked why they became the central providers of care, they had trouble coming up with answers. Most of them said, "it just worked out that way." Similarly, when we interviewed young adults whose parents had recently divorced, these young adults found it very painful to consciously recognize their own implicit dependence on the parents (Cooney, Smyer, Hagestad, & Klock, 1984). One young man exclaimed: "This just isn't fair! Instead of me leaving home, home left me!" A classic illustration of implicit scripts is provided by poet Robert Frost in *The death of a hired man*:

> Home is the place where, when you have to go there,
> they have to take you in.

The best way to understand implicit contracts might be to examine instances when they are not met, "when the contract fails," to use Foner's (1993) term, as in the case of the young adult cited above. When we consider implicit contracts across generations, we return to the "Arab proverb question" but give it a new twist. What happens to such contracts when the fundamental social conditions under which they were formed are altered? Such questions should be compelling reasons to study intergenerational patterns in countries that have recently experienced cataclysmic transformations of their political, economic, and social systems. Often, individual resources, as well as societal safety nets that were taken for granted, disappear almost overnight. There are also good reasons to study societies that have experienced less dramatic, but nevertheless profound, cultural and policy changes. An example would be men's growing involvement in parenting in the Nordic countries. Will these "new" fathers mature with a new set of implicit contracts? Will they become a new kind of older man, in relationships to aging parents, adult children, and grandchildren?

A Macro View of Interdependence

We now need to acknowledge that interdependence is not merely a matter of individuals in close, primary relationships. The family is more than a primary group; it is also a social institution that shapes social ties and roles in complex and powerful ways. Laws and policies often create a web of life-course contingencies across institutional domains and among family members (Hagestad, 1992; Millar & Warman, 1996; Rostgaard & Fridberg, 1998).

Sociologist Elias (1978) would most likely argue that level myopia limits our understanding of contemporary family life. Elias contends that in modernity, "chains of interdependence become more differentiated and grow longer; consequently they become more opaque and, for any single group or individual, more uncontrollable" (p. 68). Much work is needed to deepen our understanding of how basic structural conditions define and shape patterns of family interdependence. I have previously discussed examples of interdependence scenarios created by social policies that are based on age and duration criteria in other institutions (Hagestad, 1992):

> *A's rights or duties are based on B's age.* A spouse has a right to the partner's pension based on the partner's age. Because of age differences between husbands and wives, it is not uncommon to find women "pensioners" under the age of 40.

> *Member A's rights and duties are based on member B's duration.* In Norway, an expectant mother who wants full maternity leave must have worked for a given number of months before the birth. For the child's father to qualify for a fully paid parental leave, he, too, is dependent on the mother meeting the work duration requirement.

> *Member A's durations are in conflict with member B's durations; as a result, B may miss out on rights.* A family member who has a period of illness requiring care may prevent another member from accumulating the continuous duration of work required for certain social rights, such as unemployment benefits, sick pay, or pension. Women's entitlements, such as pensions or unemployment benefits, are often profoundly affected by care responsibilities, which are reinforced through social policy (Sørensen, 1991; Walker, 1993).

Esping-Andersen (1997), whose discussion of welfare state regimes spearheaded lively international debates, has recently urged scholars to see lives and relationships across societies within a matrix of life-course regulating policies: services and transfers to the old, arrangements for the care of children, support of parenting in young families.

Bridging Macro and Micro Levels

The unfortunate discussions of "intergenerational equity," especially evident in the United States (for an overview, see Bengtson & Achenbaum, 1993), have tended to examine allocation of societal resources as a zero-sum game that pits age groups against each other. As Heclo (1988), among others, has argued, the fates of young and old alike are closely interconnected in the family realm. We need to explore the interplay between interdependencies on macro and micro levels. To what extent does social policy protect micro-dependencies? Family leaves recognize that parents and children in up to three generations depend on one another. The clearest, and most common, public recognition of private interdependence is the relationship between young children and their parents (Marin, 2000). However, in cases of parents who do not live up to their responsibilities, the state steps in through agencies of child protection.[2] In some such instances, other family interdependencies are honored; in others, they are not. A case in point relates to grandparents and grandchildren. Some states will put children into protective services and foster care without considering existing interdependence between grandparents and grandchildren. In contrast, other states *mandate* such interdependence, without consideration of relationship qualities. An example is the state of Wisconsin's "grandparent-deeming" law. Under the law, if a minor gives birth to a child, her own parents are responsible for the grandchild until the new mother comes of age. On the other hand, we find states in which strong intergenerational interdependencies receive no public support or protection. In many cases, grandparents on the non-custodial side have no legally protected visitation rights following divorce. Similarly, step-relationships receive no public support. Parents and grandparents who have put strong efforts into building viable bonds to stepchildren and step-grandchildren find that such ties have no legal protection when the marriage that established the relationship in the first place breaks up.

Recent scholarship has pointed to the study of intergenerational transfers as a fertile area for understanding the intersection between family and state, private and public. Transfers are defined broadly and include the exchange of time, care, and material resources. I would also add skills and knowledge, and I would regard socialization as a transfer process. This requires thinking in a fairly rich matrix of what is being transferred in both private and public spheres, and that we consider the consequences of transfers for the well-being of families and individuals, as well as for individual life-course decisions and transitions. It has been argued that past discussions of transfers in the welfare state have tended to focus on cash benefits and neglect social services (Daatland, 1999; Esping-Andersen, 1997; Rostgaard & Fridberg, 1998). Both have strong implications for intergenerational transfers in families.

A number of nations have "familistic" social policies (Esping-Andersen, 1997; Leisering & Leibfried, 1999) that hold adult children responsible for their aging parents. The Nordic countries have no such laws, but they have access to an extensive set of community-based social services for the old. They also have high rates of labor force participation for middle-aged women, the most likely candidates for the "sandwich" position. In contrast, Greece, Italy, Portugal, and Spain—all of them aging societies—have family obligation laws, little use of public services for the old, and relatively low labor force participation among

---

[2] The term "state" is used here to cover both nation-states and individual states in the United States.

women between the ages of 45 and 64 (Daatland, 1999). These countries have all experienced dramatic drops in fertility. Esping-Andersen (1997) comments: "The irony is that what is considered as pro-family social policy in these countries maintains family responsibilities by force (or by the lack of alternatives), but at the expense of family formation" (p. 67). Menken (1985), in her presidential address to the Population Association of America, stated the same point a bit more cautiously: "Might it not be appropriate to interpret recent fertility change in part as representing an awareness of the lasting nature of families of origin and the private dependency burden—the extent of responsibilities that we owe to our mothers, to our daughters, to ourselves?" (p. 481).

Past considerations of the interplay between public and private transfers, benefits as well as services, have often started with a "substitution hypothesis"—a view that public transfers "crowd out" those in the private sphere. Recently, we have moved toward a "complementarity hypothesis" (Attias-Donfut & Wolf, 2000; Foner, 2000; Kohli, 1999). In a comparison of four Western nations and Japan, Künemund and Rein (1999) conclude that the most significant family support of older people is found in societies with generous welfare arrangements for this age group. Kohli, Künemund, Motel, and Szydlik (2000) even suggest that a reason for the high support for public transfers is, indeed, that they enable families to redistribute resources. Public transfers may facilitate and even strengthen private transfers because they allow capital to be preserved and transmitted to the younger generations—what one author calls "the double circuit" (Attias-Donfut, 1995, 2000). While bequests are typically distributed equally between children (often because the law requires it), inter-vivo transfers are typically based on *perceived need* (Attias-Donfut & Wolf, 2000; Kohli et al., 2000) Thus, families are arenas that may redress society's priorities with regard to transfers based on age or the life course. Foner (2000) sums it up: "While entitlements for older adults are financed and dispensed at the macro-level, a different process is at work in the age-integrated family at the micro-level" (p. 274).

Foner brings up an important, but sorely neglected, topic: age integration, and its opposite, age segregation. Many aging societies are characterized by age segregation, both in residential patterns and institutional arrangements (Hagestad, 1998). The "tripartite life course" (Kohli, 1986) channels children, adults, and old people into distinct and separate institutional settings, where they spend much of their time surrounded by age peers. Such segregation limits opportunities for cross-age interaction, deprives all age groups of valuable socialization experiences, and may breed ageism (Coleman, 1982; Hagestad & Dannefer, 2001; Uhlenberg, 2000). The family may be the only truly age-integrated social institution, facilitating long-term ties and complex personal knowledge across age and cohort lines. Some authors have begun to express optimism that intergenerational bonds in the family can foster age integration in the wider society (Attias-Donfut, 2000; Foner, 2000; Uhlenberg, 2000). One aspect of such integration is mutual socialization.

Members of different generations often serve as "cohort bridges" for one another. While older generations provide windows to the past, the young may help making a rapidly changing present manageable and understandable. Two studies, one in France (Attias-Donfut, 2000) and one in the United States (Hagestad, 1984), found that women are more likely than men to report being socialized by children and grandchildren. The most common type of influence are various forms of help related to "keeping up with the times." In contemporary families, the obvious example of such socialization from young to old would be help with computers, the internet, and e-mail.

In spite of such intra-family socialization, I would argue that the effects of age segregation are likely so profound and extensive that the family cannot "do it all" in creating necessary age and cohort agoras. More societal arenas that facilitate stable contact, understanding, and mutual learning across age lines might actually bolster intergenerational cohesion and foster fruitful negotiations in the family. Those of us who teach courses on adult development or the family hear students comment that course material made them see parents and grandparents in a new light. One discovery is that what they thought were personal idiosyncrasies actually may reflect common historical experiences or developmental preoccupations typical of a given life stage with its transitions.

Many questions need to be asked about how the age composition and degree of age segregation in social contexts affect intergenerational ties in the family, and to what extent negative and positive experiences in the family realm color cross-age relationships in other spheres. For example, to what degree do parents in age-heterogeneous work settings experience "spillover" in their family relationships? Do cross-age friendships occur because individuals introduce their peers to older and younger family members? How often do young people "adopt" the grandparent of a friend?

FINAL REFLECTIONS

The life-course perspective encourages us to create a rich, multidimensional portrait of old people and their families as they begin to negotiate the terrain of the early 21st century. To use a concept from photography, the perspective also requires *depth of field*. Researchers are urged to take *a long view,* both in portraying individual lives, linked lives, and chains of interconnected relationships. That means thinking histories and history. Both are punctuated by times of transition.

In our part of the aging world, the first decades of the new century will be marked by the exit of cohorts and generations in which many lives were marked by times of hardship and uncertainty. The bulk of the "great gray wave" will have no memory of war and will have had more opportunities for life planning and choice than their parents and grandparents did. They have children who to an even greater extent have seen themselves as their own life-course architects, and grandchildren who seem to have the negotiation skills of union lawyers.

And yet, the field also includes countries—neighbors and allies—for which the last decades of the 20th century brought profound shake-ups of the social order and the basic conditions of life. Some of them will not celebrate long lives and co-longevity, but will instead somberly face a steady shortening of average life length, especially for men. More than ever, we need to look beyond our own time and place in order to better understand the social forces that shape contours of lives and webs of family connections.

REFERENCES

Attias-Donfut, C. (1995). Le double circuit de transmission. In C. Attias-Donfut (Ed.), *Les solidarités entre généreations: Viellesse, familles,* Ètat (pp. 41-81). Paris: Nathan.

Attias-Donfut, C. (2000). Cultural and economic transfers between generations: One aspect of age integration. *The Gerontologist, 40*(3), 270-272.

Attias-Donfut, C., & Wolff, F. C. (2000). The redistributive effects of generational transfers. In S. Arber & C. Attias-Donfut (Eds.), *The myth of generational conflict: The family and state in ageing societies* (pp. 22-46). London: Routledge.

Beck, U. (1995). eigenes Leben- Skizzen zu einer biographischen Gesellschaftsanalyse. In U. Beck, W. Vossenkuhl, & U. E. Ziegler (Eds.), *Eigenes Leben-Ausflüge in die unbekannte Gesellschaft, in der wir leben* (pp. 164-174). Munich: C. H. Beck Verlagsbuchhandlung.

Beck, U. (2000). Living your life in a runaway world: Individualisation, globalisation and politics. In I. W. Hutton & A. Giddens (Eds.), *On the edge: Living with global capitalism* (pp. 164-174). New York: The New Press.

Bengtson, V. L., & Achenbaum, W. A. (1993) (Eds.). *The changing contract across generations.* New York: Aldine De Gruyter.

Bengtson, V., & Allen, K. (1993). The life course perspective applied to families over time. In G. Boss, W. Doherty, R. LaRossa, W. Schumm, & S. Steinmetz (Eds.), *Sourcebook of family theories and methods: A contextual approach* (pp. 469-498). New York: Plenum Press.

Bengtson, V. L., Rosenthal, C., & Burton, L. (1996). Paradoxes of families and aging. In R. H. Binstock & L. K. George (Eds.), *Handbook of aging and the social sciences* (pp. 254-282). San Diego, CA: Academic Press.

Blenkner, M. (1965). Social work and family relationships in later life, with some thoughts on filial maturity. In E. Shanas & G. F. Streib (Eds.), *Social structure and the family* (pp. 46-59). Englewood Cliffs, NJ: Prentice-Hall.

Brody, E. M. (1982). Women in the middle and family help to older people. *The Gerontologist, 21,* 471-480.

Burton, L. (1996). Age norms, the timing of family role transitions, and intergenerational caregiving among aging African-American women. *The Gerontologist, 36,* 199-208.

Christian, S. (1984). Grandparent anxiety. *Modern Maturity, 26*(6), 32-35.

Coleman, J. S. (1982). *The asymmetric society.* Syracuse, NY: Syracuse University.

Cooney, T., Smyer, M. A., Hagestad, G. O., & Kock, R. (1984). Parental divorce in adulthood: Some preliminary findings. *Journal of Orthopsychiatry, 58,* 470-477.

Cooney, T., & Uhlenberg, P. (1990). The role of divorce in men's relationships with their adult children after mid-life. *Journal of Marriage and the Family, 52,* 677-688.

Daatland, S. O. (1999, July). *Community services and family norms in a comparative perspective.* Paper presented at the European Congress of Gerontology, Berlin.

Dykstra, P. (1997). *Employment and caring.* Working paper 7. The Hague: NIDI.

Dykstra, P. (1998). The effects of divorce on intergenerational exchanges in families. *The Netherlands Journal of Social Sciences, 33,* 77-93.

Elder, G. H., Jr. (1974). *Children of the Great Depression: Social change in life experience.* Chicago: University of Chicago Press.

Elder, G. H., Jr. (1985) Perspectives on the life course. In G. H. Elder, Jr. (Ed.), *Life course dynamics, trajectories and transitions: 1968-1980* (pp. 23-49). Ithaca, NY: Cornell University Press.

Elder, G. H., Jr. (1998). The life course and human development. In R. M. Lerner (Ed.), *Handbook of child psychology: Theoretical models for human development* (pp. 939-991). New York: John Wiley & Sons.

Elder, G. H., Jr., & Bailey, S. L. (1988). The timing of military service in men's lives. In J. Aldous, & D. Klein (Eds.), *Social stress and family development* (pp. 157-174). New York: Guilford Press.

Elias, N. (1978). *What is sociology?* New York: Columbia University Press.

Esping-Andersen, G. (1997). Welfare states at the end of the century: The impact of market, family and demographic change. In P. Hennesy & M. Peersen (Eds.), *Family, market and community: Equity and efficiency in social policy* (pp. 63-76). Paris: OECD.

Finch, J., & Mason, P. (1993). *Negotiating family responsibilities.* London: Routledge.

Fischer, L. (1982). Transitions in the mother-daughter relationship. *Journal of Marriage and the Family, 43,* 613-622.

Foner, N. (1993). When the contract fails: Care for the elderly in nonindustrial cultures. In V. L. Bengtson, & W. A. Achenbaum (Eds.), *The changing contract across generations* (pp. 101-118). New York: Aldine De Gruyter.

Foner, A. (2000). Age integration or age conflict as society ages? *The Gerontologist, 40,* 272-276.

Gautun, H. (in progress). *Familiebånd i en vippegenerasjon* (Family ties in a "tipping generation"). Doctoral dissertation, Department of Sociology, University of Oslo.

Gee, E. M. (1986). The life course of Canadian women: A historical and demographic analysis. *Social Indicators Research, 18,* 263-283.

Gee, E. M. (1987). Historical change in the family life course of Canadian men and women. In V. Marshall (Ed.), *Aging in Canada* (pp. 265-287). Markham, Ontario: Fitzhenry & Whiteside.

Giddens, A. (1991). *Modernity and self-identity: Self and society in the late modern age.* Cambridge, UK: Polity Press.

Glick, P. C. (1977). Updating the family cycle. *Journal of Marriage and the Family, 39,* 5-13.

Grundy, E., Murphy, M., & Shelton, N. (1999). Looking beyond the household: Intergenerational perspectives on living kin and contacts with kin in Great Britain. *Population Trends, 97,* 19-27.

Gullestad, M. (1996). From obedience to negotiation: dilemmas in the transmission of values between the generations in Norway. *Journal of the Royal Anthropological Institute, 2,* 25-42.

Gutmann, D. (1987). *Reclaimed powers: Towards a new psychology of men and women in late life.* New York: Basic Books.

Hagestad, G. O. (1984). The continuous bond: A dynamic, multigenerational perspective on parent-child relations between adults. In M. Perlmutter (Ed.), *The Minnesota symposium on child psychology: Parent-child interaction and parent-child relations in child development* (pp. 129-158). Hillsdale, NJ: Lawrence Erlbaum Associates.

Hagestad, G. O. (1990). Social perspectives on the life course. In R. H. Binstock & L. K. George (Eds.), *Handbook of aging and the social sciences* (pp. 151-168). San Diego, CA: Academic Press.

Hagestad, G. O. (1992). Assigning rights and duties: Age, duration and gender in social institutions. In W. R. Heinz (Ed.), *Theoretical advances in life course research* (pp. 261-279). Weinheim, Germany: Deutscher Studien Verlag.

Hagestad, G. O. (1998). Towards a society for all ages: New thinking, new language, new conversations. *Bulletin on Aging, 2*(3), 7-13.

Hagestad, G. O., Dannefer, D. (2001). Concepts and theories in aging: Beyond microfication in social sciences approaches. In R. H. Binstock & L. K. George (Eds.), *Handbook of aging and the social sciences.* San Diego, CA: Academic Press.

Hagestad, G. O., & Neugarten, B. L. (1985). Age and the life course. In E. Shanas & R. H. Binstock (Eds.), *Handbook of aging and the social sciences* (pp. 36-61). New York: Von Nostrand & Reinhold Company.

Hagestad, G. O., Smyer, M. A., & Stierman, K. (1984). Parent-child relations in adulthood: The impact of divorcing in middle age. In R. Cohen, S. Weissman, & B. Cohler (Eds.), *Parenthood: Psychodynamic perspectives* (pp. 246-262). New York: Guilford Press.

Hareven, T. K. (1977). Family time and historical time. *Daedalus, 106,* 57-70.

Hareven, T. K. (1982). *Family time and industrial time.* Cambridge: Cambridge University Press.

Heclo, H. (1988). Generational politics. In J. L. Palmer, T. M. Smeeding, & B. B. Torrey (Eds.), *The vulnerable* (pp. 381-411). Washington, DC: Urban Institute Press.

Henretta, J. C., Grundy, E., & Harris, S. (1999, August). *Socioeconomic differences in numbers of living parents and children: A U.S.-British comparison of middle-aged adults.* Paper presented at the European Population Conference, The Hague.

Hess, B. B., & Waring, J. M. (1978). Parent and child in later life: Rethinking the relationship. In R. M. Lerner & G. B. Spanier (Eds.), *Child influences on marital and family interaction* (pp. 241-274). New York: Academic Press.

Hogan, D. P., Eggebeen, D. J., & Snaith, S. M. (1996). The well-being of aging Americans with very old parents. In Hareven, T. K. (Ed.), *Aging and generational relations over the life course* (pp. 327-346). New York: Walter de Gruyter.

Johnson, C. (1993). Divorced and reconstituted families: Effects on the older generation. In L. Burton (Ed.), *Families and aging* (pp. 33-41). Amityville, NY: Baywood.

Knipscheer, K., Dykstra, P., Utasi, A., & Cxeh-Szombathy. (2000). Aging and the family. In G. Beets & K. Miltenyi (Eds.), *Population aging in Hungary and the Netherlands* (pp. 181-199). Amsterdam, The Netherlands: Thela Thesis.

Kohli, M. (1986). The world we forgot: An historical review of the life course. In V.W. Marshall (Ed.), *Later life* (pp. 271-303). Beverly Hills, CA: Sage Publications.

Kohli, M. (1999). Private and public transfers between generations: Linking the family and the state. *European Societies, 1,* 81-104.

Kohli, M., Künemund, H., Motel, A., & Szydlik, M. (2000). Families apart? Intergenerational transfers in East and West Germany. In S. Arber & C. Attias-Donfut (Eds.), *The myth of generational conflict* (pp. 88-99). London: Routledge.

Künemund, H., & Rein, M. (1999). There is more to receiving than needing: Theoretical arguments and empirical explorations of crowding in and crowding out. *Ageing and Society, 19*, 93-121.

Lawton, L., Silverstein, M., & Bengston, V. (1994). Affection, social contact, and geographic distance between adult children and their parents. *Journal of Marriage and the Family, 56*(1), 57-68.

Lehr, U., & Schneider, W. (1983). Fünf-Generationen-Familien: Einige Data über Ururgrosseltern in der Bundesrepublik Deutschland. *Zeitschrift für Gerontologie, 5,* 200-204.

Leisering, L., & Leibfried, S. (1999). *Time and poverty in Western welfare states: United Germany in perspective.* Cambridge: Cambridge University Press.

Lestheaghe, R. (1983). A century of demographic and cultural change in Western Europe: An exploration of underlying dimensions. *Population and Development Review, 9*(3), 411-435.

Lüscher, K., & Pillemer, K. (1998) Intergenerational ambivalence: A new approach to the study of parent-child relations in later life. *Journal of Marriage and the Family, 60,* 413-425.

Maas, I., Borchelt, M., & Mayer, K. U. (1999). Generational experiences of old people in Berlin. In P. B. Baltes & K. U. Mayer (Eds.), *The Berlin Aging Study: Aging from 70 to 100* (pp. 83-110). Cambridge: Cambridge University Press.

Marin, M. (2000). Generational relations and the law. In S. Arber & C. Attias-Donfut (Eds.), *The myth of generational conflict: The family and state in ageing societies* (pp. 100-114). London: Routledge.

Mayer, K. U., & Müller, W. (1986). The state and the structure of the life course. In A. B. Sørensen, F. E. Weinert, & L. Sherrod (Eds.), *Human development and the life course: Multidisciplinary perspectives* (pp. 217-245). Hillsdale, NJ: Lawrence Erlbaum Associates.

Mead, M. (1972). *Blackberry winter: My earlier years.* New York: Simon and Schuster.

Menken, J. (1985). Age and fertility: How late can you wait? *Demography, 22,* 469-484.

Millar, J., & Warman, A. (1996). *Family obligations in Europe.* London: Family Policy Studies Center.

Moen, P. (1996). Gender and the life course. In R. Binstock & L. George (Eds.), *Handbook of aging and the social sciences* (pp. 171-187). San Diego, CA: Academic Press.

Newman, K. S. (1986). Symbolic dialects and generations of women: Variations in the meaning of post-divorce downward mobility. *American Ethnologist, 13,* 230-252.

Nydegger, C. (1991). The development of paternal and filial maturity. In K. Pillemer & K. McCarthney (Eds.), *Parent-child relations throughout life* (pp. 93-112). Hillsdale, NJ: Lawrence Earlbaum Associates.

Oppenheimer, V. K. (1981). The changing nature of life-cycle squeezes: Implications for the socio-economic position of the elderly. In R. W. Fogel, E. Hatfield, S. B. Kiesler, & E. Shanas (Eds.), *Aging: Stability and change in the family* (pp. 47-82). New York: Academic Press.

O'Rand, A. M., & Henretta, J. (1999). *Age and inequality: Diverse pathways through later life.* Boulder, CO: Westview Press.

Parrot, T. M., & Bengtson, V. L. (1999). The effects of earlier intergenerational affection, normative expectations, and family conflict on contemporary exchanges of help and support. *Research on Aging, 21*(1), 73-105.

Plath, D. W. (1980). Contours of association: Lessons from a Japanese narrative. In P. B. Baltes & O. G. Birm, Jr. (Eds.), *Life-span development and behavior* (pp. 287-305). New York: Academic Press.

Prins, A. H. J. (1953). *East African age-class systems.* Groningen, Netherlands: J. B. Walters.

Ragin, C. (2000). *Fuzzy-set social science.* Chicago: University of Chicago Press.

Riley, M. W., & Riley, J. W., Jr. (1993). Connections: Kin and cohort. In V. L. Bengtson & A. Achenbaum (Eds.), *The changing contract across generations* (pp. 169-189). New York: Aldine de Gruyter.

Riley, M. W., & Waring, J. (1976). Age and aging. In R. K. Merton & R. Nisbet (Eds.), *Contemporary social problems* (pp. 357-410). New York: Harcourt, Brace, and Jovanovich.

Romøren, T. I. (1999, July). *Courses of disability in the years before death in a population 80+.* Paper presented at the 4th European Congress of Gerontology, Berlin.

Rosenmayr, L., & Majce, G. (1998, November). *What can the generations offer each other? Doubts and hopes for the future.* Paper presented at an international conference on "Aging in Europe: Intergenerational Solidarity—A Basis of Social Cohesion," Vienna.

Rosenthal, C. (1985). Kin-keeping in the family division of labor. *Journal of Marriage and the Family, 45,* 509-521.

Rosenthal, C., Matthews, S. H., & Marshall, V. W. (1986, November). *Assessing the incidence and prevalence of "women in the middle."* Paper presented at the annual meeting of the Gerontological Society of America, Chicago.

Rossi, A., & Rossi, P. (1990). *Of human bonding: Parent-child relations across the life course.* New York: Aldine de Gruyter.

Rostgaard, T., & Fridberg, T. (1998). *Caring for children and older people: A comparison of European policies and practices.* Copenhagen, Denmark: The Danish National Institute of Social Research.

Roth, J. A. (1983). Timetables and the life course in postindustrial society. In D. W. Plath (Ed.), *Work and the life course in Japan* (pp. 248-260). Albany: State University of New York Press.

Roy, K. M. (1999). *On the margins of family and work: Life course patterns of low-income single fathers in an African American family.* Unpublished dissertation, Human Development and Social Policy, Northwestern University, Evanston, IL.

Ryder, N. (1965). The cohort as a concept in the study of social change. *American Sociological Review, 30,* 843-861.

Schutz, A. (1971). *Collected papers.* The Hague: Nijhoff.

Settersten, R. A., Jr., & Hagestad, G. O. (1996). What's the latest? Cultural age deadlines for family transitions. *The Gerontologist, 36*(2), 178-188.

Silverstein, M., & Bengtson, V. L. (1997). Intergenerational solidarity and the structure of adult child-parent relationships in American families. *American Journal of Sociology, 103*(2), 429-460.

Sørensen, A. (1991). The structuring of gender relations in an aging society. *Acta Sociologica, 34,* 45-55.

Taylor, C. (1989). *Sources of the self: The making of the modern identity.* Cambridge, Massachussetts: Harvard University Press.

Tobin, S. S. (1996). A non-normative old age contrast: Elderly parents caring for offspring with mental retardation. In V. L. Bengtson (Ed.), *Adulthood and aging: Research on continuities and discontinuities* (pp. 124-142). New York: Springer.

Turner, R. H. (1970). *Family Interaction.* New York: John Wiley & Sons.

Uhlenberg, P. (1996). Mortality decline in the twentieth century and supply of kin over the life course. *The Gerontologist, 36,* 681-685.

Uhlenberg, P. (2000). Integration of old and young. *The Gerontologist, 40*(3), 276-279.

van den Akker, P., Halman, L. , & de Moor, R. (1993). Primary relations in western societies. In D. Ester, L. Halman, & R. de Moor (Eds.), *The individualizing society. Value change in Europe and North America.* Tilburg: Tilburg University Press.

van den Kaa, D. J. (1994). The second demographic transition revisited: theories and expectations. In G. C. N. Beets, J. C. Brekel, R. L. Cliquet, G. Dooghe, & J. de Jong, (Eds.), *Population and family in the low countries.* Lisse: Swets & Zeitlinger.

Waerness, K. (1999). Aging and modernization in the Nordic countries. In S. Grønmo & B. Henrichsen (Eds.), *Society, university and world community: Essays for Ørjar Øyen* (pp. 151-165). Oslo: Scandinavian University Press.

Walker, A. (1993). Intergenerational relations and welfare restructuring: the social construction of an intergenerational problem. In V. L. Bengtson & A. W. Achenbaum (Eds.), *The changing contract across generations* (pp. 147-162). New York: Aldine De Gruyter.

Walker, A. (2000). Public policy and the construction of old age in Europe. *The Gerontologist, 40,* 304-308.

Watkins, S. C., Menken, J., & Bongaarts, J. (1987). Demographic foundations of family change. *American Sociological Review, 52,* 346-358.

Whiting, J. W. M. (1981). Aging and becoming an elder: A cross-cultural comparison. In R. W. Fogel, E. Hatfield, S. B. Kiesler, & E. Shanas (Eds.), *Aging: Stability and change in the family* (pp. 83-90). New York: Academic Press.

Williams, T. T. (1991). *Refuge: An unnatural history of family and place.* New York: Pantheon Books.

Winsborough, H. (1980). A demographic approach to the life-cycle. In K. W. Back (Ed.), *Life course: Integrative theories and exemplary populations* (pp. 65-75). Boulder, CO: Westview Press.

CHAPTER 6

What Life-Course Perspectives Offer the Study of Aging and Health

Linda K. George

Health and illness are states, but they are also processes that develop and have consequences over time. At one level, this is well understood. There is virtual consensus that both studies that focus on the impact of social and behavioral processes on health and those that examine the social and behavioral consequences of illness require longitudinal data to legitimate claims of causal inference. And, although they remain less plentiful than desirable, the research base on social factors and illness now includes a large number of longitudinal studies. Despite this, our understanding of the dynamics of social factors and health rests almost entirely on *short-term* longitudinal data. The temporal intervals most frequently examined are changes over one or two years—and the number of studies (other than those examining the predictors of mortality) that include more than ten years of data are exceedingly small.

The focus of this chapter is *long-term* patterns of social factors and illness. Although no specific time interval will be used, the emphasis is on patterns that emerge over many years, typically spanning more than one life stage as they are typically defined (i.e., childhood, adolescence, early adulthood, middle-age, early old age, and advanced old age). This long view takes us beyond the usual theoretical foundations of studies of social factors and illness which focus on relatively short-time intervals. Thus, this chapter has two primary goals: 1) to make a theoretical or conceptual case for examining long-term trajectories that result in differential vulnerability/resistance to illness and variable illness outcomes (e.g., recovery, chronicity, disability, mortality), and 2) to demonstrate that the concepts, insights, and methods of life-course research offer important tools for conceptualizing and empirically examining those long-term trajectories.

The chapter includes several sections. It begins with a brief overview of some of the essential characteristics shared by life-course perspectives. The next section summarizes a major theoretical paradigm—the stress process—underlying a large proportion of research on social factors and illness. Then, the discussion will turn to an exploration of how the stress model might be supplemented and elaborated via cross-fertilization with life-course perspectives; three promising areas of inquiry are highlighted. Throughout this section, conceptual and methodological issues are addressed in tandem. The last section presents some final thoughts about options for integrating life-course perspectives into the study of social factors and illness.

LIFE-COURSE PERSPECTIVES: CENTRAL PRINCIPLES

As Elder, George, and Shanahan (1996) note, three major principles are the common denominator of life-course perspectives. First, the life course consists of long-term sequences of transitions and periods of stability that form distinctive trajectories. As described below, this is probably the key and certainly the most complex of the three life-course principles. Second, life-course perspectives focus on the intersection of history and/or social conditions and personal biography. As such, life-course scholars emphasize the interplay of macro-, meso-, and micro-level factors in human lives. Third, life-course perspectives emphasize linked lives, or the ways that the interdependence of human lives shapes the life course. Each of these principles merits closer examination.

Life-Course Trajectories

Life-course trajectories are simply long-term patterns of change and stability. They are typically punctuated by occasional transitions, but also include periods of relative stability or change that is more gradual than that triggered by major transitions. Life-course trajectories may be isolated for specific domains of experience (e.g., health trajectories, family trajectories) or they may span multiple domains (e.g., trajectories of family and work involvement). Trajectories are not synonymous with the sociological concept of *careers*. Unlike careers, trajectories are not expected to follow specific steps or stages that lead to a specific outcome (as, for example, occupational careers do). Moreover, careers refer to patterns in one life domain whereas trajectories may span multiple domains.

Trajectories can be characterized in at least four ways. Most commonly, trajectories are defined on the basis of age or *timing*. For example, trajectories of family formation for a cohort or other group might be defined on the basis of average age at first marriage, birth of first child, birth of last child, departure of first child from the parental home, and departure of last child from the parental home. To the extent that cohorts or other groups (e.g., racial/ethnic groups) differ in the timing of these transitions, distinctive trajectories have been observed.

Trajectories also can be characterized on the basis of *duration* in a specific state. Among professors, for example, occupational trajectories can be formed on the basis of years as assistant professor, years as associate professor, and years as full professor. It is tempting to conclude that duration is simply another form of timing, but such is not the case. Using our example, given that assistant professors enter their careers at different ages, duration is a more accurate way to characterize career trajectories than average age at promotions. Defining trajectories on the basis of duration also is especially useful if transitions are duration-dependent (i.e., the odds of making a transition differ depending upon how long one has occupied a specific state). Some transitions, such as mortality, are monotonic over time—the longer individuals live, the more likely that they will die in the near future. For other transitions, however, duration dependence takes a curvilinear form. In this society, marriage is characterized by a curvilinear pattern of duration dependence. During early adulthood, every year that individuals have not married increases the odds of marriage in the near future. There comes a time, however, when individuals who have not married are likely to never marry—and the odds of marriage continue to decline after that.

A third method of characterizing trajectories is by the *sequencing* of transitions. This approach has been commonly used in studies of the "transition to adulthood" in which the order in which individuals complete their education, obtain their first full-time jobs, marry, and, in some studies, enter parenthood is observed. The rationale for measuring trajectories in terms of sequencing is the expectation that different sequences will have both different precursors and different consequences.

Finally, trajectories can be characterized in terms of the *density* of transitions at specific times or ages. Dense trajectories are those in which multiple transitions occur at or about the same time; in less dense trajectories, transitions are spaced further apart. It is typically possible to study trajectory density only if multiple life domains are examined. In this regard, the transition from adolescence to young adulthood is often viewed as especially stressful precisely because several major transitions typically occur within a short period of time.

How does an investigator choose which way(s) to characterize trajectories? As in all research, the most appropriate approach is best determined by consideration of the research question. If one wants to compare cohorts or groups on major milestones, trajectories based on timing are often most appropriate. If a researcher wants to know how the odds of a transition change over time, as a function of time spent in a given state, duration is the best way to construct trajectories. Similar arguments can be made for when it is most appropriate to construct trajectories on the basis of sequences or density.

Unfortunately, data limitations often constrict the trajectory construction choices available to the investigator. The timing intervals used in the vast majority of longitudinal studies are decided on non-scientific grounds (e.g., to meet the convenience of the investigator or the funding available). Thus, the decision to interview participants in a long-term longitudinal study at five-year intervals typically is not based on evidence that five years is the most appropriate interval to observe change and stability in (a) specific variable(s) of interest. Problems of trajectory construction are confounded even further by the fact that investigators seldom ask respondents about the timing of changes that occur between measurements. For example, existing data sources often make it possible for us to know that a respondent married between interviews, but seldom ascertain the date of the marriage. Without specific information about the temporal occurrence of transitions, it is impossible to construct accurate trajectories—and constructing trajectories based on sequences or density, in which the timing of multiple transitions is likely to occur in a relatively short time interval, is precluded. As a result of data limitations, trajectories often must be grossly measured and even timing and duration can seldom be ascertained with accuracy. Nonetheless, there is now sufficient research based on long-term trajectories, typically defined by timing, to document the power of such trajectories for illuminating the complex ways that experience early in life has persisting effects years—and even decades—later.

Life Course as the Intersection of History and Biography

It is well known in aging research that, in the absence of longitudinal data, aging and cohort effects cannot be disentangled. And it is quite common for investigators to attribute differences between age groups as cohort effects. There is much less recognition, however, that the term "cohort effects" is non-specific and non-explanatory. Documentation of cohort effects should be a first step in a process of investigation that ultimately identifies what accounts for cohort differences. An important mission of life-course scholarship is to take seriously the task of identifying the mechanisms that account for cohort differences.

To simplify, albeit fairly, two types of mechanisms have been shown to explain cohort differences: composition differences and exposure to historical experiences. Composition differences refer to cohort characteristics that distinguish cohorts from those before (and perhaps after) them. Examples of such characteristics include cohort size, percentage of the cohort who are foreign-born, and median levels of education. A substantial research base addresses the effects of cohort composition on a variety of social, psychological, and health outcomes. Very few, however, take the life-course approach and document the ways compositional factors play out over long periods of time.

Cohorts also differ in historical experience, which covers an immense territory. The most obvious examples of historical experience are dramatic events such as wars, the Great Depression, and major public policies (e.g., the enactment of Social Security, Medicare, and Medicaid). The volume of research that has examined the processes by which historical events affect life-course patterns is modest in size, but exceptionally rich and compelling. Less obvious cohort differences in historical experience that have received little, if any, research attention include targeted policies such as Civil Rights legislation and the availability of financial aid for college students, less dramatic changes in the economy, and the effects of technological change.

Again, it should be noted that only a (probably small) proportion of research on the effects of cohort composition and/or historical experience is life-course research. The unique contribution of life-course studies is their focus on both the short-term *and* long-term consequences of cohort characteristics and experience. It also is important to recognize that such studies provide a rare integration of macro- and micro-level factors as determinants of individual attitudes, behavior, and well-being.

Linked Lives

There is abundant evidence—especially, perhaps, in research on social factors and health—that social relationships are intricately involved in individuals' lives. Primary groups, especially the family, are major determinants of our socioeconomic status, our social and political attitudes, and the ways that our lives unfold over time. From birth to death, significant others are of critical importance to nearly every facet of our lives. Even less intimate relationships can have powerful effects on our lives, as evidenced in the "strength of weak ties" as originally developed by Granovetter (1973) and subsequently investigated widely.

Life-course investigators acknowledge the importance of social bonds in the trajectories of individuals. Thus, information about social relationships is central to understanding the life-course trajectories of individuals. Attention to linked lives is important for another reason as well. Primary groups, such as those found in the family, on the job, and in the community, are meso-level structures. And, indeed, primary groups are often the bridge by which macro-level structures and events affect individual lives.

A Note on Heterogeneity

The need for detailed data covering long periods of time is not the only challenge in life-course research. Trajectories tend to be highly variable across individuals. For example, in an important study addressing variability in life-course patterns, Rindfuss, Swicegood, and Rosenfeld (1987) examined role sequences for eight years after high school graduation for a cohort of young adults. Only five role transitions were examined: work, education, homemaking, military, and a residual "other." They report that 1100 sequences were required to describe the experiences of the 6700 men in the sample; 1800 sequences were needed to capture the patterns of the 7000 women in the sample. Even the simple, two-event sequence of education followed by work applied to only slightly more than half the men and to less than half of the women. This level of heterogeneity challenges analyses that attempt to characterize "typical" trajectories of specific cohorts or other groups.

The issue of heterogeneity has led to a bifurcation in research that is typically subsumed under the label of "life course research" (George, 1993). Some investigators, especially demographers, focus on the "big picture"—modal patterns in large groups, typically specific cohorts—and seem content to ignore the fact that most group members' trajectories do not resemble the modal pattern. Other investigators make the heterogeneity of trajectories the focus of their efforts, attempting to understand how social factors and conditions help to shape trajectories that take a myriad of forms. The decision to examine aggregated or disaggregated trajectories has important statistical implications, given that very different analytic techniques are needed to study the two forms of trajectories. These techniques will be discussed later in this chapter.

THE STRESS PROCESS: A KEY PARADIGM FOR STUDYING SOCIAL FACTORS AND ILLNESS

Stress theory is arguably the dominant paradigm in research that focuses on the role of social and behavioral factors as antecedents of health and longevity. In a now classic article, Pearlin, Lieberman, Menagham, and Mullan (1981) brought conceptual order to a field that already had literally hundreds of published studies. In essence, the generic components of their stress model are stressors, health outcomes, mediators, and moderators. Stressors are events (acute stressors) and conditions (chronic stressors) that tax the individual's ability to handle his or her life and, consequently, have the potential to harm health. Health outcomes are the parameters of health and well-being expected to be affected by stress. Depending on the research question, health outcomes will range from the very general (e.g., mortality, self-rated health) to the highly specific (e.g., onset of a specific illness, inability to achieve glycemic control among persons with diabetes). Mediators are the social and psychological factors that intervene between stressors and health outcomes. As such, mediators tend to fall into two classes: 1) social and psychological resources that can minimize or prevent illness in the face of stress, and 2) mechanisms by which stressors affect morbidity and mortality (e.g., by affecting health behaviors).

Moderators are conceptually similar to mediators in that they are social and psychological factors expected to alter the likelihood that stressors will harm health. The conceptual difference between the two is that moderators are expected to statistically interact with stressors to affect health and mediators are expected to have direct effects on health. Social support has received most attention with regard to efforts to determine whether its salubrious effects on health are direct or interactive. If it is a mediator of stress and illness, social support will always be associated with better health, regardless of levels of stress. If it is a mediating variable, social support will help protect health during times of stress, but be irrelevant to health in the absence of stress. These are not, of course, mutually exclusive hypotheses. It may be that supportive social relationships promote health at all times, but are especially powerful during times of stress.

A critical feature of Pearlin et al.'s (1981) model of the stress process is their emphasis on the social structural antecedents of both stress and resources. First they argued against an exclusive focus on life events. Chronic stressors, they suggest, are more likely than acute stressors to have significant effects on health; a proposition now supported empirically in numerous studies (e.g., Krause, 1986; Norris & Murrell, 1987). Equally important, chronic stressors tend to emerge in social structural contexts, especially those in which major role obligations are incurred (e.g., work, family). Second, both social and personal resources for handling stressors are related to one's position in social structures. Thus one's ability to cope with even "random" life events (Aneshensel, 1992) that are not grounded in structural conditions will be influenced by the resources to which one has access, which is in part determined by social location.

Space limitations preclude a comprehensive overview of research based on stress theory. Three major themes in the research base will be highlighted. I will return to them later in discussion of the potential cross-fertilization of life-course perspectives and research on social factors and illness.

Social Causation and Social Selection

A critical issue in research on social factors and illness is verifying what is cause and what is effect. The social causation hypothesis posits that social factors are the causal agents—that social factors affect health both directly and, in some cases, indirectly through more proximate causal agents. The social selection hypothesis suggests the reverse—that illness has social consequences. For more than 50 years, these competing hypotheses have been tested in the context of the relationship between socioeconomic status (SES) and health. The social causation hypothesis claims that low socioeconomic status is a cause of illness (e.g., Link & Phelan, 1995); the social selection hypothesis suggests that illness leads to downward mobility (e.g., Waldron, Herold, Dunn, & Staum, 1982). Similar claims and counter-claims can be made for the relationships between health and employment, marital status, participation in voluntary and religious organizations and other social factors.

Although the social causation and social selection hypotheses are typically viewed as competing, both can be valid. That is, there can be reciprocal paths of influence such that social factors are valid risk factors for illness and illness can lead to changes in social risk factors. Clearly, these are empirical questions. In the studies to date that have tested both hypotheses, evidence is typically found for both, although the effects of social causation are generally stronger (e.g., Johnson, 1991; Pugliesi, 1995; Ross & Mirowsky, 1995). A critical element needed to test these hypotheses is longitudinal data in which social factors are measured before and after illness onset. That fact has been widely recognized in research on social factors and illness. Beyond that, however, issues of timing, duration, and other critical elements of life-course perspectives have largely been ignored. In the next section, the potential benefits of using life-course perspectives to better understand the dynamics of both social causation and social selection are described.

Differential Exposure and Differential Vulnerability

One of the persisting challenges in medical sociology has been to identify the explanations for group differences in rates of illness and longevity. Explaining SES differences in morbidity and mortality has been of most concern, but race and gender differences also have received substantial attention. Social stress has been a prime candidate for explaining group differences. Social disadvantage—whether indexed by SES, race/ethnicity, or gender—is likely to be associated with exposure to stress. Consequently, stress may be a major mechanism by which social disadvantage translates into poorer health and shorter life. Most studies have shown that exposure to (or amount of) stress can explain some, but not most of the differences in morbidity across groups (e.g., Cohen, 1988; Krause, 1998; Schmader, Studenski, MacMillan, Grufferman, & Cohen, 1990).

Following the lead of Kessler (1979), group differences in illness that are not explained by differential exposure to stress have been attributed to differential vulnerability to stress (e.g., McLeod & Kessler, 1990; Roberts, Duncan, & Haug, 1994; Ulbrich, Warheit, & Zimmerman, 1989). Typically, greater vulnerability is assumed to be a function of fewer personal and social resources that are useful in confronting, alleviating, and minimizing the effects of stress. These are not mutually exclusive hypotheses—that is, some individuals may both experience more stress and be more vulnerable to it. Nonetheless, they often are posed as competing hypotheses for explaining group differences in illness and longevity.

One of my dissatisfactions with the differential vulnerability hypothesis is that it is a post hoc explanation. That is, whatever variance shared by group membership (e.g., SES, gender, race/ethnicity) and health outcomes that is not explained by differences in exposure to stress is attributed to differential vulnerability to stress. However, as noted above, the stress process model that dominates research on this topic specifically incorporates the kinds of psychosocial resources that are expected to mediate and/or moderate the effects of stress on health (e.g., social support, social integration, self-efficacy, and self-esteem). A substantial number of studies have included both stress and psychosocial resources; in them, the combination of stressors and resources has failed to fully explain group differences in morbidity and mortality (e.g., Ensel, 1991; Holahan & Moos, 1991; Roxburgh, 1996). Despite this, differential vulnerability continues to be offered as the major explanation for group differences in health and longevity.

The differential exposure and differential vulnerability hypotheses have been examined within both cross-sectional and longitudinal research frameworks. Most longitudinal studies, however, have been short-term and few include more than two measurement occasions. Measures of all the independent variables, including stressors and psychosocial resources, have typically been taken at a single (early) point in time and used to predict either health at a later time or health changes over time. As such, although the temporal distinction between independent and dependent variables is clear-cut in these studies (i.e., health cannot be the cause of stress and resources), the dynamics of the independent variables remain unaddressed (and unaddressable). Possible causal pathways that remain to be explored include the following: that 1) psychosocial resources may decrease the likelihood of experiencing stressors, 2) over time, repeated exposure to stress may deplete psychosocial resources, and 3) over time, repeated exposure to stress may strengthen psychosocial resources (a resilience hypothesis rather than a depletion hypothesis). As discussed in the next section, life-course perspectives provide the conceptual and empirical armamentaria for addressing such issues.

Broadening the Conceptualization of Stress

There has been growing concern about the validity of assuming that group differences in health and longevity are largely the result of differential vulnerability to stress. Turner, Wheaton, and Lloyd (1995) issued an especially compelling warning that dismissing or down-playing the role of exposure to stress as an explanation for group differences in health may be premature. They argue instead for broadening the definition of exposure to stress.

Even before Turner et al.'s warning, the need to broaden the concept of stress beyond an exclusive focus on life events was recognized. Pearlin et al. (1981) discussed the importance of both chronic stressors and "acute" life events, pointing out that 1) an appropriate test of the effects of stress on health must include both chronic and acute stressors, and 2) chronic and acute stressors are often causally linked. Avison and Turner (1988), in an attempt to disentangle the effects of acute and chronic stressors, found that individuals often report that the effects of life events persist over long periods of time, blurring the distinction between chronic and acute stressors. Thoits (1994) also reported that life events can have persisting effects, depending on whether the individual views them as "resolved" or "unresolved." In the case of unresolved events, individuals continue to experience negative effects on mental health long after occurrence of the stressful event.

Turner et al. (1995) broadened the concept of exposure to stress even further, introducing the concepts of "operant stress" and "cumulative stress." Operant stress refers to the total number of stressors affecting an individual at a given point in time and includes recent life events, more distal life events that individuals report continue to affect their lives, and chronic stressors. Cumulative stress refers to the combination of operant stress and the experience of traumas that are believed to be so significant that they become permanent sources of stress (e.g., sexual abuse, physical violence). In studies to date, both operant stress and cumulative stress have been 1) stronger predictors of depression than more conventional measures of life events, and 2) shown to significantly mediate the relationships between group membership and depression (Turner et al., 1995; Turner & Lloyd, 1999). As yet, the concepts of operant and cumulative stress have not been used in studies of stress and physical health outcomes.

Renewed attention to exposure to stress also has been spurred by recent work on stress proliferation (Pearlin, Aneshensel, & LeBlanc, 1997). Stress proliferation refers to the propensity for stressors to multiply and to "spill over" into life domains beyond that in which the original stressor occurred. Pearlin et al. refer to the original stressor as a "primary stressor." "Secondary stressors" result from the original stressor, but in other life domains. Stress proliferation occurs when a primary stressor either leads to other primary stressors or generates secondary stressors. Using the experience of providing informal caregiving to AIDS patients as an illustration, Pearlin et al. demonstrate that the primary stressor of taking on caregiving responsibilities often results in other primary stressors as the illness progressed (role overload, role captivity) and in secondary stressors (work strain, constriction of social and leisure activities). The primary and secondary stressors operated cumulatively to increase depressive symptoms. Like the concepts of operant stress and cumulative stress, stress proliferation provides a broader, more detailed view of stress exposure than is obtained using conventional measures of acute and chronic stress. It demonstrates that stress not only increases the risk of depression, but also the risk of additional stressors. As yet, the effect of stress proliferation on physical health has not been examined.

Implicit recognition of life-course patterns clearly underlies recent efforts to broaden the conceptualization and measurement of exposure to stress. The key factor in recent concepts of operant stress, cumulative stress, and stress proliferation is recognition that a focus on purely current conditions does not capture the full range of factors affecting current health and well-being. As discussed in the next section, tools from life-course perspectives might provide additional capacity to understand the dynamics of social factors and illness via explicit attention to timing, duration, and density of stressors.

SOCIAL FACTORS AND ILLNESS: POTENTIAL CONTRIBUTIONS OF LIFE-COURSE PERSPECTIVES

It is the thesis of this chapter that life-course perspectives have the potential to greatly enrich the study of social factors and illness. For purposes of illustration, three specific issues that integrate life-course principles and methods with important research issues in the study of social factors and illness will be examined. Because there has been little research that merges life-course perspectives with mainstream medical sociology/psychology, discussion will focus primarily on the *potential* contributions of life-course research for understanding the social antecedents of health and illness.

Trajectories as Pathways of Vulnerability and Resilience

As noted previously, trajectories are long-term patterns of experience in one or more life domain. Before turning to the potential of trajectories to inform our understanding of health and illness, a few conceptual and methodologic issues need to be briefly reviewed. Most importantly, two general approaches have been used to define and analyze trajectories.

The *aggregated approach* is based on construction of trajectories that best describe long-term patterns of stability and change for a sample. Consider the hypothetical example of a representative sample of persons age 65 and older at baseline who are interviewed five times, at two-year intervals. Study investigators want to identify long-term patterns of disability, impairments to Activities of Daily Living (ADL), and determine if those patterns are predicted by a set of social risk factors. Using the aggregated approach, a single trajectory that best describes the pattern of ADL impairment in the sample over the nine years of the study is generated. An analysis of latent growth curves, conducted in a hierarchical linear modeling framework, would be the best option for identifying the aggregated trajectory for the sample and its predictors (e.g., Bryk & Raudenbush, 1992). This technique involves two stages of analysis. In the first, the trajectory that best fits the sample data is identified; the trajectory takes the form of a line that best describes the ADL scores over time for the sample as a whole. In the second stage, a set of independent variables is entered. An independent variable is statistically significant to the extent that it is associated with differences in the intercept or slope of the aggregate trajectory. For example, if gender is a significant predictor of the disability trajectory, either the intercepts or the slopes (or both) of the trajectory differ for men and women.

In contrast, the *disaggregated approach* involves the identification of several distinctive patterns of change and stability within the sample. The trajectories can be formed either by hand coding of each sample member's trajectory or by using computer programming to implement a set of decision rules developed by the investigator. In the example above, investigators may observe several distinct patterns of change and stability in ADL scores—for example, consistently high levels of ADL impairment (a chronic disability trajectory), consistent absence of ADL impairments (a trajectory of no disability), a period of no ADL impairments followed by an increase in them (a disability onset trajectory), a period of no ADL impairments followed by an increase in them and a subsequent return to no ADL impairments (a disability onset and recovery trajectory). Because these trajectories are discrete categories, a categorical form of analysis (e.g., cluster analysis, multinomial logistic regression) must be used to examine the relationships between the disability trajectories and social risk factors.

Both approaches have advantages and disadvantages—and, importantly, both are more labor-intense than more conventional analytic methods. The major advantage of the aggregated approach is that hierarchical linear models offer a more sophisticated form of statistical modeling than those appropriate for the disaggregated approach. The advantages of the disaggregated approach are that the discrete trajectories are more intuitively appealing and highly specific comparisons can be made that are not possible using hierarchical linear modeling and related techniques (e.g., the investigator can identify variables that distinguish between those who recover after the onset of disability and those who do not). A final advantage of the aggregated approach is that trajectories of predictors (e.g., stress trajectories) can be used to predict trajectories of illness (e.g., trajectories of depressive symptoms).

Health Trajectories as Outcomes

The example above illustrated health trajectories as the dependent variables in studies of social factors and health. Health trajectories can be identified over varying time intervals (e.g., patterns of symptoms over days or weeks, trajectories depicting health during adulthood). Trajectories that cover large segments of the life course are well-suited to answering questions about the illness experiences that individuals bring to late life. In cross-sectional and short-term longitudinal studies of older adults, "health histories" are a potentially important source of unmeasured heterogeneity that may be related to current and future health status. That is, two older adults who are identical in terms of current status (e.g., have no ADL impairments), but who have different life-course patterns of health and illness, may be at differential risk for the onset of specific chronic illnesses, disability, or death.

Analyses of health trajectories that span shorter time intervals can also be informative. Studies of the effects of social factors on illness course and outcome is an important but understudied issue. Trajectories spanning months or years of an illness provide a potentially important way of identifying complex patterns of chronicity, recovery/remission, and relapse. Social and clinical factors can be assessed in terms of their power to predict different illness trajectories.

Earlier in this chapter, I noted several ways of conceptualizing the characteristics of trajectories. Each of these carries the potential to yield important information about social factors and illness. The *timing* of health transitions (e.g., the age at which they occur) may have important consequences for illness course. The illness course is also likely to be *duration* dependent. For example, in the course of clinical depression, some evidence suggests that the likelihood of recovery increases with time for approximately six months; after that, however, the likelihood of recovery falls off sharply (e.g., Keller, Lavori, & Rice, 1986;

Wells, Stewart, & Hays, 1989). The *sequencing* of health transitions also may be important for the outcome of an illness episode. For example, cognitive impairment is associated with poorer outcome for a number of health conditions (e.g., George, Landerman, Blazer, & Anthony, 1991). Thus, health trajectories in which cognitive impairment occurs after the onset of other chronic conditions may be less problematic than those in which cognitive impairment develops prior to the onset of other chronic conditions. Finally, the *density* of health transitions may be important for understanding illness outcome. It is well known that comorbid illnesses are associated with poorer outcome (e.g., Katz, 1996). In previous research, however, comorbidity has been determined by the presence of other illnesses at the time that the health condition of interest is measured. Little attention is paid to the onset of new health problems after the baseline assessment. The concept of density reminds us that multiple transitions may occur in a relatively short period of time and that the temporal concentration of multiple transitions can have important consequences.

Although there have been numerous studies of health transitions, studies of health trajectories have been rare and virtually all of them appeared in the last decade. Studies using the aggregated approach are more common than those using the disaggregated approach. Some examples may further illustrate the potential importance of health trajectories for understanding the relationships between social factors and health. Using data from three waves of the Children of the National Longitudinal Surveys of Youth, McLeod and Shanahan (1996) examined the relationship between poverty and trajectories of children's mental health. Latent growth curve analysis (LGCA) was used to depict the trajectory of mental health symptoms over five years. The amount of time the children lived in poverty was examined as a predictor of mental health trajectories. The results indicated that persistent poverty was associated with accelerating increases in mental health symptoms. Trajectories of disability in late life have been examined by several investigators; one of these studies will be summarized here. Mendes de Leon and colleagues (1997) used data from two EPESE (Established Populations for Epidemiologic Studies of the Elderly) sites, one in the northeast and one in the south, to examine the course of disability over a seven- to nine-year interval and determine if there were significant differences between blacks and whites. The aggregate trajectory that best fit both samples was one of "functional decline followed by recovery." This finding alone is important as it debunks the usual stereotype of late life as a time of monotonic declines in functional capacity. For both sites, blacks were more likely than whites to experience significant functional declines. However, when SES was controlled, this race difference was reduced in the northeast sample and eliminated in the southern sample.

Studies using the disaggregated approach to depict health trajectories are rare. Two studies illustrate this approach. Using data from the Terman men, covering 40 years (with eight times of measurement), Clipp, Pavalko, and Elder (1992) identified five major trajectories for physical illness and six for mental illness: stable good health, stable poor health, improving health over time, declining health, and fluctuating levels of health. These trajectories were related in predictable ways to specific illnesses, self-reported energy and vitality, and alcohol use.

Similarly, Singer, Ryff, Carr, and Magee (1998) used data from a subset of women in the Wisconsin Longitudinal Study to identify four trajectories of mental health, which they labeled as healthy, depressed, vulnerable, and resilient pathways. "Healthy" women had low levels of life-course stress and consistently high levels of mental health. "Depressed" women experienced both high levels of stress and high levels of depression over time. "Vulnerable" women were those who reported little stress, but had high levels of depression across time. "Resilient" women experienced high levels of stress over time, but consistently reported few depressive symptoms. Their elegant analysis profiles these four groups in terms of education and occupational characteristics, personality traits, and social relationships (including marriage and parenthood).

It is interesting to note that two sets of investigators who initially used aggregate trajectories later turned to disaggregated trajectories for more fine-grained analyses. Maddox and Clark (1992) used LGCA to examine the trajectories of functional impairment in approximately 2700 older persons in the Longitudinal Retirement History Study. In a subsequent paper, however, they expressed the desire for more detailed comparisons than those available in LGCA and relied on event history analysis to identify race and gender differences in the timing of disability onset (Maddox, Clark, & Steinhauser, 1994). Crystal and Sambamoorthi (1996) used data from nine time points to examine the course of physical functioning among a sample of AIDS patients. They first used HLM to produce an aggregate trajectory for the sample. The results suggested a month-to-month worsening of functional status over time. Concerned that a single trajectory might not do justice to the heterogeneity in the sample, they then reanalyzed the data using disaggregated trajectories. These results indicated that the most common trajectory was a course of worsening functional status—but a course that was variable and episodic rather than characterized by consistent decline. They caution readers against assuming that sample patterns translate to individuals and discuss the clinical implications of relying on aggregated data to guide expectations of illness course. These studies suggest that disaggregated trajectories provide a level of detail unavailable in aggregated trajectories. However, the choice of aggregated or disaggregated trajectories is probably best made on the basis of the research question under investigation.

Clearly, health trajectories hold substantial promise for addressing research questions about the role of social factors in health and illness that cannot otherwise be studied. However, there is one important limitation of studies in which health trajectories are used as dependent variables. Precisely because health trajectories cover long periods of time, it is difficult to maintain temporal clarity between them and the independent variables that might be expected to account for them.

In general, temporal clarity and, hence, causal inference is restricted to the relationships between health trajectories and independent variables that are fixed characteristics of sample members (e.g., race, sex) or were measured at baseline. For example, although baseline levels of stress that predict subsequent health trajectories might be a legitimate causal claim, levels of stress observed at subsequent test dates would have occurred *after* the starting point for the health trajectory. Therefore, it would not be clear whether stress was playing a causal role in the form of the health trajectory or, vice-versa, whether health conditions had a causal role in subsequent patterns of stress. Thus, it is not an accident that studies of health trajectories to date have included few independent variables other than fixed characteristics of sample members.

Trajectories of Risk Factors as Predictors

In addition to treating health trajectories as outcomes, it is also possible to construct trajectories of social risk or protective factors and to then use those trajectories to predict specific health outcomes. Again, either aggregated or disaggregated trajectories can be used in this fashion. When trajectories are used as independent rather than dependent variables, statistical analyses are simpler and more familiar estimation techniques can be used (e.g., conventional regression analysis).

Given this, it is surprising that so little attention has been paid to trajectories of risk factors in studies of health and longevity. From a theoretical perspective, risk factor trajectories are ideally equipped to address an especially important and neglected issue: length of exposure to risk factors. It is a core principle of epidemiologic research that one must not only ascertain information about current exposure to risk factors for illness, but also measure the length or intensity of exposure to those risk factors. For example, if epidemiologists had been content to ask study participants if they had smoked a cigarette today (or even in the last year), it is doubtful that the relationship between smoking and heart and lung disease would have been observed. It is long-term exposure to cigarette smoking that poses significant health risks. Thus, epidemiologists developed the concept of "pack years" of smoking to capture the length or intensity of individuals' exposure to this risk factor. An alternative technique would have been to construct trajectories of cigarette smoking. Social and behavioral scientists have been remarkably sanguine about measuring social factors that are hypothesized to affect health in ways that are comparable to knowing whether their respondents smoked a cigarette today (or, in the case of standardized life events scales, in the past year). There are impressive bodies of research demonstrating that factors such as SES and supportive social ties are robustly related to morbidity and mortality. But virtually nothing is known about long-term patterns of socioeconomic achievement or social relationships and their effects on health outcomes. This is undoubtedly an important source of unmeasured heterogeneity in health research (e.g., some individuals who currently report multiple satisfying social relationships will have a long history of such relationships; others will have established successful social bonds only recently).

With the exception of fixed characteristics of individuals (e.g., race, sex), almost all social factors hypothesized to affect health could be examined, given suitable data, in the form of trajectories. Socioeconomic status could be conceptualized and measured as socioeconomic history. Rather than focusing solely on current marital status, marital history trajectories could be related to health outcomes. Long-term patterns of social networks and social support may be related to health in different or stronger ways than is now known. Indeed, several authors have based post hoc explanations for unexpected relationships between social support and health on the lack of long-term longitudinal data. For example, some authors have observed a positive rather than negative relationship between social support and illness. Rather than concluding that supportive social ties place one at risk of illness, they suggest that we are seeing the "tail end" of a long process in which persons who are ill and need social support are receiving it from friends and relatives.

Trajectories of stress could therefore be constructed to determine how long-term exposure to stressors affects health. There is increasing evidence that employment benefits health (e.g., Pugliesi, 1995; Ross & Mirowsky, 1995). But in what form(s)? It is unlikely, for example, that those benefits kick in on the first day on the job. Examining employment trajectories could help to identify the amount of time in the labor force required before the health-promoting benefits of employment are experienced. Similarly, there now is strong evidence that attending religious services on a regular basis benefits health and longevity with a wide variety of other risk factors statistically controlled (e.g., Idler, 1987; Koenig, Hays, Larson, George, Cohen et al., 1999; Strawbridge, Cohen, Shema, & Kaplan, 1997). Again, it is doubtful that attending services for two weeks has the same benefits as regular attendance over a period of years, but until long-term patterns of religious participation (and non-participation) are carefully examined, we cannot know the point at which health benefits are discernable. The same logic could be used to determine if and when ceasing regular religious service attendance leads to increased risk of illness.

Thus, trajectory characteristics have the potential to further our understanding of the complex relationships between social factors and health. In terms of *timing,* the age at which specific transitions in social factors may affect health. In line with attachment theory (e.g., Bowlby, 1980), for example, loss of a parent at very young ages may have stronger effects on health during adulthood than loss of a parent at later ages. *Duration,* of course, is the essence of length of exposure and most of the above examples concerned the amount of time one must be exposed to a social factor to experience its benefits or liabilities for health. The *sequencing* of transitions in the context of a larger trajectory also may affect health. For example, the sequencing of marriage and parenthood may have implications for the health of the mother and/or child. Finally, the *density* of transitions also may have health consequences—for example, the experience of multiple loss events in a relatively short period of time may have greater effects on health-related outcomes than if those same events are experienced over a longer interval.

As noted above, very little research has examined the effects of risk factor trajectories on health outcomes. In fact, I am aware of only one study that has taken this approach. (There are a number of studies of transition sequencing and density in early adulthood, but the outcomes in those studies have related to socio-economic achievement and marital stability rather than health.) Barrett (1999) examined the effects of marital history on two mental health outcomes: depression and anxiety. She identified nine primary marital trajectories that were suffi-ciently common to permit multivariate analysis: 1) never married; 2) continuously married; 3) married and then divorced/separated; 4) married, divorced, remarried; 5) married, divorced, married, divorced; 6) married and then widowed; 7) married, widowed, and then remarried; 8) married, widowed, remarried, then widowed; and 9) married, divorced, remarried, and then widowed. Space limitations preclude detailed description of the findings of this study, including the significant gender and race differences observed. Two findings that I believe highlight the impor-tance of marital history trajectories will be briefly summarized.

First, Barrett (1999) observed that women who had remarried after a divorce had significantly higher levels of depression than women who were continuously married. This relationship held true regardless of how long the women had been remarried (and controlling on other risk factors for depression). This single finding demonstrates the added value of examining marital history rather than marital status in relation to depression. If marital status were the social factor examined, as is typical in studies of social factors and illness, these two groups of women would be included in the same category of "currently married." There would be no way to know about the unmeasured heterogeneity in this group that is due to different marital trajectories that lead to being currently married.

Second, there were interesting differences between the women in the once-widowed (excluding the trajectory that included one divorce and one widowhood) and twice widowed trajectories (Barrett, 1999). Twice-widowed women exhibited higher levels of depression and anxiety than their once-widowed counterparts. Mental health symptoms dissipated more quickly, however, among twice-widowed women than among first-time widows. This finding demonstrates that *levels* of symptoms are related differently to marital history than is *duration* of symptoms.

Risk Factor Trajectories Predicting Health Trajectories

It is possible to combine trajectories of independent and dependent variables in the same analysis using hierarchical linear modeling and related techniques.

Given the small volume of trajectory-based research in medical sociology/ psychology, it is not surprising that almost no attention has been paid to including trajectories on "both sides" of predictive models. However, there is reason to believe that such investigations may have substantial payoff. Ge, Lorenz, Conger, Elder, & Simons (1994) examined the relationship between trajectories of stressful life events and symptoms of depression over four years in a sample of adolescents, and Lynch and George (in press) examined the relationship between trajectories of loss-related events and depressive symptoms over five years in a sample of older adults. Both studies reported strong relationships between the two trajectories: the *rate* of occurrence of life events predicted the *rate* of increase in depressive symptoms over time. It thus appears that depressive symptoms are highly sensitive to the pacing of acute stressors. Clearly this technique could be used with other risk factor and health trajectories and would generate new information about the sensitivity of health to changes in risk factors.

Tracing Long-Term Pathways: Non-Trajectory Approaches

The impact of social factors on long-term patterns of health and illness can be studied only if trajectory-based analyses are used. However, there are valid non-trajectory approaches to studying the long-term pathways by which social factors affect health. Although considerable space has been devoted to the contention that trajectory-based analysis has substantial potential for furthering our understanding of social factors and health, other techniques that do justice to life-course principles also merit consideration.

Given data that cover long periods of time, several analytic strategies that do not involve trajectories can be used to answer specific types of questions about the long-term antecedents of health outcomes. Two approaches in particular have yielded important contributions: time series analysis and path analysis.

By time series analysis, I refer to analytic designs in which the same variables are related to each other over multiple time points (a minimum of three, but more than that are preferable) (e.g., Rossi & Freeman, 1989). An example will demonstrate the utility of time series analysis for understanding social factors and health. It is well established that subjective perceptions of social support adequacy are more strongly related to health outcomes, especially depression and self-rated health, than other social support dimensions (e.g., instrumental support, size of social network) (e.g., Lin, Dean, & Ensel, 1986; Wethington & Kessler, 1986). Critics have argued that these relationships are inflated because both are based largely on affect (e.g., Henderson, 1984; McLean & Link, 1994). Thus, one might expect strong relationships between depression and subjective social support because depressed people will perceive their lives, including their support networks, in negative terms. I have previously referred to this as the "contamination hypothesis" (George, Blazer, Hughes, & Fowler, 1989).

One way to address this criticism is to use time series analysis to model the relationships between subjective social support and depression over time. This analysis strategy can answer two questions: Are both variables equally stable over time? and Is there a dominant direction of influence between the two variables? Two studies have addressed these questions using time series analysis. Holahan and Moos (1991) examined the relationships among acute stressors, subjective social support, and depressive symptoms over a four-year interval (four times of measurement) among a sample of community-dwelling older adults. Blazer, Hughes, and George (1992) examined the relationship between subjective social support and depressive symptoms over one year (three times of measurement; six-month intervals between test dates) among a sample of clinically depressed middle-aged and older adults, all of whom were hospitalized at baseline. The studies yielded consistent results: 1) in both, perceptions of social support were more stable over time than were depressive symptoms, and 2) the dominant direction of influence was from subjective social support to depression, rather than the opposite. These findings represent a strong rebuttal to the contamination hypotheses. There are certainly robust relationships between subjective social support and depression, but they do not change in tandem and there is a clear path of causal influence that refutes the contamination hypothesis.

This is an illustration of the potential of time series analysis to provide important information about the interrelationships among variables over multiple times of measurement. It is surprising how rarely time series analysis has been used in the study of social factors and illness. Undoubtedly, the lack of data from a sufficient number of time points is one obstacle to its use. I would like to see it used more frequently, especially with data covering large segments of the life course to examine continuities and discontinuities over time, as well as for identifying the social conditions that lead to stability and change.

A second, much more commonly employed technique for tracing life-course patterns is path analysis. Using path analysis, investigators develop and test a model that includes stages of successively more proximal predictors of an outcome of interest. The stages of predictors can be based on conceptual definitions of relative causal proximity, on temporal assessments of the variables of interest, or both. When data permit, path analysis can be a powerful tool for tracing the pathways from temporally distant to temporally proximal predictors of outcomes. Typically, both conceptually and temporally proximate predictors have stronger effects on the dependent variable than more distal predictors. This does not imply that the distal factors are unimportant, however: if one wants understand the complex processes that underlie the linkages between social factors and illness, all components of the causal chain are important.

Much, perhaps most life-course research is based on path analytic models. Some of the extant research base focuses on health outcomes. Space limitations preclude a comprehensive survey of that research. Studies of the conditions under which traumas experienced relatively early in life have persisting effects on physical or mental health provide examples of the contributions of life-course perspectives to our understanding of health later in life. Evidence is most plentiful for two types of traumas: childhood traumas and combat experience.

There is substantial evidence that a variety of childhood traumas—especially parental divorce, physical abuse, and sexual abuse—are significantly related to mental health problems during adulthood (e.g., Harris, Brown, & Bifulco, 1990; Kessler & Magee, 1994; Winfield, George, Swartz, & Blazer, 1990). Similarly, combat exposure during war is a risk factor for mental health problems and, to a lesser extent, physical health problems throughout adulthood (e.g., Elder & Clipp, 1989; Kulka, Schlenger, Fairbank, Hough, Jordan et al., 1990). Evidence of the persisting health effects of early traumatic experiences is itself testimony to life-course principles. Even more useful, however, is what life-course studies have taught us about the pathways by which early traumas are linked to mental health decades later. Research on both childhood traumas and combat experience suggests that the effects of those traumas on health are mediated by two types of subsequent experience: the immediate aftermath of the trauma and the accumulation of post-trauma resources (George, 1999).

The Immediate Aftermath of Trauma

There is considerable evidence that the ways that early traumas are handled are related to the likelihood that the trauma will generate a pathway of persisting vulnerability. For example, the extent to which parental divorce affects subsequent mental health is largely determined by the quality of care the child receives after the divorce (e.g., Harris et al., 1990) and economic hardship resulting from the divorce (e.g., Landerman, George, & Blazer, 1991). Other investigators have identified a cognitive style that is often adopted by children who are victims of abuse. This style, sometimes referred to as "emotional reactivity," is characterized by hypersensitivity to actual or implied criticism and a tendency to anger easily and out of proportion to the situation. This cognitive style is associated with persistent interpersonal stress and mental health problems in adulthood (e.g., Rutter & Rutter, 1993). Life-course studies of combat stress also provide evidence that what happens immediately after military service affects the likelihood of later mental health problems. In particular, veterans who do not have problems securing employment, who obtain higher status jobs, and who have lower levels of overall life stress in the years immediately following military service exhibit better physical and mental health in middle and late life (e.g., Elder & Clipp, 1989; Elder, Shanahan, & Clipp, 1994).

Accumulation of Post-Trauma Resources

There also is substantial evidence that the accumulation of social resources after early trauma can lessen the risk of subsequent mental illness. When victims of childhood traumas can accumulate resources during adulthood—especially socioeconomic achievement and high quality interpersonal relationships—the effects of those traumas are reduced or eliminated (e.g., McLeod, 1991). Similarly, accumulation of social resources reduces the effects of combat stress on subsequent physical and mental health. Among combat veterans, stable careers, higher levels of educational attainment, and higher income reduce the impact of war stress on subsequent health (e.g., Elder & Clipp, 1989; Elder et al., 1994). Establishing supportive relationships, especially high-quality marriage, after military service also decreases the risk of later health problems (e.g., Elder & Clipp, 1989; Kulka et al., 1990).

Path analysis, as a method of tracing the effects of distal and proximal predictors on health, is familiar to researchers studying social factors and illness. Given this, there appear to be two primary obstacles to increased attention to life-course patterns and later health. First, investigators need to develop conceptual models of the social antecedents of health and illness that include temporally distant predictors, which will be discussed in the next section. Second, longitudinal data are needed on larger segments of the life course and on both health and factors expected to affect health, an issue which is taken up in the final section.

Social Selection as Life-Course Processes

Investigators interested in the relationships between social factors and health implicitly subscribe to a social causation model. That is, nearly all research on this topic focuses on the ways in which social factors either place individuals at risk of illness or protect them from it. The alternate postulate of social selection is viewed as either a competing hypothesis to be ruled out or as a methodological nuisance that precludes the firm causal inferences desired. There is no question that social selection poses problems for inferences of social causation. Virtually all of the social factors that have been demonstrated to be robustly related to morbidity and mortality (e.g., SES, social stress, social support) are phenomena that are not amenable to experimental manipulation (i.e., they cannot be randomly assigned to individuals). Consequently, one can never be absolutely sure that the relationships between social factors and health are not the result of selection factors that determine SES, exposure to stress, social support, and other relevant risk factors. Conventional ways of dealing with this problem include 1) statistically controlling variables that may confound the relationships between social factors and health, and 2) making statistical adjustments for specific and known selection effects.

In contrast, life-course scholars tend to take a different view of selection processes. Rather than considering them to be methodologic nuisances, they take these processes as things to be modeled, as processes that characterize or underlie pathways of vulnerability and resilience. In other words, social selection is a substantive focus of life-course research, and life-course scholars would argue that these selection processes should be empirically examined rather than statistically controlled or "adjusted for." Thus, life-course perspectives literally transform social selection from a methodologic problem to a valuable topic for scientific inquiry. Two areas of research demonstrate the utility of examining selection processes associated with differences in social risk factors.

Antecedents of Social Support

First, a limited research base addresses the precursors of social networks and social support. Pearlin (1989) argues that variations in the availability of social support are a result of both contemporary and developmental experiences. With regard to developmental experience, relationships in the family of orientation play a critical role in developing the skills, motivations, and expectations that individuals carry forward to broader social contexts (see also Sarason, Pierce, & Sarason, 1990). During adulthood, social relationships develop largely in the context of social location, especially via role settings—a postulate supported by the empirical work of Turner and Marino (1994), among others.

Lin, Dean, and Ensel (1986) also emphasize the importance of social structure in the availability of social support. One of their primary theses is that, although subjective perceptions of support are the most powerful predictors of health and well-being, the *origins* of those perceptions are structural. Their work documents the strong links between detailed characteristics of individuals' social networks (e.g., size, density, composition) and perceptions of support availability and adequacy.

Using longitudinal data (two times of measurement, seven years apart), Stoller and Pugliesi (1991) examined the effects of older adults' changes in health on both receipt of social support and structural characteristics of the social network. They report that the onset or worsening of health problems increased the amount of social support received by older sample members, but had no effect on the social network. These results are contrary to the hypothesis of some scholars that increased need for social support will tend to deplete support provision and/or reduce the social network to those persons willing to make long-term commitments of unbalanced support. This hypothesis, however, may be true for other groups or illnesses (e.g., depressed people may be interpersonally difficult and drive away sources of support).

This limited research suggests that it is possible to identify antecedents of social support. None of this research, however, has used life-course perspectives to examine long-term patterns of social support. More fine-grained studies that focus on social ties across the life course would almost certainly provide important information about the life experiences associated with variations in the availability of social support.

Selection Processes and the Effects of Combat Exposure

In their work on the health effects of combat stress with World War II veterans, Elder and colleagues have consistently paid attention to pre-military

experiences and characteristics associated with combat experience and its consequences. They identified three important pre-military characteristics that were
associated with either exposure to combat or with increased risk of health
problems after combat exposure. First, SES prior to induction in the military was
significantly related to the likelihood of combat exposure (Elder et al., 1994).
Compared to their more advantaged peers, men of low SES were more likely to be
exposed to combat. Even in wars with nearly universal participation by men of
certain ages, such as World War II, SES is a strong predictor of the odds of
experiencing combat. A broad body of research indicates that low SES is a risk
factor for mental health problems in general (e.g., Kessler, 1979; Link & Phelan,
1995; Pearlin et al., 1981). This research suggests that, during war, low SES also
predicts exposure to combat stress, which is a predictor of mental health problems
independent of SES. Second, although the military typically will not accept men
with obvious psychiatric histories, Elder et al. (1994) found that post-military
mental health problems were more common among veterans with a pre-military
history of psychological problems—a pattern also observed for Vietnam War
veterans (Kulka et al., 1990).

Third, age of entry into the military also affected the likelihood of post-
military mental health problems (Clipp & Elder, 1996). Older age at entry
was associated with greater life-course disruptions (specifically, higher rates of
divorce and lower levels of socioeconomic achievement) which, in turn, increased
the likelihood of long-term mental health problems. Interestingly, older age at
induction was associated with mental health problems despite the fact that older
inductees had higher levels of education and were less likely to be exposed to
combat than their younger peers.

Hopefully, these examples illustrate the importance of studying rather than
controlling away or adjusting for selection processes. We have learned much about
health and longevity by focusing on contemporaneous and recent social factors.
But we lack critical information about how and why individuals come to be at
differential risk of illness. Temporally, proximate risk factors do not emerge
full-blown at the time they are measured; nor can we assume that these factors
represent characteristics that have been stable across the life course. A more
realistic assumption is that life-course experiences generate trajectories of vulnerability and resilience that culminate in different levels of health and well-being. If
this assumption is taken seriously, selection processes are an integral part of these
pathways and merit increased empirical attention.

FINAL THOUGHTS

The purpose of this chapter has been to demonstrate the benefits of integrating life-course principles and methods into the study of aging, social factors,
and illness. The life-course perspective is one that is best used in conjunction with
other social and behavioral paradigms. It is not so much a separate research topic

as it is a set of conceptual and methodologic tools for enriching our understanding of the many domains in which human lives unfold.

There appear to be strong, "natural" links between life-course perspectives and the study of social factors and illness. The notion of process has long been a part of the lexicon of research in this tradition (e.g., the stress process, illness course and outcome). Life-course perspectives augment this process orientation by suggesting that even longer views of human lives will provide valuable information about health and longevity.

Without question, the greatest obstacle to integrating life-course perspectives into the study of social factors and illness is the lack of data covering long periods of time. A number of major longitudinal studies are now reaching the point of covering multiple decades of participants' lives (e.g., the Longitudinal Surveys of Labor Market Experience, the Wisconsin Longitudinal Study). Unfortunately, these data sets typically include limited data on health, although additional information about health is often being added over time, as the individuals in these samples age. Moreover, these data sources generally provide excellent opportunities for constructing trajectories of risk factors. Thus, some data resources for this purpose already exist or will eventually mature to the point of being useful.

In the meantime, a variety of interim steps can be taken to further our understanding of the life-course antecedents of health. Although the validity of retrospective data is always suspect, judicious use of retrospective accounts can provide a wealth of information with which to explore life-course issues. Although it is best to avoid retrospective accounts of highly subjective variables, one can have more confidence in the accuracy of reports of relatively objective phenomena. Marital, occupational, and military histories are examples of retrospective data that is worth obtaining. In addition, whenever possible, dates should be obtained for important events and life changes (e.g., if marital status changes between test dates in a longitudinal study, obtain the date of the status change). The availability of dates opens the doors to types of statistical analysis that cannot otherwise be conducted—including studies of "time till" an event (e.g., using functional status measures to predict time till institutionalization), and analyses of duration dependence (e.g., how the odds of dying change with duration in specific health states).

Finally, life-course perspectives take us a bit closer to studying the "whole person" because the emphasis is on the whole life—a characteristic that some scholars have described as "person-centered" rather than "variable-centered" (Bergman & Magnusson, 1997; Singer et al., 1998). Although some level of aggregation is a prerequisite of scientific inquiry, the closer we can come to incorporating the complexities and dynamics of individuals lives, the better our science will be. I believe that life-course perspectives will greatly enrich our understanding of the precursors of health and illness. The validity of this belief awaits additional empirical inquiry—but it is a belief worth testing.

REFERENCES

Aneshensel, C. S. (1992). Social stress: Theory and research. *Annual Review of Sociology, 18,* 18-38.

Avison, W. R., & Turner, R. J. (1988). Stressful life events and depressive symptoms: Disaggregating the effects of acute stressors and chronic strains. *Journal of Health and Social Behavior, 29,* 253-264.

Barrett, A. M. (1999). *The effects of marital history on mental health: A life course perspective.* Doctoral dissertation, Duke University, Durham, North Carolina.

Bergman, L. R., & Magnusson, D. (1997). A person-oriented approach in research on developmental psychopathology. *Development and Psychopathology, 9,* 291-319.

Blazer, D. G., Hughes, D. C., & George, L. K. (1992). Age and impaired subjective support: Predictors of depressive symptoms at one-year follow-up. *Journal of Nervous and Mental Disease, 180,* 172-178.

Bowlby, J. (1980). *Attachment and loss: Volume III: Loss, sadness, and depression.* New York: Basic Books.

Bryk, A., & Raudenbush, S. (1992). *Hierarchical linear models: Applications and data analysis methods.* Newbury Park, CA: Sage.

Clipp, E. C., & Elder, G. H. Jr. (1996). The aging veteran of World War II: Psychiatric and life course insights. In P.E. Ruskin & J.A. Talbott (Eds.), *Aging and posttraumatic stress disorder* (pp. 119-143). Washington, D.C.: American Psychiatric Press.

Clipp, E. C., Pavalko, E. K., & Elder, G. H. Jr. (1992). Trajectories of health: In concept and empirical pattern. *Behavior, Health, and Aging, 2,* 159-177.

Cohen, L. H. (Ed.) (1988). *Life events and psychological functioning.* Beverly Hills: Sage.

Crystal, S., & Sambamoorthi, U. (1996). Functional impairment trajectories among persons with symptomatic HIV disease: A hierarchical linear models approach. *Health Services Research, 31,* 467-486.

Elder, G. H. Jr., & Clipp, E. C. (1989). Combat experience and emotional health: Impairment and resilience in later life. *Journal of Personality, 57,* 311-341.

Elder, G. H. Jr., George, L. K., & Shanahan, M. J. (1996). Psychosocial stress over the life course. In H. B. Kaplan (Ed.), *Psychosocial stress: Perspectives on structure, theory, life course, and methods* (pp. 247-292). San Diego: Academic Press.

Elder, G. H. Jr., Shanahan, M. J., & Clipp, E. C. (1994). When war comes to men's lives: Life course patterns in family, work, and health. *Psychology and Aging, 9* (special issue), 5-16.

Ensel, W. M. (1991). "Important" life events and depression among older adults. *Journal of Aging and Health, 3,* 546-566.

Ge, X., Lorenz, F. O., Conger, R. D., Elder, G. H. Jr., & Simons, R. L. (1994). Trajectories of stressful life events and depressive symptoms during adolescence. *Journal of Health and Social Behavior, 30,* 467-483.

George, L. K. (1993). Sociological perspectives on life transitions. *Annual Review of Sociology, 19,* 353-373.

George, L. K. (1999). Life course perspectives on mental health. In C. S. Aneshensel & J. C. Phelan (Eds.), *Handbook of the Sociology of Mental Health* (pp. 565-583). San Diego: Academic Press.

George, L. K., Blazer, D. G., Hughes, D. C., & Fowler, N. (1989). Social support and the outcome of major depression. *British Journal of Psychiatry, 154,* 475-485.

George, L. K., Landerman, R., Blazer, D. G., & Anthony, J. A. (1991). Cognitive impairment: Prevalence, correlates, and consequences. In L. N. Robins & D. A. Regier (Eds.), *Psychiatric Disorders in America* (pp. 291-327). New York: Free Press.

Granovetter, M. S. (1973). The strength of weak ties. *American Journal of Sociology, 78,* 1360-1380.

Harris, T., Brown, G. W., & Bifulco, A. (1990). Loss of parent in childhood and adult psychiatric disorder: A tentative overall model. *Development and Psychopathology, 2,* 311-328.

Henderson, A. S. (1984). Interpreting the evidence on social support. *Social Psychiatry, 19,* 49-52.

Holahan, C. J., & Moos, R. H. (1991). Life stressors, personal and social resources, and depression: A 4-year structural model. *Journal of Abnormal Psychology, 100,* 31-38.

Idler, E. L. (1987). Religious involvement and the health of the elderly: Some hypotheses and an initial test. *Social Forces, 66,* 226-238.

Johnson, T. P. (1991). Mental health, social relationships, and social selection: A longitudinal analysis. *Journal of Health and Social Behavior, 32,* 408-423.

Katz, I. R. (1996). On the inseparability of mental and physical health in aged persons: Lessons from depression and medical comorbidity. *American Journal of Geriatric Psychiatry, 4,* 1-16.

Keller, M. B., Lavori, P. W., & Rice, J. (1986). The persistent risk of chronicity in recurrent episodes of nonbipolar major depressive episode: A prospective follow-up. *American Journal of Psychiatry, 143,* 24-28.

Kessler, R. C. (1979). Stress, social status, and psychological distress. *Journal of Health and Social Behavior, 20,* 259-272.

Kessler, R. C., & Magee, W. J. (1994). Childhood family violence and adult recurrent depression. *Journal of Health and Social Behavior, 35,* 13-27.

Koenig, H. G., Hays, J. C., Larson, D. B., George, L. K., Cohen, H. J., McCullough, M. E., Meador, K. G., & Blazer, D. G. (1999). Does religious attendance prolong survival? A six-year follow-up study of 3,968 older adults. *Journal of Gerontology: Medical Sciences, 54A,* M370-M376.

Krause, N. (1986). Social support, stress, and well-being among older adults. *Journal of Gerontology, 41,* 512-519.

Krause, N. (1998). Early parental loss, recent life events, and changes in health among older adults. *Journal of Aging and Health, 10,* 395-421.

Kulka, R. A., Schlenger, W. E., Fairbank, J. A., Hough, R. L., Jordan, B. K., Marmar, C. B., & Weiss, D. S. (1990). *Trauma and the Vietnam war generation: Report of findings from the National Vietnam Veterans Readjustment Study.* New York: Brunner/Mazel.

Landerman, R., George, L. K., & Blazer, D. G. (1991). Adult vulnerability for psychiatric disorders: Interactive effects of negative childhood experiences and recent stress. *Journal of Nervous and Mental Disease, 179,* 656-663.

Lin, N., Dean, A., & Ensel, W. J. (1986). *Social support, life events, and depression.* Orlando: Academic Press.

Link, B. G., & Phelan, J. (1995). Social conditions as fundamental causes of disease. *Journal of Health and Social Behavior, extra issue,* 80-94.

Lynch, S. M., & George, L. K. (in press). Interlocking trajectories of loss-related events and depression among elders. *Journal of Gerontology: Social Sciences.*

Maddox, G. L., & Clark, D. O. (1992). Trajectories of functional impairment in later life. *Journal of Health and Social Behavior, 33,* 114-125.

Maddox, G. L., Clark, D. O., & Steinhauser, K. (1994). Dynamics of functional impairment in late adulthood. *Social Science and Medicine, 38,* 925-936.

McLean, D. E., & Link, B. G. (1994). Unraveling complexity: Strategies to define concepts, measures and research designs in the study of life events and mental health. In W. R. Avison & I. H. Gotlib (Eds.), *Stress and mental health* (pp. 15-42). New York: Plenum.

McLeod, J. D. (1991). Childhood parental loss and adult depression. *Journal of Health and Social Behavior, 32,* 205-220.

McLeod, J. D., & Kessler, R. C. (1990). Socioeconomic status differences in vulnerability to undesirable life events. *Journal of Health and Social Behavior, 31,* 162-172.

McLeod, J. D., & Shanahan, M. J. (1996). Trajectories of poverty and children's mental health. *Journal of Health and Social Behavior, 37,* 207-220.

Mendes de Leon, C. F., Beckett, L. A., Fillenbaum, G. G., Brock, D. B., Branch, L. G., Evans, D. A., & Berkman, L. F. (1997). Black-white differences in risk of becoming disabled and recovering from disability in old age: A longitudinal analysis of two EPESE populations. *American Journal of Epidemiology, 145,* 488-497.

Norris, F. H., & Murrell, S. A. (1987). Older adult family stress and adaptation before and after bereavement. *Journal of Gerontology, 42,* 535-542.

Pearlin, L. I. (1989). The sociological study of stress. *Journal of Health and Social Behavior, 30,* 241-256.

Pearlin L. I., Aneshensel, C. S., & LeBlanc, A. J. (1997). The forms and mechanisms of stress proliferation: The case of AIDS caregivers. *Journal of Health and Social Behavior, 38,* 223-236.

Pearlin, L. I., Lieberman, M. A., Menagham, E. G., & Mullan, J. T. (1981). The stress process. *Journal of Health and Social Behavior, 22,* 337-356.

Pugliesi, K. (1995). Work and well-being: Gender differences in the psychological consequences of employment. *Journal of Health and Social Behavior, 36,* 57-71.

Rindfuss, R. R., Swicegood, C., & Rosenfeld, R. A. (1987). Disorder in the life course: How common and does it matter? *American Sociological Review, 52,* 785-801.

Roberts, B. L., Duncan, R., & Haug, M. (1994). Physical, psychological, and social resources as moderators of the relationship of stress to mental health of the very old. *Journal of Gerontology: Social Sciences, 49,* S35-S43.

Ross, C. E., & Mirowsky, J. (1995). Does employment affect health? *Journal of Health and Social Behavior, 36,* 230-243.

Rossi, P. H,. & Freeman, H. E. (1989). *Evaluation: A systematic approach* (fourth edition). Newbury Park, CA: Sage.

Roxburgh, S. (1996). Gender differences in work and well-being: Effects of exposure and vulnerability. *Journal of Health and Social Behavior, 37,* 265-277.

Rutter, M., & Rutter, M. (1993). *Developing minds: Challenge and continuity across the life span.* New York: Basic Books.

Sarason, B. R., Pierce, G. R., & Sarason, I. G. (1990). Social support: The sense of acceptance and the role of relationships. In B. R. Sarason, G. R. Pierce, & I. G. Sarason (Eds.), *Social support: An interactional view* (pp. 97-129). New York: Wiley.

Schmader, K., Studenski, S., MacMillan, J., Grufferman, S., & Cohen, H. J. (1990). Are stressful life events risk factors for herpes zoster? *Journal of the American Geriatrics Society, 38,* 1188-1194.

Singer, B., Ryff, C. D., Carr, D., & Magee, W. J. (1998). Life histories and mental health: A person-centered strategy. In A. Raftery (Ed.), *Sociological Methodology, 1998* (pp. 312-347). Washington, DC: American Sociological Association.

Stoller, E. P., & Pugliesi, K. L. (1991). Size and effectiveness of informal helping networks: A panel study of older people in the community. *Journal of Health and Social Behavior, 32*, 180-191.

Strawbridge, W. J., Cohen, R. D., Shema, S. J., & Kaplan, G. A. (1997). Frequent attendance at religious services and mortality over 28 years. *American Journal of Public Health, 87*, 957-961.

Thoits, P. A. (1994). Stressors and problem-solving: The individual as psychological activist. *Journal of Health and Social Behavior, 35*, 143-160.

Turner, R. J., & Lloyd, D. A. (1999). The stress process and the social distribution of depression. *Journal of Health and Social Behavior, 40*, 360-376.

Turner, R. J., & Marino, F. (1994). Social support and social structure: A descriptive epidemiology. *Journal of Health and Social Behavior, 35*, 193-212.

Turner, R. J., Wheaton, B., & Lloyd, D. A. (1995). The epidemiology of social stress. *American Sociological Review, 60*, 104-125.

Ulbrich, P. M., Warheit, G. J., & Zimmerman, R. S. (1989). Race, socioeconomic status, and psychological distress: An examination of differential vulnerability. *Journal of Health and Social Behavior, 30*, 131-146.

Waldron, I., Herold, J., Dunn, D., & Staum, R. (1982). Reciprocal effects of health and labor force participation among women: Evidence from two longitudinal studies. *Journal of Occupational Medicine, 24*, 126-132.

Wells, K. B., Stewart, A., & Hays, R. D. (1989). The functioning and well-being of depressed patients: Results from the Medical Outcomes Study. *Journal of the American Medical Association, 262*, 914-919.

Wethington, E., & Kessler, R. C. (1986). Perceived support, received support, and adjustment to stressful life events. *Journal of Health and Social Behavior, 27*, 78-89.

Winfield, I., George, L. K., Swartz, M. S., & Blazer, D. G. (1990). Sexual assault and psychiatric disorders among women in a community sample. *American Journal of Psychiatry, 147*, 335-341.

PART IV

Promises for Social Policy

CHAPTER 7

Rethinking Social Policy: Lessons of a Life-Course Perspective*

Richard A. Settersten, Jr.

This chapter examines the intersection between human development and social policy. It considers the role that social policies play in facilitating or constraining development and in structuring the life course. It shows how greater attention to life-course concepts, principles, and methods might change the ways in which social policies are developed, implemented, evaluated, and reformed. In turn, it suggests that these changes carry significant potential to improve human development and social welfare. The term "social policy" refers to a broad array of policies, programs, interventions, and services tied not only to the federal government, but also to state- and local-level governments and to private organizations and firms. These linkages are demonstrated through examples drawn from the central policies of the American welfare state and a variety of other policies related to education, work, family, and health.[1] While American social policies are used to illustrate these connections, the questions posed here are nonetheless relevant to those of other nations.

The intersection between social policy and the life course draws attention to macro-sociological phenomena—to large, distal forces that impact lives. This view is consistent with recent emphases in the social sciences on the "macro-micro

*Special thanks are due to Tanetta Andersson, Rich Carpiano, and Judy Reardon for their research assistance. I am also indebted to Lisa Dobransky, Amy Wisniewski, and students in my autumn 1998 seminar on "The Life Course" (at Case Western Reserve University) for exploring the relationships between social policy and the life course as part of that seminar.

[1] I will briefly draw on specific policies to illustrate points. Many of these policies are under constant debate, particularly during an election year (2000). As a result, the details of some policies may have changed by the time of publication.

link." The life-course framework also emphasizes this link, as it stresses both proximal and distal social forces that shape the experiences of individuals and groups. These forces guide, and even dictate, the movement of individuals and groups through roles, positions, and statuses. While distal social forces are more difficult to study than proximal ones, they are critical forces to be reckoned with as we struggle to understand and improve human development.

The state and its policies are among the most important of these forces. In fact, there is evidence that lives have become increasingly "institutionalized"— that is, structured by separate institutional spheres (e.g., education, work, and family) and by the state's regulation of these spheres (Settersten, 1999). The life course might even be conceptualized as a series of "status passages" monitored by, and embedded in the structure of, the state (Heinz, 1998; see also Mayer & Müller, 1986). From this vantagepoint, the social processes that move people between state-regulated positions, and the experiences individuals have as they move between these positions, must be better understood. Besides state regulation, institutionalization also occurs through established pathways in educational settings and work organizations.

The institutionalization thesis assumes that these forces, while often constraining lives, are largely positive. These forces provide a blueprint for life, and they integrate experiences across life spheres and foster continuity in experiences over time. Ultimately, these functions enhance the development of the self. Of course, these forces may also reduce the range of potential options available to individuals and groups, thereby "canalizing" lives over time. Yet, in limiting a set of pathways, and in keeping individuals focused on specific tracks, these restrictive processes might maximize potential gains and minimize potential declines.

While such arguments can be made, many developmental scientists consider these constraints negative and even oppressive. These restrictions are problematic because individuals, and entire classes of people, are systematically denied certain options or are forced onto negative pathways with little or no opportunity to leave them. Either way, one thing is certain: The life course can no longer be portrayed as if it exists in isolation of social policies. To the contrary, social policies likely lend the life course much of its shape and presumably equip it with a standard set of expectations and meanings.

In addition to the debate about institutionalization, two other debates on the rhythm of the life course in modern societies are pertinent here (see Settersten, 1999). One debate relates to the "chronologization" of lives—that is, the degree to which time and age are central dimensions of individual and social life. The other debate relates to the "standardization" of lives—that is, the degree to which central life transitions, and larger pathways through education, work, and family, are regular and predictable. Taken together, these three debates have led some scholars to argue that the life course, as a whole, is rigidly structured and experienced. Others have argued the opposite: that the life course is, or at least has the potential to become, flexibly structured and experienced. Social policies have affected and been affected by these trends, and much remains to be learned about these connections.

ANALYZING THE INTERSECTION BETWEEN HUMAN DEVELOPMENT AND SOCIAL POLICY

This chapter introduces a framework, driven by concerns central to a life-course perspective, with which developmental scientists and policy-makers and -analysts can better address the intersection between human development and social policy. The questions that comprise this framework are compiled in Table 1, and each question will be discussed in turn.

At What Life Sphere(s) is a Policy Aimed?
What Specific Dimension(s) of Human Development Does a Policy Address?

The life-course perspective emphasizes the fact that development occurs in multiple spheres and along multiple dimensions, and that these spheres and dimensions interact. Extending these points to an analysis of social policy, we must consider the primary life sphere at which a policy is aimed and, more specifically, the dimension(s) of development at which it is aimed. A policy might be generally directed at the sphere of family, work, education, health, or finances. For example, Medicare, Medicaid, and Food Stamps are directed at the sphere of health. The Paycheck Fairness Act, which enforces equal pay laws for men and women who do equal work, and Unemployment Insurance, which provides assistance to those who are out of work, are directed at the sphere of work. The Earned Income Tax Credit (EITC), which reduces the economic "penalty" associated with marriage, and tax credits for childcare improve the economic statuses of families.

Some policies are aimed at specific aspects of physical, psychological, or social development. For example, a program such as Head Start not only seeks to improve school achievement, but also social, health, and life skills. It also actively promotes the physical health of youngsters, through formal and informal screenings, immunizations, and inoculations, and through the provision of breakfast and lunch. Similarly, Comer's School Development Program (SDP) is directed at improving specific aspects of children's development, especially for poor, minority children (see Anson, Cook, Habib, Grady, Haynes, & Comer, 1991; Comer, 1988). Its immediate goals are to increase self-efficacy and confidence, affirm individual and ethnic identities, build interpersonal skills, foster attachment to school and cultural institutions, and create positive relationships with adults inside and outside of school. Through these short-term improvements, SDP hopes to raise academic performance, increase conventional social behavior and decrease deviant behavior, and improve mental health in the long run. Both Head

Table 1. A Framework for Analyzing the Intersection Between
Human Development and Social Policy

• At what life sphere(s) is a policy aimed?
• What dimension(s) of human development does a policy address?

• Does a policy intend to ameliorate, or even eliminate, something negative?
  Does it intend to actively promote something positive? Or does it intend to
  do both?

• Is the temporal view of a policy more prospective or retrospective?
  Is it focused more on the past, present, future, or some combination of
  these?

• What model of the life course underlies a policy?
• Does a policy relate to a certain segment of life or to the life course as a
  whole?
• Is its vision of the life course rigid or flexible?
• To what degree does a policy promote or prevent innovation in the life
  course?

• Does a policy intend to reinforce, change, or reflect life patterns?
• To what extent does a policy lag "behind the times"?
• To what degree can we extrapolate future policies on the basis of current
  policies?

• Whom does a policy target, whom does it exclude, and why?
• What are its underlying assumptions about who is "at risk," for what, and
  why?
• What are its underlying assumptions about who should be helped (or who is
  worthy for help)?

• At what level(s) is a policy implemented?

• How do the effects of a policy come about? And who is affected?
• Are its effects temporary or permanent?
• What should occur in the short- and long-term?
• What unintended effects might occur? And for whom?

• What are the costs associated with a policy? And for whom?
• What are the costs associated with not developing a policy? And for
  whom?

Start and SDP draw attention to the fact that policies aimed at particular dimensions of development may also impact other dimensions. Indeed, both programs are unusual in that they are multidimensional and specific about which aspects of development they intend to affect. Researchers and policy-makers too often take a fragmented view of individuals, focusing on a single characteristic or a small set of characteristics, rather than tending to the whole. How might we better account for people in all of their complexity?

The life-course framework draws attention to the interconnections between the spheres of education, work, and family, and to the fact that individuals participate in multiple spheres simultaneously. Some policies account for the interconnectedness of life spheres. For example, the stated goals of Temporary Assistance to Needy Families (TANF) are aimed at work-family connections. TANF intends to provide assistance to needy families so that children can be cared for in their own homes; reduce dependency on the state by promoting job preparation, work, and marriage; prevent out-of-wedlock pregnancies; and encourage the formation and maintenance of two-parent families.

Similarly, proposals related to restructuring work assume that time gained will be devoted to family or educational pursuits. This is especially true of flextime policies in many corporations, which are offered to help single parents or working couples better juggle work and family demands, or to permit employees to enroll in courses or gain additional training during the work day. A policy such as the Family and Medical Leave Act (FMLA) also explicitly addresses the work-family intersection. FMLA is a federal law that allows unpaid leaves to eligible employees so that they may care for family members or themselves for approved family and medical conditions. It protects employees by guaranteeing their right to return to work after the leave, and it prevents employers from discouraging or preventing employees from taking a leave under specified conditions. It prohibits employers from discriminating against or discharging an employee for matters related to the leave. And it ensures that all benefits, such as health insurance coverage, are maintained under the same terms and conditions that existed while the employee was working. Social policies must not only take connections such as these into account, but they should facilitate experiences in one sphere or along one dimension without compromising experiences in or along others.

As we consider intersections between the spheres of education, work, and family, we must confront the gender-, race-, and social class-based nature of the life course. For example, the structure and experience of men's and women's lives continues to be different, despite significant gains for women in recent decades (Sørensen, 1991). Women continue to take responsibility for the care and raising of children, which strongly conditions their educational attainment and their attachment to the labor market. In addition, the position of women in the labor market remains one of marked disadvantage, even net of skills and qualifications, family roles and responsibilities.

Policy-makers and -analysts must therefore consider how social policies might create or reduce opportunities and experiences in education, work, and family as a function of gender. They might consider how social policies might be developed or reformed to encourage men to take equal responsibility for the care and raising of children, and to create greater demand for and place more value on women's labor. To do so, the demands placed upon men, especially around work, must also change. A parallel set of questions might be asked about how to reduce the sorting of opportunities and experiences by race, social class, and other dimensions of social stratification.

A central proposition of the life-course framework is that single experiences cannot be adequately understood if they are considered in isolation of others. Yet social policies are largely aimed at specific experiences and transitions. For example, research and policy related to the transition to adulthood has largely treated five transitions separately – leaving home, finishing school, entering work, getting married, and having children. However, these transitions are interrelated. Young adults make decisions about when to marry and have children based on when they expect to finish school and enter work. And when young adults marry or have children before they expected to do so, work and school experiences are affected thereafter. These experiences must be understood as a cluster. In addition, new markers of adulthood might now exist to supplement or replace those in the traditional set, given that the demography of each of these transitions has changed significantly in the past few decades.

Similarly, a specific life period (e.g., adolescence, adulthood, or old age) cannot be adequately understood if it is considered in isolation of others. Yet policy-makers conveniently split the life course into discrete periods and develop initiatives around the special circumstances and needs of individuals in those periods. For example, the transition to old age has long been exclusively defined by retirement or, more generally, in terms of age-of-eligibility for receipt of Social Security and pension benefits. Like the transition to adulthood, the demography of the transition to retirement has changed significantly in the past few decades. Individuals have increasingly found alternatives to moving directly to full-time retirement, such as "bridge jobs," part-time work, and limited-time returns to work during retirement (see also Chapter 3). Rather than treat the transition to old age in terms of retirement, new markers of old age might now exist to supplement or replace it. More importantly, individuals' statuses and options in later life are tied to earlier experiences, especially their family, work, and savings histories.

These points reinforce other concerns central to the life-course framework: The importance of understanding people in whole (over time) and as wholes (studying larger profiles of traits and characteristics rather than single variables). The dynamics of loss and gain (and their interdependence) across spheres and dimensions of development. And the need to take an interdisciplinary approach to understanding the dynamics of human growth and change.

Does a Policy Intend to Ameliorate, or Even Eliminate, Something Negative?
Does It Intend to Actively Promote Something Positive?
Does It Intend to do Both?

Most social policies are problem-focused and seek to ameliorate or eliminate an existing negative condition. These policies take a more responsive and palliative approach, focusing on relieving a problem that has recently occurred, and assisting individuals as they move through what is taken to be a transitory state. The intended effect is to foster continuity (or at least reduce discontinuity) over time. The model at the heart of these policies is one of homeostasis: The policy seeks to restore individuals or groups to a prior state, or to equip them with additional resources as they face challenging transitions or periods of risk. These resources also reduce the degree to which individuals are dependent on others as they manage hard times. Policies that provide money or in-kind assistance to those without jobs, health insurance, food, or housing are good examples of these types of policies. Yet this results in a series of policies related to specific transitions or life periods rather than the life course as a whole.

In contrast, other policies seek to ensure a more positive future. These policies are more preventive and curative in that they equip individuals and groups with skills and resources *from early on* in an effort to reduce the likelihood of later negative outcomes. They are based on probabilities and are inherently temporal. These policies may also increase the likelihood of positive outcomes by putting individuals and groups on more positive pathways from the start. Head Start (for children aged three to five) and Early Start (up to age three) are good examples of this, given their early intervention into the lives of disadvantaged children.

Still other policies have both preventative and corrective components. These are often aimed at correcting problematic aspects of the past, with the hope that, from that point on, the likelihood of negative states will diminish and positive states will increase. Job training programs or educational interventions are good examples of these types of policies. The Job Training Partnership Act (JTPA) targets disadvantaged or unemployed adults whose characteristics serve as barriers to finding gainful employment, such as having poor English language skills, low educational levels, or few "life skills." It also assists displaced workers in upgrading existing skills or equipping them with new skills. The program develops individualized training programs that combine classroom training, on-the-job-training, work experience, and supportive services. And it teaches job-seeking skills and assists trainees with job searches and relocation. In the long run, the program should result in steady workers who are better skilled and more confident, which ultimately benefits individuals, families, employers, and the community.

These approaches correct or prevent problematic developmental statuses or improve the likelihood of more positive outcomes (or at least make them less negative). Yet we might also consider how the existing positive states of those individuals might also be improved. Similarly, while it is important to target populations with special needs, the circumstances of individuals who hover above special-needs thresholds might also be better addressed. While the development of these individuals may not be in jeopardy to the same degree or in the same ways as those who fall within established thresholds, they may nonetheless gain a great deal from assistance. Issues related to the inclusiveness or exclusiveness of policies will be addressed later.

Is the Temporal View of a Policy More Prospective or Retrospective? Is It Focused on the Past, Present, Future, or Some Combination of These?

The life-course framework emphasizes the importance of understanding dynamics related to time. It points to the challenges of understanding lives prospectively (forward in time) and retrospectively (backward in time), and of examining the current circumstances of individuals or groups within the context of both past and anticipated circumstances. For example, pension plans and Social Security have both prospective and retrospective aspects of time at their core. These policies are future-orientated in that they are ultimately aimed at improving income security in later life (under the assumption that old age is a period of retirement and leisure, as it is currently structured in most Western nations). At the same time, and perhaps more importantly, these policies are bound to the past in that benefit levels in later life are intimately tied to an individual's work history, especially the duration of continuous full-time work and earnings levels.

For example, in "defined benefit" plans, pension levels are generally a function of the duration of service and the last few years of earnings (Henretta, 1994; see also Chapter 3). Vesting rules may result in a complete loss of benefits if the employee leaves the position before the vestment period has passed, and they may penalize workers who leave before official retirement ages. In "defined contribution" plans, on the other hand, the employer makes an annual investment based on a percentage of the employee's annual income, and these plans generally have much shorter vesting periods and are often portable. As a result, defined contribution plans do not penalize those with discontinuous work careers (e.g., alternating between full- and part-time status, taking leaves, changing jobs) to the same degree as defined benefit plans. While the shift toward "contingent" models of work, to be discussed shortly, has been accompanied by a shift toward defined contribution plans, the majority of covered workers continue to have defined benefit plans (Quadagno & Hardy, 1996). The shift toward contingent models of work has also been accompanied by an increase in the proportion of workers who are not only without pension coverage, but without benefits of any kind.

Whether individuals are entitled to Social Security benefits, and how much they receive, also depends on a number of factors. These include an individual's birth year, age at retirement, average career earnings in employment covered by Social Security, and a work history that spans a minimum number of 40 quarters. Social Security benefits increase in value with longer, more continuous work (Burkhauser & Quinn, 1994). This again means that workers with discontinuous work careers are penalized. (One of the latent consequences of this structure is that it puts certain groups, especially women and minorities, at a disadvantage.)

In addition, spousal Social Security benefits are not only tied to the spouse's work history, but to the marital history of the couple (especially duration of marriage). This has especially important implications for women's lives. Social Security rules are based on a "traditional" family model in which men are the sole wage earners and marriages start early and last for life. These rules served to protect current and past cohorts of older women because most women did not have earnings histories of their own on which to draw (or at least not at the required level of participation). What these women did have was long-term marriages to men with continuous work histories, and they could therefore draw benefits through their husbands. Nonetheless, this policy devalued the contributions of women. Spousal benefits are generally equivalent to about half of the husband's entitlement. Such a model is clearly disadvantageous for caregivers, divorced women, and some widows.

But it also leaves vulnerable women who are currently married. Indeed, for future cohorts of older women, the model on which Social Security is built may create even greater problems. Under current Social Security regulations, women can only draw on spousal benefits if their marriages lasted a minimum of 10 years. To be eligible for individual Social Security benefits (rather than spousal benefits), individuals generally need to have worked 10 years. While women from recent cohorts have longer work histories than their predecessors, they nonetheless continue to cycle in and out of the labor force in response to family demands. More importantly, marriages of recent cohorts of women have been of shorter duration. In the end, the coupling of these patterns may place recent and future cohorts of women at greater risk than their predecessors.

This example illustrates the fact that policies are often based on assumptions about others to whom individuals are tied, the nature of those ties, and how those ties condition opportunities. Warranted or not, these assumptions relate to a central life-course proposition: the interdependence of lives. Individual lives are not lived in isolation but are intimately bound to others. To build a complete view of the life course, these ties must be taken into account.

The policies just described relate to the particular work and marital histories of *individuals*. Yet benefits and entitlements are often based on those of a *group*. For example, policies may be based on the fact that opportunities of larger social groups who have experienced discrimination in the past must be treated with full respect and protected by law. These kinds of "identity politics" (Wolfe & Klausen, 1997) are matters of heated debate. Good examples are affirmative action policies related to race and gender, the Americans with Disabilities Act, and other non-discrimination policies pertaining to age, religion, and, at times, sexual orientation (e.g., Employment Non-Discrimination Act [ENDA], Local Law Enforcement Act).

Similarly, benefits and entitlements may be based on the likelihood that members of a group will have a particular experience (or set of experiences) in the future. For example, most "risk"-based policies are tied to the fact that certain groups of people are more likely to experience certain negative outcomes in the future. An important function of developmental science, then, is to discover the factors that place these groups at risk, and to work with policy-makers, -analysts, and practitioners to design and implement interventions before the undesirable experiences occur. Risk-based policies naturally take a longer view of lives.

In contrast, many policies related to old age, such as Social Security and pension policies, are inherently more retrospective because they are explicitly tied to the past. Of course, one could argue that all age-based policies for older adults are at least implicitly tied to the past in that an individual must survive to old age in order to draw upon the resources. Yet old-age policies like Social Security and Medicare are implicitly based on the notion that old age, irrespective of the resources at an individual's disposal, brings significant financial and health-related risks. This point is also debatable. Old-age policies are built on the assumption that the process of aging inevitably brings these risks. This assumption is based on the experiences of past cohorts whose financial and physical conditions were worse than those of current and future cohorts. The statuses of older persons have, on average, improved significantly in recent decades. Yet the proportion of "near-poor" elderly—those hovering just above the poverty line—has increased. In addition, improvements in mortality and morbidity have extended the period of old age, thereby increasing the period of potential age-related risk for these groups.

One could also argue that need-based programs for older adults are also tied to the past in that resources in later life are generally a direct function of prior resources. (The tensions between age- and need-based policies will be discussed shortly.) In fact, older people as a group exhibit significant heterogeneity in financial status. This heterogeneity may be the result of the accumulation of advantage and disadvantage over the life course (Dannefer, 1987).

Concerns about cumulative advantage and disadvantage depend on the segment of the life course on which we are focused. In understanding the welfare of the old, we are interested in understanding how prior experiences—experiences that span six or more decades—lead to statuses in old age. For the old, time-already-lived is long and time-left-to-live is (relatively) short. Time-already-lived is very relevant to old-age policies, particularly where pathways resulted in problematic outcomes in later life. In contrast, to understand the welfare of children, adolescents, and young adults, we must understand how early experiences play critical roles in shaping the future.

For the young, time-already-lived is short and time-left-to-live is long. As a result, many child-oriented policies are future-oriented and preventative in that they provide young people with important experiences and skills that facilitate more positive pathways through life. Policies related to the young are more often focused on prevention than correction.

Social policies themselves may contribute to the accumulation of advantage and disadvantage over the life course. For example, tracking practices through primary and secondary schools have implications for later educational and occupational options. In many countries, educational tracks are explicit and an individual's performance at critical junctures determines the track onto which the individual is placed (Rosenbaum, Kariya, Settersten, & Maier, 1990). The practice of tracking goes against American ideals of equality and individualism, and its existence in the United States is often denied. However, educational tracking does exist, and these tracks are often simply "hidden" from students and parents (Rosenbaum, 1976). This serves as a reminder that individuals may be unaware of policies that significantly affect their lives. Ultimately, each educational track determines the range of educational and occupational options open in the future. Where educational tracks are explicit and strong, the individual has little or no opportunity to veer from it once it has been assigned.

Similarly, promotional practices in many organizations are based on an individual's age and tenure. An individual's current or future chances at promotion are dependent on her or his prior promotional record and successful movement through a series of hierarchical positions (Rosenbaum, 1987). Many professions (e.g., in law, medicine, or the academy) are structured by a set of "nested" or prerequisite positions or experiences that need not be (and generally are not) restricted to a single organization. These policies make promotions dependent on full-time continuous work histories, leave little room for educational or other pursuits, and make late entry into some occupations very difficult. These examples underscore the need to understand long-ranging trajectories and remain sensitive to two time-related parameters: age and duration.

In addition, the tuition policies of many work organizations, when available, often provide tuition assistance *only* when the courses taken relate directly to the employee's current position. While these policies provide some opportunity for adults to refresh their skills in job-related areas, they work against flexibility in that they reinforce *existing* occupational positions and pathways. These policies do not allow individuals to seek training for new occupational positions or careers or to simply enrich themselves by taking courses of interest. Many policies also require employees to pay tuition up front, and the company later reimburses the employee depending on the final grade(s). These policies make educational pursuits difficult and risky for many adults, especially those already hesitant to return to school.

What Model of the Life Course Underlies a Policy?
Does a Policy Relate to a Certain Segment of Life or to the Life Course as a Whole?
Is Its Vision of the Life Course Rigid or Flexible?
To What Degree Does a Policy Promote or Prevent Innovation in the Life Course?

Models of the life course that underlie social policies must be made clearer. We must bring to the surface the "lay" theories of human development that are implicit in policy-makers' judgments about the needs of individuals in different periods of life. In discussing policies on aging, Walker (1999) takes the controversial stance that old age itself may be a product of public policy, that "in the 20th century, older people have been often the unwitting victims of policy" (p. 362). We would benefit a great deal from a more thorough examination of questions such as these. To what degree are different life periods (e.g., childhood, adolescence, young adulthood, midlife, or old age) created and reinforced through social policy, and in what ways?

Policies must be sensitive to the entire life course, to the ways in which they dictate the experiences of people of a given age, and how the activities, opportunities, and constraints of early periods set the stage for later ones. We must consider whether a policy relates to a certain period of life or the life course as a whole, and whether its vision of the life course is rigid (confining educational, work, leisure, and other experiences to specific periods) or flexible (promoting these experiences throughout life).

For example, international scholarship on the life course has noted the widespread segmentation of the life course into three separate periods: An early period devoted to education and training, a middle period devoted to continuous work and economic activity, and a final period devoted to retirement and leisure. In such a regime, work organizes the life course, and educational, work, and leisure experiences are age segregated (see Chapter 1). This age-differentiated structure is convenient in that it creates predictability in the entry to, and exit from, social roles and activities. At the same time, it restricts opportunities for various types of activities to specific life periods and results in an inflexible life course. Of course, for current cohorts of people in their later years, this "tripartition" may be more characteristic of the structure of men's lives than women's lives. For younger cohorts, it may also characterize the life structures of many women, though there is some evidence that this structure may be crumbling even for men.

In contrast, family experiences are assumed to extend across the entire life course. However, the nature of these experiences clearly changes as family members grow older. Many policies are oriented toward special family circumstances that emerge at particular points in life. For example, policies are often targeted at periods when families are being formed (e.g., maternity or paternity leave), children are young (e.g., childcare, child abuse, child support, custody, or parental leave), children are adolescents and young adults (e.g., school vouchers, financial aid to college students), or parents are old (e.g., eldercare).

Similarly, health experiences are assumed to extend across life, though these concerns also differ by life period. Health-related policies seem especially focused on the two ends of life, under the assumption that children and the elderly are dependent groups for whom access to health care must be ensured. On the early end, a wide variety of policies regulate and promote the health of children and adolescents, including policies related to nutrition and physical health, mental health, physical abuse, pregnancy, and drug abuse.

On the other end of life, a single major program of the American welfare state—Medicare—provides minimal health insurance coverage to the elderly. Medicare was originally designed to cover acute care needs. While the basic benefits package has changed little since the program began, many services are not delivered beyond traditional acute-care settings. However, most Medicare recipients need supplemental coverage, whether Medicaid (for the poor), coverage through former employers as part of their retirement plans, or Medigap.[2]

However, during most of adult life, access to health insurance hinges on the good fortune of having a full-time job with an employer that provides health insurance benefits, or of being legally attached (as a spouse or dependent) to someone who does. An important exception is Medicaid, which provides medical and health-related services to specific groups of eligible Americans, especially the poor.[3] Apart from Medicaid, American social policy concerns itself very little with the health of gainfully employed lower- or middle-income adults whose jobs do not come with health insurance coverage. For these and other reasons, there are more than 40 million Americans without health insurance, and many more who are underinsured. In 1997, Congress passed the Children's Health Insurance Program (CHIP) so that workers who do not have health care coverage at least have the option to provide it for their children.

The policies of the Food and Drug Administration (FDA), the United States Department of Agriculture (USDA), and other bodies also play critical roles in protecting health. These policies regulate the quality of the air we breathe, the water we drink, the food we eat, the medical treatments we receive, the prescriptions we take, and the buildings in which we live, learn, and work. These policies affect people of all ages.

[2] Medigap is private insurance that is available to Medicare beneficiaries to help pay for services and costs not covered in Parts A or B of Medicare. Part A relates to Hospital Insurance, and is an earned benefit for most people and requires no premium upon eligibility. Part B relates to Supplementary Medical Insurance, participation in which is voluntary and carries a monthly premium.
[3] Operating within broad federal guidelines, each state establishes its own eligibility standards; determines the type, amount, duration, and scope of services; sets the payment rate for services; and administers its own program.

Policy-makers must be more attentive to how the education-work-retirement tripartition is changing and how these trends might be related to, or altered by, social policies. Consider the shifting boundaries of the three boxes. The trend toward early retirement at the upper end of work life, coupled with an extension of schooling at the lower end of work life, has shortened the period of gainful work in the middle. In addition, early retirement, coupled with increased longevity, has lengthened the period of retirement at the end. Policies that regulate these boundaries may be at odds with one another. For example, organizational policies and practices have often encouraged individuals to retire early or take "bridge jobs," while Social Security and Medicare rules have reinforced age 65 as the appropriate age at which to move into the third box. However, in the case of Social Security, later age-eligibility thresholds are now being phased in.[4] In addition, longstanding earnings penalties to Social Security recipients were also recently lifted, bringing to an end a policy that has, since the time of the Depression, devalued and discouraged the work of older adults.

The changing content of the three boxes might also be considered. For example, an important shift seems to be occurring in the organization of work itself. This shift has particularly important implications for policies based on age-structured "lifetime" models of work (Henretta, 1994; see also Chapter 3). In lifetime models of work, the employer and employee invest in a long-term partnership. The longer the amount of time the employee spends in the firm, the more the employee gains important training, and the greater the individual's wages, job security, job mobility, and pension. Lifetime models contain a hier- archical sequence of positions, with a clear entry point and a strong emphasis on promotion from within the organization. As a result, age- or tenure-based rewards and security characterize these models. In addition, because much of an indi- vidual's training is specific to the organization, the skills acquired may not be transferable to other organizations. This leaves little opportunity for work reduction or for temporary exits from work, and it reduces incentives to receive training outside the firm, shift to positions on other tracks within the same firm, or completely change the direction of one's career.

Lifetime models of work are dissolving and being replaced by "contingent" models of work (Henretta, 1994; see also Chapter 3). Contingent models of work stand in direct contrast to lifetime models. Contingent models are characterized by time-bound contracts with no promise of work beyond those parameters. Movement toward contingent models of work has been driven by technological change, foreign competition, concerns about the cost of labor, the decline of

---

[4] For people born before 1938, the retirement age for full benefits is 65. Beginning in the year 2003, those who were born in 1938 or later will have their benefits delayed by two months for each year, which will move the threshold to 66 and eventually to 67, with a similar process set to begin in 2021. There has also been some discussion about instituting parallel changes in Medicare eligibility, though as of yet no formal action has been taken.

manufacturing, and the emergence of service-sector positions, which offer few benefits and low wages, and are generally not unionized. The result is that employers keep fewer employees in their lifetime pools and more employees in their contingent pools. This shift carries dramatic implications for social policy and the security of individuals and families. For example, it means that health care coverage, pension plans, and Social Security benefit levels may be jeopardized or significantly lowered. Because careers have become more disjointed, it may also mean that individuals need Unemployment Insurance more often and for longer periods. Changes such as these not only affect specific individuals, but also spouses, partners, and children.

In the sphere of education, recent tax-reform debates in Congress have included proposals to tax tuition scholarships, including graduate-level fellowships and tuition waivers. These reforms have major implications for the likelihood of educational pursuits in adult life. For students at private universities with high tuition, these tax bills are sizeable and may make education unaffordable. Most scholarships, federal grants, work-study funds, and low-interest loans are also generally only awarded to full-time degree-seeking students, which most adults cannot be. As a result, expenses for educational activity must be paid out-of-pocket, making a return to school unaffordable for many adults.

With prolonged education at the lower end of the life course, individuals from more recent cohorts also get a late start in building private and public pension funds. This likely reduces an individual's resources in old age, a problem exacerbated by the fact that gains in longevity have also extended the retirement period.

Given that many policies have created and reinforced the education-work-leisure tripartition, we must explore how existing policies might be reformed, and new policies mounted, in an effort to dismantle it, should this be desired. To what degree is this structure restrictive, for whom, and why? How does it place individuals or groups in positions of relative advantage or disadvantage? Given current economic and demographic realities, is this model outdated and inappropriate? To what degree does it strip individuals of opportunities to actively create their lives as they choose?

We must consider how social policies might remove age barriers to social roles and activities and maximize opportunities for people of all ages. The time has come to begin developing what Hirschhorn (1977), once described as "social policy for the fluid life cycle." Societies have much to gain by developing policies that allow and even encourage life-course flexibility "by softening the penalties for movement, increasing tolerance for deviance, and creating incentives for innovation" (Hirschhorn, 1977, p. 447). Several questions should be asked as we develop, implement, and evaluate policies to increase flexibility. How is flexibility to be achieved? What are important barriers to achieving it? How will new-found flexibility be used? What benefits will it provide, and for whom? With what losses will flexibility come, and for whom? And who should bear the financial burden?

Does a Policy Intend to Change, Reinforce, or Reflect Life Patterns? To What Extent Does a Policy Lag "Behind the Times"? To What Degree Can We Extrapolate Future Policies on the Basis of Current Policies?

Social policies may promote certain life patterns, prevent other patterns, or reflect emerging patterns in an effort to "keep up with the times." Consider, for example, the remarkable reminder that it is only in the past century that basic civil rights were granted to women and racial minorities, and that these changes came with great resistance. More recently, similar turmoil has emerged around ensuring civil rights for another vulnerable group: Gays and lesbians. We have witnessed the emergence of the Defense of Marriage Act, which denies same-sex unions the basic set of rights extended to heterosexual marriages. And with California's Proposition 22, these same rights were recently struck down as they were put onto the ballot and into the hands of voters, rather than in the courts and into the hands of judges. These are good examples of the fact that lives have changed rapidly in this century, but social policies have often not kept pace with social change. This creates asynchrony between lives as they are supposedly lived (as reflected in assumptions underlying social policies) and lives as they are actually lived (which may be at odds with those assumptions).

At the same time, Vermont's House of Representatives recently approved a landmark bill recognizing same-sex "civil unions." Many cities, corporations, and universities now extend insurance and tuition benefits to domestic partners, though some offer these benefits only to same-sex partners (given that opposite-sex couples have the opportunity to marry), while others extend these benefits to both same- and opposite-sex couples. Similarly, some corporations and universities have taken the lead in developing "family friendly" policies including benefits related to the provision of child care or parent care, assistance with and leaves for adoption, job-sharing and flextime, and slowing timetables around promotion and tenure for family-related reasons.

These issues relate to another lesson of the life-course framework: that individual lives must be understood within the contexts of historical time and the birth cohorts to which they belong. Cohort size and composition, in particular, are important in determining the implications a cohort holds for the opportunities and constraints its members face, and the implications it holds for social institutions and social policies. Abrupt changes in cohort size and composition result from significant shifts in fertility, migration, or mortality. As an example of the strain that large cohort size may have on the social system, consider the "baby boom" cohort (see Ryder, 1965). As this group has grown up and older, it has strained educational institutions and job and housing markets. These factors may have shaped other life decisions, such as whether and when to marry, whether and when to have children, or how many children to have. These experiences may also have had cumulative effects over time, shaping the social, family, and economic states of individuals later in life. Warranted or not, there is significant public concern about the potential strain that baby boomers will place on the Social Security and Medicare programs as they retire. The characteristics of a cohort set parameters not only on the lives of its members, but on the lives of adjacent and distal cohorts. Cohorts do not stand in isolation from one another, for their lives are inextricably linked through many social settings. While school environments and social groups tend to be age-segregated, families, work places, and communities are more age-integrated.

Cohort-specific conditions create challenges for social policy. To what degree can the needs of future cohorts be anticipated based on the experiences of current cohorts? Similarly, how might policies themselves have differential effects across cohorts? For example, changes in the indexing of Social Security have had an inequitable impact on the financial benefits paid to members of different cohorts (see Schultz, 1995). Changes in the organization of state-supported medical programs such as Medicare and Medicaid also likely create different health care experiences and options for members of different cohorts. These are matters of inter-cohort variability. At the same time, we must also be sensitive to matters of intra-cohort variability. How might individuals within a cohort be different, and might policies have differential effects on them?

Cohort seems especially important where old-age policies are concerned. The elderly are a large and diverse group with many decades of life behind them. Each successive cohort of elders has also had dramatically different experiences in history. In contrast, cohort differences seem less problematic for policies related to childhood and adolescence, not only because the number of years children and teens have lived are few, but because this period of life is relatively short. Development during childhood and adolescence is more predictable—many systematic physical, psychological, and social changes occur during these years. However, this does not mean that cohort is unimportant for policies related to child and adolescent development. For example, recent cohorts of children eligible for Head Start are undoubtedly different from those who entered the program in the 1960s—they face different lives and have different needs, and the world is now a different place. As a result, what it means to have been exposed to the Head Start program has also changed. Indeed, the program itself has changed in its three decades of existence. This serves as a reminder that longstanding policies, like people and their environments, are dynamic entities.

Besides cohort, we must be more sensitive to other dimensions of social stratification, particularly sex, race, and social class. Through its policies, the state allocates resources and sets parameters on the statuses of these groups. Understanding variability along these dimensions is central to the life-course framework. New census projections for the next century indicate that the United States and the world at large will shift dramatically in both size and composition (U.S. Bureau of the Census, 2000). For example, the resident population of the U.S. is expected to nearly double. Hispanics will triple by 2050 and become the largest minority group; Asians and Pacific Islanders will more than triple; and African-Americans will increase by 70 percent. The population age 65 and older will increase 137 percent by 2050, while the proportion of children will decline to 24 percent of the population. Key demographic parameters (such as mortality, morbidity, and fertility) are also expected to shift slightly in the next century. For example, childbearing among women should remain close to present levels, and mortality should decline gradually. Racial differences in childbearing and mortality should diminish. How might these shifts require new kinds of policies, and how might existing policies need to be reformed in light of them?

Whom Does a Policy Target, Whom Does It Exclude, and Why?
What are Its Underlying Assumptions about Who is "At Risk," for What, and Why?
What are Its Underlying Assumptions about Who Should be Helped?

Social policies often carry the assumption that certain statuses come with different types and degrees of "risk." Significant attention has been devoted to identifying the factors that place individuals at risk for a variety of negative developmental experiences or "disordered behaviors," especially those that come early in life. That catalog of risk factors is diverse and includes genetic, biological, psychological, social, and economic variables.

The risk factors most often examined are "background" or "demographic" characteristics. For practical purposes, policies are often based on ascriptive (versus achieved) statuses such as sex, race, or age. They are based on statuses such as marriage (e.g., divorcees, widows), parenthood (e.g., single mothers, childless women), or economic characteristics (e.g., poverty, families with two wage earners). Most of the former statuses are permanent (or relatively so), while most of the latter ones are dynamic (or at least carry the potential to change). This approach might be described as "class-theoretical" (Bronfenbrenner, 1988) because the phenomena under study are somehow "explained" by the categories themselves. This approach is problematic in that it assumes that these individual characteristics serve as important proxies for "social structure" and an individual's experiences within it. What is it about being a member of a particular category that makes it important? What about a category justifies basing policies on it? To answer these questions, attention must be turned to the types of outcomes associated with a category, and to the social processes and mechanisms through which it brings about those outcomes. Ultimately, greater attention to social processes and mechanisms, which are also central to the life-course framework, should lead to more effective interventions.

Because risk-based policies are generally aimed at populations, they also generally assume that all individuals who possess a risk factor (or set of factors) are at equal risk. This assumption is clearly questionable. Policies must become more sensitive to the number of risks to which an individual is exposed, to the specific types of risks to which an individual has been exposed, the degree of exposure to those risks, and the timing and duration of exposure. The latter two time-related parameters are central to the life-course perspective. For example, while contemporary developmental scientists now largely reject the idea of fixed "critical" periods of development, there may nonetheless be "sensitive" periods during which individuals are particularly susceptible to positive or negative influence, bringing about marked gains or losses.

To complicate matters further, a single risk factor may predispose an individual to multiple negative outcomes, just as a single negative outcome may be linked to multiple risk factors. Both approaches to understanding risk factors and their consequences must be fully explored. Some of these factors may not themselves raise the risk of a specific outcome or set of outcomes, but they may disturb psychological functioning which, in turn, causes the outcome(s) (Rutter, 1993). That is, it may not be prior experiences or risk factors that lead to negative outcomes, but the ways in which individuals respond to stressors that does (Garmenzy, 1993). This makes the policy-making process more difficult: Adaptable, individual-level responses are not the stuff from which policies are made.

These points also demonstrate the need to conduct longitudinal research, a design that stands at the core of the life-course framework. Longitudinal research allows an examination of "escape" from risk, in that some individuals exposed to a risk or set of risks manage to move through life without serious problems, presumably buffered by a set of "protective" factors. It allows an examination of direct and indirect chains of effects. And it permits the scrutiny of important junctures at which individuals change direction along a trajectory (whether onto, or off of, an adaptive or maladaptive path) or at which the nature or extent of risk may be especially high or low. These, too, are important temporal dynamics that must be understood to better develop social policy.

Another serious challenge is what Leibfried (1998) described as "the problem of binary statuses." Social policies often categorize individuals in binary "0,1" terms—as being either fully in or out of a status (e.g., in or out of the labor force; in or out of school). As a result, a mismatch may occur between the actual statuses of individuals (which are more complicated than simple dichotomies) and the ways in which policies deal with statuses and categorize individuals. In reality, individuals hold multiple statuses simultaneously, and their commitments to roles are best conceptualized along a continuum (rather than in discrete terms) and change over time (rather than remain stable). Yet in Leibried's (1998) terms, social policies are designed to be "rough instruments" rather than "continuous adjusters." As life patterns exhibit greater variability, statuses and their categorizations will become increasingly complex.

Risk should be understood not only in terms of individual characteristics, but also in terms of social settings, which are central to a life-course framework. Settings themselves may place individuals at risk or buffer them from it. For example, risk might be based on characteristics of the setting (e.g., dilapidated schools, crime-ridden neighborhoods) or on the characteristics of the people in the setting (e.g., schools or neighborhoods with a high percentage of African-Amercian students or families). In fact, rather than a personal characteristic uniformly becoming a risk (or buffer), it would seem as if personal characteristics become risks (or buffers) *in conjunction with* a set of social contexts. For example, an African-American teen living with a single mother in public housing and attending a low-quality school faces a different kind of future than an African-American teen living with two parents in a middle-class neighborhood and attending a high-quality school.

This type of reasoning underlies Chicago's landmark Gautreaux program, which moves inner-city black families from high-rise public housing to subsidized housing in white middle-class suburban neighborhoods (e.g., Rosenbaum, 1995). After nearly two decades, the success of that program led the federal government to design the Moving to Opportunity program, which is implemented by the U.S. Department of Housing and Urban Development. Its primary intentions are to improve both the short- and long-term chances of these children. In the short term, it puts children in contact with good schools, safe neighborhoods, quality health care, and more conventional peers. In the long run, it hopes to result in greater educational attainment, lead to better and higher-paying jobs, raise self-esteem, and improve other personal traits.

This underscores the fact that social policies must become more sensitive to the social settings in which individuals exist. Contexts, like individuals, are changing, multidimensional, interactive, and interdependent, and they, too, must be the targets of policies. Certain types of individuals may be sorted or self-select themselves into multiple contexts that are all of poor quality, and whose presumably negative effects may accumulate across contexts and over time. Similarly, certain types of individuals may be sorted or self-select themselves into multiple good contexts, and these positive effects may also accumulate across contexts and over time. Still others may develop in contexts of discrepant quality, some of which may be negative and place the individual at some developmental "risk," and others of which may be more positive and "buffer" the individual from potentially damaging factors.

It is important to consider whether and how phenomena of interest are especially open to the influence of particular environments at particular points in time. It is also important to consider whether and how the strength of contextual effects on target phenomena change over time, as well as how long individuals have been exposed to those contexts. Consider an educational intervention: To what degree does exposure to a program change children in positive and permanent ways? Once children leave a program, do its effects diminish and even vanish? How long do children need to be exposed to the program for it to work? Are the effects of a program greater for some children than for others (e.g., for children of particular age, sex, race, socioeconomic status, or ability)?

Research has emphasized the role that genetic factors play in determining individuals' behaviors, particularly those behaviors that shape and select their environments (e.g., Scarr, 1993). Of course, problems construed to be the result of genetic factors may ultimately lead to claims that social policies meant to compensate for them are worthless because they do not change the forces responsible for individuals' opportunities or life conditions, which are not environmental. This raises the question of "plasticity"—the degree to which certain aspects of human development are modifiable, and the extent to which interventions can or cannot help. When an aspect of development is understood to be the result of "nature" rather than "nurture," we are not as likely to intervene. Consider the statement, "*X* could be improved *if. . .*" (Riley, 1998). When parts of the *if* are focused on social characteristics and processes, this would suggest that *X* is at least partially a function of forces outside of the individual, and it might provide important insights about how we might intervene. Similarly, certain spheres of life might be more amenable to outside intervention than others. For example, the family sphere is often considered more "private" and less amenable to (and appropriate for) state intervention, whereas more "public" spheres, such as education or the economy, are viewed as more amenable to (and appropriate for) state intervention.

Some have viewed the "at-risk" label as a wolf in sheep's clothing, viewing it as an "implicitly racist, classist, sexist, ageist, and ableist . . . model which locates problems or 'pathologies' in individuals, families, and communities rather than in institutional structures that create and maintain inequality" (Swadener & Lubeck, 1995, p. 3). To define groups of people as "at-risk" can indeed be damaging in these ways. This serves as a reminder that interventions aimed at improving human development and welfare can have both intended *and* unintended consequences. Yet it is clear that policies must, for practical reasons, be targeted toward clearly defined groups of people. Until we manage to eliminate the social processes that create and maintain inequalities, we must find sophisticated but convenient ways of targeting groups of people in need of assistance. To illustrate many of these challenges, consider the question of age- versus need-based social policies.

Challenges Related to Developing Policies Based on Age and Need

Many policies are based on age, under the assumption that individuals at particular ages have a common set of needs and are "at risk" by virtue of their age. Social policies often use age or age groups as a basis for providing opportunities and allocating resources in the spheres of education, work, family, or health care, and these age rules and preferences condition the structure and experience of life in a society. For example, many rights and duties are often explicitly based on age, including age regulations around voting, driving, drinking, working and retiring, marrying, compulsory school, or seeking public offices. Discussions about legal ages often center around how soon in life individuals should be granted adult rights and obligations, or how late in life adult rights and obligations should be maintained (Cain, 1976). Some of these age rules also seem at odds with one another, such as when 16-year-olds are allowed to marry but not vote, or 18-year-olds are allowed to vote but not drink. The two ends of life are viewed as dependent periods (or, in the case of old age, as a period during which individuals are at risk of becoming dependent). There is little attention to the space of life between early adulthood and old age with the exception that the welfare of little children is targeted vis-à-vis their adult parents and, increasingly, the welfare of elderly parents is targeted vis-à-vis their adult children.

Recent years have brought significant, and even heated, discussion about whether to move away from age-based policies, even for policies originally conceived as old age policies. Shall government assistance continue to be granted on the basis of age without acknowledging 1) the possibility that age may become increasingly irrelevant in contemporary and future societies, and 2) that specific age groups, and especially older people, exhibit significant variability on most biological, psychological, and social indicators? Both of these points have been emphasized in recent scholarship on the life course, and they seemingly make it unreasonable to use age alone as a basis for determining eligibility for benefits and entitlements. While age-based policies may elevate the status of a group as a whole, they overlook differences across sub-populations within an age group, some of whom may be in much greater need than others and who remain at a relative disadvantage even after they receive age-based benefits and entitlements. An age-based approach to social policy may also have the unintended consequences of labeling specific age groups as problematic, institutionalizing new forms of ageism, and creating age divisiveness (Neugarten, 1974, 1982).

To what degree do policies serve to tear generations apart rather than pull them together? Consider the controversial intergenerational equity debate that surfaced in the 1980s. (For reviews, see Bengtson & Achenbaum, 1993; Marmor, Smeeding, & Greene, 1994.) Intergenerational equity refers to the idea that different generations should receive similar treatment and have similar access to societal goods and services. Do elderly people, as some have argued, receive more than their fair share of the federal budget, especially given the costs of Medicare and Social Security? Do they ultimately receive age-based benefits at the expense of groups that are more needy and deserving, such as children? This thesis is linked to the fact that elderly people, as a group, have experienced increases in economic well-being over the last several decades, while younger age groups, especially young children, have experienced declines. This has fostered the perception of older people as "greedy geezers." Proponents of this thesis have argued that the elderly have coupled their gains in economic power with gains in political power, granting them the ability to secure a greater share of public services for themselves.

On the other side of the debate stand those who believe that this thesis is predicated on false assumptions. It assumes that older people, as a group, have the same needs and share the same interests. It assumes that older people are self-interested. It assumes that older people do not represent a significant economic burden. And it assumes that given the chance, both the public and legislators would happily decrease or even eliminate old age benefits and entitlements.

In response to the high costs of health care for older people, several contro-versial proposals have rationed health care expenditures in advanced old age, especially expensive life-prolonging procedures (e.g., Callahan, 1987). The rationale underlying such proposals is that human beings now naturally live somewhere between 80 and 85 years; beyond this threshold, these procedures prolong life in unnatural ways. Cain's notion of "counting backwards" (that is, of determining access to resources based on one's anticipated number of "years yet to live") is simultaneously more complicated and provocative than proposals related to the rationing of resources, though it is nonetheless certain to be controversial (see Chapter 11).

Of course, there are other ways to ration health care besides age, including ability to pay, the likely effectiveness of a procedure, judgments about quality versus quantity of life, waiting lists, first-come first-served, or how much one has contributed to society (Moody, 2000). Relative to age, these alternatives seem significantly more difficult to define and measure. And each solution, including those anchored in age, brings its own set of ethical dilemmas. Despite its problems, chronological age is an attractive dimension on which to build social policies: It is convenient, easily measured, practical, objective, and universal. Still, age-based policies often seem arbitrary and unjust.

Other alternatives turn more exclusively to need, or use need in combina-tion with age. Need-based approaches also bring significant challenges, especially in determining what constitutes "need" and how it should be demonstrated. The debate about drawing the poverty line can readily be extended to these questions (see Ruggles, 1990). For example, in identifying the needy, should absolute, relative, or subjective measures be used? How should those thresholds be set? How should adjustments be made for changes in prices, relative incomes, and consumption of "necessary" goods over time? How should adjustments be made for differences in family needs? Whose income should be counted—individuals, families, or households? And what should be counted—income, non-cash income, non-market income, financial assets, non-financial assets, or intangible assets?

Other pitfalls may occur with need-based approaches, particularly if the means for demonstrating need demean or stigmatize recipients. In the United States, individuals who draw on certain need-based policies such as Food

Stamps or TANF are often stigmatized and feel shame. However, in restructuring "welfare" as "welfare-to-work," eligibility periods have been shortened and work requirements have been added. These and other reforms seem to have improved public perceptions of these programs.

This leads to a critical question that researchers, policy-makers and -analysts must consider: What does it mean to have been targeted by the state and to have received benefits associated with its policies? To answer this question, the addition of qualitative methods would seem especially useful. In listening to the voices of recipients, we might better understand the pathways through which individuals end up in vulnerable or dire circumstances; how policies help or hinder the progress of individuals and families in the short and long term; and how drawing on policies affects how recipients view themselves.

Most American policies are intended to only provide temporary support. For example, in the case of TANF, individuals must be employed after two years on assistance, and there is a five-year (cumulative) limit on receiving cash assistance. Unemployment Insurance generally provides assistance for 13 weeks while individuals who have been fired or laid off, or who are out of work for some reason other than their own doing, search for employment. (Under certain conditions, this time period can be extended to 26 weeks.) The Family and Medical Leave Act permits employee leaves for up to 12 weeks within a one-year period.

Most American policies are also intended to provide only minimum levels of support. For example, for most individuals, Unemployment Insurance benefits typically amount to only half of one's usual salary (though benefits are capped at the upper end). Similarly, the initial intent of Social Security was to protect older adults from poverty. Its architects assumed that elderly people would provide most of their income through savings and private pensions. Yet it is clear that the Social Security program is no longer used in this way. In fact, most older Americans rely on Social Security as their largest source of income: More than 50 percent rely on Social Security to provide more than half of their income.[5] Programs such as Medicare and Social Security, in particular, serve to keep the majority of older Americans from falling into poverty (Kingson, 1994).

Assumptions about Who Should be Helped

It is important to bring to the surface the set of assumptions that underlie policies about which types of individuals, unions, and families are "legitimate" and worthy of support and protection, and which are not. How do social policies promote opportunities for certain types of people, and overlook and even deny

---

[5] There is a large group of "near poor" older people hovering just above the official poverty line, and who slip in and out of poverty over time. There is also a sizable group of "'tweeners" who are not in good financial shape but are not poor enough to receive SSI or Medicaid (Smeeding, 1986).

them to others? Consider policies that prevent the extension of benefits to same-sex or unmarried heterosexual couples, the adoption of children by same-sex or unmarried heterosexual couples, or inter-racial adoption. These are good examples of policies that carry strong assumptions about types of unions and families not worthy of the support and protection of the state. And even when there are no formal policies to prevent these things from happening, informal "practiced preferences" often do.

Unmarried partners, whether heterosexual or homosexual, are unprotected with respect to Social Security and many pension benefits, which are granted only to surviving legal spouses. They are also generally not recognized in nursing home arrangements, hospital policies, or medical insurance coverage. And they face many significant legal complexities around inheritance, assets, power of attorney, and other issues. Of course, heterosexual couples at least have the opportunity to marry and therefore have access to the bundle of rights that come with marriage. Long-term gay and lesbian couples are explicitly denied those rights. Yet little if anything is done to scrutinize the legitimacy and quality of legal unions between men and women. As a case in point, consider the recent television show "Who Wants to Marry a Millionaire," in which beautiful women entered a competition to be instantly married to a man whom they never met but knew to be rich. Within minutes, that union was granted the "sanctity" of marriage and awarded a bundle of over one hundred legal rights. Ironically, as one observer noted, same-sex couples who have been together for decades are "legal strangers" to one another (Humm, 2000).

Gay and lesbian elders face serious challenges in many areas of life that have largely been ignored in social policy. They may feel out of place in housing environments that are heterosexual in orientation. Indeed, the presence of an openly gay or lesbian elder may make other residents and staff members uncomfortable. In the realm of health care, gay and lesbian elders may have reservations about being "out" to health care providers for fear that this will prevent them from getting services they need. They may lack social support because they have no children or because they have been estranged from parents, siblings, or other relatives. Gay and lesbian elders with partners may have great difficulty coping with illness or bereavement, in that others may not acknowledge the partner, or the partner's importance, when she or he becomes ill or dies.

Once underlying assumptions such as these are made more explicit, we will be better positioned to alter existing policies that disadvantage these groups and to develop new policies that might facilitate their development. Surely, as family and family-like relationships become more complex, policy-makers must face difficult questions about (and hopefully enlarge) the social and legal definitions of "family." These examples also reinforce the earlier point that we must be sensitive to the ways in which social policies may be used to actively promote certain life patterns, actively prevent others, or reflect new patterns in an effort to "keep up with the times."

At What Level(s) is a Policy Aimed and Implemented?

The life-course framework emphasizes the need to consider multiple levels of analysis (e.g., micro, meso, and macro), and the bridges between them, in an effort to build a more comprehensive understanding of human development. As social policies are made and evaluated, those efforts must be sensitive to the levels at which policies are aimed and implemented, and their effects across levels. For example, a policy might affect individual development through a combination of meso-level settings—such as partnerships between work and family, school and family, or neighborhood and school. We earlier discussed the fact that development takes place on multiple levels and in multiple spheres, yet policy initiatives seldom target these complexities.

And just as environments are interdependent, so too are individuals. What happens to one person is a function of what happens to another person, and this inevitably creates unpredictability. This taps one of the hallmarks of the life-course framework: the "interdependence of lives" (or "linked lives"). Some policies do take these others into account—especially where parents, young children, and spouses are concerned. More attention must be paid to the ways in which policies are (or might be) designed to affect targeted individuals via their relationships to others. For example, some policies are exclusively or largely implemented at the level of parents, but are ultimately aimed at improving the lives of children in that the effects are expected to "trickle down" from parents to children. A program like TANF is based on the assumption that the economic conditions in which children live affect their development, and that improving the financial state and security of parents in turn improves the development of children. Similarly, a program such as Early Start teaches parents good parenting skills, including learning about the play and discipline of children, nutrition, how to cook, and where and how to access food through government programs—all with the ultimate hope of improving the development of their children.

How do the Effects of a Policy Come About? And Who is Affected?
Are Its Effects Temporary or Permanent?
What Should Occur in the Short- and Long-Term?
What Unintended Effects Might Occur? And for Whom?

As noted earlier, the life-course framework draws attention to the need to better understand and specify the processes and mechanisms through which effects come about. Generally, these are neither well specified in theory or research, nor in social policies and interventions. Greater attention to issues such as these will clearly aid the design and implementation of more successful interventions. Also as discussed earlier, the life-course framework raises awareness of the interdependence of lives, and the ways in which individuals, via their relationships with others, may be targeted by social policies. Similarly, more attention must be paid to the ways in which others beyond the recipient might be affected by a policy. That is, a policy may have "ripple effects" on others to whom the individual is tied. For example, changes in eligibility rules and indexing procedures for Social Security benefits have real effects on spouses, particularly for divorced or widowed women who do not have Social Security benefits of their own on which to draw.

The remaining questions also relate to elements that are central to the life-course framework: Understanding long-ranging trajectories, proximal and distal causes, and proximal and distal effects. As part of this, greater attention might be paid to "domino" (or "chain") effects (subsequent effects brought about by an initial one) and "sleeper" (or "delayed") effects (effects that lie dormant for many years and emerge much later). Greater consideration must also be given to both intended and unintended effects. Policies may not only fail to achieve intended effects, but they may produce unintended, and even opposite, effects.

What are the Costs Associated with a Policy? And for Whom? What are the Costs Associated with Not Developing a Policy? And for Whom?

Social policies always carry financial costs. They are therefore often met with controversy because they require financing through tax money and public resources. Yet we seldom consider the costs associated with *not* having or developing certain policies, and we must begin to think in these terms. An interesting illustration of this logic is Cohen's (1998) economic analysis of the monetary value of "saving" at-risk youth. When interventions are evaluated, we inevitably ask whether their costs outweigh their benefits. We generally know something about the financial costs of an intervention, but we often know little about its financial benefits. Cohen examines these potential benefits by estimating the lifetime costs associated with the typical "career criminal," heavy drug abuser, and high school dropout. Because controlled experimental data are seldom gathered on the number of career criminals, abusers, or dropouts who are averted by a program, we might instead ask how many of these individuals must be "saved" before the program would "pay for itself." The costs caused by individuals in each of these categories are staggering: between $1.3–$1.5 million for a career criminal; between $370,000 to $970,000 for a heavy drug user; and between $243,000 and $388,000 for a high school dropout. Once Cohen accounts for overlap between these three states, he estimates that the overall value of saving *just one* high-risk youth is an overwhelming $1.7 to $2.3 million. The financial costs of many programs aimed at serving high-risk adolescents and young adults are therefore very trivial to the financial costs of not having those programs, especially when the cumulative tolls to individuals, families, and society are taken into account. Much can be gained by extending this logic to evaluations of other types of policies, especially those that have been met with great resistance or have become matters of significant debate, including Medicare and Social Security. And much can be gained by estimating other types of costs in this way as well—whether physical, psychological, or social.

We must also begin to analyze whether the continued support of a policy takes significant tolls on individuals, families, and society. Consider the birth of a child. Many insurance providers and work organizations classify childbirth as a physical condition from which a woman must recover, not as a taxing period of transition for the parent(s). Under these circumstances, supported leaves are permitted only for women and, more specifically, only for women who have physically birthed a child. Similar support is not offered to biological fathers, nor is it extended to individuals or couples who adopt a child. As another example, consider the fact that Maine is only state in America that is now prepared to offer Medicaid benefits to HIV-positive individuals *before* they become disabled (Peregrin, 2000). In the remaining states, HIV-positive individuals cannot qualify for benefits until they are classified as disabled, at which point treatments may no longer be effective. Similar tragedies are created by health insurance policies that deny individuals essential, even life-saving, treatments for pre-existing conditions. Policies such as these obviously conserve a great deal of money. But at what costs do they come?

Many policies are oriented toward achieving social justice in that they inherently seek to equalize life chances, reduce inequality, or "normalize" statuses. Social justice policies are vitally important. But should we not hope to do more than simply close the gap between individuals at average or higher levels and individuals below those levels? Might we more often find ways to facilitate and even optimize the development of all people, regardless of their starting points or current levels? While it is impossible to develop social policies on individual bases, these are nonetheless important questions.

Of course, the possibilities offered in response to these questions will vary according to the political ideology of a state and its conception of civil society. For example, should education, especially higher education, be a universal right for each citizen regardless of abilities or resources? Or should it be the privilege of a few? What about access to a livable wage, decent health care, or leisure? Answers to these questions also depend on economic and social climates of the times, as certain policies will be more or less popular during periods of hardship or prosperity, liberalism or conservatism.

CONCLUSION

This chapter has presented a framework with which developmental scientists and policy-makers and -analysts might better address the intersection between human development and social policy. Driven by core life-course concepts, principles, and methods, this framework has illustrated how greater attention to these questions will dramatically change the ways in which American social policies are developed, implemented, evaluated, and reformed.

To move forward, the link between the research and policy processes must be facilitated. Theory and research on human development have something important to offer as policies are designed and implemented to reduce or eliminate problems and even promote "successful" development. Similarly, well-crafted evaluation research may, in turn, not only shed further light on theory, but it will teach us important lessons about how to reform policies in the future.

One major problem is that good data are seldom available on most programs to know whether they work. This is because intervention efforts are generally not backed by solid evaluation research, which is admittedly very costly. Evaluation efforts—when they occur—are seldom systematic or comprehensive. For example, one of the many challenges in evaluating a program such as Head Start is that state governments have begun to play a larger role in providing services. This has resulted in a set of initiatives that vary widely in design, implementation, and quality (Ripple, Gilliam, Chanana, & Zigler, 1999). Similarly, the wide variety of ways in which researchers operationalize outcomes is also problematic. Again in the case of Head Start, it has, from its inception, claimed children's social competence as a primary goal of intervention. Yet researchers have yet to settle on a definition of social competence that can be used consistently across evaluation efforts (Raver & Zigler, 1997).

Because evaluation efforts are rarely longitudinal, little or nothing is known about the range, strength, shape, and dynamics of effects over time. For many reasons, this is true even of Head Start, despite the fact that it may be the most popular and "extensively evaluated social program in American history" (Zigler & Styfco, 1994, p. 129), and despite the fact that it has existed for more than three decades.

The possibility of doing good evaluation research is also made difficult by the imprecision of the policies themselves. Policies are designed with surprisingly little specification as to what is to happen, how it is to happen, what outcomes should come about, when and how these outcomes should come about, for whom they should come about, or how long they should last. Under these circumstances, high-quality programs and high-quality evaluation research cannot be expected.

It is therefore imperative that we more systematically analyze policies by asking questions in line with the framework presented here. In the process, we must also explicitly compare the policies of nations to examine innovative policies that have been mounted elsewhere and with what success they have been mounted. Policy and institutional structures vary widely across nations, and they set parameters on the ways in which lives are lived and experienced. We have important lessons to learn from other nations.

Another important barrier is the difference between how scientific research is conducted and how social policies are made. Developmental science, in particular, is immensely complex and time consuming. Social policies generally cannot afford to be. The conclusions we draw in research are seldom definitive, as we hedge them with contingencies related to research designs, samples, measures, and analyses. Policy-makers instead want and need quick, clear bottom-line answers and hard, fast solutions. As a result, social science research cannot be used optimally at any point in the policy process.

These factors serve as barriers to the development and implementation of good social policy. There are surely other barriers that are psychological, sociological, economic, political, or geographic in nature (Gallagher, 1996). Greater attention to these barriers, and to the kinds of questions posed in this chapter, are critical to effectively bridge the gulf between science and practice. We have nothing to lose and a great deal to gain. Indeed, the development and welfare of individuals, families, and societies is at stake.

REFERENCES

Anson, A. R., Cook, T. D., Habib, F., Grady, M. K., Haynes, N., & Comer, J. P. (1991). The Comer School Development Program: A theoretical analysis. *Urban Education, 26* (1), 56-82.

Bengtson, V., & Achenbaum, A. (1993) (Eds.). *The changing contract across generations.* New York, NY: Aldine de Gruyter.

Bronfenbrenner, U. (1988). Interacting systems in human development: Research paradigms, present and future. In N. Bolger, A. Caspi, G. Downey, & M. Moorehouse (Eds.), *Persons in context: Developmental processes* (pp. 25-49). New York: Cambridge University Press.

Burkhauser, R., & Quinn, J. (1994). Changing policy signals. In M. W. Riley, R. L. Kahn, & A. Foner (Eds.), *Age and structural lag: Society's failure to provide meaningful opportunities in work, family, and leisure* (pp. 237-262). New York: John Wiley & Sons.

Cain, L. D., Jr. (1976). Aging and the law. In R. H. Binstock & E. Shanas (Eds.), *Handbook of aging and the social sciences* (pp. 342-368). New York: Van Nostrand Reinhold Company.

Callahan, D. (1987). *Setting limits: Medical goals in an aging society.* New York: Simon & Schuster.

Cohen, M. A. (1998). The monetary value of saving a high-risk youth. *Journal of Quantitative Criminology, 14* (1), 5-33.

Comer, J. P. (1988). Educating poor minority children. *Scientific American, 256* (11), 42-48.

Dannefer, D. (1987). Aging as intracohort differentiation: Accentuation, the Matthew effect, and the life course. *Sociological Forum, 2,* 211-236.

Gallagher, J. J. (1996). Policy development and implementation for children with disabilities. In E. F. Zigler, S. L. Kagan, & N. W. Hall (Eds.), *Children, families, and government: Preparing for the twenty-first century* (pp. 171-187). New York: Cambridge University Press.

Garmenzy, N. (1993). Developmental psychopathology: Some historical and current perspectives. In D. Magnusson & P. Casaer (Eds.), *Longitudinal research on individual development* (pp. 95-126). Cambridge, UK: Cambridge University Press.

Heinz, W. R. (1998, May). *Work and the life course: Cross-cultural research perspectives*. Paper presented at "Restructuring Work and the Life Course: An International Symposium," University of Toronto, Toronto, Ontario.

Henretta, J. (1994). Social structure and age-based careers. In M. W. Riley, R. L. Kahn, & A. Foner (Eds.), *Age and structural lag* (pp. 57-79). New York: John Wiley & Sons.

Hirschhorn, L. (1977). Social policy and the life cycle: A developmental perspective. *Social Service Review, 51,* 434-450.

Humm, A. (2000, February 19). "Sacred" TV marriage. *New York Times,* Op. Ed.

Kingson, E. (1994). Testing the boundaries of universality: What's mean? What's not? *The Gerontologist, 34* (6), 736-742.

Leibfried, S. (1998, May). *Policy challenges*. Paper presented at "Restructuring Work and the Life Course: An International Symposium," University of Toronto, Toronto, Ontario.

Marmor, T., Smeeding, T., & Greene, V. (1994) (Eds.). Economic security and intergenerational justice: A look at North America. Washington, D.C.: Urban Institute Press.

Mayer, K. U., & Müller, K. (1986). The state and the structure of the life course. In A. B. Sørensen, F. E. Weinert, & L. R. Sherrod (Eds.), *Human development and the life course: Multidisciplinary perspectives* (pp. 217-245). Hillsdale, NJ: Lawrence Erlbaum Associates.

Moody, H. R. (2000). *Aging: Concepts and controversies* (3rd edition). Thousand Oaks, CA: Pine Forge Press.

Neugarten, B. L. (1974). Age groups in American society and the rise of the young-old. *Annals of the American Academy of Political and Social Science, 187,* 187-198.

Neugarten, B. L. (1982). *Age or need? Public policies for older people*. Beverly Hills, CA: Sage.

Peregrin, T. (2000, 9 March). Maine expands HIV care: Medicaid program sets national example. *Windy City Times,* p. 1.

Quadagno, J., & Hardy, M. (1996). Work and retirement. In R. Binstock & L. George (Eds.), *Handbook of aging and the social sciences* (4th ed., pp. 325-345). San Diego, CA: Academic Press.

Raver, C. C., & Zigler, E. F. (1997). Social competence: An untapped dimension in evaluating Head Start's success. *Early Childhood Research Quarterly, 12* (4), 363-385.

Ripple, C. H., Gilliam, W. S., Chanana, N., & Zigler, E. F. (1999). Will fifty cooks spoil the broth? The debate over entrusting Head Start to the states. *American Psychologist, 54* (5), 327-343.

Riley, M. W. (1998). A life course approach. In J. Giele & G. H. Elder, Jr. (Eds.), *Methods of life course research* (pp. 28-51). Thousand Oaks, CA: Sage.

Rosenbaum, J. E. (1976). *Making inequality: The hidden curriculum of high school tracking*. New York: John Wiley & Sons.

Rosenbaum, J. E. (1987). Structural models of organizational careers: A critical review and new directions. In R. L. Breiger (Ed.), *Social mobility and social structure* (pp. 272-307). New York: Cambridge University Press.

Rosenbaum, J. E. (1995). Changing the geography of opportunity by expanding residential choice: Lessons from the Gautreaux Program. *Housing Policy Debate, 6* (1), 231-270.

Rosenbaum, J. E., Kariya, T., Settersten, R. A., Jr., & Maier, T. (1990). Market and network theories of the high school-to-work transition: Their application to industrialized societies. *Annual Review of Sociology, 16,* 263-299.

Ruggles, P. (1990). *Drawing the line: Alternative poverty measures and their implications for public policy.* Washington, D.C.: The Urban Institute.

Rutter, M. (1993). Developmental psychopathology as a research perspective. In D. Magnusson & P. Casaer (Eds.), *Longitudinal research on individual development* (pp. 127-152). Cambridge, UK: Cambridge University Press.

Ryder, N. (1965). The cohort as a concept in the study of social change. *American Sociological Review, 30,* 843-861.

Scarr, S. (1993). Genes, experience, and development. In D. Magnusson & P. Casaer (Eds.), *Longitudinal research on individual development* (pp. 26-50). Cambridge, UK: Cambridge University Press.

Schultz, J. H. (1995). *The economics of aging* (6th ed.). Westport, CT: Auburn House.

Settersten, R. A., Jr. (1999). *Lives in time and place: The problems and promises of developmental science.* Amityville, NY: Baywood.

Smeeding, T. (1986). Nonmoney income and the elderly: The case of the 'tweeners. *Journal of Policy Analysis and Management, 5* (4), 707-724.

Sørensen, A. B. (1991). The restructuring of gender relations in an aging society. *Acta Sociologica, 34,* 45-55.

Swadener, B. B., & Lubeck, S. (1995). The social construction of children and families at risk: An introduction. In B. B. Swadener & S. Lubeck (Eds.), *Children and families "at promise": Deconstructing the discourse of risk* (pp. 1-14). Albany, NY: State University of New York Press.

U.S. Bureau of the Census (2000, January 13). Census Bureau projects doubling of nation's population by 2100. http://www.census.gov/population/www/projections/natsum.html

Walker, A. (1999). Public policy and theories of aging: Constructing and reconstructing old age. In V. L. Bengtson & K. W. Schaie (Eds.), *Handbook of theories of aging.* New York: Springer.

Wolfe, A., & Klausen, J. (1997) Identity politics and the welfare state. In E. F. Paul, F. D. Miller, Jr., & J. Paul (Eds.), *The welfare state* (pp. 231-255). Cambridge, England: Cambridge University Press.

Zigler, E. & Styfco, S. J. (1994). Head Start: Criticisms in a constructive context. *American Psychologist, 49* (2), 127-132.

PART V

Promises for Understanding
Successful Aging

CHAPTER 8

Contextualizing Successful Aging: New Directions in an Age-Old Search*

Eva Kahana and Boaz Kahana

Gerontologists have long endeavored to unravel elements of successful aging. They have invoked diverse conceptualizations regarding the outcomes of successful aging and have considered challenges faced by aging persons in attaining these outcomes, as well as facilitators of goal attainment (Featherman, Smith, & Peterson, 1990; Rowe & Kahn, 1998). Less attention has been directed at the processes of successful aging (Baltes & Baltes, 1990), particularly beyond the attainment of medical outcomes such as longevity, physical health and mental health. Furthermore, gerontological research has clung closely to exploration of late-life. Few scholars have considered events or adaptations occurring throughout life that shape successful aging, or the societal contexts within which successful aging takes place.

In this chapter, we explore alternative directions for models of successful aging, and the conceptual and methodological challenges faced in this quest. We make these directions and challenges concrete by contextualizing our previous model of Preventive and Corrective Proactivity (PCP) (Kahana & Kahana, 1996). We cannot shy away from acknowledging the definitional problems associated with conceptualizing and operationalizing constructs related to successful aging. We consider these problems within the context of our model and the work of others.

*The work reported in this manuscript has been supported by two grants from the National Institute on Aging, "Buffers of Impairment/Disability Cascade Among the Old-Old" (AG10738) and "Adaptation to Frailty Among Dispersed Elderly" (AG-07823).

Particularly in the last decade, gerontological research began to examine the positive aspects of aging. Prior to that, much of it was focused on identifying the problems of aging. Successful aging is more than the absence of problems. It must be considered in the context of comprehensive multidimensional models of health and wellness (Lawton, 1980; Pearlin, Lieberman, Menaghan, & Mullan, 1981).

Despite the emphasis on "aging well" in recent literature, few testable conceptual frameworks address the nature and antecedents of successful aging among the "old-old" (Baltes & Baltes, 1990). The propensity of older adults to respond passively to environmental influences has been the focus of dependency models of aging (Kahana, Kahana, & Kinney, 1990). This view is reflected in studies of caregiving burden, disablement, and dependency. Only recently has gerontological research recognized older persons as proactive, drawing upon and enhancing their resources and shaping their environment (Lawton, 1989).

Successful aging has been conceptualized as maximizing benefits associated with aging and minimizing losses (Baltes & Baltes, 1990). Others have emphasized the adaptive resources of the evolving self (e.g., Brandtstädter, Wentura, & Greve, 1993) or productive activity (e.g., Butler, 1994; Caro, Bass, & Chen, 1993). While our notions of proactivity emphasize continued adjustments and adaptation to the environment, other researchers have noted the important roles played by cognitive processes, such as social comparisons and goal adjustments (Franks, Herzog, Holinberg, & Markus, 1999). Common to all of these formulations is the recognition that older people can and must be active and proactive if they are to age successfully.

In this chapter, we review our prior model of successful aging and then contextualize and expand it in time and space, two dimensions central to a life-course perspective (Settersten, 1999). We tend to time by considering the influences of history and biography, and we tend to space by considering demographic and ecological contexts. We illustrate the usefulness of our expanded model with data from longitudinal research that focuses on the relationship of gender to stress exposure and proactivity (Kahana, King, Meehan, Smith, Boswell, Newell, Kahana, Kercher, & Borawski, 1996). We then consider alternative perspectives that fall outside our specific stress-based paradigm. We address the limitations of existing approaches and suggest directions for overcoming them. Our major goal is to advance understanding of successful aging by invoking conceptual and methodological contributions of a life-course perspective. These efforts provide a more comprehensive framework for understanding the aging process and the attainment of successful aging.

BRIEF OVERVIEW OF THE PREVENTIVE AND CORRECTIVE PROACTIVITY (PCP) MODEL OF SUCCESSFUL AGING

Our earlier model of Preventive and Corrective Proactivity (PCP) is anchored in the stress paradigm (Kahana & Kahana, 1996). This model is depicted in

Figure 1. It takes the normative stressors of aging to represent important challenges for older adults. Unique normative stressors of aging include illness, social losses, and lack of person-environment congruence.

Traditionally, the stress paradigm has emphasized the adverse influences of life change on health and psychological well-being (Dohrenwend & Dohrenwend, 1974). These models have also called attention to the buffering roles played by both internal resources (e.g., adequate coping strategies, self-esteem) and external resources (e.g., formal and informal social supports) (Pearlin et al., 1981). Internal and external resources are conceptualized as moderators and serve important functions in ameliorating the negative consequences of stressful life situations on diverse outcomes. Our model further developed and differentiated traditional notions about how internal and external resources enhance quality of late-life. We focused on buffering roles played by proactive behaviors, such as health promotion, planning ahead, and helping others, and view these behaviors as cornerstones of successful aging. We distinguished proactive behaviors from personality and dispositional characteristics that are generally subsumed under the category of "internal resources" (e.g., Cumming & Henry, 1961; Neugarten, 1964), and from external resources, such as social supports (e.g., Jackson, Antonucci, & Gibson, 1990). We further differentiated proactive adaptations, which serve preventive functions, from corrective adaptations, which are aimed at ameliorating adverse outcomes of stress exposure. Preventive adaptations are useful because they can diminish or delay the onset of late-life stressors, and they can also help build external resources. Corrective adaptations occur once stressors have arisen and diminish the impact of stressors through actions such as marshalling support, role substitution, and environmental modifications.

Our PCP model provided a differentiated taxonomy of enduring dispositions (personality and cognitive characteristics) that facilitates the emergence of proactive adaptations (Fleishman, 1984). We also expanded quality of life outcomes beyond traditional conceptions, which have been anchored primarily in measures of morale or psychological well being (Lawton, 1971), to encompass finding meaning in life, maintaining valued social activities and relationships, and achieving an array of positive outcomes. Our focus on preventive proactivity emphasized the ways in which individuals avoid, delay, or minimize stress exposure, how they can build their external resources, and how success in meeting life's challenges can be an important source of positive well-being. By specifying the causal linkages among elements of our model, we attempted to provide a testable and falsifiable framework for understanding elements of successful aging.

LIMITATIONS OF THE PREVENTIVE AND CORRECTIVE PROACTIVITY (PCP) MODEL

While our PCP model achieved many conceptual and empirical strides, it nonetheless stopped short of addressing the broader temporal and spatial contexts

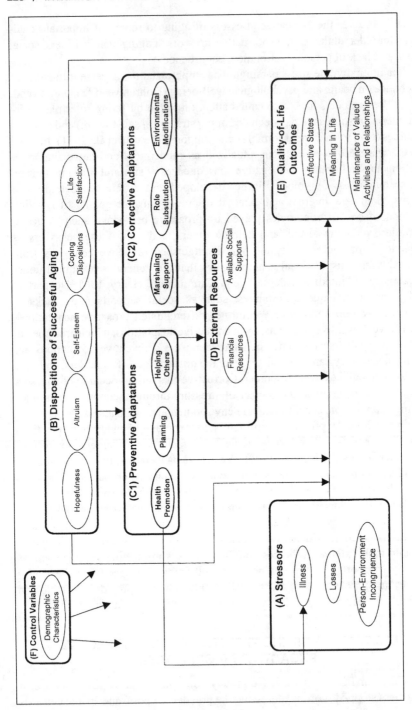

Figure 1. Successful aging: model of preventive-corrective proactivity. Adapted from Kahana, E., & Kahana, B. (1996).

within which successful aging occurs. In our original model, we broadly noted the importance of social structure (as reflected in demographic characteristics) and that these factors impinge on every element of successful aging. We suggested that demographic background factors be controlled in order to assure the recognition of their impact on specific components of the model. The necessity of including demographic variables in models of successful aging is dictated by research that emphasizes the differential life experiences of the elderly by gender, race, and social class (Stoller & Gibson, 2000). To simplify the presentation of the original model, recursive causal pathways were not depicted in Figure 1, though empirical studies must take alternative causal pathways into account (e.g., the proposition that external resources and well being may reduce stress exposure). Demographic characteristics (which we take to reflect social structural influences) and other features of the environment can also impact stress exposure, proactivity, or quality-of-life outcomes.

In our original PCP model, we also briefly noted that different types of normative stressors or challenges might exist during different life stages. Yet we stopped short of exploring how stressors endured earlier in life (be they normative or idiosyncratic) also influence successful aging. In a subsequent discussion, we began to explore the cumulative aspects of stress exposure (Kahana & Kahana, 1998). Given the limitations of our earlier model, we now propose our contextualized model.

THE CONTEXTUALIZED MODEL OF SUCCESSFUL AGING

The PCP model of successful aging emphasized agency and initiative in the form of proactive adaptations (Kahana & Kahana, 1996). The contextualized model extends the PCP model in both time and space, providing a more comprehensive, ecologically valid, and textured depiction of successful aging. In placing stress exposure, proactivity, and external resources within temporal and spatial contexts, we note that defining these contexts is highly complex. It is beyond the scope of this discussion to fully explore the benefits and limitations of alternative definitions of temporal and spatial contexts. Many of these alternative frameworks have been comprehensively reviewed by Settersten (1999).

In regard to temporal influences, our major emphasis is on stress exposure and its effects, not only in old age but throughout the life course. This generally implies gathering retrospective data about major life events, changes, and trauma occurring earlier in life. While this approach has obvious limitations related to recall or attempted reduction of cognitive dissonance (Festinger & Carlsmith, 1996), it is preferable to ignoring significant earlier events. For example, loss of a parent early in life may influence subsequent stress exposure, coping behaviors, and external resources. An orphaned child may experience stresses posed by new stepparents, lack external resources such as stable finances and social supports, and be required to cope with demands of a difficult home environment. These early life experiences likely have important effects on adaptations and resources throughout life.

Stress exposure, proactive adaptations, and resources are also influenced by social contexts. We consider demographic influences, which have been viewed in sociological research as reflecting aspects of social stratification for the individual. And we explore influences of central ecological contexts including characteristics related to residential, family, community, and cultural settings. Demographic influences and social settings influence both stress exposure and proactivity, as well as the resources at an individual's disposal for meeting challenges of late life. To simplify our discussion, we draw on examples from two spatial domains, those of gender influences (reflecting demographic characteristics) and age-segregated versus age-integrated community environments (representing the ecological context). We describe how temporal and spatial contexts influence elements of the original PCP model. The contextualized PCP model is depicted in Figure 2. The newly added model components, which contextualize the original PCP model (Figure 1), are shown in "bold" frames in Figure 2.

CONTEXTUALIZING STRESS EXPOSURE

Temporal Context of Stress Exposure

The temporal context introduces the background and influences of "biography and history" (Mills, 1959) on successful aging. It recognizes that challenges to aging persons are not limited to stresses that occur in later life. Rather, the influence of late-life stressors must be considered alongside cumulative stress exposure (Kahana & Kahana, 1998; Wheaton, 1996). Exposure to such stressors may have arisen based on historical events or personal history. In addition, chronic enduring stressors often arise from traumatic stressors. Sequelae of trauma include psychological and social residues such as hyper-vigilance, isolation, or stigma. These characteristics are incorporated into the traumatized individual's psyche and contribute to the spectrum of stressors confronted by elderly individuals (Kahana, Kahana, Harel, Kelly, Monaghan, & Holland, 1997).

Researchers have increasingly recognized the relevance of the life-course perspective to understanding exposure and adaptation to stress (e.g., Aldwin, 1991; Rodin, 1987). Prior stress experience likely alters responses to subsequent stress exposure, increasing or diminishing the impact of future stressors. Proponents of the vulnerability hypothesis have emphasized that earlier stress exposure may deplete one's social and psychological resources, which in turn may increase the likelihood of exposure to future stressors (e.g., Lin & Ensel, 1989; Wheaton, 1983). A variety of mechanisms might underlie these effects, ranging from having limited abilities to recognize or withstand future stressors (Pearlin et al., 1981) or to occupy high-risk roles or statuses (Turner, Wheaton, & Lloyd,

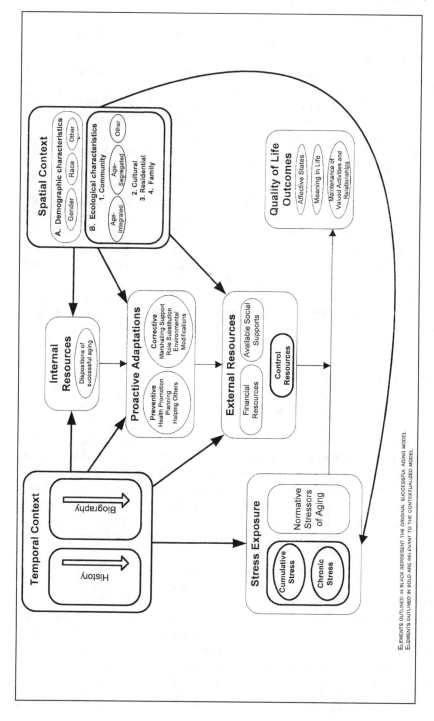

Figure 2. Contextualized model of successful aging.

ELEMENTS OUTLINED IN BLACK REPRESENT THE ORIGINAL SUCCESSFUL AGING MODEL.
ELEMENTS OUTLINED IN BOLD ARE RELEVANT TO THE CONTEXTUALIZED MODEL.

1995). The latter may be exemplified by divorce or widowhood, predisposing single parents to economic or role strains as they simultaneouly juggle roles of worker and parent.

Conversely, proponents of the inoculation hypothesis have suggested that early stress may diminish the adverse effects of later stress, based on enhanced coping skills and abilities to meet life's challenges (e.g., Garmezy, 1983; Turner & Roszell, 1994). For example, Roszell (1996) suggests that there is considerable interdependence between initial and later stressors in predicting adverse outcomes, so that exposure to loss early in life may diminish the potentially adverse outcomes of later losses.

Extensive empirical evidence links a variety of stressors to adverse physical and mental health sequelae. These stressors include lifetime trauma, recent stressful life events, chronic stress, role strain and daily hassles (e.g., Pearlin, 1983; Pearlin et al., 1981; Turner et al., 1995). However, stress researchers have predominantly focused on recent life events. Even when they acknowledge potential long-term influences of early life stressors, they seldom consider both early and recent life events (Kahana & Kahana, 1998).

However, one finding relevant to a life-course perspective is that childhood adversity is often predictive of adult depressive symptoms (Kessler & Magee, 1994; Rutter, 1989). Similarly, in our research on elderly survivors of the Nazi Holocaust (Kahana et al., 1997), we called attention to the long-term influences of this earlier trauma. We also considered the normative stressors these individuals endured in the context of their unique biography and the historical periods through which they lived. Normative influences on elderly Holocaust survivors included childhood life stressors and adult life stressors, including stressors of immigration and acculturation. These normative stressors were layered on the trauma-related stressors endured during the pre-war period, during the Holocaust, and during the post-war period. Individuals who, because of historical events, experienced great trauma early in their lives, carry secondary, trauma-induced chronic stressors with them over time. Such chronic stressors include intrusive memories of trauma, living with fear and distrust, isolation, and stigma. The latter are likely to influence their appraisal of normative stressors of late-life and their late-life adaptation. Additionally, even less stressful life experiences not bound to historical events contribute to cumulative stress and subsequent adaptation.

In the original PCP model, we considered illness and loss as the most important challenges to successful aging. Following up on our earlier example, the impact of such normative stressors would be magnified for individuals whose lives during the Holocaust were in jeopardy if they showed signs of illness or weakness. Therefore, the temporal context of early experiences is an important precursor to understanding how survivors appraise normative stressors of later life. Elderly survivors of the Holocaust may also have experienced further threats during prior illness episodes. Based on the trauma they endured, they may fear that illness makes them vulnerable, and they may mistrust the health care system and those in charge of their care. Consequently, the quality of later life for these individuals would be challenged not only by normative late-life stressors of illness, but by cumulative and chronic stressors that comprise lifetime stress exposure.

There are numerous cumulative stressors that impact adults as they age, even those who did not endure extreme trauma early in life. The social losses that occur with aging may pose threats to psychological well being by decreasing the number of roles that older people are able to occupy (Linville, 1987). Multiple role involvements during younger years allow individuals opportunities to maintain high self-esteem (Breytspraak, 1984). Social isolation, which may come about as people age and lose friends and family members, may also result in negative mental health effects by reducing the multiple identities that promote well being throughout life (Thoits, 1983). Age-based social institutions, such as school and work, also lose salience as people grow older. Greater awareness of patterns of stress exposure during different life stages can strengthen understandings of successful aging by pointing to the cumulative nature of stress and coping.

Spatial Influences on Stress Exposure

Stress exposure throughout life is also shaped by the individual's placement within social structures and the environment. Our approach to the spatial context is divided into two broad categories as depicted in Figure 2: demographic characteristics and ecological contexts. *Demographic characteristics* are routinely considered by sociologists as representative of the enduring influences of social structures on individuals (Stoller & Gibson, 2000). Age, gender, race, and ethnicity are seen as master statuses, which define how social stratification impinges on every aspect of an individual's life. Yet, in spite of their appeal and ease of measurement, it is difficult to tell to what extent demographic characteristics reflect cultural, economic, biological, psychological, or socialization factors. In fact, reflexive and simplistic consideration of demographic or other ecological variables has been criticized as being reductionist (Settersten, 1999).

Expanding the PCP model in space is timely, as recent work has suggested that epidemiological variability in psychological well being and mental health may stem from differences in social support, which is influenced by differential placement in the social structure (e.g., Eaton & Muntaner, 1999; Turner & Marino, 1994). Similarly, evidence of differential stress exposure, based on social-structural characteristics, has also been underscored in recent sociological research (e.g., Turner & Roszell, 1994; Wheaton, 1983). Men, women, and people from different racial or ethnic backgrounds are differentially exposed to stressful life events, such as being victims of crime or experiencing role overload.

The *ecological context* refers to extrinsic milieu represented by cultural, social, or physical environments. Ecological units may range from the macro level, defined by the cultural context within which aging occurs (Cain, 1964), to the meso level of community, family, and residential context (Bronfenbrenner, 1979;

234 / INVITATION TO THE LIFE COURSE

Brown, 1997). On the macro level, societies that provide few roles for elders create stressors through role loss (Rosow, 1974). Societies may also limit or maximize social supports and financial resources available to older adults. Societal and cultural influences are also strongly expressed through social policies toward the aged. Provision of health insurance programs, such as Medicare in the United States, may protect older adults from normative stressors of illness. Alternatively, social policies may contribute to stress exposure in late-life, through retirement policies that may rob older adults of opportunities for meaningful engagement in work.

Meso-level characteristics are also relevant to stress exposure of older adults, and particularly characteristics of the "suprapersonal" environment, such as age-integrated versus age-segregated environmental settings (Lawton, 1980). Age-integrated living may minimize explicit or implicit rituals and shared experiences about status passages that accompany the normative stressors of later life. For example, social losses, and particularly widowhood, may be differentially experienced in age-integrated versus age-segregated communities. In age-segregated retirement communities, these transitions are shared by many members of the community, providing opportunities for older widows and widowers to congregate, go out for dinner, talk about grieving, and, in some cases, experience new-found independence (Streib, Folts, & LaGreca, 1985). In contrast, individuals in age-integrated environments may experience these transitions alone (Cain, 1964). The family context also contributes to stress exposure in late life by supplying either insufficient or excessive social supports (Stephens & Hobfoll, 1990). Similarly, the residential environment may contribute to stress exposure as the needs of the older person change, and as incongruence develops between the demands of the social environment and the abilities or needs of the older adult (Kahana, 1980).

Person-environment incongruence may characterize the life situation and stress exposure of an older person at a given point in time. Person-environment fit can be conceptualized in terms of physical or social characteristics. On the one hand, there can be incongruence between the residential environment and the older individual's needs, preferences, or abilities (Kahana, 1980). On the other hand, incongruence may also exist between role expectations, imposed by the social environment, and the capacities or preferences of the older individual (Kahn, 1979). A major area for development in gerontological theory and research is to better classify the salient environments of later life, and to understand the ways in which the features and practices of these environments promote or prevent stress exposure and place constraints on or facilitate adaptation. Person-environment incongruence may result not only from excessive demands in the environment, but also from insufficient demands, as in having too little responsibility or influence or too few opportunities to help others (Kahn, 1979). Accordingly, an unexplored avenue for the scholarship on successful aging is to cast stress exposure within the framework of ecological contexts, and especially in terms of how these contexts promote stress exposure through lack of person-environment fit.

CONTEXTUALIZING PROACTIVITY

Proactivity is the most distinct element of our PCP model because it captures preventive and corrective behavioral adaptations. Proactivity represents the major "process" component of the model and allows us to define successful aging independent of outcomes. It also permits us to consider the intersection between micro (person-based) and meso/macro (environment-based) variables in models of successful aging. Through proactivity, individuals can shape their environments, even though these environments may simultaneously constrain or facilitate their coping. The advantages of a process-based (rather than outcome-based) view include an ability to recognize success based on agency, even when negative outcomes ensue due to factors beyond the individual's control, such as heredity, adverse environments, and the temporal context of lives. While agency is a central component of the model, individuals are not to be blamed for adverse outcomes.

Temporal Context of Proactivity

A distinct feature of the original model was its focus on proactive adaptations that minimize or delay future stressors, as well as those they invoke to deal with stressors that have already arisen. To some extent, older adults of today lived through historical periods in which planning ahead was not possible because of extreme social upheaval, such as the Holocaust and World War II or the Great Depression. In these instances, preventive proactivity, such as planning, would have had little or no impact on one's future (Elder, 1974). Constraints on proactivity brought about by biographical influences are exemplified by family disorganization through death or divorce of parents, which curtail planful preventive proactivity in youth (Garmezy, 1983).

Historical and biographical influences are also likely to be important determinants of corrective proactivity. In the case of marshalling support, adults who were socialized during an era that stressed self-reliance may be less likely to ask for assistance than members of later cohorts. In fact, the eldest cohorts of today are reluctant to take advantage of entitlements designed to benefit them (Binstock, 1996).

In introducing an historical perspective to understanding proactive adaptations, it is useful to consider the fact that the eldest members of contemporary society entered adulthood in an era when people naturally engaged in physical activity as part of daily living. Walking, carrying groceries, and doing gardening and housework all constituted naturally occurring and demanding forms of exercise that were not specifically undertaken for health benefits. With the advent of the car, sedentary work patterns, and greater emphasis on passive pursuits (such as watching television), physical exercise increasingly became viewed as an activity undertaken to improve health (Elward & Larson, 1992). As new cohorts enter old age, we will likely witness shifts in the type and range of health promoting activity.

Similarly, the proactive adaptation of helping others is likely shaped by historical changes in the value of social attachments and in views about providing help to others, both within and outside the family. Within the family, older adults have often provided help in taking care of their grandchildren, at least before extensive patterns of social and geographic mobility among adult children rendered this type of involvement impractical (Adams, 1971). Interestingly, there is a resurgence of active grandparental involvement in child-rearing in urban areas, particularly among minority and low income families (Stanford, 1990).

There are marked differences between the ways that different cohorts age. Many cohort differences may be seen as resulting from or reflecting social change. The characteristics of a cohort also bring about social change. For example, increasing numbers of very old individuals, and of people with functional limitations, place demands on the health care system and on service sectors of society. Greater numbers of disabled individuals, coupled with the increasing clout of the American Association of Retired People (AARP), may have contributed to the enactment of legislation resulting in the Americans with Disabilities Act. In turn, greater accessibility of buildings and other accommodations for the disabled may enhance opportunities for activity and environmental modifications, which constitute corrective adaptations in our model.

The PCP model also emphasizes the value of role substitution as a corrective strategy. Corrective strategies are based on the expectation that the negative outcomes that may result from relinquishing one valued role might be offset when other valued roles are undertaken (Franks et al., 1999). To the extent that valued social roles, such as worker or volunteer, may be differentially available to the aged during different historical periods, opportunities for corrective proactivity may be enhanced or limited during particular times.

Spatial Context of Proactivity

Proactive adaptations are shaped in enduring ways by both demographic characteristics and ecological contexts. We first turn to an example of the ecological (community) context represented by age-integrated versus age-segregated living. We later illustrate the importance of demographic context using empirical data from our ongoing research.

Age-segregated retirement communities supply residents with a meaningful reference group, thereby eliminating one of the major problems posed for the elderly: the "social breakdown syndrome" postulated by Kuypers and Bengtson (1973). Retirement community living fosters social interaction among neighbors (Longino & Lipman, 1983). Being in close proximity facilitates mutual assistance, and leisure-oriented lifestyles reinforce the value of helping others as a means of maintaining attachments and social involvements. In these environments, providing help to age peers may be a form of preventive proactivity.

While it is natural for the young to be socialized by the old, it is less clearly accepted that the old also learn from the young (Cain, 1964). In modern industrialized societies, with increasing reliance on technology, the young often become gatekeepers to the full array of proactive adaptations, which are needed for health promotion practices or for planning ahead. To the extent that older adults migrate to age-segregated Sunbelt retirement communities, their exposure to members of the younger generation becomes limited (Jacobs, 1975). At the same time, older adults may be more open to socialization by age peers. For example, they may be more likely to take up new physical activities that are popular among age peers, such as golf, than they might be to join a health club frequented by younger individuals. These examples make it evident that characteristics of the community context likely impinge on the types of proactive activities in which individuals engage.

The symbolic-interactionist sociological tradition (e.g., Blumer, 1969) focuses on the ongoing and creative participation of individuals in social interactions. One can anticipate that role substitutions actively undertaken by individuals, as posited in the corrective proactivity component of our model, can be useful in helping older people sustain positive self-images and maintain identities in the face of role losses that come with aging (Lemon, Bengtson, & Peterson, 1972). However, the opportunities for role substitutions may be differentially available to older adults depending on their community contexts. Opportunities for finding part-time employment after retirement are less available in age-segregated retirement communities than age-integrated settings. Retirement communities also provide fewer opportunities to fulfill family roles, such as grandparenthood. On the other hand, age-segregated settings provide an abundance of opportunities for leisure activities. Depending on the types of functions that are lost with advancing age, the community context will differentially support possibilities for role substitution.

The formation of a retirement subculture in age-segregated retirement community settings (Streib et al., 1985) reflects the dynamics of social change in terms of changing characteristics of subsequent cohorts of elders and social response to these changes. The migration of large numbers of affluent older adults to the Sunbelt supports the formation of new community options, such as health clubs and swimming pools which, in turn, can support health-promoting lifestyles (Renwick, Brown & Nagler, 1996). As migrants to the Sunbelt age, and as retirement communities are increasingly populated by very old residents, amenities and services change, as exemplified by new transportation systems and placement of benches along popular routes in the community (Kahana, Kahana, Kercher, King, Lovegreen, & Chirayath, 1999). These environmental resources, in turn, enable frail older adults to continue functioning. Frail elders may get around by taking frequent breaks as they walk through their communities. It is also important to recognize that options for age-segregated Sunbelt retirement community living have largely remained closed to African-American and other minority elders (Kahana et al., 1999). Furthermore, retirement community living does not protect older adults from the ageism of better functioning elders who may separate themselves from functionally impaired peers, thereby constraining the opportunities of those most in need of social support. Further exploration of the ways in which ecological contexts prohibit or facilitate opportunities for proactivity are needed.

Contextual influences also significantly impact an individual's ability to alter an environment so that it is more congruent with personal needs and states. Moving to a more congruent setting is one way a person can escape an incongruent environment. However, moves may also create new and different types of stressors (Schulz & Brenner, 1977). Yet the opportunities, and even inclinations, to move are impacted by factors related to history, biography, demographic characteristics, and community contexts.

CONTEXTUALIZING EXTERNAL RESOURCES

In the original PCP model, external resources for successful aging were based on economic and social resources. Both temporal and spatial influences likely impact each of these resources. To illustrate these influences, we focus on the social support components of external resources.

Temporal Influences on External Resources

In gerontological research, social supports are typically viewed as resources available in old age. However, these resources are based on lifelong interactions between individuals and others. To the extent that individuals succeed in building a "convoy" of social supports throughout life, it is likely that such supports will be available when they reach old age (Antonucci & Akiyama, 1991). The availability of social supports in old age is largely a function of an individual's network of friends and family. The original PCP model recognized that both individual proactivity (such as marshalling support) and stress exposure (such as bereavement) influence the availability of social supports. Our contextualized model calls attention to an older adult's prior history of social relationships, which likely leads to the availability (or lack thereof) of social supports in later life. This history is impacted by historical events, which may have limited family size or opportunities for marriage, as well as personal proactivity. Working women from cohorts in which few women worked outside the home may have had fewer opportunities to develop families and close circles of friends than women who took more traditional family-based pathways (Troll, 1994). Consequently, these women may find themselves with more limited social support networks in old age.

Spatial Influences on External Resources

The availability of social supports in old age is also influenced by the demographic characteristics of individuals and the community context. For example, women are widowed at younger ages than men. Widows are more likely to rely on formal support networks and may have increased service needs as their health declines. Similarly, the community context impacts the availability of both formal and informal social supports. For example, older adults living in age-segregated communities might first rely on a network of friends for support, while those living in the age-integrated communities might first turn to family members.

The ecological context not only influences the availability of social supports from friends and family, but also resources for independent living, which are critical for maintaining quality of life among frail older adults. As noted above, in the original PCP model, external resources were defined primarily in terms of economic resources and social support. In the contextualized model, we also call attention to "control resources." For elderly people who face frailty or the potential loss of independence, control resources may include the availability of a driver, consumer-directed helpers, assistive devices, and good access to health care. These are more concrete, disability-specific definitions relative to more traditional definitions anchored in adequate social supports and finances. Our discussion of the community context of successful aging has highlighted the importance of differential access to control resources in different living environments and family contexts. Control resources affect social-structural features, which in turn affect meaning in life and the maintenance of valued activities and relationships. Understanding the ecological contexts within which proactive adaptations occur helps us appreciate the degree to which older adults experience real limits on control. The gerontological literature has directed considerable attention to locus of control, mastery, and efficacy beliefs as potential facilitators of successful aging (Seligman, 1975).

GENDER INFLUENCES ON SUCCESSFUL AGING:
AN EMPIRICAL ILLUSTRATION ACROSS
MODEL COMPONENTS

We now illustrate how gender—one dimension of demographic influences under spatial context—impinges on elements of the model. Alternative theoretical orientations within sociology may be extended to gender differences in adaptation to aging. Expectations of differential social roles for men and women arise from structural functionalist theories (e.g., Parsons & Bales, 1955). In this view, men are assigned to instrumental roles while women fulfill expressive roles. This division of labor, which is seen as adaptive for society, results in women and men developing different styles of adaptation that may persist throughout life.

Another formulation arises from conflict theory. Based on this view, women have experienced many social disadvantages and stressors throughout life because they are relegated to less valued roles and suffer economic and social discrimination. This perspective has been articulated as the "double jeopardy" hypothesis for older women. Being both female and old, and, in some cases having minority status, add to greater risk for stress exposure (Stoller & Gibson, 2000).

A less deterministic and more process-oriented view of gender roles derives from symbolic interactionism (e.g., Goffman, 1959). This view takes into account both structural constraints and the individual's role in defining their situations. Men and women define criteria they find meaningful for role performance based on internalized representations of their social environments. This perspective is better suited to micro-level social-psychological analyses and is compatible with the stress paradigm. The stress paradigm acknowledges that gender-related differences in social roles result in different levels and types of stress. In particular, the increasing numbers of roles played by women are seen as increasing the likelihood of stress. Furthermore, role conflicts likely pose stress at the intersection of multiple roles. Because women are more linked to expressive roles and friendship networks, they may benefit from more extensive social supports. At the same time, women are more exposed to losses as friends become ill or die. Men, in contrast, may be more insulated from such losses (Helsing, Szklo, & Comstock, 1981).

In addition to stress exposure, gender differences likely exist in stress appraisal. Women, who are more embedded in family roles may react more adversely to events such as divorce of an adult child, which may bring the potential for increased role responsibility. Men, however, may have greater difficulty in dealing with work-related losses, which may decrease their role responsibilities.

A major area of gender differences relates to coping resources and strategies that correspond to proactive adaptations in the proposed model. Prior literature does not provide clear directives about the nature of gender differences in adaptive strategies. Some studies report more effective coping strategies among men, and others suggest that women possess more flexible and effective coping repertoires (Stoller & Gibson, 2000).

We have considered elements of successful aging in an ongoing study of 1,000 retirees to the Sunbelt of the United States. The findings reported here are from the first wave of our study, when the mean age of respondents was 79.3 years. Data from this project permit us to explore gender differences in elements of the PCP model, and our findings illustrate the pervasiveness and complexity of gender differences throughout it.

HEALTH-RELATED STRESSORS

Instrumental Activities of Daily Living

In our generally healthy sample, respondents indicated little difficulty with instrumental activities of daily living. Statistically significant differences existed between men and women in total Instrumental Activities of Daily Living, with women exhibiting greater difficulty ($p < .01$, alpha = .87). An examination of specific items in this scale (with a range of 1 to 4, where 1 reflected "never having difficulty" and 4 reflected "always having difficulty"), indicated that women had significantly more difficulty walking up and down stairs (1.5 for women versus 1.3 for men, $p < .05$), doing housework (1.6 for women versus 1.3 for men, $p < .05$) and shopping for groceries (1.2 for women versus 1.1 for men, $p < .05$). There were no differences between men and women in getting from room to room, going out of doors, and preparing their own meals.

PROACTIVE ADAPTATIONS

Health Promotion

Men engaged in regular exercise significantly more than women (at least 3 times per week) (69.3 percent of men and 45.6 percent of women; $p < .001$). In regard to other health promotion activities, a reverse trend was observed. Significantly more women reported avoiding harmful substances (48.6 percent of women compared to 35.4 percent of men; $p < .01$). We found no gender differences in other health behaviors. The striking gender differences in exercise may be a function of socialization for this older cohort, where men were encouraged toward active lifestyles and had the opportunity to devote leisure time to self-enhancing pursuits. Our findings of greater risk avoidance in the health behaviors of women support prior findings by Antonucci, Akiyama, and Adelmann (1990).

Planning Ahead

Overall, both men and women in this sample were found to be planful regarding provisions for future care. Women planned more for future disability (64.7 percent of women and 51.7 percent of men, $p < .001$). These plans extend from considering housing options to advanced directives. However, when considering general future plans, the relationship between gender and planning was found to shift. Men planned more for travel and new purchases (45.9 percent for men versus 39.0 percent for women). Plans for visits to children did not differ by gender, and this finding held even after marital status was controlled. Differences in patterns of planning likely reflect the interaction between situational demands and personal tendencies. Women who anticipate widowhood or are already widowed have a greater need to plan for their own care. Men, in contrast, may more readily assume that they will be cared for by current or future wives.

Helping Others

Volunteering

There was a high level of volunteering among respondents, with 40 percent having volunteered an average of six hours per week during the past year. No significant differences were found between men and women in the propensity to volunteer.

Assisting Friends and Family

Prior research suggests that men at all age levels belong to more volunteer organizations, while women are more involved in providing personal assistance to others (Gallagher, 1994). Throughout their lives, women are more likely to be called upon for caregiving (Kastenbaum, 1993), and men are usually socialized to delegate hands-on caregiving tasks (Matthews & Rosner, 1988). In our research, gender differences were observed in selected areas of providing assistance to others. Men and women provided similar levels of help to friends who were in need of transportation (45.3 percent of women and 46.7 percent of men, $p < .001$). However, consistent with prior research, women more often helped friends with shopping (33.5 percent of women and 25.2 percent of men) and household tasks (6.2 percent of women and 2.8 percent of men, $p < .05$). In assisting family members, men and women gave similar levels of assistance with finances (14.5 percent of women and 21.0 percent of men, $p < .05$) and household chores (15.1 percent of women and 17.0 percent of men). However, women more often provided extensive help when a family member was sick (11.6 percent of women and 5.6 percent of men). Overall, women provided more assistance to both friends and family.

CORRECTIVE PROACTIVE ADAPTATIONS

Gender differences were also considered along two of the three dimensions of proactive adaptations: marshalling support and environmental modifications. The third proposed dimension, role substitution, was not measured in the first wave of our study.

Marshalling Support

Women more often expressed difficulty in asking for assistance when they experienced problems (52.1 percent of women versus 39.4 percent of men, $p < .05$). These findings differ from general expectations that women would be able to marshal support more readily than men, based on their greater extroversion (Barer, 1994), self-disclosure (Pennebaker, 1995), and emotion-focused coping styles (Vingerhoets & Van Heck, 1990). It is possible that if women required greater assistance, then their response reflects the reality of their experiences, while men may have responded to a hypothetical situation.

Environmental Modifications

Modifications to home environments (e.g., installation of a shower chair) were made about equally by men and women. These findings suggest that environmental modifications may be less important for both men and women in a structured retirement community designed for aging than they might be in non-planned communities. Furthermore, there would be little reason to expect that gender should play a major role in the propensity to modify the physical environment.

EXTERNAL RESOURCES OF SUCCESSFUL AGING

Available Social Supports

Almost all men and women in our study have a confidant (94.8 percent of men and 95.2 percent of women), though the types were found to differ for men and women. Men more often listed their wives as their only confidantes (2.9 percent of women and 12.3 percent of men). Men also more often listed their sons as confidants (19.2 percent of men as compared to 10.5 percent of women), and women listed their sisters (7.9 percent of women as compared to 3.0 percent of men). Women also more often listed friends as their confidants (35.3 percent of women as compared to 23.0 percent of men).

Men and women also differed in the amount of emotional support they received from spouses, family and friends (scale range of 1 to 5, with 1 reflecting "none" and 5 reflecting "very much"). Men received more support from their spouses (3.9 for women versus 4.5 for men, $p < .01$), while women received more support from family (3.8 for women versus 3.5 for men, $p < .05$) and friends (3.2 for women versus 2.9 for men, $p < .01$). The latter findings are consistent with prior research, which indicate that women tend to receive more informal support than men, particularly after age 75, and that women identify more kin in their social networks than men (McDaniel & McKinnon, 1993).

These data provide useful insights into the gendered nature of late-life adaptation. Rather than suggesting simple and clear-cut advantages for men or women as they age, our data underscore the complex influences of socialization, differences in opportunity structures, and, most importantly, resilience and adaptability, which evolve out of differential life experiences. A model of successful aging which has proactive adaptation as its core allows us to understand the specific needs of male and female elders. Consistent with growing emphasis in the field on diversity in patterns of aging, greater attention to differences in elements of successful aging helps specify processes that underlie diversity. We learn that, out of their unique life circumstances, women and men develop adaptations tailored to their special circumstances.

It is also important to recognize that socialization is a lifelong process (Rosow, 1974). For future cohorts of older adults, there are increasing options to move away from long-term social and physical environments. The reliance on family for daily assistance might be altered for those who live at great distances from their children, and particularly for those in age-segregated settings. As these elders develop new support systems among their peers, women may have a distinct advantage based on their well-honed nurturing roles. Their greater propensity to aid others may result in greater success in establishing a network of peers to help in times of need.

The findings of our research are also consistent with tenets of cultural feminism (Andersen, 2000), given that they point to some basic differences in value orientations, behavior patterns, and adaptation between men and women. However, our data do not provide evidence for one gender portraying superior adaptive skills than the other. Rather, they suggest that each gender adapts in ways tailored to their life experiences and value orientations.

Our gender-related findings also call attention to the multidimensionality of elements of the successful aging model. It is necessary to go beyond unidimensional generalizations about health promotion, planning, or helping in order to appreciate gender influences in each area. In the area of health promotion, exercise and substance avoidance yield different gender-linked patterns. In regard to planning, we must differentiate planning for dependency from normal role-related planning in order to understand gender influences. In terms of helping others, both "domains" and "targets" of helping must be considered for understanding the gendered nature of the adaptation.

In evaluating our findings about gender differences, we acknowledge that residents of retirement communities represent a unique group. They are older adults who self-selected to relocate in late-life to age-homogenous settings generally at a distance from their families. The retirement community is designed for leisure-oriented lifestyles, and both men and women are removed from instrumental worlds of work and expressive worlds of family. Such settings may thus foster convergence in lifestyles and adaptations of men and women. Nevertheless, the fact that clear differences do emerge attests to the powerful roles of lifelong gender socialization. Our contextualized model of successful aging brings many complex challenges. We now discuss some of these complexities and acknowledge ambiguities inherent in it.

CHALLENGES AND OPPORTUNITIES FOR THE STUDY OF SUCCESSFUL AGING

Overlap between Elements of Context

The first challenge is to recognize that elements of the temporal and spatial contexts may not always be independent of elements of the basic model. In developing traditional models of stress, social scientists have typically incorporated some aspects of social context as major model elements. For example, aspects of social support, which in our model are represented by external resources of available social supports, are inherently tied to ecological characteristics of family, community, and residence. Each of these external resources sets parameters on the type and availability of support (Settersten, 1999). Similarly, one might find areas of overlap between ecological contexts of community or residence and degree of stress exposure experienced by an individual throughout life. Certain environmental characteristics, such as crowded or impoverished communities, may be inherently stressful. In spite of these areas of potential overlap, we find it useful to retain core elements of the traditional stress paradigm in our basic model while recognizing that components of social context impinge on these elements.

Linking Individuals and Social Structure

Scholarship on the life course should establish linkages between individuals and society by focusing on differential distributions of opportunities for growth and to human development (Settersten, 1999). These differences may be based on differential distribution of economic and cultural resources, such as educational opportunities (Dowd, 1980). In extending the successful aging paradigm in space, specifying how sociodemographic influences constrain or facilitate opportunities for proactivity and the availability of external resources, we move closer to attending to person-structure interactions. Ultimately, our hope is to connect temporal and spatial dimensions of context in our model. Sociodemographic or ecological factors may influence successful aging by contributing to both lifetime stress exposure and to socialization into proactivity throughout life. Interaction effects such as these are exemplified as we consider differential childhood socialization patterns for men and women into exercise and other health-promoting activities that may carry over into old age. Our finding that elderly women exercise less than elderly men may be a function of lifelong activity patterns that were shaped by a society that values exercise more for men than women. Indeed, gender differences in expectations about exercise may have been reinforced in early school and family experiences (Strawbridge, Camacho, Cohen, & Kaplan, 1993).

Stress-based models of successful aging invoke interactions between individuals and their social contexts in that these models focus on ways in which older adults are able to marshal personal and social resources to ameliorate the adverse effects of stress. Successful aging has been conceptualized by Baltes and Baltes (1990) as reflecting a maximization of benefits associated with aging together with a minimization of losses. Baltes and Baltes' work has emphasized the ways in which older adults may optimize their situations through selectivity and compensation. For example, older adults who experience limited energy may prioritize involvement in sports and hobbies. They may reduce involvement in less valued activities so as to devote their remaining energies to their favorite sports or organizations.

Influences on social structure and successful aging may also be illustrated through cohort effects. Recent research on wisdom in later life points to some of the benefits associated with being a member of older cohorts (e.g., Ardelt, 1997). Older adults were socialized prior to the advent of the technological have unique skills for handling household tasks. They also possess basic mathematical skills, as they seldom rely on calculators. Thus, older adults may derive self-esteem from possessing skills that are scarce among today's youth.

Stressors, and particularly major life events, have been viewed as key dynamic forces that propel individuals along life pathways (Riegel, 1975). Our prior work has also explored differential stress exposure to recent life events based on the individual's placement in social structure (Kahana, et al., 1999). Within the PCP model, we implicitly recognized the influences of social structure when we outlined normative stressors of aging. Normative life changes, such as retirement, may be propelled by social structural influences and pose challenges to aging individuals. We also noted that human agency, in the form of proactive adaptation, reflects the ongoing propensity of individuals to anticipate and cope with elements of the environment. These notions are even more explicit in the contextualized model.

DISTAL ANTECEDENTS AND PROJECTIONS
OF THE FUTURE

An important challenge to future research and theory on successful aging relates to considering both proximal and distal antecedents of current adaptations. We cannot assume that patterns of successful aging are independent of experiences and adaptations forged throughout life. Nor can we assume that older adults are incapable of invoking new adaptations that facilitate success in later life. Our PCP model focused on specific proactive adaptations that facilitate coping with normative stressors associated with aging, and socialization during childhood and earlier periods of adulthood likely has important influences on late-life proactivity.

For example, where modes of health promotion, such as exercise or low fat diets, were not salient during early socialization of today's elders, and particularly women, they may require new socialization to adopt health-promoting behaviors in late-life. Those who move to retirement communities where peer socialization promotes formal exercise may even initiate these behaviors for the first time during later life. For those older adults who received reinforcement for excelling in sports activities early in life, such early reinforcements may be important distal antecedents of late-life proactivity.

While we generally study successful aging in the present, expanding our paradigm temporally helps us recognize connections to both the past and projected future. The degree to which individuals are able to draw on dimensions of past, present, and future may, in and of itself, reflect flexibility important to successful aging. Indeed, preventive proactive adaptations, such as planning ahead and pursuing health-promoting lifestyles, require a positive anticipation of the future.

OTHER CHALLENGES FOR FUTURE RESEARCH

Contextualizing models of successful aging provides a greater understanding of the complex influences of both time and place. However, these complexities pose challenges to empirical work that seeks to test these models. Nevertheless, the causal pathways outlined in both our original and contextualized PCP models (Figures 1 and 2) readily allow us to test the elements of these models. Our presentation in here has been, of necessity, generic. Empirical investigations will benefit from better specifying parameters related to time and space, both of which impinge on each component of the model. For example, research might usefully focus on specifying temporal influences such as stress exposure during childhood and adolescence, which likely has negative effects on late-life pro-activity or other outcomes. Broader tests of the model might consider proposed causal linkages in different community settings or for different racial or gender groups. The task of testing the broader model represents a promising agenda for cumulative empirical studies.

Our own research has begun to move in these directions. We have noted racial similarities in proactive adaptations, such as planning and helping others when comparing White and African-American respondents (Kahana et al., 1999). In addition, we have found support for long-term benefits of both pre-ventive adaptations of health promotion (Kahana, Lawrence, Kahana, Kercher, Stoller, & Stange, 2000) and of helping others (Kahana, Midlarsky, & King, 1998). Spatial contextualization of our model led us to recognize that our findings based on age-segregated community contexts must also be explored in age-integrated community settings.

Furthermore, we should reiterate that the examples provided in this chapter have, of necessity, been selective. We have paid attention to only one ecological context—the community, and to one of its primary characteristics—age-segregation versus age-integration. Our broad model also presents many possibilities for the study of other contexts, such as family or residential contexts. Selectivity is needed to guide empirical research and explore the effects of specific variables, and of specific causal sequences, that can be empirically isolated and compared. The causal pathways specified in both the original and the proposed contextualized model of successful aging suggest approaches to multivariate and path analytic studies. The specification of recursive paths may be explored using structural equation modeling in the context of longitudinal studies. Models of successful aging tend to be complex, and contextualizing these models only adds to their complexity. For researchers, such complexity may suggest the fruitfulness of testing each component of the model separately. It is also important to emphasize that there is considerable room for qualitative approaches to our model. Temporal expansion of the model and concomitant assessment of cumulative life stress lends itself well to in-depth life history interviews. Consideration of spatial context, particularly for older adults living in institutional settings, opens the way for strategies that explore the multitude of ways in which institutional living constrains proactivity. For example, how might one age successfully in the nursing home? Goffman's (1961) classic work on total institutions provides us with ample reasons to expect that these settings likely constrain proactivity. Even amidst scattered therapy programs, proactive adaptations such as planning, helping others, role substitution or environmental modification may become nearly impossible.

Recognizing the ways in which ecological contexts may shape stress exposure and place constraints on adaptive strategies calls for an exploration of these models in alternative ecological contexts. Urban versus rural settings, age-integrated or segregated communities, and assisted living or nursing home environments are likely to lead to differential stress exposure and permit different expressions of adaptive strategies. By conceptualizing successful aging as a process, we are permitted to examine and capture the selectivity of these processes, as individuals move from independent living to assisted living, and as they face significant challenges and opportunities along the way. Gerontological research typically pays little attention to contextual influences and is seldom set in comparative frameworks. Similarly, closer attention to the complex influences of demographic factors on each of the elements of successful aging will provide a more differentiated portrayal of stressors, internal and external resources, and their relationship to outcomes.

BEYOND THE CONSTRAINTS OF PRIOR APPROACHES

Stress-based frameworks of successful aging, are predicated on the achievement of a broad spectrum of desirable outcomes and high quality of life. In our PCP model, we expanded the range of outcomes beyond traditional indices of psychological well being to also include meaning in life and social functioning. We also allowed for definitions of successful aging based on processes as well as outcomes. Accordingly, a person who engages in proactive corrective adaptations can be viewed as aging successfully even if progressive frailty results in lower levels of psychological well-being. Our expanded range of positive outcomes also provides a glimpse into the phenomenology of successful aging by considering meaning in life as an important outcome.

We are just beginning to more seriously consider the processes of successful aging and the phenomenology of older person's definition of stress. Prior research shows that older adults vary in the degree to which they identify themselves as old (Karp, 1988), and older people subsume a broad range of physical, social, psychological and spiritual phenomena in their personal definitions of success. When we asked our respondents about their criteria for successful aging, we obtained many existential definitions akin to Tornstam's (1997) notions of "gero-transcendence." Many elders see their success in terms of the legacy they will leave to future generations through their work and family contributions. Others cite dispositional qualities that seem independent of age, such as optimism or the moral fiber of the individual. For most, success is considered in personal terms, though it often involves the lives and accomplishments of significant others. We must also recognize that the very term "success" holds within it a Western, and largely American, view of achievement orientation in defining the goals of aging. A less restricted view of "good" aging may offer entirely different perspectives on that which is desirable for individuals, families, and society.

Our discussion has focused on successful aging of individuals. Our research has documented the prevalence of proactive adaptations and, specifically, of health-promoting behaviors among individuals who migrated to Sunbelt retirement communities (Kahana et al., 2000). The availability of peers who serve as role models and socializing agents for health-promoting lifestyles likely play an important role in supporting such lifestyles. Peers facilitate proactive adaptations above and beyond selection factors that lead to migration of proactive individuals. The confluence of environmental facilitators is thus likely to lead to the development of larger groups of successful agers.

As we seek to understand the secrets of successful aging for individuals, we must be cognizant of social influences that can reinforce behaviors of successful aging for aggregate groups of older adults. The picture of healthy and active communities of older people holds promise. But there are also dangers inherent in group-based definitions of successful aging. These notions of community may exclude individuals who can no longer keep up with group norms of success. Some of these implicit expectations for group success may be responsible for the resistance that many frail elders have to receiving services. This may result in the involuntary relocation, and even expulsion from retirement communities, of elderly persons who cannot conform to norms of activity, independence, and engagement.

A critical challenge to existing theory and research is the specification of criteria for success. Success may be viewed in common sense discussions as the attainment of something desirable. Yet in gerontological research and theory, goals of success and resources for goal attainment are often confounded. Health-based models often view health and youthfulness as the ultimate criteria for success (e.g., Rowe & Kahn, 1998). But if health is the goal of successful aging, it cannot also be viewed as the pathway for attaining the goal.

Age must also be meaningfully related to success or made relevant to issues of success. We need to distinguish the hands that older people are dealt from how they make the best of those hands. We must recognize diversity in goals and values and evaluate success relative to personal goals. For example, being surrounded by family and loved ones may be a goal for many aged persons, but one that is hard to attain in a mobile society. Being valued for expertise, wisdom, or opinions may be a goal for others, but these may be unattainable when retirement is necessary for the individual. The spectator role, in which older people derive gratification from watching activities of others or watching the world go by, may be hard to attain in isolated environments. Furthermore, spectator roles may be valued by older adults but misinterpreted by observers as reflecting disengagement.

It is ironic that the very efforts to legitimate the field of aging have largely segregated later life from prior periods of the life course (Settersten, 1999). Yet a science of old age isolated from earlier periods of life denies the very processes that give rise to it. It is imperative that studies of successful aging consider the entire life course and the processes that allow individuals to forge successful pathways through it.

We must also broaden our parameters for evaluating successful aging, distinguishing necessary but insufficient from optimal criteria. The emphasis on health and psychological well-being in American research has led to a medicalized view of successful aging. Instead, it is useful to consider multidimensional views of success, which include social as well as spiritual or existential orientations and move beyond traditional biomedical or psychological considerations. We should also recognize the limitations of culture-bound definitions of success, such as the emphasis on individual satisfaction and achievement in the United States.

Images of successful aging have been elevated to a cultural ideal through role models such as John Glenn, who undertook a space mission in old age (Minkler, 1999). The idealization of successful aging raises special new problems for adults who cannot live up to cultural ideals due to ill health or social disadvantages. We must be careful to avoid stigmatizing those who cannot attain these criteria. These risks may be minimized as gerontologists call attention to broader criteria for success. Communitarian or social definitions also hold promise. This has been reflected in some of our research on elderly Holocaust survivors in Hungary and Israel (Kahana et al., 1997). For example, among Hungarian elderly, definition of success is often expressed in generativite terms, such as leaving behind offspring who care for one another or leaving an honorable legacy to the next generation.

Among Israeli elders, reflections on successful aging include having children who serve their country and who have not abandoned it for material gain.

Goals of successful aging are also likely influenced by both the temporal and spatial contexts. Thus, success elders who lived through the Great Depression may involve having sufficient financial resources to provide for their own care and remain self-reliant. Yet for future generations, who will have lived through different economic climates (e.g., managed care and HMOs), successful aging may include the ability to shelter one's assets and ensure one's entitlements from public programs, such as Medicare or Medicaid.

Life-course scholarship holds great promise for rescuing successful aging research from its theoretical and methodological doldrums. Gerontological research must rediscover its creative roots in history, philosophy, psychology, and sociology, and it will greatly benefit from demedicalization. It can do so even while recognizing that genetic, biological, and health-care factors ultimately account for an important portion of unexplained variance in social research.

REFERENCES

Adams, B. (1971). Isolation, function and beyond: American kinship in the 1960s. In C. Broderick (Ed.), *A decade of family research and action*. Minneapolis, MN: Council on Family Relations.

Aldwin, C. M. (1991). Does age affect the stress and coping process? Implication of age differences in perceived control. *Journal of Gerontology, 46* (4), 174-180.

Andersen, M. L. (2000). *Thinking about women: Sociological perspectives on sex and gender*. Boston: Allyn & Bacon.

Antonucci, T. C., & Akiyama, H. (1991). Social relationships and aging well. *Generations, 15* (1), 39-44.

Antonucci, T. C., Akiyama, H., & Adelmann, P. K. (1990). Health behaviors and social roles among mature men and women. *Journal of Aging and Health, 2* (1), 3-14.

Ardelt, M. (1997). Wisdom and life satisfaction in old age. *Journal of Gerontology, 52B* (1), P15-P27.

Baltes, P., & Baltes, M. (1990). Psychological perspectives on successful aging: The model of selective optimization with compensation. In P. Baltes & M. Baltes (Eds.), *Successful aging: Perspectives from the behavioral sciences* (pp. 1-34). Cambridge, UK: Cambridge University Press.

Barer, B. M. (1994). Men and women aging differently. *International Journal of Aging and Human Development, 38* (1), 29-40.

Binstock, R. H. (1996). Continuities and discontinuities in public policy on aging. In V. L. Bengtson (Ed.), *Adulthood and aging: Research on continuities and discontinuities* (pp. 308-326). New York: Springer.

Blumer, H. (1969). *Symbolic interactionism: Perspective and method*. Englewood Cliffs, NJ: Prentice Hall.

Brandtstädter, J., Wentura, D., & Greve, W. (1993). Adaptive resources of the aging self: Outlines of an emergent perspective. *International Journal of Behavioral Development, 16*, 323-349.

Breytspraak, L. M. (1984). *Development of self in later life.* Boston, MA: Little, Brown.

Bronfenbrenner, U. (1979). *The ecology of human development: Experiments by nature and design.* Cambridge, MA: Harvard University Press.

Brown, V. (1997). *The elderly in poor urban neighborhoods.* New York: Garland Publications.

Butler, R. N. (1994). Dispelling ageism: The cross-cutting intervention. In D. Shenk & W. A. Achenbaum (Eds.), *Changing perceptions of aging and the aged* (pp. 137-143). New York: Springer.

Cain, L. D., Jr. (1964). Life course and social structure. In R. E. L. Faris (Ed.), *Handbook of modern sociology* (pp. 272-309). Chicago, IL: Rand-McNally.

Caro, F. G., Bass, S. A., & Chen, Y. (1993). Introduction: Achieving a productive aging society. In S. A. Bass, F. G. Caro, & Y. Chen (Eds.), *Achieving a Productive Aging Society* (pp. 3-26). Westport, CT: Auburn House.

Cumming, E., & Henry, W. (1961). *Growing old: The process of disengagement.* New York: Basic Books.

Dohrenwend, B. S., & Dohrenwend, B. P. (Eds.) (1974). *Stressful life events: Their nature and effects.* New York: Wiley.

Dowd, J. (1980). *Stratification among the aged.* Monterey, CA: Brooks/Cole.

Eaton, W. W. & Muntaner, C. (1999). Socioeconomic stratification and mental disorder. In A. V. Horwitz & T. L. Scheid (Eds.), *A handbook for the study of mental health: Social contexts, theories, and systems* (pp. 259-283). New York: Cambridge University Press.

Elder, G. H., Jr. (1974). *Children of the Great Depression: Social change in life experience.* Chicago, IL: University of Chicago Press.

Elward, K., & Larson, E. B. (1992). Benefits of exercise for older adults: A review of existing evidence and current recommendations for the general population. *Clinics in Geriatric Medicine, 8* (1), 35-50.

Featherman, D., Smith, J., & Peterson, J. (1990). Successful aging in a post-retired society. In P. Baltes & M. Baltes (Eds.), *Successful aging: Perspectives from the behavioral sciences* (pp. 50-93). Cambridge, MA: Cambridge University Press.

Festinger, L. & Carlsmith, J. M. (1996). Cognitive consequences of forced compliance. In S. Fein & S. Spencer (Eds.), *Readings in social psychology: The art and science of research* (pp. 102-109). Boston, MA: Houghton Mifflin Company.

Fleishman, J. A. (1984). Personality characteristics and coping patterns. *Journal of Health and Social Behavior, 25* (2), 229-244.

Franks, M., Herzog, A., Holinberg, D., & Markus, H. (1999). Educational attainment and self-making in later life. In C. Ryff & V. Marshall (Eds.), *The self and society in aging processes* (pp. 223-246). New York: Springer.

Gallagher, S. K. (1994). Doing their share: Comparing patterns of help given by older and younger adults. *Journal of Marriage and the Family, 56,* 567-578.

Garmezy, N. (1983). Stressors of childhood. In N. Garmezy & M. Rutter (Eds.), *Stress, coping, and development in children.* Baltimore, MD: Johns Hopkins University Press.

Goffman, E. (1959). *The presentation of self in everyday life.* Garden City, NY: Anchor Books.

Goffman, E. (1961). *Asylums: Essays on the social situation of mental patients and other inmates.* Garden City, NY: Anchor Books.

Helsing, K., Szklo, M., & Comstock, G. (1981). *Factors associated with mortality after widowhood. American Journal of Public Health, 71,* 802-809.

Jackson, J., Antonucci, T., & Gibson, R. (1990). Social relations, productive activities, and coping with stress in late-life. In M. Stephens, J. Crowther, S. Hobfoll, & D. Tennenbaum (Eds.), *Stress and coping in later-life families* (pp. 193-214). New York: Hemisphere.

Jacobs, J. (1975). *Older persons and retirement communities.* Springfield, IL: Charles C. Thomas.

Kahana, B. & Kahana, E. (1998). Toward a temporal-spatial model of cumulative life stress: Placing late-life stress effects in life course perspective. In J. Lomranz, (Ed.), *Handbook of aging and mental health: An integrative approach* (pp. 153-178). New York: Plenum Press.

Kahana, B., Kahana, E., Harel, Z., Kelly, K., Monaghan, P., & Holland, L. (1997). A paradigm for understanding the chronic stresses of post-traumatic life: Perspectives of Holocaust survivors. In M. Gottlieb (Ed.), *Chronic stress and trauma* (pp. 315-342). New York: Plenum Press.

Kahana, E. (1980). Alternative models of person-environment fit: Prediction of morale in three homes for the aged. *Journal of Gerontology, 35,* 584-595.

Kahana, E., & Kahana, B. (1996). Conceptual and empirical advances in understanding aging well through proactive adaptation. In V. Bengtson (Ed.), *Adulthood and aging: Research on continuities and discontinuities* (pp. 18-41). New York: Springer.

Kahana, E., Kahana, B., Kercher, K., King, C., Lovegreen, L., & Chirayath, H. (1999). Evaluating a model of successful aging for urban African-American and White elderly. In M. Wykle (Ed.), *Serving minority elders in the 21st century.* New York: Springer.

Kahana, E., Kahana, B., & Kinney, J. (1990). Coping among vulnerable elders. In Z. Harel, P. Ehrlich, & R. Hubbard (Eds.), *The vulnerable aged: People, services, and policies* (pp. 64-85). New York: Springer.

Kahana, E., King, C., Meehan, R., Smith, T., Boswell, G., Newell, K., Kahana, B., Kercher, K., & Borawski-Clark, E. (1996, November). *Gender and aging successfully.* Paper presented at the meeting of the Gerontological Society of America, Washington, D.C.

Kahana, E., Lawrence, E., Kahana, B., Kercher, K., Stoller, E., & Stange, K. (2000, November). *Long-term impact of preventive proactivity on quality of life of the old-old.* Paper presented at the meeting of the Gerontological Society of America, Washington, D.C.

Kahana, E., Midlarsky, E., & King, C. (1998, November). *Demographic antecedents and stability of altruism in late life.* Paper presented at the meeting of the Gerontological Society of America, Washington, D.C.

Kahn, R. L. (1979). Stress: From 9 to 5. In P. I. Rose (Ed.), *Socialization and the life cycle* (pp. 205-212). New York: St. Martin's Press.

Karp, D. A. (1988). A decade of reminders: Changing age consciousness between fifty and sixty years old. *The Gerontologist, 28* (6), 727-738.

Kastenbaum, R. (1993). Gender as a shaping force in adult development and aging. In R. Kastenbaum (Ed.), *Encyclopedia of Adult Development* (pp. 165-170). Phoenix, AZ: Oryx Press.

Kessler, R. C., & Magee, W. J. (1994). Childhood family violence and adult recurrent depression. *Journal of Health and Social Behavior, 35* (1), 13-27.

Kuypers, J. A., & Bengtson, V. L. (1973). Social breakdown and competence: A model of normal aging. *Human Development, 26,* 181-201.

Lawton, M. P. (1971). The dimensions of morale. In D. Kent, R. Kastenbaum, & S. Sherwood (Eds.), *Research, planning and action for the elderly.* New York: Behavioral Publications.

Lawton, M. P. (1980). Competence, environmental press, and adaptation of older people. In M. P. Lawton, P. G. Windley, & T. O. Byerts (Eds.), *Aging and the environment* (pp. 33-59). New York: Springer.

Lawton, M. P. (1989). Environmental proactivity in older people. In V. Bengtson & K. Schaie (Eds.), *The course of later life: Research and reflections* (pp. 15-23). New York: Springer.

Lemon, B., Bengtson, V., & Peterson, J. (1972). An exploration of the activity theory of aging: Activity types and life satisfaction among in-movers to a retirement community. *Journal of Gerontology, 27,* 511-523.

Lin, N., & Ensel, W. (1989). Life stress and health: Stressors and resources. *American Sociological Review, 54,* 382-399.

Linville, P. (1987). Self-complexity as a cognitive buffer against stress-related illness and depression. *Journal of Personality and Social Psychology, 52* (4), 663-678.

Longino, C. F., & Lipman, A. (1983). Informal supports of residents in planned retirement communities. In M. B. Kleinman (Ed.), *Social gerontology* (pp. 107-118). Basel: Karger.

Matthews, S. H., & Rosner, T. T. (1988). Shared filial responsibility: The family as the primary caregiver. *Journal of Marriage and the Family, 50* (1), 185-195.

McDaniel, S. A., & McKinnon, A. L. (1993). Gender differences in informal support and coping among elders: Findings from Canada's 1985 and 1990 General Social Surveys. *Journal of Women and Aging, 5* (2), 79-98.

Mills, C. W. (1959). *The sociological imagination.* New York: Oxford University Press.

Minkler, M. (1999). *Images of successful aging.* Paper presented at the 52nd Gerontological Society of America meetings. San Francisco, CA.

Neugarten, B. (1964). *Personality in middle and late life.* New York: Atherton.

Parsons, T., & Bales, R. F. (1955). *Family, socialization, and interaction process.* Glencoe, IL: Free Press.

Pearlin, L. (1983). Role strains and personal stress. In H. Kaplan (Ed.), *Psychosocial stress: Trends in theory and research* (pp. 3-32). New York: Academic Press.

Pearlin, L., Lieberman, M., Menaghan, E., & Mullan, J. (1981). The stress process. *Journal of Health and Social Behavior, 22* (4), 337-356.

Pennebacker, J. (Ed.) (1995). *Emotion disclosure and health.* Washington D.C.: American Psychological Association.

Renwick, R., Brown, I., & Nagler, M. (1996). *Quality of life in health promotion and rehabilitation: Conceptual approaches, issues, and applications.* Thousand Oaks, CA: Sage.

Riegel, K. F. (1975). Adult life crises: A dialectic interpretation of development. In N. Datan & L. H. Ginsberg (Eds.), *Life-span developmental psychology: Normative life crises.* New York: Academic Press.

Rodin, J. (1987). Personal control through the life course. In R. P. Abeles (Ed.), *Life-span perspective and social psychology* (pp. 103-119). Hillsdale, NJ: Lawrence Erlbaum.

Rosow, I. (1974). *Socialization to old age.* Berkeley, CA: University of California Press.

Roszell, P. (1996). *A life course perspective on the implications of stress exposure.* Unpublished doctoral dissertation, University of Toronto, Ontario, Canada.

Rowe, J., & Kahn, R. (1998). *Successful aging.* New York: Pantheon.

Rutter, M. (1989). Pathways from childhood to adult life. *Journal of Child Psychology and Psychiatry and Allied Disciplines, 30* (1), 23-51.

Schulz, R., & Brenner, G. (1977). Relocation of the aged: A review of theoretical analysis. *Journal of Gerontology, 32* (3), 323-333.

Seligman, M. E. P. (1975). *Helplessness: On depression, development, and death.* San Francisco, CA: Freeman.

Settersten, R. (1999). *Lives in time and place: The problems and promises of developmental science.* Amityville, NY: Baywood.

Stanford, E. (1990). Diverse Black aged. In Z. Harel, E. McKinney, & M. Williams (Eds.), *Black aged: Understanding diversity and service needs* (pp. 194-204). Newbury Park, CA: Sage.

Stephens, M. A. P., & Hobfoll, S. E. (1990). Ecological perspectives on stress and coping in later-life families. In M. A. P. Stephens, J. H. Crowther, S. E. Hobfoll, & D. L. Tennenbaum (Eds.), *Stress and coping in later-life families* (pp. 193-215). New York: Hemisphere.

Stoller, E., & Gibson, R. (2000). *Worlds of difference* (3rd ed.). Thousand Oaks, CA: Pine Forge Press.

Strawbridge, W. J., Camacho, T. C., Cohen, R. D., & Kaplan, G. A. (1993). Gender differences in factors associated with change in physical functioning in old age: A 6-year longitudinal study. *The Gerontologist, 33* (5), 603-609.

Streib, G., Folts, W., & LaGreca, A. (1985). Autonomy, power, and decision-making in thirty-six retirement communities. *The Gerontologist, 25* (4), 403-409.

Thoits, P. (1983). Multiple identities and psychological well being: A reformulation and test of the social isolation hypothesis. *American Sociological Review, 48,* 174-187.

Tornstam, L. (1997). Gerotranscendence: The contemplative dimension of aging. *Journal of Aging Studies, 11* (2), 143-54.

Troll, L., (1994). Family connectedness of old women: attachments in later life. In B. Turner & L. Troll (Eds), *Women growing older: Psychological perspectives* (pp. 169-201). Thousand Oaks, CA: Sage.

Turner, R. J., & Marino, F. (1994). Social support and social structure: A descriptive epidemiology. *Journal of Health and Social Behavior, 35,* 193-212.

Turner, R., & Roszell, P. (1994). Innovations in the measurement of life stress: Crisis theory and the significance of event resolution. *Journal of Health and Social Behavior, 33* (1), 36-50.

Turner, R. J., Wheaton, B., & Lloyd, D. A. (1995). The epidemiology of social stress. *American Sociological Review, 60,* 104-125.

Vingerhoets, A. J., & Van Heck, G. L. (1990). Gender, coping, and psychosomatic symptoms. *Psychological Medicine, 20* (1), 125-135.

Wheaton, B. (1983). Stress, personal coping resources, and psychiatric symptoms: An investigation of interactive models. *Journal of Health and Social Behavior, 24,* 208-229.

Wheaton, B. (1996). The domains and boundaries of stress concepts. In H. B. Kaplan (Ed.), *Psychosocial stress: Perspectives on structure, theory, life-course, and methods* (pp. 29-70). San Diego, CA: Academic Press.

PART VI

Further Promises for Scholarship on Aging and Later Life

CHAPTER 9

Whose Life Course Is It, Anyway? Diversity and "Linked Lives" in Global Perspective

Dale Dannefer

Surely, a first task of the field of life course studies is to describe key aspects of the lives of human beings in empirical terms, and to understand and interpret them in terms of social, psychosocial and individual processes. Yet it must be acknowledged that the description of life course patterns and other central preoccupations of the life course literature are largely irrelevant to the empirical reality of the existence of the majority of the present human population of the earth. Moreover, the applicability to diverse populations and diverse cultural situations of concepts such as accentuation, the life-stage principle, and other notions that seek to discern how early experiences shape later life outcomes is not clearly known. Beginning from this general observation, the aim of the present chapter is to offer a tentative exploration of the "yield potentials" of the life course perspective when its questions and principles are systematically applied to traditional societies or unusual subpopulations. A careful consideration of the lives of such populations also brings to bold relief a related point that cannot be avoided: That in a global order, the lives of those in what used to be called the third world and are now misleadingly called "developing countries" are intricately linked to those who populate late modern societies (e.g., Beck, 1994; Castells, 1996). This chapter examines life-course aspects of three alternative populations: the working children of the third world, street gang members in Los Angeles, and Amazonian shamans.

*The author thanks Elaine F. Dannefer, George Gonos, Ivor Goodson, Rick Settersten, Paul Stein, and Peter Uhlenberg for comments on an earlier draft of this chapter.

THE POPULATION OF CHILD LABORERS

I pluck cotton and chilies, harvest wheat and other crops and do whatever is asked by the landlord. . . .They beat me and keep us hungry. They say they will not give us food if we do not work. . . . I cannot leave or where will I go?

These are the words of a 12-year-old girl—a bonded laborer, who works along with her family in Sindh Province, Pakistan. "Bonded labor takes place a family receives an advance payment (sometimes as little as U.S. $15) to hand a child . . . over to an employer. In most cases the child cannot work off the debt, nor can the family raise enough money to buy the child back" (Human Rights Watch, 1995). Concerning the family of the girl above, a reporter wrote, "over time they became trapped, and now work just to pay a debt that grows each year." Bonded child labor is often illegal, yet it is widespread and institutionalized in Pakistan, India, and elsewhere in Asia. In 1995, it was estimated that 15 million children work as bonded laborers in India alone. Bonded labor describes a very specific structure of intergenerational relations (in which resource transfers from child to parent begin, without respect to anything like choice, in early childhood) and of multi-generational family patterns (since many families have been enslaved by bondage for five or more generations).

To modern sensibilities, the more general phenomenon of child labor is a matter of regret, often consoled by a hope that it is a transitory condition, an accidental "Falling Through the Cracks" (Human Rights Watch, 1999) that will surely soon be corrected or, perhaps, by a sense of inevitability. In reality, over much of the planet, child labor is an integral element of deeply institutionalized processes of production, economic, family, and labor market patterns. Rather than disappearing, these patterns are increasingly shaped and solidified by the strong exogenous forces of a globalizing economy. Consistent estimates suggest that at least 250 million children who are 14 years of age or younger work—about half of them full time—in Asia, Africa, and Latin America. This number does not count those who work "under the table" or illegally, engaged in work ranging from domestic service to prostitution. Informed estimates suggest that if those are counted, the number is 400 to 500 million (United Nations Children's Fund, 1997; see also Alam, 1997). Other experts have suggested that child labor is expanding in Eastern and Central Europe (International Labour Organization, 1996). These practices have long been integral to the economic structure of many poor or "underdeveloped" societies and to their relation to wealthier societies. One indication of the institutionalization of these child labor is that it is seen neither by employers nor by the families and children themselves, as a transitory condition in need of eradication. Rather, it is in need of refinements articulated by a range of child labor advocates—ranging from corporate spokespersons who plausibly argue that children would be "worse off" without the opportunities for work that they provide (despite its adverse features judged by Western standards), to labor organizers and child laborers themselves, who urge "not abolition but regulation" of child labor (Swift, 1997).

A consideration of the educational and work careers of children in global perspective thus reminds us that the empirically observable life-course patterns of the greater share of the earth's human population are—from childhood onward—quite different from the prevailing Eurocentric notions of either "normal human development," or of an institutionalized life course with sustained periods of schooling and retirement. The structures of relationships and opportunities encountered in much of the world may call into question the scope of applicability of favored concepts (e.g., successful aging or planful competence) and, even, accepted categories (e.g., play/leisure, retirement, volunteerism, long-term care).

Overall, the life-course patterns of child workers and of their families can generally be explained by economic, legal, and political forces; the individuals whose lives are thus constituted have been defined by a combination of policy, conscription, and familial or personal economic duress. The structural diversity of the institutionalized life course of children extends, as well, to some societies of late modernity evidenced, for example, by the working children of migrant farm workers in the United States.

THE LIFE COURSE OF HOMEBOYS

Some alternative configurations of the life course involve a limited amount of experienced choicefulness, and can be analyzed as integral aspects of alternative cultures, including cultures of resistance. For example, urban North American street gang members talk about the positive value of their gangs and the positive choices they make in regard to gang participation and activity—despite participating in a lifestyle that looks to many outsiders like an intensely undesirable situation.

Consider the following exchange between two Los Angeles gang members, chatting with each other at a detention facility, reported by the French journalist Bing's report on the lives of young people who belong to the notorious gangs, the Crips and the Bloods, in Los Angeles. Tiny Vamp is 15, G-Roc is 15 (adapted from Bing, 1991, p. 21).

Tiny Vamp: You still a little homie, or what?

G-Roc: Li'l Homie. I ain't probably gonna reach the O.G. stage for awhile yet. I got outta baby homie when I was like thirteen and a half. How 'bout you?

Tiny Vamp: I'm still a Tiny. In my set you get a rep by straight killin'. I been on drive-bys and I been stabbed.

Sidewinder, another 15-year-old Crip detained for participating in a drive-by shooting, sees himself an O.G. (Original Gangster) in 5 or 10 years (Bing, 1991, pp. 47, 50).

Here is a structure of an "objective" (in the way that Durkheim [1897] described "social facts") set of life stages: Homeboys graduate from baby to li'l homie to homie (homeboy) status by getting "jumped in." "Getting jumped in" refers to an initiation rite of passage, for which a kind of informal counseling is available from older gang members (Bing, 1991, p. 24):

> It's like when I got jumped in—all my homeboys and my cousins told me "You in now, man . . . Either you be down for it or get out now." Cause you KNOW you gonna have go to jail. You KNOW you might end up gettin' killed, gettin' stabbed, gettin' shot. You know all this. My homeboy, Li'l Lazy, just got killed, and he only sixteen.

If they survive, they may graduate again to O.G. (Original Gangster) status, in their 20s. Life-course stages beyond O.G., the mature stage of the twenties, become much less clear. On the other hand, a preoccupation with funerals, especially one's own funeral, is frequently in the foreground of consciousness of teenage and pre-teenage gang members. Each year, several hundred gang-related homicides occur in Los Angeles; many of the victims are also gang members. Gang members of every age and their extended families virtually all know people who have been killed or seriously injured through their lifestyle.

These terms are sufficiently institutionalized that they are shared across rival gangs, and formal names have given rise to an argot of abbreviations and slang or nicknames that are as taken-for-granted as are "frosh" or "preppie" in mainstream institutions. Homeboys are "homies" or "homes," gangsters are O.G.'s or T.G.

The structure of gangs as social networks emerged early in both East and West coast American cities among immigrants who were marginalized and excluded from mainstream opportunities. The *gang career* as an organizing reality for members is probably as old as the mainstream institutionalized life course. Even on the West coast, gangs developed early in the Twentieth century. There are currently estimated to be 150,000 gang members in Los Angeles county alone (Alonso, 1997), and gangs have a significant presence in more than 800 North American cities, including more than 80 cities with populations less than 10,000 (Hixon, 1999).

This is a subpopulation with its own heroes—not Martin Luther King or Malcolm X, but gang legends such as Raymond Washington or "Tookie" Williams (Alonso, 1997, p. 3)—both founding Crip leaders. In their collective memory, the Watts rebellion may hold a significance analogous to that held for many American citizens by the Revolutionary War. Even the correction officers who deal with incarcerated gang members, some of whom appear to be remarkably effective as counselors in the conventional sense, do not expect these young people to develop an appreciation of the "founders of the Republic." One officer who Bing describes as especially skilled with kids, himself logged brig time in the Marine Corps, for refusing to wear the required dress on July 4. ". . . American Independence wasn't important to me because my particular forefathers were still slaves . . . I didn't— and don't— feel a freedom based on that event" (Bing, 1991, p. 11).

Given what is known about the social-psychological processes of adaptation, it is not surprising that participants describe the gang lifestyle in positive terms. Tiny Vamp and G-Roc agree,"I wouldn't change nothin' about my life . . ." (Bing, 1991, p. 30). Such a statement is made in an insulated social context (Rosenberg & Simmons, 1971), and it may well involve a measure of denial. It cannot be reduced entirely to ignorance or to a mere coping strategy, however. Even Rider, a homeboy who, through shrewd entrepreneuring, has become an affluent member of the middle class, remains active in his Blood set (Bing, 1991, pp. 212-213). Rider places in relief the fact that a sustained experience of biculturation (Stack, 1974)—of having important and close relationships simultaneously in two social worlds and of being, therefore, frequently torn between them—irreducibly includes a bicultural life course.

Of course, the life-course pattern that is locally institutionalized in gang subcultures can be analyzed as a product of the exclusionary practices and other inequality-reproducing processes that remain powerful in schools and other major institutions in the United States. It represents a life constructed in response to limited opportunities that bears some similarities to the locally institutionalized alternative family patterns identified and analyzed by Linda Burton (e.g., Burton, 1990, 1996). Yet despite her extensive work, and despite the robustness of these life-course processes, little reference to them can be found in a life-course literature dedicated to the modal lives of modern Western citizens.

Just as child laborers are clearly undercounted in official statistics, the lives captured by Bing and described by Alonso and others are undercounted in Census and Social Survey data, and are only obliquely and anonymously reflected in educational data. Yet, it is certain that a cross-sectional census of the number of lives involved in such alternative life-course modes gives an understated impression of the magnitude of the diversity in purely human terms, since individuals in such circumstances—whether a child prostitute in Thailand or a gang member in Torrance—experience abbreviated lives. The countries most noted for the use of child labor have high mortality rates, but many of them have very high rates of population doubling. For example, Bhutan, India, Pakistan, and Sudan all have population doubling rates of under 40 years. Therefore, it is likely—barring quite radical change—that the proportion of human individuals who countenance such a life course has expanded and will continue to expand foreseeable future.

INSTITUTIONALIZED LIFE-COURSE VARIATIONS AND
THEIR INTERDEPENDENCE

Child labor, starkly inhumane by modern and humanistic standards, is an institution on which low-cost factory production processes and modern Western consumption patterns depend. The market for child labor structures the early lives of scores of millions of young people in multiple societies. The enslavement of children and entire families through the process of bondage has been reproduced over multiple generations in several Asian countries. It clearly meets the criterion of being considered an institution, and it is an institution that affects a large segment of the world's children. More generally, the often-involuntary press of children into full or part time work in factories, mines, farming, service or prostitution is sustained by its integral functional importance to the overall economic functioning of societies, economic and political relationships between societies similarly meets the criterion of institutionalization. These are mechanisms that not only lead to regularly repeated and largely taken-for-granted life-course structures; they are also supported and often, virtually dictated, by the exigencies of national economies or multi-national corporations.

In the United States, the institutionalized gang career that has provided to millions of gang members a meaningful framework for structuring their lives, and has defined and sustained the life projects of large numbers of young people— gang members—across the 20th century. Ignoring the opportunity of mainstream society from which its members perceive themselves to be alienated and excluded, its members create a positive alternative in reaction to it that society, and in the process create jobs for platoons of agents of social control (social workers, probation officers, rehab workers, etc.).

Thus, these life-course patterns share with the late modern "three boxes of life" (Kohli, 1986; Riley & Riley, 1994) key structural features of institutionalization: They are established practices; and they use age—beginning with the dependency and powerlessness of childhood—to structure the life course of individuals in articulation with economic processes.

But the manifest diversity of institutional forms of the early life course are not simply free-standing alternatives. In every case, they have emerged historically, in relation to the exigencies of economic systems, technology and politics. Increasingly, these economic processes are globally linked, so that full-time child laborers make a growing share of the products consumed by citizens of modern societies, from shoes and shirts to Mickey Mouse dolls (Lee & Brady, 1988), and child labor is utilized in the manufacture and distribution of products from electronic accessories to farm produce.

This well established set of circumstances requires that life-course concepts such as "linked lives" (Elder, 1998) be seen in global perspective, and it suggests an extension of the kinds of analysis that have been conducted within society to an international and global level. For example, the general shift of resources in the

United States away from children and toward the aged does appear to be quite well established—notwithstanding the intergenerational equity debate (Bengtson & Achenbaum, 1993; Cohen, 1993). In national perspective, it may be hypothesized that the shift of resources away from families and children and toward the aged may increase a sense of hopelessness among those families and children most in need of a minimal resource base.

It is, however, perhaps even more significant to contemplate this question in international perspective. Direct comparisons are difficult to implement, given the difficulties of obtaining reliable and comparable data, and complexities such as the sharply contrasting age structures found in different societies. However, one might hypothesize that the diminishing resources available to American children reported by Preston (e.g., 1984) would be dwarfed by the magnitude of deprivation of resources available to the children of many other countries. If that is the case, we are in a position to understand the institutionalized life course of late modern societies, including a protracted childhood and a lengthy retirement, as requiring the structuration of the activities of Asian children into life-course patterns consisting of unending long days of low-paid work.

This structural linkage of lives across the planet, connected by cruel and outrageously inequitable market processes, is perceived by many of us to be an unwelcome realization; it is, however, very real. Its reality is obfuscated by the fact that exchanges do not take place at a micro-level but through market processes managed by corporate and governmental entities on a huge scale, and on the fact that consumption is far removed in space from the site of production (e.g., Castells, 1996). Yet at any given point in time, the structural components of such processes can readily be traced.

Examining these connections in terms of cohort processes reveal some dimensions of added significance. The fact that the number of such child workers is likely to increase as a proportion of all children at any given point in time, does not exhaust the life-course implications. A further implication derives from the difference in the rate of living across these societies. Societies with higher mortality rates cycle individuals through the life course more rapidly. One result is that the numbers visible at any given point in time underestimates the number of individuals cycling through such a system within, say, a 20-year period.

THE VENERATED LIVES OF AMAZONIAN SHAMANS

I conclude by turning to late life, and to a society with a different set of institutionalizing dynamics—the tribes of the Amazon rain forest, especially the north Amazon. In the small and relatively isolated traditional communities inhabiting this region, it is not surprising that age is still venerated. The most valued knowledge base and the most efficacious nutritional and healing practices are those held by elder Shamans. In contrast to the population growth of the subpopulations from which child laborers are drawn, however, the tribal communities of the Amazon have been declining in number and size. Some have been displaced by mining, oil drilling, or deforestation (whether by logging companies or by agricultural efforts), and knowledge of the outside world has inevitably proven seductive for many young persons. The life-course patterns and the population trends of Amazonia are, thus, similarly linked to the consumption practices of late modern societies.

Here, the entire structure of the tribal social order is under assault, including the established understandings of age and the life course. A typical lament of the Shaman is that young men have no interest in the learning the complex and intricate knowledge base of plant and animal life, seasons and weather that has taken him a lifetime to master (Plotkin, 2000). Yet for some Shamans, the source of the assault on their traditional status may also be the source of a solution. A new market for the knowledge of Shamans has emerged among the trend-sensitive elites of affluent moderns, who can learn about opportunities for study with Shamans and perhaps even find healing for maladies (e.g., bursitis) that can be precisely diagnosed but not cured by current medical practice. Fax machines, cell phones and international travel are becoming part of the experience of Shamans, and a growing number of Northern clients—many of them academics and professionals who regard themselves as knowledgeable about the limits of known pharmaceuticals and the possibilities of alternative medicine—are making trips to the Northern Amazon, as consumers of a novel kind of chic alternative medicine. The range of botanical treasures and animal life forms that inhabit their rain forest (as is the also the case for those in Asia, Africa and elsewhere in the Caribbean) is much greater than that which is yet part of the knowledge base of biochemistry and botany, or the knowledge base of the Shamans themselves. Yet this knowledge base and the practices and products deriving from it may never be, as novelist Traven (1966) has so compelling illustrated in "Assembly Line," compatible with processes of mass production, since they are held to be sensitive to the most intricate knowledge of subtleties of the temporal rhythms of weather, season, and day-night.

CONCLUDING REFLECTIONS: TOWARD A GLOBAL HYPOTHESIS

Obviously, the research questions that a consideration of the institutionalized life-course patterns of homeboys or bonded child laborers readily suggest are many and provocative. It would certainly be illuminating to have more data depicting transition behavior and transition processes in traditional societies as they are being reshaped by their interaction with those of late modernity. Solid knowledge of such alternative patterns can offer a new avenue for expanding life-course scholarship "beyond microfication" (Hagestad & Dannefer, 2001), and for integrating it with other areas of sociological inquiry. I conclude by suggesting one of these, in the form of a tentative hypothesis.

Reflecting together on the categories of third-world child laborers and traditional Shamans and the relation of each of them to the late modern world, it is tempting indeed to propose that something like Preston's (1984) depiction of the shift in the resource distribution from youth to age is occurring even more powerfully—even to the point of sharp caricature of the picture Preston offers. We see that there is enormous and expanding demand for the labor of growing populations of children, which is bought very cheaply; at the same time there is a renewed appreciation for the wisdom—more specifically the putative healing powers—of the Shaman, who is almost by definition aged, and whose powers are presumed to increase with age, due to the richness and complexity of the knowledge on which they are based. This knowledge is, of course, a scarce commodity that is personally, and in most cases locally, administered. Thus, outside of the indigenous communities in which it is based, it is available only to those with the stylish knowledge and material affluence to afford travel to exotic and remote locations. Clearly, then, the rebirth of the wisdom of age is materially rewarded by those with the resources and cultural capital to avail themselves of it, while the mass-production bondage of the growing masses of children who are deprived the "normal" opportunities to gain knowledge through education and community-based and collective work is created by the same consumerist impulses of late modern citizens seeking cheap goods in the marketplace. One might ask, can the future of the life course include consideration of these grotesque but globally linked discrepancies in the life-course patterns and opportunities afforded by the institutional structures of a globalizing world? One might even ask, will—or indeed should—there be a future of life-course studies in which we do not begin to grapple with the range of life-course patterns found globally and what they reveal about opportunities for human development and full human participation?

REFERENCES

Alam, S. (1997, July). Thank you, Mr. Harkin, sir! *New Internationalist, 292,* 12-14.

Alonso, A. A. (1997). *Territoriality among street gangs in Los Angeles.* Unpublished master's thesis, University of Southern California, Los Angeles, California.

Beck, U. (1994). *Ecological enlightenment: Essays on the politics of the risk society.* Atlantic Highlands, NJ: Humanities Press.

Bengtson, V. L., & Achenbaum, W. A. (1993). *The changing contract across generations.* New York: Aldine de Gruyter.

Bing, L. (1991). *Do or die.* New York: HarperCollins.

Burton, L. (1990). Teenage childbearing as an alternative life-course strategy in multi-generation black families. *Human Nature, 1,* 123-143.

Burton, L. (1996). Age norms, the timing of family role transitions, and the intergenerational caregiving among aging African American women. *The Gerontologist, 36,* 199-208.

Castells, M. (1996). *The network society.* Malden, MA: Blackwell.

Cohen, L. M. (Ed.) (1993). *Justice across generations: What does it mean?* Washington, D.C.: Public Policy Institute, American Association of Retired Persons.

Durkheim, E. (1938[1897]). *The rules of sociological method.* New York: Free Press.

Elder, G. H., Jr. (1998). The life course and human development. In R. M. Lerner (Ed.), *Handbook of child psychology: Vol. 1. Theoretical models of human development* (5th ed., pp. 939-991). New York: John Wiley & Sons.

Hagestad, G. O., & Dannefer, D. (2001). Concepts and theories of aging: beyond microfication in social science approaches. In R. Binstock & L. George (Eds.), *The handbook of aging and the social sciences* (5th Edition). San Diego, CA: Academic Press.

Hixon, A. (1999). Preventing street gang violence. *American Family Physician, 59* (8), 2121.

Human Rights Watch. (1995). *Contemporary forms of slavery in Pakistan.* New York: Human Rights Watch.

Human Rights Watch (1999). Children's Rights Division [on-line]. Available: http://www.hrw.org

International Labor Organization. (1996). *Child labour: What is to be done?* Geneva: International Labor Organization.

Kohli, M. (1986). Social organization and subjective construction of the life course. In A. B. Sørensen, F. Weinert, & L. Sherrod (Eds.), *Human development: Multidisciplinary perspectives* (pp. 271-292). Hillsdale, NJ: Erlbaum.

Lee, D., & Brady, R. (1988). Long hard days—at pennies an hour. *Business Week* (Industrial Technology Edition), *3077*, 46-47.

Plotkin, M. J. (2000). *Medicine quest: In search of nature's healing secrets.* New York: Penguin.

Preston, S. (1984). Children and the elderly in the United States. *Scientific American, 251* (6), 44-49.

Riley, M. W., & Riley, J. W. (1994). Structural lag: past and future. In M. W. Riley, R. L. Kahn, & A. Foner (Eds.), *Age and structural lag: Society's failure to provide meaningful opportunities in work, family and leisure* (pp. 15-36). New York: John Wiley & Sons.

Rosenberg, M., & Simmons, R. G. (1971). *Black and white self-esteem; the urban school child.* Washington, D.C.: American Sociological Association.

Stack, C. B. (1974). *All our kin: Strategies for survival in a black community.* New York: HarperCollins.

Swift, A. (1997). *Children for social change.* Nottingham, England: Educational Heretics Press.

Traven, B. (1966). *The night visitor and other stories.* New York: Hill and Wang.

United Nations Children's Fund (UNICEF). (1997). *The state of the world's children.* New York: UNICEF.

CHAPTER 10

The Life Course as a
Cultural Construct

Christine L. Fry

A persistent complaint about research on aging is its atheoretical nature and its focus on the most painful parts of old age, disability and caregiving. The "old" in research on aging has been incorporated into a number of paradigmatic approaches that seek to link the issues to broader sociocultural phenomena that define them. One such perspective is the life-course perspective which, as early as the 1960s, began to revolutionize the way we look at aging. Early work by Cain (1964) and subsequent work by Riley and her colleagues (Riley, Johnson, & Foner, 1972) and Neugarten (Neugarten & Datan, 1973) combined to portray the promise of this perspective. As individuals age, their lives can be understood, to a great degree, by linking them to the social and historical contexts in which they are embedded. Paradigmatically, the promise is there, but in the past four decades, have we made any real theoretical breakthroughs? Settersten's (1999) synthesis demonstrates that considerable progress has been made, but that we still have a long way to go.

Many of the cardinal principles of the life-course framework reveal its complexity. First, the life course is exactly that: all of the events, discontinuities, and continuities that make up the unfolding trajectory of an individual's life. At the same time, lives are also to be understood in a context that embraces higher order phenomena, namely society and culture. In taking the common sense notion of a life course and rendering it into a researchable paradigm, a number of propositions have been delineated to codify the phenomena. Settersten (Chapter 1) and Elder and Johnson (Chapter 2) offer more comprehensive discussions of these central principles. To simplify, the life course as a scientific construct must address the following four issues: temporal, individual, sociocultural, and complex phenomena.

TEMPORAL PHENOMENA

If our view of the life course is to be lifelong, time becomes a central dimension of inquiry. All creatures experience their lives in time; all of the changes that punctuate lives and periods of relative continuity happen in time. If we are interested in figuring out how earlier experiences or conditions have consequences in later life, we must explicitly deal with time. The life course and age have become increasingly linked. Age, itself, is only a temporal measure of events that have or should happen across a life or lives. This is a topic that will be explored below.

INDIVIDUAL PHENOMENA

Individuals experience a life course and our data are generally aimed at the individual level. Individual-level data demand attention to two issues: 1) variability, and 2) human agency. By definition, individuals are unique and highly idiosyncratic. Consequently, diversity and variability are to be expected even in the most homogenous groups or settings. Conceptually, variability is one of the tasks that a life-course paradigm is designed to explain. Further complicating this task is the fact that humans are not passive puppets in managing their lives. To the contrary, they actively navigate their worlds and negotiate their lives together with others.

SOCIOCULTURAL PHENOMENA

Although individuals experience life courses, they do not invent them from scratch starting at birth. Life courses are institutionalized within social and cultural contexts. The institutions that have received the most attention within life-course scholarship are education, work, family, and the social policies of a state. One learns the path ahead by observing and interacting with parents and other adults. Of course, this too is variable, depending on culture, historical circumstances, and the other lives that intersect with one's own.

COMPLEX PHENOMENA

Any research agenda that embraces the first three issues becomes quickly complicated. It involves multiple dimensions (e.g., biological, psychological, sociocultural) and their interactions over time. It therefore involves active multidisciplinary and interdisciplinary efforts.

Do any of us disagree that the life course is comprised of complex temporal phenomena that are both individual and sociocultural in nature? Few can disagree. The four issues outlined above are rather axiomatic, laudable, challenging, and downright exciting. However, are they too general, too all-inclusive, to direct research? The life course is one of the greatest challenges to scrutinize scientifically. To put it simply: the study of lives is a messy business. In opening those doors, and in glimpsing at these complexities, we might be tempted to shut the door in terror. Theories meant to capture both micro and macro phenomena through time are mind-boggling. The data necessary to evaluate these theories are not only complex, but they seem exceedingly difficult to manage in practice. Multiple measurement at different times introduces complicated management issues. Tracking individuals through time brings problems related to attrition, missing data, and incomparable data. With time, our analytic tools and technology change, and our theoretical paradigms and questions of interest are also revised. Added to this, the life course is cultural and, consequently, is subject to diverse meanings, definitions, and interpretations. Is understanding the life course too big a structure to erect? Have we been so enticed by its promise that we have rushed to the top of the building without paying enough much attention to its foundations?

Nearly 20 years ago, I was the senior author on a paper "The Life Course as a Cultural Unit (Fry & Keith, 1982). In that paper, Jennie Keith and I reviewed what was known about cultural diversity and the promise of the life course for cross-cultural research. Thereafter, we and our colleagues spent a decade engaged in a comprehensive study of the meanings and uses of age and aging across seven sites in four countries: Project AGE (Keith, Fry, Glascock, Ikels, Dickerson-Putnam, Draper, & Harpending, 1994). In our cross-cultural test of the life-course framework, we encountered some instructive but unanticipated surprises. Namely, that respondents in smaller-scaled contexts had difficulty with our instruments. The task we presented to respondents was to sort cards describing *social persona* (culturally meaningful individuals) into age groups. In contrast, respondents in large-scaled urban and industrial societies experienced few problems in the sorting task. We concluded that the life course, as it is known in the scientific literature, is cultural and is appropriate for societies of Europe and North America in the 19th and 20th centuries. For those not fully integrated into the institutions that dominate these societies (namely, an industrial labor market), this model of the life course is not appropriate or is marginal at best.

If the life course is a cultural model, then we should examine the "deep structure" cultural premises on which it is based. The intent of this chapter is to explore cultural assumptions of the life-course model and the corresponding assumptions made in behavioral and social scientific research on the life course. Put simply, understanding the life course is about understanding lives through time. Yet with few exceptions (Hendricks, 1982; Hendricks & Hendricks, 1976; Neugarten, 1979; Schroots & Birren, 1990), time has not been a focus of our discourse. Even in the study of aging, which is obviously a temporal phenomenon, time is taken as a given. It is viewed a physical property of the universe in which lives take place, and it is therefore not viewed as problematic. A notable exception to this trend has been the discussion of methodological confounds that result when we consider multiple temporal variables simultaneously (e.g., age, period, cohort; e.g., Nydegger, 1981; Schaie, 1965).

In this chapter, I consider time to be problematic. First, I examine time as a set of phenomena and how these phenomena are appropriate for the study of aging and lives. Second, I look at the issue of how time is measured and the cultural knowledge that is the foundation of chronological age. Third, I explore how time and age are used to create age norms and life stages, which themselves are further subject to cultural interpretation and variation. Fourth, I ask questions about how to disentangle temporal and cultural complexities so that we might ask theoretically productive questions. Finally, I raise questions about the phenomena that we are or should be investigating in our attempts to understand aging and the life course in contemporary times.

THE PROBLEMS OF TIME

Time is an enormous topic, primarily because of its ubiquity. Interestingly, while humans live through time and are concerned with time, we have no specialized senses with which to perceive time. Take away the cultural devices that measure time (clocks and calendars), and the precision for estimates of time begin to crumble. No human has the "on board" clocks of the observers in Einstein's famous thought experiments. Yet humans perceive time with the same senses we use to observe things in spatial dimensions. Einstein's hypothetical observers, besides informing us of the relativity of time, also determined time as the fourth dimension (in addition to the spatial dimensions of height, width, and depth). Because we can only perceive spatial phenomena, we derive time from events that happen in our spatial context. Theoretically, time, as the fourth dimension, is the dimension through which space and things in it move. Consequently, when we discuss time, we resort to spatial metaphors.

More practically, what is it that humans use to discern time? Scholarship on the subject points to continuities/discontinuities (Benedict, 1938) and to periodicity/duration (Leach, 1961). Persistence and change are at the heart of how we process time. Continuity or the duration of a pattern, punctuated by change, enables us to discern the passage of time. Most familiar are sequences that are a product of the location of the earth in the solar system and universe. Day is replaced by night. The cold season (winter) is replaced by the warm season (summer). In some locations, seasonality means that wet is replaced by dry. The stars, such as the Pleiades, appear in the same location in the night sky only once as the earth orbits around the sun. Many things display continuity/discontinuity and periodicity/duration and, consequently, diverse kinds of time run throughout human lives and culture. These range from chemical time, such as radioactive carbon we use to date the past, to the sidereal or stellar time we use to calibrate the yearly round. We must also include the time of human lives and culture. If there were only discontinuities, there would be chaos. If there were only continuities, it would be impossible to tell time because there would be no way of knowing about it. We process the passage of time through continuities or discontinuities. Without change and stability, we would have no way of experiencing time, much less a means for interpreting it.

Most of the work on the philosophy of time belongs to the philosophy of science, and particularly to physics; but it has little of relevance to how humans experience time. Of relevance are two positions that have emerged to reflect different ways of approaching time. These are labeled by the rather non-descriptive terms of "A-Time" and "B-Time." A-Time was introduced in the work of Gale (1967, 1968; for an extended discussion of the relevance of this distinction for the social sciences, see Gell, 1992).

Briefly, A-Time views time as a line composed of a past, present, and future. Many languages of the world have rules on verb tenses requiring their speakers to make distinctions between past, present, and future. English is one such language. Metaphorically, this view of time is best represented in a short story by Jorge Borges, *The Book of Sand* (1998 [1975]). Unlike paper, the pages in the book of sand do not retain their organization. Once a page is turned, it is impossible to find that page again. It is a book without a beginning or an end. As one searches for end points, pages always well up or recede. The book of sand is an infinite book, and its owner wisely gets rid of it by leaving it in a library. At this point, the metaphor breaks down because time is not infinite. A-Time does, however, reflect how time is experienced. In its extreme, all that exists is the present. The past falls into disorganization and is replaced by new forms of the present. The future has yet to be formed from the structure of the present. A difficulty with A-Time that renders it problematic in the social sciences is the fact that the time line is relative. The present was some past's future and will become another future's past. Conceptually, we need a conception of time that is less fluid and relativistic.

B-Time, on the other hand, is different in that its time line is not as complex and has points that are more fixed. B-Time is simply something happens before another something. In its most elementary form, B-Time considers two points on a time line: before and after. Regardless of how it is measured, and from any perspective on a time line, B-Time is not relativistic. An event can only happen before or after another. Although B-time is probably not the way we experience time, it simplifies time-related phenomena considerably, which means these phenomena can be handled more adequately in social scientific research. It reminds us that, in investigating temporal phenomena, we search for sequences of patterns that precede or follow one another.

Time is neither an enigma nor a conceptual problem. Time has to do with the organization of the phenomenal world. It is a world that is forever changing, but it is also a world that is characterized by transformations that are sufficiently gradual so that we are nonetheless able to see stability. When stationary patterns are altered, we experience discontinuities that are comprehended as cycles or as transformations. In our spatial world, we therefore experience time. When humans try to control time by measuring it or putting it to social use, it becomes part of culture—where it is interpreted, refined, and loaded with assumptions. I now turn attention to cultural assumptions about age and life stages.

TIME AND THE INVENTION OF CHRONOLOGICAL AGE

Chronological age is under attack as an empty variable simply because its units (years) are a measure of sidereal time. Accumulating cycles around the sun would appear to be irrelevant to a meaningful social world. Interestingly, this supposedly empty variable is an essential criterion in rationalizing the enormous populations of contemporary industrial capitalist states. Age in years is a simple and impartial standard to define the rights and responsibilities of citizenship. The ability to know one's age is the result of an incredible multicultural effort to measure time. The crown jewel of this effort is the Gregorian Calendar (Duncan, 1998).

The major problem that has to be dealt with in any calendar is that lunar cycles and solar cycles are not congruent with one another, and they are not easily divisible into each other or into days. For instance, the lunar year is 354.3672 days in length and the solar year is 365.242199 days. It took well over two millennia to figure this out and depended on work by Babylonians, Egyptians, Romans, Hindus, Arabs, and Europeans. The solution of the Gregorian reform in 1582 was to reset the calendar by eliminating the 10 days of "creep" from the older Julian Calendar, and to institute a leap year rule for century years. Only century years that are divisible by 400 have a leap year (e.g., 1600, 2000, 2400). Although not perfect, this calendar has been adopted by most nations. It is the calendar used to schedule market days and holidays and to date contracts. Alternative calendars that are more concerned with the quality of time (than with the counting of time) are also frequently used, such as that which exists in Bali (Geertz, 1973) or in Japan. Astrology informs us of days that are good for different kinds of activities, and days we avoid different kinds of activities. Friday the 13th is one of the few cycles of days and numbers that forecasts bad luck in the Gregorian Calendar.

The Gregorian calendar enables us to determine chronological age. With secularization, this calendar provides us with a measured time line that appears to be extra-societal. In other words, the construction of days, months, and years are no longer in the hands of Priests or the State. The cycle of days, months, and years has lost its significance as Saint's Days and symbols of political importance. Its workings are understood by nearly everyone, and the abundance of published calendars objectify the time line. The Gregorian Calendar also employs the remarkable invention of a fixed point to begin the numbering of years. In the 6th Century (531 A.D.), a little-known monk, Dionysius Exiguus (Little Dennis), with very little fanfare modified the Christian Calendar to begin with the birth of Christ. Before this, the yearly count began with the installation of the current ruler. For instance, the year 1984 in the Gregorian Calendar would be the 2nd year of the rule of President Clinton in the United States and the 32nd year of the rule of Queen Elizabeth II in the United Kingdom. With the fixed point (year 1), we count forward the years classed as A.D. (the years of our Lord) and backward the years labeled B.C. (before Christ).

With this long extra-societal (but not extra-cultural) time line, the calculation of chronological age is quite simple. To determine one's age, one needs to know the year of birth and subtract it from the present year. Knowledge of one's birth year also requires considerable cultural data. Without written records, the past becomes imprecise and blurred. Certainly, the earliest records were Church recordings of baptisms, weddings, and deaths. Later (primarily in the 19th century), vital statistics (e.g., birth and death certificates, marriage licenses) were routinely gathered along with national census data. With these trends, chronological age also became increasingly important.

From the perspective of the 21st century, it is difficult to imagine a world without years or chronological age. Yet humans survived for millennia without precision in temporal measurement. Calendars and chronological age are inventions of large-scale state-level societies that appeared around 3,000 B.C. at the earliest. Small-scale societies are not organized bureaucratically. In these simpler societies, individuals have extensive personal knowledge about nearly everyone in a given "social field." Age is viewed not in chronological terms, but is instead viewed in terms of birth order and relative seniority. Age is mostly expressed in the language of kinship and is best seen as a generational difference. Of course, generations have no precise temporal definition other than as a line of descent. In small-scale societies, age may serve to index maturity or seniority but is otherwise irrelevant.

Can we dismiss chronological age as an "empty" variable? If we take the view that the Gregorian Calendar is extra-societal and therefore an objective count of solar cycles, age would appear to be a largely meaningless measure of time and duration of life. However, the Gregorian Calendar is a rather major and very successful cultural invention. Likewise, chronological age is a remarkable cultural innovation. We cannot dismiss either one of them. Instead, we must understand how these temporal measurements are used within a culture. A real strength of chronological age is that it is both numeric and linguistic (Crump, 1990). Numbers are relational, and language enables us to translate them into other dimensions. The real complaint about chronological age is the way it is used as a proxy for an individual's developmental state(s) and position(s) in the life course. Bureaucratically, chronological age functions to shape and rationalize a large heterogenous population into a skilled and manageable labor force. Opportunities to acquire skills and knowledge are obtained in educational institutions that recruit and sort their participants in terms of chronological age. Likewise, workers enter and exit the work force primarily on age-related terms. We now turn our attention to the question of how age is used normatively to shape the life course.

AGE NORMS AND LIFE STAGES

Social time, as outlined by Neugarten and Datan (1973), differentiates a sociocultual notion of time that is clearly distinct from biological and historical phenomena. Social time is based on a cultural notion of age grading—the "recognized divisions of the life of an individual as he passes from infancy to old age" (Radcliffe-Brown, 1929). Age grades are social categories that roughly mirror biological maturity in terms of physical abilities. Age grades, however, are more than biological maturity, in that cultural values, meanings, and assumptions are built into them. Age grades are more like genealogies (social categories), which reflect the biological facts of a pedigree (genetic facts of descent). At times, social categories can be inconsistent with biological facts (such as adoption, or aunts and uncles who are the same age as an ego). Genealogies and age grades are more accurate maps of the social world, and of assumptions made about families and the life course, respectively.

Age norms give definition to age grades. Norms are expectations about how the social world *should* work. The early work of Neugarten clearly demonstrated that Americans in the 1950s had clear ideas about the timing (age) norms for specific events and transitions (Neugarten & Peterson, 1957). More recently, the work of Settersten has reaffirmed these norms, which demonstrate a remarkable degree of continuity 40 years later (e.g., Settersten & Hagestad, 1996a, 1996b). Norms are rather basic in the construction of social phenomena. As Durkheim (1938[1897]) argued long ago, social norms 1) have a social end; 2) exist external to and prior to individuals; and 3) exert constraint upon individuals. In order to discover the "age" in age norms, we must not only identify the norm, but we must also ask about its functions and the mechanisms that enforce it. If norms are to be effective, there must be either anticipated or real consequences for those who violate them (Settersten, 1999).

Many age norms are quite informal. Admonitions to "act your age" are often informal jokes designed to modify behavior and stimulate awareness of what is appropriate for one's age grade. At worst, an individual so chastised is embarrassed by direct confrontation or suffers the effects of negative gossip. Other age norms are more formalized legal norms embedded in the law, for which violators experience clearer-cut sanctions. For instance, driving, drinking, or marrying at ages younger than those legally defined will result in fines and even jail time. Likewise, falsification of age to receive age-related entitlements gets the counterfeiter into serious legal trouble.

If social time is a key to the life course, then it is critical that we be able to model social time. These models should reveal the assumptions made about age and how age is structured into a society. Cultural meanings and definitions of age should be brought to the surface, and the social purposes of those meanings and definitions should be understood. How might we model social time?

Social time is more basic than either age grades or age norms. Both age grades and age norms are constructed using notions about time, age, and social life. Much of our thinking about social time—age grades, age norms, age statuses— is heavily influenced by ethnographic literature anchored in what we now identify as "age class societies." Descriptions of societies from East Africa, Australia, and Native North and South America fascinated researchers because age and age grades are a formal feature of social organization. For example, age is a prominent feature of recruitment of males into an age-stratified political life. Despite of considerable variability in the form and function of age classes, men are recruited into corporate groups that dominate their passage through adulthood (see Bernardi, 1985). Boys are recruited and initiated into an age set that is then closed and bounded. This set will then collectively move through a stratified system of seniority, replacing the next senior set until it reaches the most senior status and most of its members have died (for a detailed example of the Maasai, see Spencer, 1988).

Borrowing models from an ethnographic literature of a very different cultural type leaves us prone to inappropriate theoretical formulations. What is true for the age classes of East Africa is not an appropriate model for industrialized capitalistic societies (Spencer, 1990). First, notions of time are very different in that time in East Africa is expressed in terms of generational differences between fathers and sons, not in terms of chronological age. Secondly, East African age classes do not translate well into life stages or age grades. Thirdly, East African age classes function to resolve and manage generational conflict.

To construct a model of age, we need to design a framework that uses time. We have to return to the basics and look at time as a set of cultural phenomena. In Figures 1 through 4, I develop a notion of age/time by exploring three questions. First, how is time involved in social life? Second, how is time involved in age-related status change? Third, how is time involved in dividing the life course into meaningful categories?

Time in social life (Figure 1). In embracing age grades and age norms as defining features of social time, we put the proverbial cart before the horse. If we subscribe to age as temporal, and we are most interested in the social aspects of age, then we should be focused on time. As I have argued above, B-Time is the most appropriate for use in the social sciences. Social time then becomes social events or things that display continuity and discontinuity, events and things that come before or after each other. It is the predictability created by culture that makes the life course a meaningful unit to study. Graphically, this can be represented with the horizontal axis representing continuity and the vertical axis discontinuity (see Figure 1). In the resulting figure, the plotted line appears as steps on a stairway. As one moves from left to right, time passes—one event happens before another.

Age/time in status change (Figure 2). If social events or things enable us to recognize the passage of social time, then what are these social events and things?

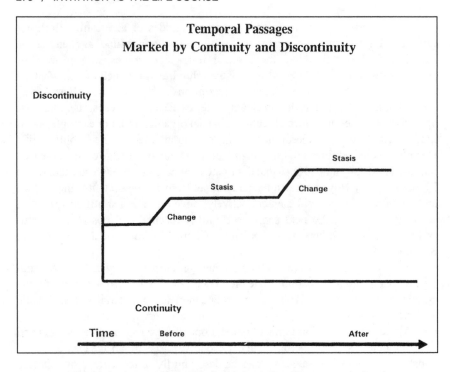

Figure 1. An age/time graph representing time as periods of
relative stasis punctuated by change.

Age grades and life stages are not random events or even happenings in daily life. Instead, age-related social phenomena are made up of events and things that are far more elementary. As Nydegger has argued, the life course is, in essence, a role course (Nydegger, 1986). In looking at Figure 2, an age/time graph, the lines of continuity become statuses that an individual has and activates, while the lines of discontinuity become transitions. Let us examine just one event—marriage. The lines of continuity or status occupation are "single" and "married," with the lines of discontinuity representing the "engagement" and "wedding." In this case, because an age norm presumably exits, it is represented by an intersection with time, which is now chronologized with a time line and with age calculated by the difference between birth year and the present.

Marriage is but one example. If we want to know what these social events are, we must inform ourselves ethnographically. We must discover the markers of the social clock that operate in specific settings. In Project AGE, we were interested in learning what information individuals need in order to make judgments about another person's age or life stage. People in societies organized by industrialized capitalism need remarkably little information in order to make these judgments. In

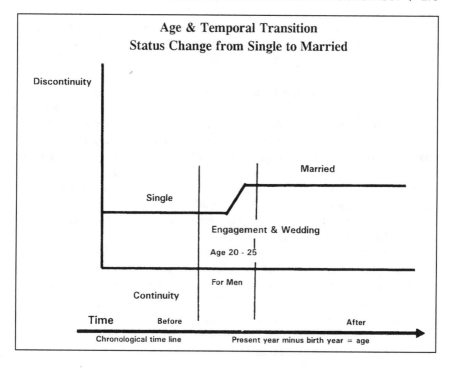

Figure 2. An age/time graph representing time as an element
in an age-related status transition.

communities in the United States (Swarthmore and Momence), Ireland
(Blessington and Clifden), and Hong Kong, the vital age-relevant information
related to education, work status, marital status, and status as parents (children's
status). To a lesser extent, it also related to participation in a community's organizational structure, status of one's parents (in terms of their work or health status),
and a financial life course (payment of mortgages). Not surprisingly, these are
quite similar to markers that have been used in classic and contemporary studies of
age norms (e.g., Neugarten, Moore, & Lowe, 1965; Settersten & Hagestad, 1996a,
1996b). In Botswana (!Kung and Herero), the story is quite different. Although
information about marriages, children, and the ability to work are important, they
are not nearly as age-based as they are in industrialized societies.

What is it about education, work status, marital status, and the status of
children that bind this information to age? Formal (legal) age norms codify rights
based on chronological age and govern entry into and exit from these statuses.
Clearly, the state institutionalizes a life course (Kohli, 1986a; 1986b; Meyer, 1986;
Settersten, Chapter 7), which is to say the life course *as researchers in North
America and Europe have come to know it*. In a temporal framework, we might call

this *legislative time.* The social purpose of these norms is to define the rights and duties of citizenship. At two points in the lives of citizens, norms become especially effective: first, in the transition from adolescence to adulthood; and second, in the transition between adulthood and old age.

The rights of adulthood (Figure 3). Adolescence is a time of denial of adult privilege and waiting for the arrival of full adult status. There are very clear laws about what adolescents can and cannot do. For instance, drinking and smoking are risky behaviors, and young people cannot purchase offending substances until they are deemed old enough to make informed decisions. Voting, driving, work, and marriage all assume cultural competence. Along with capability comes responsibility. Adults are accountable for their actions. In legal terms, they have reached the age of majority. Minors are children who are dependent on parents, and adolescents acquire education to become culturally competent. When adolescents violate these norms, the state quickly intervenes.

The rights of old age (Figure 4). Old age has come to be defined as a period in which people so defined withdraw from the adult status of "working" and enter the older adult status of "retirement." In addition, the responsibility for dependent

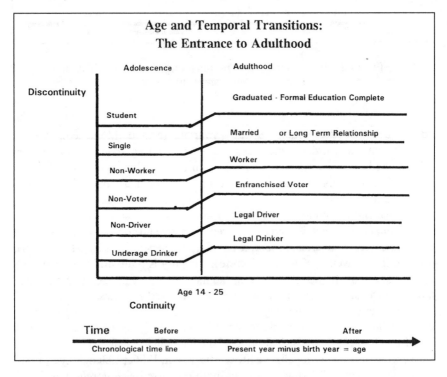

Figure 3. An age/time graph representing the density of age status transitions from adolescence into adulthood.

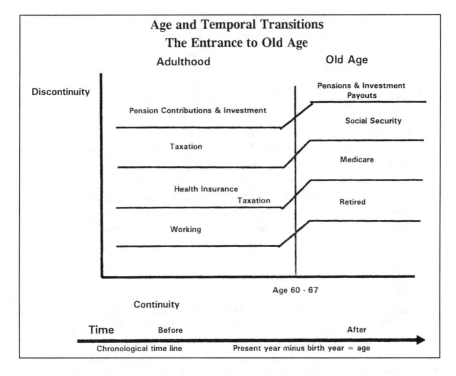

Figure 4. An age/time graph representing the density of age status transitions from adulthood into old age.

children has usually concluded by this time. The state compensates its citizens for the loss of 'income and health insurance that result from the loss of work. To activate entitlements, explicit age requirements must be met (e.g., in the United States, Social Security between the ages of 62 and 67 and Medicare after the age of 65). There are also explicit age requirements that regulate other aspects of the financial life course (e.g., for private pensions, IRAs). If an older person violates these norms, they do not get too far.

It would appear as if little happens to regulate the time between entry into adulthood and entry into old age. To the contrary, the norms of work and specific corporate structures come into play. It is simply that workplace norms are occupation-specific and even corporation-specific, not society-wide. However, norms around marriage, and norms concerning compulsory education of children, are society-wide. Children are required to attend heavily and finely age-graded educational institutions. Indirectly, parental status is defined in terms of their children's educational statuses.

Individuals in capitalist nation-states use information on work, education, marriage, and parental status to estimate age, adding or subtracting years with each new piece of information learned. Thus, they take known exits from education, add a few years for work and marriage, and then add specific years for the educational status of the oldest child. It is not very difficult to make a reasonable guess about another person's age once we have these types of information. Likewise, information about retirement, pensions, Social Security, or Medicare, and (less precise) information on grandparental or health status, yield accurate guesses about ages in later life.

In these societies, legal age norms lie at the foundation of the life course. Clearly, statuses that make up the life course are sequenced (before/after) through time in a fairly standardized fashion. This sequencing is so clear that three life stages are demarcated with marked discontinuity and density in transitions between them. These stages are pre-adulthood (childhood and adolescence), adulthood, and post-adulthood (old age). This division and associated rights of citizenship distribute education, work, and leisure expenses unevenly across life. As Settersten (Chapters 1 and 7) and Hendricks and Cutler (Chapter 4) have indicated, the assumptions that define this division may no longer be warranted or desirable in contemporary Western societies.

What about further distinctions beyond adolescence—during adulthood and old age? People in industrialized societies are certainly capable of making further refinements. Gerontologists routinely differentiate old age into "young-old," "old-old," and "oldest-old" categories. In Project AGE, respondents in the United States, Ireland, and Hong Kong divided adulthood into three to five stages. The presence of five or more categories was statistically rare, yet fewer than three was nearly nonexistent. Researchers who have examined age grading or life stages (beyond the three divisions indicated above) are impressed by variability not only in the number of divisions, but also in the age thresholds that mark movement from one age to the next. To understand the structure in data such as these, statistical techniques that use the composition of groupings, such as cluster analysis or multidimensional scaling, are needed. As meaningful cultural categories, age grades are clusters of age-relevant statuses. In Western societies, age is heavily bound legislative time and is therefore highly standardized. Yet beyond the tripartite division into adolescence, adulthood, and old age, the meanings of age may become variable and idiosyncratic.

For people in non-industrialized societies, information about education, work, marriage, and children provides very little specificity about age. In the Kalahari Desert of Botswana there are few schools, and most are limited to the primary grades. Participation in an age-graded educational system is not universal, nor is attendance mandated by the state. Work does not 'involve a national labor market for wages. Instead, individuals are engaged in subsistence activities of foraging, hunting, gardening, and herding cattle. Marriage is not regulated by age, as adults arrange marriages for their children as young as eight years of age. The most important information on children is their physical size (little or big) and how many there are, given that there is almost no participation in an educational system. Thus, these similar statuses do not encode age because legislative time does not shape these respective roles.

If venturing beyond the legislative time of the state and chronological age leads us into less standardization and more variability, how are we to make the life course a theoretical construct that is researchable and empirically meaningful? Of course, a strength of science is it approaches a set of phenomena in explicit and systematic ways. I now turn to the prospect of using age/time to construct theories of the life course. In Figures 1 through 4 I presented the notion that age is time. Temporal passage brings many continuities and discontinuities. A window to investigating the cultural aspects of age is to explicitly link age to time. One goal is to move beyond culturally-specific understandings and to instead develop theoretical constructs that apply to a wide range of societies.

THEORY CONSTRUCTION AND LIFE COURSES

Human lives through time present a complicated picture. The complexity is that there are many kinds of temporal change and continuity that shape lives. Societies change. Populations change. Opportunities change. Personal networks change. Bodies change. Amidst all of this change, continuity or stasis makes for an interpretable order. Humans use culture to explain and muddle through life. Our understandings of the world around us and of our immediate circumstances guide our decisions and the actions we take.

We must construct theory to understand phenomena as complex as life courses. The primary advantage of theory construction is that logic and abstraction simplify and make explicit how ideas or variables are to be generated. Attention is paid to making generalizations so that they are falsifiable and empirically verifiable. A little theory construction goes a long way in improving our chances of making the life course a researchable unit. Within this context, I focus on two issues: 1) the life course as a theoretical construct, and 2) the kinds of time that underlie and intersect with life courses.

The Life Course as a Theoretical Construct

In the past three decades of its development, scholarship on the life course has taken the life course to be a universal feature of all human societies and something that is relatively culturally-neutral. Since the 1960s, the "life course" replaced the "life cycle," which had been used most often up to that point, particularly in ethnographic literature. In planning Project AGE, we hoped to use the life-course framework to unearth cross-cultural views of social times and social clocks. Instead of finding working-class American time and middle-class American time, or Irish time or Hong Kong time, or !Kung or Herero time, we learned that the life-course framework was not as culturally-neutral as we thought it might be. In other words, our ideas about the life course were not appropriate for non-industrialized communities (!Kung and Herero) or for those marginal to industry (e.g., Clifden, Ireland) (Keith et al., 1994). In using the standards of theory construction (namely classification) to analyze this situation, it became clear that the life course as *we* know it is but one variant of life courses. Cross-cultural research suggests there are at least three kinds of life courses: 1) staged life courses, 2) generational life courses, and 3) age-classed life courses (for further discussion, see Fry, 1999).

Staged Life Courses

The "staged" life course has become the accepted definition of the life course. This kind of life course has also been referred to as the "institutionalized" life course. It assumes that age grades are life stages with which people plan their lives. The "age" in the age norms that shape the life stages are anchored in a social clock based on chronological age and legislative time of the institutions of industrial societies. Age grades divide this life course into three distinct segments: childhood and adolescence, adulthood, and old age. Life plans in this course relate to preparing and then launching oneself into adulthood. Adulthood is a long period of working, nurturing children, and launching them into adulthood. Old age is a period of withdrawal from the world of work and of benefiting from state-supported entitlements and the accumulation of one's prior resources (financial and otherwise).

Generational Life Courses

A "generational" life course is not widely recognized, simply because the life course in small-scaled societies has not received as much attention. A notable exception here is the study of kinship. Generational life courses are defined in the web and language of kinship (see also Hagestad, Chapter 5). In this case, social time is linked to kinship position and combined with physical abilities that come with maturation (not chronology). Age grades are not sharply defined. Generations are defined by descent (birth order), but boundaries between generations are often difficult to define because families are large and long periods of reproduction increase the ambiguity of generational markers. Although it is possible to make these distinctions in small-scaled societies, people in these societies seldom do. Within generational life courses, the life plan is to mature into adulthood, have a family, work in subsistence, and simply live.

Age-Classed Life Courses

"Age-classed" life courses attracted the attention of early researchers who formulated concepts of age norms and age grades. Ethnographically, these have been well documented but are not recognized as a decidedly different life course. For the few societies in which age is formalized into classes, it is very difficult to argue that it is age per se that defines those classes. Instead, it more often seems based on kinship. Age-classed life courses are a variant of generational life courses. For all the variability, the minimal rule governing class membership is that father and son must belong to a different class. Hence, the kind of time that is important is generational (kinship) time. Classes have sharp boundaries through the recruitment of membership and the closed corporate structure of the class. For example, a generalized life plan among the Maasai is for a male to first spend the initial set fighting and attracting the attention of women. Then, he becomes a householder, herds cattle, and raises a family. Then, he ascends into eldership and influence, and moves closer to (and finally joins) his ancestors in death.

Thus, by taking what would appear to be a theoretical construct that could well be a cultural unit applicable to all cultures, we discover that our initial idea is loaded with cultural assumptions. For these three categories of life courses, we see significant differences in the basis for social time, the social purposes for which they are used, the resulting social classification, and the life plans individuals generate based on them.

Time and Life Courses

If we are serious about constructing theories of the life course, we must take a careful look at the issues related to time. Time is not necessarily a flat linear dimension. Some of the objections to our extreme reliance on chronological age concern the fact that it makes unidimensional that which is inherently multidimensional. As noted earlier, time expressed in years is bound to the Gregorian Calendar, which measures sidereal time. Although this calibration has objectified our experience of time, we must realize that there are other kinds of time. Time is comprehended through the continuity and discontinuity of the phenomena we are investigating. Events are experienced in a before-and-after (sequenced) fashion (B-Time). It is highly probable that non-sidereal times can be expressed in sidereal time much as the familiar 3-sided (or more sided) ruler. In fact, a theoretical breakthrough in the study of life courses has been the recognition of at least three kinds of time—life time, social time, and historical time (Neugarten & Datan, 1973). Indeed, we have been stimulated by the challenge of temporal complexity, but we have not gone far enough. The intricacies of time as expressed in age/period/cohort or in life/social/historical time all point to the enormous job of understanding the life course scientifically in a single culture, let alone across multiple cultures. The reason this task appears nearly impossible is that the levels of the phenomena we have tried to incorporate are far too general to handle theoretically and methodologically.

An important task of theory construction is the creation of ideas that are logically and empirically testable and falsifiable. We cannot examine the whole universe at once. We must use our abilities of abstraction to investigate discrete aspects of phenomena that we can manage logically and empirically. To further the productivity of our questions, I propose that we embrace the idea that many different kinds of time are integrated within the construct of the life course. Obviously, many things happen in time. If we recognize the continuities and discontinuities in these happenings as specific temporal dimensions, then the life course consists of several kinds of time with distinctive calibrations. Some may be more closely expressed and synchronized with sidereal time while others may be only roughly indexed by this kind of time.

If we accept this proposal, our next challenge is to isolate these different kinds of time. Given what we already know about the life course, this is not as difficult as it might appear. The institutional framework in which lives are lived is an excellent place to begin our inquiry. In fact, the chapters of this book provide an excellent springboard from which to explore different kinds of times that comprise lives.

If the purpose of theory is to model something in the phenomenal world, then what is it that we seek to model with the life course? A prevalent theme the authors in this book have used is that of a trajectory. The image of the life course is of an object being transmitted through time, space, or another medium. Trajectories do not have well-defined paths. For life, there is no career or script to follow at every turn. At best, the life course is guided by cultural scripts but remains general enough to be implemented flexibly at the individual level. When we talk about the life course at the level of society, we are modeling the rules of the game and temporal reward structures in specific social contexts. Yet variability and disorder at the individual level make this extremely difficult (see George's discussion in Chapter 6 of Rindfuss, Swicegood, and Rosenfeld's (1987) analysis of young adult role sequences following graduation).

In taking a temporal perspective, we ask questions in a before-and-after framework. For example:

1. If/Then Statements (coincidence):
   If L, M, N happen/are present at time A, then X, Y, Z are found at time B.
2. Causal statements (one set of variables creates change in another set of variables):
   Conditions L, M, N at time A cause X, Y, Z at time B.

These arguments can be cast in a probabilistic framework. The hypothesis can be either prospective (predictive), using time A as the starting point; or retrospective (remembered), using time B as the point. Multiple hypotheses can be linked into chains, provided they can be arrayed in time (in a before-and-after fashion). We have the tools to do this, for concepts such as timing, duration, sequencing, spacing, and density can be operationalized in fairly straightforward ways. As noted above, roles exist in time and are clustered in ways that lend lives some patterning, increase predictability, and make sense of serendipity.

If we are modeling the rules of the game (norms) that individuals use in organizing and interpreting life trajectories, then we must look at the institutional structures in which they spend portions of their lives. At this point, I turn my attention to the contributions of this volume. The focus of this work is in a specific type of society, that of industrial capitalism or "late modern" societies. Four topics organize the section that follows: 1) time and the world of work; 2) time and the domestic world of families; 3) time and consequences for health and well-being; and 4) history and context.

Time and Work Life

Capitalist societies with an industrial mode of production are work societies. Capitalism is but one transformation in a long line of economic evolutionary innovations to increase human productivity through work and technology. The blueprint for capitalism is the vision Adam Smith outlined in *The Wealth of Nations,* which was written at the time of the American Revolution (1960 [1776]). Smith's prophecy was that wealth and productivity would be increased through an extensive division of labor. Of course, the establishment of capitalism required a number of now familiar things to happen—such as the commodification of land, money, and work, along with the creation of a free market. By the 20th century, the life course that was institutionalized is the tripartite division of preparation for work, work, and retirement that Henretta (Chapter 3), Hendricks and Cutler (Chapter 4), Settersten (Chapter 7) and others discuss.

Although this tripartite life course has been called the "'institutionalized" life course, it is really a work course. Our image is one of young people being launched into a world of work where they will spend the majority of their adult lives until they retire in later life. As noted above, this trajectory is calibrated through *legislative time.* States improve the skill level of their labor pools by rewarding adolescents (or at least certain groups of adolescents) to attend schools with the promise of bettering their chances in the labor market. Prolonged education, of course, delays entry into the labor force and is also a method for regulating the size of the labor pool. The legislative time of the state directly calibrates the life course by controlling the timing and density of the transitions, such as entry into and exit from work roles. Another kind of time is implicit in this life course: *financial time.* The immediate reward is that, with entry into the work force, one gains enough income to provide personal autonomy and security for self and family. In the long term, one should accumulate sufficient wealth to meet both emergencies and scheduled expenditures and have enough left over to provide security in old age once one has retired.

Another kind of time also underlies the rhythm of work. For lack of a better term, one aspect of *work time* is *schedule time* because it relates to the coordination of workers. An extensive division of labor requires rational schedules. Time clocks and punch clocks regulate the workday. The week is defined so that there are workdays and non-workdays for personal time (leisure). (The weekend was invented primarily to end the practice of "St. Monday"—the recovery needed following Sunday's feasting, drinking, and merry-making [Rybcznski, 1991].) Companies need workers to arrive and depart at predictable times. Thus, in this scenario, leisure is defined as the opposite of work. As the converse of work, leisure is distributed unevenly across adult life; while this is problematic, there is also evidence that this may change (Hendricks & Cutler, Chapter 4).

Now that the 20th century is over, does this model still work? As Henretta (Chapter 3) indicates, when the rules are changed, individuals generally accommodate. The historical shift from "lifetime jobs" to "contingency jobs" has implications for the financial security of individuals and families in both the short and long term. The same is true of the parallel historical shift from defined pension benefits to contributory pension plans. As rules change, so, too, do life trajectories. Because society-wide temporal institutionalization is based on the legislative time of the state, assumptions about timing, sequencing, duration, spacing, and density must be reexamined to reflect changes in the work course and questions of equity (see Settersten, Chapter 7).

Time and Domestic Life

Relative to work trajectories, family trajectories are more difficult to delineate. Generations constituting families are extremely vague societal-wide units. With the evolution of capitalism, families lost many of the political and economic functions they had in archaic states and smaller-scaled societies. Families operate as consumption units and as entities from which workers are recruited. Despite their diminished power, families, in all their diversity, remain extraordinarily important as the locus of support and intimacy, and homes as private spaces within which individuals are free to be themselves.

Family life is calibrated by *generational time.* Births of parents must precede that of their children. As Hagestad (Chapter 5) indicates, families have trajectories or domestic cycles of formation, expansion, and contraction. Through reproduction, generational time is linked to *life time* through biological possibilities. Although the computation of the age difference between parents and children is straightforward, the translation of generational membership into an age-related unit is problematic. For instance, a child born to an 18-year-old mother will be 30 years older than another child born to the same mother when she is 48. The age difference between the two siblings is almost two times that of the eldest child and the mother!

Families link lives across time. As Hagestad notes, dramatic shifts in the mortality rate over the past century have slowed generational turnover so much so that up to five generations within a family may be alive at once. If one is old (Omega generation), one looks down to descendants. Children (Alpha generation) look up to the ascending generations. The middle (Janus) generation looks both directions. Through written records, it is possible to look up to ascending generations as far back as 400 or more years. Before the 1500s in Europe, surnames were not used and the records were not kept because taxation was not systematic. On the other hand, Chinese genealogies often extend over 1000 generations.

Family time also intersects with legislative time and work time. Through its policies, the state legislates the acceptable form of families (monogamy between individuals who are not related more closely than second cousins) and timing (age) of formation. The state also enforces norms of parental responsibility. Most obvious is the enforcement of rules concerning the age of children's participation in educational institutions. Work time also impacts decision-making about fertility and the spacing of children, which creates nightmares for scheduling and coordination in families with two working parents.

Especially when viewed from a comparative, global perspective, families are resilient, multipurpose, and extremely diverse. Families present challenges to life-course researchers precisely because lives are linked in domestic contexts and because generational time intersects biological time and various other types of time. Hagestad outlines some of the challenges initiated by increased longevity, reduced fertility, high divorce rates, and the private norms of family life.

Time, Health, and Successful Aging

Health and successful aging in a temporal framework take us into relatively uncharted territory. Our temporal constructs of timing, duration, sequencing, and density will encounter very fertile ground and high pay-offs. Both the chapter by George (Chapter 6) and the chapter by the Kahanas (Chapter 8) employ a stress framework, which paradigmatically argues that past events (stressors) are related to present and future outcomes (health/quality of life). A duration variable as elegant as "pack years" links past behavior to present disease states (see George, Chapter 6). By considering successful aging in temporal and spatial contexts, the Kahanas' model of "preventive-corrective proactivity" is entirely transformed (Chapter 8).

When it comes to managing complexities related to time, the spheres of health and quality of life present even greater challenges than the spheres of family and work. Let me highlight two potential difficulties. First, much of the behavior that impacts health and quality of life is habitual. If we had to think before every action taken throughout the day, we would exhaust our brain's resources. We rely on routines to get through our days. We "go on automatic" because what we do is often a repeat of what we have done before. What should I eat for breakfast? Should I fasten the seat belts? What route should I take to work? What newspaper should I buy? And so on. Responses to these questions are largely handled by habit. This might even be considered another kind of time: *habitual time.* This is related to *schedule time* simply because it is repetitive. Habitual behavior associated with nutrition, risk-taking, sleeping, or addiction will certainly affect health and quality of life if they are of particularly long duration. Most habits are also initiated culturally. For instance, tobacco addiction begins with a decision to start smoking, which is probably triggered by peer pressure, image, or identity issues. Once hooked, it becomes habitual. But our main difficulty is in disentangling cultural factors from the habitual ones. The two go hand in hand. This is a particularly interesting challenge. If we were to consider the "internal resources" component of the contextualized model of successful aging to be a routinized response pattern, how much is cultural and how much is idiosyncratic and habitual?

A second related point is that much of what we take to be healthy or high quality-of-life outcomes are rooted in a cultural interpretation. Culture always presents us with challenges. While we may seldom be aware of it, culture is constantly at our side, offering a framework within which we interpret the phenomenal world. Clearly good health and quality of life call for cultural interpretation. It defines what constitutes the "good" in good health and the "quality" in quality of life. A vexing part of culture is that when we add time to that framework, its complexity increases exponentially. From time A to time B, we want to know how to get there in good health and with high quality of life. Cultural knowledge provides for alternatives and compensations. There are many different ways to get from time A to time B. If one path does not work, individuals use culture to find alternatives. For instance, there are a number of ways to make a left turn when the rules prohibit turning left. Also, the meaning of "good life" can shift in definition or can change with technological or other support. Consequently, what are hypothesized to be fairly direct relationships are deflected by cultural compensation, and researchers therefore see only very weak linkages. An example of this is the elusive link between age and well-being. Obvious declines in health and functionality seem to have little impact on levels of well-being, primarily because of culture.

History and Context

Historical time is another pervasive theme reflected in the chapters of this book. Historical time is a very different kind of time. Although consequential, historical time may not be as central to life-course studies as one might think. What happened in history is a quality of the sociocultural contexts in which lives are lived. In an A-Time framework, historical data from the patterns of the past fall into disorganization as the present emerges. Probes into the distant past reveal greater and greater disarray. For instance, a community that existed 12,000 years ago is difficult to reconstruct, but one that existed 120,000 years ago is even more difficult. History is important in three ways. First, present patterns come from the past. We therefore need to know about them to discover the processes through which the present was created. Secondly, historical patterns provide important contrasts (similarities and differences) to the present. Historical comparisons bring the here and now into sharper focus. Historical research is another variety of comparative research. Third, recent history exists in the memories of individuals who experienced that past. These experiences have consequences for the ways they view and understand the world. However, we need to tap much more than historical time if we are to adequately develop and adopt a life-course framework.

The life course as a cultural construct makes good intuitive sense for late-modern capitalist societies. But we need to move beyond our common sense and scientific modeling of the rules of the game. That is precisely what a book like this does. It calls for reflection on what we have accomplished from a number of perspectives. In this book, perspectives from sociology, psychology, and anthropology are well represented. Its vantage points range from historical syntheses of the life course to the institutional sectors that shape lives: work, leisure, family, nation-states, and health. A volume like this also calls for innovation, particularly through the rethinking of established knowledge.

A healthy dose of skepticism will only make our models, which are inherently cultural, increasingly congruent with the world we seek to explain. Dannefer (Chapter 11) offers some very interesting challenges to the model of the institutionalized life course. In the case of working children in the third world, the rules of adolescent denial and preparation are absent. These children will not, in all probability, experience a tripartite life course. A globalized labor force is in many respects similar to subsistence work, except that one harvests very low wages. Los Angeles gang members experience lives that share some parallels with age classes in East Africa. Although a gang's age-classes are not corporate, they are characterized by risk-taking and initiation feats, which creates an age-stratified system for these males. The alternative courses that Los Angeles gang members have worked out for their early adult years have very little to do with work. With globalization, we might expect world markets to become more homogenized and integrated. Indeed, the 19th and 20th centuries have seen the destruction and transformation of small-scaled societies. As the case of the Amazon shaman indicates, global markets dislocate local cultures but offer new opportunities that alter life trajectories. Cases such as those described by Dannefer illustrate that mainstream models of the life course do not work well for many peoples of the world. We should use theory construction to look beyond the institutionalized life course and toward to diversity of life-course patterns and the various times and processes that shape them.

AGE/TIME AND LIVES

I have always been fascinated by the language we use to describe and explain our subject matter. Gerontology shifted from the specific study of old age to the larger study of aging. In a recent conversation with Hyam Hazan (personal communication, 1999), we were both impressed by one advantage that those who study gender have over those who specialize in aging. Both fields are largely defined by biological or ascriptive roles: sex and age. However, gender, as a construct, is more than sex. Gender recognizes phenotypic differences but focuses on cultural elaboration and diversity. For age, there is no parallel. A quick review of a dictionary or thesaurus reveals a culturally-negative evaluation of age and a conclusion that is not in line with what we study. While frailty and disability are certainly part of our field, they are not necessarily the exclusive phenomena of age. There are virtually no synonyms for age. If gender is the phenomenon based on sex, what is the parallel for age?

Searching for an appropriate label for the phenomena we study is an interesting and important question. By way of conclusion, I will take a stab at providing an answer. In a volume such as this, a very tempting answer is the life course. Unfortunately, the life course is not the same as gender. While gender connotes cultural phenomena, it is not anchored in a single context. Gender invites us to examine diversity. As we have seen, the life course is a cultural construct. It is based on cultural definitions of time and uses of age which, in turn, set parameters on the lives of members of those societies (namely industrial-capitalist nations). It is clear that we must study human lives the long way—through time and through culture. It is also clear that we must study age—dynamically, aging is the time of our lives. When we do this, we study one kind of time: age/time. Yet there are many other kinds of time, including solar time, lunar time, biological time, DNA time, radiocarbon time, and the like. As with all temporal phenomena, they happen simultaneously. In addition, one kind of time is likely linked to, or even translatable into, other types.

Until we come up with a better notation, I propose we use "age/time." Neologisms, unfortunately, have a habit of becoming jargonistic, which can make communication more precise but also inhibit interaction with wider audiences. Like gender, age/time has the advantage of embracing the ascriptive. Age/time points us in the direction of the cultural without all the cultural baggage that comes with culturally-specific notions of the life course. And it has the advantage of embracing a wide variety of questions. Age/time, especially the "time" part of the term, reminds us that age *is* temporal. Theoretically, age/time is a window to our phenomena. Age/time incorporates other kinds of time that are relevant to lives. As we have seen above, these types of time include biological time, habitual time, schedule time, generational time, legislative time, historical time, and possibly many other kinds of time. In essence, age/time captures the many *times* that comprise our lives.

REFERENCES

Benedict, R. (1938). Continuities and discontinuities in cultural conditioning. *Psychiatry 1*, 161-167.

Bernardi, B. (1985). *Age class systems: Social institutions and polities based on age* (D. I. Kertzer, Trans.). Cambridge: Cambridge University Press.

Borges, J. L. (1998[1975]). *Jorge Luis Borges collected fictions* (A. Hurley, Trans.). New York: Penguin Books.

Cain, L. D. (1964). Life course and social structure. In R. E. L. Faris (Ed.), *Handbook of modern sociology* (pp. 272-309). Chicago: Rand-McNally.

Crump, T. (1990). *The anthropology of numbers.* Cambridge: Cambridge University Press.

Duncan, D. E. (1998). *Calendar: Humanity's epic struggle to determine a true and accurate year.* New York: Avon.

Durkheim, E. (1938[1897]). *Rules of the sociological method.* New York: Free Press.

Fry, C. L. (1999). Anthropological theories of age and aging. In V. L. Bengtson & K. W. Schaie (Eds.), *Handbook of theories of aging* (pp. 271-286). New York: Springer.

Fry, C. L., & Keith, J. K. (1982). The life course as a cultural unit. In M. W. Riley, R. P. Ables, & M. S. Teitelbaum (Eds.), *Aging from birth to death: Sociotemporal perspectives* (pp. 51-70). Boulder, CO: Westview Press.

Gale, R. (Ed.) (1967). *The philosophy of time.* New York: Doubleday.

Gale, R. (1968). *The language of time.* London: Routledge.

Gell, A. (1992). *The anthropology of time: Cultural constructions of maps and images.* Oxford: Berg.

Geertz, C. (1973). *The interpretation of cultures.* New York: Basic Books.

Hendricks, J. (1982). Time and social science: History and potential. In E. H. Mizruchi, B. Glassner, & T. Pastorello (Eds.), *Time and aging* (pp. 12-45). New York: General Hall.

Hendricks, C. D., & Hendricks, J. (1976). Concepts of time and temporal construction among the aged with implications for research. In J. F. Gubrium (Ed.), *Time, roles and self in old age* (pp. 13-49). New York: Human Sciences Press.

Keith, J. K., Fry, C. L., Glascock, A. P., Ikels, C., Dickerson-Putnam, J., Draper, P., & Harpending, H. (1994). *The aging experience: Diversity and commonality across cultures.* Thousand Oaks, CA: Sage.

Kohli, M. (1986a). The world we forgot: A historical review of the life course. In V. Marshall (Ed.), *Later life* (pp. 271-393). Beverly Hills, CA: Sage.

Kohli, M. (1986b). Social organization and subjective construction of the life course. In A. B. Sørensen, F. E. Weinert, & L. R. Sherrod (Eds.), *Human development and the life course: Multidisciplinary perspectives* (pp. 271-292). Hillsdale, NJ: Lawrence Erlbaum Associates.

Leach, E. R. (1961). *Rethinking anthropology.* New York: Humanities Press.

Meyer, J. W. (1986). The self and the life course: Institutionalization and its effects. In A. B. Sørensen, F. E. Weinert, & L. R. Sherrod (Eds.), *Human development and the life course: Multidisciplinary perspectives* (pp. 199-216). Hillsdale, NJ: Lawrence Erlbaum Associates.

Neugarten, B. L. (1979). Time, age and the life cycle. *American Journal of Psychiatry, 136,* 887-894.

Neugarten, B. L., & Datan, N. (1973). Sociological perspectives on the life cycle. In P. B. Baltes & K. W. Schaie (Eds.), *Life span developmental psychology* (pp. 53-69). New York: Academic Press.

Neugarten, B. L., Moore, J. W., & Lowe, J. C. (1965). Age norms, age constraints and adult socialization. *American Journal of Sociology, 70* (6), 710-717.

Neugarten, B. L., & Peterson, W. L. (1957). A study of the American age-grade system. *Proceedings of the Fourth Congress of the International Association of Gerontology, 3,* 497-502.

Nydegger, C. (1981). On being caught up in time. *Human Development, 24,* 1-12.

Nydegger, C. (1986). Age and life course transitions. In C. Fry & J. Keith (Eds.), *New methods for old age research* (pp. 131-162). New York: Bergin & Garvey.

Radcliffe-Brown, A. R. (1929). Age organization terminology. *Man, 21.*

Riley, M. W., Johnson, M., & Foner, A. (1972). *Aging and society, Volume 3: A sociology of age stratification.* New York: Russell Sage Foundation.

Rindfuss, R., Swicegood, C., & Rosenfeld, R. (1987). Disorder in the life course: How common and does it matter? *American Sociological Review, 52,* 785-801.

Rybcznski, W. (1991). *Waiting for the weekend.* New York: Penguin Books.

Schaie, K. W. (1965). A general model for the study of developmental problems. *Psychological Bulletin, 64,* 92-107.

Schroots, J., & Birren, J. E. (1990). Concepts of time and aging in science. In J. E. Birren & K. W. Schaie (Eds.), *Handbook of the psychology of aging* (pp. 41-64). San Diego, CA: Academic Press.

Settersten, R. A., Jr. (1999). *Lives in time and place: The problems and promises of developmental sciences.* Amityville, NY: Baywood.

Settersten, R. A., Jr., & Hagestad, G. O. (1996a). What's the latest? Cultural age deadlines for family transitions. *The Gerontologist, 36* (2), 178-188.

Settersten, R. A., Jr., & Hagestad, G. O. (1996b). What's the latest? Cultural age deadlines for educational and work transitions. *The Gerontologist 36* (5), 602-613.

Smith, A. (1960[1776]). *The wealth of nations.* London: J. M. Dent & Sons LTD.

Spencer, P. (1988). *Maasai of Matapato: A study of rituals and rebellion.* Bloomington: Indiana University Press.

Spencer, P. (Ed.) (1990). *Anthropology and the riddle of the sphinx: Paradoxes of change in the life course.* New York: Routledge.

CHAPTER 11

Age-Related Phenomena: The Interplay of the Ameliorative and the Scientific

Leonard D. Cain*

This chapter draws upon personal experiences and five decades of scholarship directed toward understanding age-related phenomena from two distinctive perspectives. At times I have performed as a sociologist of age status and the life course, at other times as a social gerontologist. This dual identity, and my periodic effort to consider a convergence of sociology and gerontology, are reflected in this chapter, as I consider whether and how these perspectives might meld. The primary difference between these two approaches is that gerontologists generally focus on the elderly, whereas sociologists of age and the life course are concerned about the lives of people of all ages, as they move from "the cradle to the grave."

Another significant difference is that social gerontology from its inception has focused on "amelioration," advocating for rights and protections for older people and for public policies to support those benefits. In contrast, the sociology of age status and the life course has focused on age status systems, intergenerational interaction patterns, transitions along the life course, and the like; it has focused more on what "is" than on what "ought to be." Over four decades ago, I therefore labeled gerontology a "social movement" (Cain, 1959, 1964), intending to convey the sense that the goal of gerontology was to improve the well-being of older persons and that sound research was integral.

*I would like to express my deep gratitude to my mentor and friend of a half-century and longer, Gideon Sjoberg, who, as a recent avocation, has mastered my specialty better than I, and has given me tips and encouragement and cautions as this manuscript has evolved. And to my daughter, Diedre, who, as a teacher of English as a Second Language has been both demanding and persistently tender and patient not only with refugees and immigrants, but has provided her skills and kindness in pointing out flaws in composition to one who has used English as a first language for many years.

At that time, I noted that gerontological research did not address the needs of younger people. Two early experiences affirm this point. First, during 1970 I taught in a summer gerontology program. At the convocation, speakers exhorted students to mount vigorous efforts to energize Congress to support legislation to benefit the elderly. I rose to my feet to gain recognition to speak. My intended message was simple: In the process of lobbying for the elderly, remember that children also need special consideration, given current conditions. I had hoped to encourage students to expand their vocabulary to include young as well as old. Before I was able to explain my position, a raucous chorus of boos and hisses emanated from the audience. I was stunned.

A second experience occurred in 1981 in a meeting room in Washington, D.C., during the annual meeting of the Gerontological Society of America (GSA). The theme of this session was how to take advantage of the assemblage of gerontologists in the nation's capital. Panelists discussed several bills before Congress, offered advice about how to advocate for each bill, and urged attendees to visit their Senators and Representatives. When a pause for discussion occurred, I rose to urge gerontologists to also support legislation to improve the status of children. There were no boos and hisses, only puzzled and hostile stares. Within seconds, lobbying for the elderly agenda resumed, as though I had never spoken.

Other attempts to link the needs of children to those of the elderly led to charges that I somehow hoped to pit the young against the old in order to reduce federal involvement in programs that serve the elderly. Rather, my goal has always been twofold: to seek justice for both young and old, and to point out that if today's young are not provided with opportunities for a quality education and good health, they may have neither the ability nor the willingness to serve and sacrifice for the emerging elderly. To serve the elderly adequately, we cannot focus on the elderly alone, for the young of today will one day be old.

Since then, a peculiar paradox has emerged. On the one hand, the success of the Gerontology Movement can properly be celebrated, and the continuing increase in the percentage of the elderly in the population portends increased power for the elderly. On the other hand, the elderly seem increasingly "commodified" in that they have become objects for commercial purposes as well as subjects for study with ameliorative goals in mind. This has shifted the focus away from enhancing their dignity. As examples, witness the increasing presence of merchandising at the annual meeting of GSA or the themes of recent TV commercials.

My first mentor in sociology made an observation over a half-century ago that has guided my scholarship in my dual role as both a sociologist of age and the life course and as social gerontologist:

> The sociologist struggles so hard to become a scientist that he [or she] often forgets the side of his subject which is akin to the humanities. The sociologist tries so hard to validate that he not infrequently fails to illuminate

his principles. The literary [person] may move too rapidly in the opposite direction. The dream [I have] is one of exploring roads both may travel together (Porterfield, 1957).

Much of my effort has been aimed at promoting a more "scientific" foundation for "ameliorative" gerontology, and a more humanistic foundation for "scientific" sociology of age status and the life course. That is, gerontologists need to be more fully aware of the scientific understanding of the "is," and sociologists more aware of the challenge and opportunity to contribute to the "ought to be." When wearing a sociological hat I have directed critical remarks toward gerontology; when wearing a gerontological hat I have sought to design an ameliorative research agenda for sociology. This continuing "dialog with myself" will become clear as I reflect on some of the themes developed in an early work, "Life Course and Social Structure" (Cain, 1964), which appeared in the *Handbook of Modern Sociology* (hereafter referred to as the Faris chapter). These themes have become increasingly central to these fields in the intervening years, and they continue to pose challenges for contemporary scholarship.

In developing this chapter, I asked myself what led me to propose a course in sociology of age status in the early 1950s, at a time when there was meager theoretical and substantive work by sociologists on the topic. I also reminisced about my early life experiences. As a child of parents who experienced sharecropper childhoods, a child of the Great Depression, and a combat infantryman in World War II, many personal experiences raised my awareness of the connection between personal history and the life course, of the victimization of the very young and the very old, and other facets of interdependence. As I began my sociological studies under the GI Bill, I was already equipped with a myriad of age-related experiences and inchoate ideas.

Fortunately, during my scholarly journey I escaped the pressures of the "publish or perish" mandate. I have avoided the constraints that "calls for proposals" impose upon researchers. And I have used research methods that are no longer *en vogue*. For instance, one of my fondest memories as professor came in the late 1970s, after I had conducted a local colloquium. A statistician and computer specialist approached me and asked, "Professor Cain, how can you do all that writing without any data?" I explained that we are all steeped in "institutional" data, especially about issues related to age; that those interested in ideas need to nurture an historical curiosity; that there are alternatives to, and supplements to, our dependency on survey research and processed data. In short, I invited her to use "sociological imagination" (Mills, 1959). I share this story because I am concerned about the "commodification" of older human beings for profit, and about their commodification in social research. I continue to be disturbed by the rush to quantify all social phenomena, particularly when the issues at hand properly call for open-ended curiosity—for example, questions about identity, about hopes and fears related to aging.

Indeed, four decades ago (Cain, 1959) I put my sociological imagination to work by envisioning a merger between the perspectives of social gerontology and of sociology of age status. I approached the prospect of collaboration, if not a merger, between these two perspectives, asserting:

> It is apparent that social gerontology, as a social movement and as a source of sociological data, is rather far advanced and continuing to enrich a socio- logical perspective. Closely allied with social gerontology, but with some distinct origins, interests, and development, is a sociology of old age. . . . A sociology of ageing, or, possibly, age status, is also evident in the litera- ture. . . . This, as a special field within sociology, properly encompasses the entire life cycle,[1] and includes movement from one age status to another (rites of passage) and patterns of interaction among those of different age categories (generations) (pp. 65-66).

Before assessing themes iterated in my chapter in Faris' *Handbook of Modern Sociology,* a brief report on the circumstances that led to its drafting is in order. Before proposing an undergraduate course on the "Sociology of Age Status" in the early 1950s, I surveyed the literature and drew upon many materials, from anthropology, demography, history, and social welfare; fewer materials from sociology were available. There were studies of the family cycle, of career patterns and seniority and retirement, of human development, and of biological aging. Sociologist Parsons (1942) and anthropologist Linton (1942) had written pioneering articles, but neither had pursued the issues they raised. There was great disappointment in discovering that *Sociological Abstracts* during its early years had no "age" or "aging" category. Textbooks on Introductory Sociology displayed little awareness of age. A few textbooks on social problems dealt with adolescence or old age. Missing from sociological literature was curiosity about the general significance of age and its role in establishing social structures and value systems.

I felt great joy, however, when I discovered Davis' insightful articles on childhood (Davis, 1940), adolescence (Davis, 1944), and old age (Davis & Combs, 1950), and a chapter that introduced the rudiments of a sociology of age status (Davis, 1948). I was inspired to write Professor Davis, asking for reprints of other relevant pieces. Brazenly, I added the recommendation that he write a text for my class. Davis told me that I had found all of his relevant writings, adding that, "If you are smart enough to locate my articles, you are smart enough to write the textbook yourself."

Although his suggestion did not lead me to write a textbook, the many notes and reprints I accumulated were filed under several themes with chapter- like headings: Conditions—Biological, Demographic; Institutions—Family,

---

[1] The term "life cycle" was in common use at this time. Yet I had already concluded that this term did not represent what transpired with aging. I therefore advocated the concept of "life course" in subsequent work.

Economic, Political, Educational, Religious, Legal; and Social Change—Social Movements, Generations. These were the foundation from which I began the Faris chapter.

The current chapter is based primarily upon a reconsideration of some of the themes introduced in that early chapter. Here I emphasize the following: 1) age status as an institution; 2) generational phenomena and birth cohort analysis; 3) aging and the law; and, to a lesser degree; 4) aging and the family. I conclude by reiterating a few "intemperate remarks" I made in the past, and by speculating about future prospects for integrating the endeavors of social gerontologists with those of sociologists of age status and the life course.

AGE STATUS AS AN INSTITUTION

Each society confronts the aging of its members, and the age differences of its members, by developing distinctive patterns of age-linked roles, distinctive means of learning those roles, and distinctive means of effecting transitions to successive age-related roles as the life course unfolds. These patterns, designed to meet a "functional prerequisite" for societal survival, may be called the age status institution. Concepts such as "invention," "modification," and "asynchronization" assist in the analysis of this institution.

In my early work, I did not foresee the importance that would be given by social scientists to issues of age and aging. Rather, I was simply aware that sociologists had virtually overlooked and seemingly cast aside concerns about age and aging. Apart from the "trend report" noted above (Cain, 1959), the Faris chapter was my first opportunity to explore these matters. I began by pointing out that poets and essayists for centuries had shown astuteness in understanding age, aging, and the life course. Anthropologists had been capturing the centrality of life course and age status phenomena of preliterate societies. There was, indeed, a sturdy bedrock on which to build. My task became that of bringing diverse contributions together, of producing a useable set of conceptual tools for the ordering tasks ahead.

In an effort to begin corralling the abundance of information to design an effective set of tools, I emphasized that (Cain, 1964, pp. 272, 287):

> A social structure may be viewed as a system of statuses, and among the universal criteria in the articulation of a status system is the age of its members. . . . Societies confront not only the existential factors of having members who, because of age differentials, have varying potentials and strengths, and of having a particular demographic composition, but also the factor of aging of individuals. Every member of a society is called upon to move through a succession of age statuses. Every society, therefore, has the tasks of preparing individual members for subsequent age statuses, of absorbing them into the successive statuses along with removing them from the formerly occupied status, and of proclaiming to, or

providing other means of communicating to, the society that the transfers have been accomplished. . . . The coherence and persistence of social structure and institutions undergo continuous strain from demands generated by age and aging phenomena.

The Invention and Modification of Age Statuses

My graduate study in the post-World War II era was dominated by emphasis on "the coherence and persistence of social structure," on the "social system," on "culture," on "normative order," on "strain toward consistency," on "functional analysis." There were, of course, theories of social change, illustrated by social movements. Marx, among others, reminded us of the centrality of conflict. Thus, in the Faris chapter I asserted that societies strive for persistence in defining the attributes and needs of various age categories. The ongoing maintenance of a distinctive status or series of statuses for children, for adults, and for the elderly, permits efficiency, predictability, and planning.

Yet even before the Faris chapter, I had begun to struggle with themes of institutionalization, and possible re-institutionalization, of age statuses. For my dissertation (Cain, 1955), one of the case studies I examined was the Townsend Movement, which during the Great Depression proposed a pension for old age (see also Cain, 1986). While combing through its newsletter, *The Townsend Weekly,* I discovered the movement's slogan—"Youth for work: age for leisure," which advocated a distinctive status for old age and promoted what I would subsequently identify as an age status. The role of the Townsend Movement in promoting a Social Security program in the United States remains debatable, yet the argument for reducing the span of years of adulthood and constructing the status of "old age" was clear.

My invitation to establish "a status system for the aged on new premises" (Cain, 1959) now leads me to ponder whether the words represent gerontology or sociology. I am confident that my intention at the time was to be sociological. But is there not at least a hint of the "ought to be" rather than the "is," of the ameliorative and advocative? Regardless of what label is affixed, it is clear that the search for an equitable set of "new premises" remains an ongoing process. And it is clear that, both for scientific and justice reasons, gerontologists need to adopt a life-course framework to study these processes.

Another example that served as a capstone experience for my interest in age status as an heuristic device to explore social change, or "invention," came when I served as a consultant to the Federal Council on the Aging in 1976. My assignment was to explore the feasibility of institutionalizing a status, "frail elderly," as a means of extending services to the elderly. Specifically, I was asked to explore whether a chronological age, such as age 75, could serve as a defensible proxy for the onset of frailty; and to determine if there were any precedents in law or in practice for advancing multiple statuses for old age, rather than a blanket of

"65 and older." Additionally, I considered practical functional criteria for determination of frailty.

I discovered that some jurisdictions, especially in establishing safety standards for life care facilities, had begun to recognize multiple statuses for the residents, through different sets of fire safety standards and rules for the "well elderly" wing, the "assisted living" wing, and the "hospital" wing. Thus, I argued, a three-status rather than a two-status model for old age was emerging (based on Neugarten's (1975) ideas about the "young-old" and "old-old"). On occasion I was called upon to testify. To convey this three-stage model, I, without any intention of caprice, coined the phrases: the "frisky stage," the "frail stage," and the "fragile stage."

Student editors of a gerontological newsletter at Brandeis University, upon learning of the introduction of these three terms in testimony before the Federal Council on Aging in May, 1976, reprimanded the (unidentified) user of the terms severely (October, 1976). I responded by accepting responsibility for coining two of the three terms. Then I sought to explain that (Cain, 1976b, p. 8):

> Members of the Federal Council have very perceptively recognized that national policy has essentially overlooked the special needs of the elderly who are no longer capable of maintaining autonomy without assistance but who do not need the services of a nursing home. [It is important] (1) to understand more fully how the Gerontology Movement has wound up supporting programs for the well, active elderly primarily; (2) to identify the distinctive needs of the frail elderly and to isolate the best indicators of the onset of frailty; and (3) to find precedents of rationale in jurisprudence for the establishment of a multi-tiered rather than single-tiered legal status for the elderly. The terms "frisky," "frail," and "fragile" evolved, not for the serious purpose of denying dignity to the elderly . . . but for the purpose of abetting a proposal which I continue to maintain is among the more exciting, and radical, that I have encountered in gerontology. . . . However, I cannot claim originality for subdividing the status of the elderly into three components. I have been reminded that someone else has already suggested that three stages of old age might be called the "go-go" stage, the "slow-go" stage, and the "no-go" stage.

A quarter-century later, Congress has not yet institutionalized a multi-status system for the elderly, although both sociological data, and gerontological concern for justice for the elderly, surely confirm the need for policy that would move beyond conceptualization of old age as a singular status.

More recently, I provided further rationale for identifying the development of an age status system as meeting a functional prerequisite in the maintenance of every society (Cain, 1995; for a critique of the concept of "age stratification," see Cain, 1987). I have emphasized 1) the persistent aging of its members, both as individuals and as cohort collectivities; 2) variations among individuals and cohorts in moving through life-course stages, or successive age statuses, "on time"; 3) variations in the pace of maturation and aging among its members; and

4) the prospect that members may be called upon to move through the life course at an asynchronous pace (which will be discussed below). I argued that as society responds to these challenges, the institutionalization of an age status system emerges, and that the adaptation and revision of this system appears to be pervasive, at least in bureaucratized societies.

Much remains to be learned about the historical roots of specific statuses within the age status institution. More importantly, social science knowledge must be actively used to anticipate the need to adjust or redesign components of the age status institution to meet the needs of individuals, groups, and society at large.

Age Statuses and Asynchronization

In the Faris chapter (Cain, 1964, p. 288), I introduced the concept "age status asynchronization":

> [S]eparate institutions have been assigned responsibility for establishing age status sequences, frequently with the result that individuals experience asynchronization in moving through the life course. The use of age for defining legal status, for example, may not result in a status pattern synchronous with career patterns, and family responsibilities do not synchronize with earning capacity; a married student may simultaneously be a student pre-adult.

My awakening to this phenomenon originated shortly after D-Day in 1944. I was a private in an armored infantry battalion, in training to be transferred to combat duty overseas. Several of us, mostly teenagers, anxiously discussed reports of the heavy casualties on Normandy's beaches and wondered how many of us would be assigned to a "repple depple" (replacement depot) for immediate insertion into combat units that had suffered heavy losses. This possible fate came at a time when, due to our youth, we were ineligible to vote in the November presidential election.

I had penned a brief poem to my parents, which began: "An eighteen year old in uniform? 'Preposterous,' Americans once said. But times have changed, and here we are; And many of us lie dead." My mother shed many tears because she thought I was blaming her for my moody prognosis. She should have been embarrassed at her son's ignorance of military policy of active recruitment of 17-year olds. The "old enough to fight, old enough to vote" slogan was validated, for 18 to 20-year olds, some years later.

Anthropologists had reported that preliterate societies generally conducted rites of passage, which changed the age status of, for example, a set of children into adults. In contrast, there is abundant evidence that individuals in more complex societies do not move through the life course synchronously. A child may become an adult within the religious institution by age 12; a delinquent act by a 14 year old may be identified as a criminal act if perpetrated by a 15 year old; a 16 year old may operate an automobile, but not a factory machine until two or more years later.

Likewise, movement into the old age status may be achieved piecemeal, at successive chronological stages (Cain, 1974b). It has puzzled me that gerontologists in particular have not seemed curious about such ambiguity and confusion, since identity seems to be of major concern, and since older persons are assigned, and assign themselves, to an old age status at various chronological ages.

Elaboration of one illustration must suffice. Professor Ambrose Klain, of The Pennsylvania State University, was forced to retire upon becoming 65 years of age, although he had responsibility for the welfare of two minor children. He filed a lawsuit against the university to appeal his mandatory retirement (Klain vs. Pennsylvania State University, 1977). Arguments from my Affidavit to the Court in support of Professor Klain identify not only details the asynchronization at issue but some possible remedies—that is, counter-system models (see Sjoberg & Cain, 1971). Born in Eastern Europe, Klain had been victimized by Nazi invaders. His youth service in his nation's military organization and his confinement in a Nazi concentration camp consumed eight years of his life. Several years of recovery from illness followed release from captivity. By the time he adjusted to immigration to the United States and had earned a doctorate, he was older than most in his birth cohort in preparing to enter a profession. His late marriage and subsequent parenthood contributed to the circumstances of his suit.

The Affidavit pointed out that if "Plaintiff [Klain] were younger, unemployed, and eligible to receive child welfare payments rather than pension payments, our officials would exert strong pressure for him to work rather than approve his forced removal from the work force." To strengthen the argument, there was a drawing upon "counter-system" recommendations made in another court case. In that instance, a man, Mr. Murgia, had been forced to retire at age 50 on the grounds that his position called for physical assets that normally begin to decrease by that age (Cain, 1976b, p. 247):

> Courts have been repeatedly pressed in recent years to declare mandatory retirement practices unconstitutional, and they have generally resisted. . . . In the meantime, lawmakers should be invited to consider factors typically overlooked that may ease burdens now associated with forced retirement. One factor is the number of dependents an older worker may have as he/she faces impending retirement. As marriage and remarriage patterns shift it is evident that a sizeable number of male and female workers are approaching the age of 60 or 65 with dependent children in the household.

The asynchronization problem faced by Professor Klain led to drawing from the Murgia case for a proposal to the court:

> [A] worker's previous unemployment pattern, early or late start in career, interruptions for childbearing, military service, education, injury or illness are seldom introduced in deliberations on retirement schemes. Possibly establishment of the principle of the right to work for a specified number of years would promote justice (p. 247).

In this illustration, there is an invitation for those interested in social geron-tology, and in other age statuses as well, to include in their methodological repertoire not only probability theory, but also "possibility theory." That is, there is an invitation to explore alternative futures as means for overcoming the contra-dictions and ambiguities that may emerge in age status institutions.

GENERATIONAL PHENOMENA AND COHORT ANALYSIS

This section focuses on anticipatory gerontology and social change through use of the concepts "generation" and "cohort." If gerontologists were to adopt a life-course approach, studies of cohorts and generational phenomena could isolate the attributes and needs of those not yet old. Equipped with this knowledge, we could then design programs to meet the needs of individuals and cohorts as they move through adulthood and into old age.

The Static and the Dynamic

As I sought to fit the age status system into both social structure and social change, the duality of society's task began to emerge. On the one hand, a society is likely to want to maintain order, to preserve continuity, to promote predictability, and to develop a socialization strategy of "like parent, like children," that main-tains the institutionalization of age status. On the other hand, the continuing flow of successive generations (also conceived differently as cohorts) invites social change that modifies the inherited age status pattern.

From early on, I argued that the concept of generation carries significant potential for a sociology of aging, particularly with refinements in cohort analysis, new uses of public opinion data, and continued interest in inter-generational patterns in the family. A sociology of aging has much to gain by incorporating generational analysis into its basic fabric (Cain, 1959). Of course, the concept of "cohort analysis" gradually began to compete with "generational analysis" as a tool for explaining social change in age status systems and life-course patterns. Ryder's (1965) classic article on "Cohort as a Concept in the Study of Social Change" was particularly important in prompting this shift. In the Faris chapter, I pointed to generational phenomena advanced by Strauss (1959). Like Ryder, Strauss argued that efforts to isolate a well-regulated set of age statuses yielded a static, non-historical view of the life course in which generation succeeds generation without appreciable alteration. This model, Strauss insisted, is too simple to be useful for studying modern societies. It is critical to recognize that social structure and institutions undergo continuous strain from demands generated by age and aging phenomena. These create, and are created by, new life-course patterns emerging among successive generations.

In the Faris chapter, I listed "generational phenomena" as one of five major "status accommodations" to the age continuum of populations and the aging of members of societies. Since that time, this particular "accommodation" has evolved considerably for me. In 1964, I summarized Mannheim's (1952[1928]) two perspectives on generational phenomena: the "positivist" tradition and the "romantic-historical" tradition. Strauss and Howe's (1991) view that in America there has been a new generation every 22 years or so is a recent illustration of the "positivist" tradition. The "romantic-historical" tradition, in contrast, loosely accepts the view that a generation lasts as long as it lasts; that is, it lasts as long as a distinctive life style or value position dominates society. In the Faris chapter, I avoided confronting the ambiguity advanced by Mannheim, suggesting that "patterns of interaction between generations . . . and factors contributing to ad hoc age sets, or peer groups, which may in time be identified as generational phenomena, clearly need thorough examination by sociologists" (p. 303).

At the time, this concept was one of the most difficult, yet necessary, to locate under the rubric of sociology of age status and the life course. Historians and political scientists interested in conflict and social change have long engaged in generational analyses. But their approach has not fit easily into a model of social systems or social structures. It is age differences, not aging (or age changes), that has been at the core of their interest. Although life-course concepts such as "socialization" and "rites of passage" addressed ideas related to social change, there was need for a conceptual tool to capture a comprehensive dynamism related to age. Therefore, "generational phenomena" were vital in my early view. However, it has been the concept of "cohort" and the analytic strategies associated with it that have proved to be effective in dealing with dynamic dimensions of age-related phenomena (discussed below).

Ryder (1965) was an advocate of the concept "cohort" as a supplement to, not as a replacement for, the concept "generation." Ryder's discussion of cohorts assisted me with two questions I had been working on for some time. First, are those entering old age in subsequent decades significantly different from those already old? This question was stimulated by observations made several years before by my wife, that my parents, born in 1896 and 1900, seemed more like grandparents than parents to her, whereas her parents, born in 1903 and 1905, seemed to fit their title. Since all four had similar ethnic, religious, rural, and social class backgrounds, could there be a cohort difference? Could 1900 be a generational watershed? How is my own cohort (say, 1916-1925) distinctive from those who came before or after? Is being a child of the Depression significant? What about the impact of military experience in World War II? What about the children of the children of the Depression, the Baby Boomers? In pursuing the first question, I arbitrarily chose 1890-1899 and 1900-1909 as cohort termini; in pursuing the second question I chose 1916-1925. In both cases, I chose convenient definitions over substantive ones. Serious methodological challenges remain in defining and measuring cohort, and in separating the effects of cohort from those of maturation (aging) and time of measurement (period).

In Search of a Generational Watershed

In an early article entitled "Age Status and Generational Phenomena" (Cain, 1967), I suggested that sociologists are confronted with the task of interpreting the relationship between social statics and social dynamics, between the persisting and the changing. The concept "generation" offered great promise in assisting in this task. My concern at the time was with the dynamic:

> [A] frequent use of "generation" . . . is that associated with the formation of distinctive life styles among discrete groups. Crises, . . . intellectual or technological "breakthroughs," . . . or modifications in social structure seem to force those coming of age during the crisis or the breakthrough or the change in social structure to develop responses to life different from those just older. This suggests what might be called a "historical hinge," or a "generational watershed." . . . Thus, the "needs" of institutions (as manifested, for example, in age status systems) and the "needs" of generations (as manifested in innovation and protests by the young) may periodically be in conflict (Cain, 1967, p. 83).

In examining whether 1900 might be a "generational watershed," I hypothesized that Americans born in the years before the turn of the 20th century are distinct from those born just after the turn of the century. I captured two groups, one born between 1890-1899 ("Cohort A") and the other born between 1900-1909 ("Cohort B"). Put in generational terms, I proposed that a historical "hinge" or "watershed" developed at the end of World War I that directed Cohort A down one path and Cohort B down another. Using data on educational achievement, fertility, employment and working conditions, and immigration from sources of the United States Census, I found evidence suggesting a "watershed" had, indeed, produced a new generation as the new century began. The data hinted that the 1900-1909 cohort had been a "favored" generation. Its members had not had to fight a war. They had fared better than other age groups during the Depression. They filled the lucrative defense jobs of World War II and rode a crest of unprecedented prosperity. They had fewer children to educate and more double paychecks. All of this pointed to the fact that gerontologists needed—and continue to need—to ask new types of questions, use new methods, and use their imagination in new ways if they hope to serve the aged in optimal ways.

In other papers, I directed my attention to my own birth cohort—1916-1925—and our children, the Baby Boomers (e.g., Cain, 1968a, 1968b; 1970). In part, this was an exercise in attempting to understand my cohort, my children, and myself. During the student revolt of the 1960s, sociologist Flacks conducted research on the background of student participants on various campuses (e.g., Flacks, 1967; see Cain, 1968b). He found that a large percentage of the protesters were from middle and upper-middle class backgrounds, with parents who displayed divergence from conventional middle-class values. That is, their parents were especially permissive and democratic in relationships with their children. Therefore, Flacks concluded, the students were participating in an emergent cultural tradition generated by their parents, and not repudiating their values.

Flacks suggested that traditional middle-class values emphasized occupational achievement, complete with a futuristic orientation, a well-regulated emotional life, and concern for the opinions of others about oneself. In contrast, the emergent humanistic sub-culture emphasized experimentation, expressiveness, spontaneity, creativity, and stressed concern for the social condition of others. In brief, the traditional culture emphasized self-control, the emergent culture, self-expression.

Since Flacks made no effort to isolate the origins of the new humanistic subculture, I chose to investigate the impact of recent historical events on these innovative parents. My focus was on the 1916-1925 birth cohort, which I presumed included a sizeable percentage of the parents of student activists. I am a member of this cohort. Excerpts from my "findings" indicate what I predicted for the Baby Boomers (Cain, 1968b, pp. 35-36):

> The parents of youths "under thirty" [as of the mid-1960s, let us say those in the 1916-1925 cohort], experienced the Great Depression as children old enough to remember its agonies, and World War II as young soldiers or their wives and sweethearts. . . . It is my contention that the parents of today's youth—from middle and lower classes too—have made a vital breakthrough by their recognition of the bankruptcy of inherited ideologies, but have been able to go only "half way" in capitalizing on the breakthrough. Many parents, I submit, are quite aware of the deficiencies of chauvinism in today's nuclear world, but are not able to repudiate the old patriotism; are sensitive to the inadequacies of moralistic, socially irrelevant religion, but are not yet prepared to accept the death of their confined God and to venture into a Godly community of love and tenderness for mankind; are aware of the invitation to leisure and creativity provided by automation, but cannot support an alteration in the reward system which would de-emphasize work as justification for a paycheck; are fully aware that war, especially the Vietnam type, is cruel and improper, but cannot quite ovecome their awe for the authority vested in the presidency and the military; are aware that the Negro in America has been treated unjustly, but cannot support fair housing and equal protection of the laws; . . . Herein lies a problem.

This hardly orthodox method of seeking to identify a generational watershed turned to consideration of the impact of "half-way" measures of the parents on their children (Cain, 1968b, p. 36):

> Depression horrors have been erased by the "considerate" refusal of parents to transmit the facts of those years to their children. The protective strategy is

now crumbling, as the children raised in suburban environs which ill equip for confrontation with potential tragedies—nuclear annihilation, racial genocide, the arrogance of power, poverty in the midst of plenty—turn to new religious expressions and new political moods and new life styles in quest of means to overcome their deprivation. The culturally deprived children of affluence are experimenting with new models of institutions in an attempt to understand afresh man's proclivity to make institutions which fail to nurture man's potential for good and for creativity.

Shortly after my commentary on Flacks, I undertook a more sociologically orthodox effort to understand the 1916-1925 cohort and its children (Cain, 1970). I had witnessed a heated discussion on the so-called generation gap. The story told by one of the participants, a man in his late forties (born c. 1920), provided the introduction:

When I was a kid during the Depression I had a bath once a week. Since my brother was older than me, I had to use his left-over bath water every Saturday night. I can still remember how cold and greasy the water always felt. So, I vowed that when I had children they would have their own bath water. I worked hard to get a college degree, and I've worked hard ever since so I could provide my children with things I did not have as a child. Now my teenage children take a bath every day, in their own warm water, and change their clothes every day too. But, they and their friends have begun to accuse me of being an evil materialist, of consuming a wasteful amount of natural resources such as water and of polluting our rivers with soap and detergent. How can a father these days win?

Let current researchers, who have mature Baby Boomers in their midst, determine if there was any accuracy whatever in those observations of more than three decades previous.

My research on Americans born between 1916-1925 suggested that this group experienced the vagaries of history in unique ways, made a break with the past, and were beneficiaries of the new age of affluence. They gave birth to the Baby Boom, supplied the majority of combat troops during World War II, expanded labor force opportunities for women, increased both marriage and divorce rates, and earned high school and college degrees in record numbers. Their political aspirations were destroyed by the assassinations of John and Robert Kennedy, Medgar Evers, and Malcolm X, and the disabling of George Wallace.

The most important contribution of my explanations of "generational watersheds" is the criticism it posed of the common practice of using those who are already old as the universe for aging research, and the use of results from that research to propose public policies for the aged. This practice is flawed in that those who were, at that time, "coming of old age" were on the other side of a generational watershed from those already old. Policies based on studies of the older generation are applied to those who follow at some risk. This latter challenge remains critical for research, policy, and practice today. We cannot assume that the experiences of old age for past cohorts will be similar to those of future cohorts. As a result, the policies and practices based on prior cohorts of elderly people may not, and likely will not, fit cohorts of elderly in the future.

Differences between Cohort and Generation

In early papers, I used the terms "cohort" and "generation" alternatively, although not entirely interchangeably. Nearly a decade after the Faris chapter, I better captured my understanding of each (Cain, 1973). I argued that cohort analysis begins as an operational assignment—take a segment of a population with a common attribute, frequently chronological age or age span; then, ask a question about the performance of that segment (or birth cohort), say, its median years of education, the fertility of its women, the political persuasion of its members; then, measure changes in members of the cohort at successive intervals or compare the performance of the cohort with cohorts older and younger. The operation has methodological rigor. But, as the results of the analysis flow, new invitations present themselves, invitations to probe history to ascertain reasons for the differences among cohorts, invitations to ponder whether it is chronological age or the historic age in which the cohort matured that offers explanation of the change, and invitations to modify and refine arbitrarily drawn age spans for the cohorts, as the data indicate.

At one extreme, historians have advanced the concept "periodization" to partition time; typically, decades, even centuries, are utilized in the determination of the duration of successive epochs. At the other extreme, pundits may hasten to label a passing fad among youth as evidence of a new generation. Somewhere in between these two extremes, those interested in cohort analysis and the study of generational phenomena are found. If we are to make sense out of the world, and if we are to equip people to encounter the emergent world more effectively, cohort analysis, in particular, is a vital tool.

The generational analyst locates historical brackets and puts them around an era of history. The cohort analyst puts methodological brackets around a segment of the population to determine if new historical eras are emerging. The generational analyst declares that he or she has isolated the brackets for a distinctive cohort. The cohort analyst seeks evidence that generational brackets have been isolated. Generational analysts compartmentalize that which is essentially a continuum; cohort analysts interrupt a continuum to determine if there is significant unevenness along the continuum, and in finding unevenness provide indication of the termini of generational phenomena. Cohorts test the efficacy and the efficiency of a society's age status institution. Generational phenomena are in themselves evidence of both the inefficacy and the inefficiency of that institution.

In the time that has elapsed since I made sense of these concepts in these ways, sociologists have brought a methodological sophistication to generational studies and cohort analysis vastly beyond my crude efforts. Yet two fundamental weaknesses remain. The first relates to the absence of "flavor," of a grasp of lives of people other than that embodied in survey research and demography, of the drama of the dynamics of everyday life. The second weakness—in which I myself have excelled—is that there has been inadequate recognition that year of birth alone does not capture the differences in experiences and opportunities and perspectives of rich and poor, majority and minority ethnic groups, rural and urban, and the like. Indeed, age groupings reveal some factors that clarify age-related phenomena. But there is more to know if there is to be adequate under-standing of age and aging processes in their entirety.

What I have sought to convey about generational phenomena is that there is an omnipresent threat to the effort to institutionalize age status, to provide predictability to the life course. For example, societies are called upon to establish notions of childhood, adulthood, and old-age that will persist over time, so that schools can be developed, careers designed, social security systems placed in operation. At the same time, societies must learn to deal with persistent challenges to the institutionalized patterns adopted.

The challenge to scientists is to understand how societies navigate between these two imperatives, the needs of institutions and the needs of generations. Cohort analysis stands ready to enrich understanding of social change and to reveal repeated tests of the adequacy of institutionalized age status patterns. Perhaps most importantly, there is a practical application of these substantive concerns and methodological advances: to move toward creating an anticipatory gerontology, in which we have the means to predict the needs in old age of those who are not yet old. The prospect holds tremendous promise for policy-making and social planning.

AGING AND THE LAW

Most scholarly literature on age-related phenomena has lacked curiosity about the legal basis for the status of various age categories, especially the elderly. It has appeared as though we naturally understand who the elderly are, when they became elderly, and what their legal rights are or ought to be. Gerontology textbooks reveal very little, if any, attention to the role of legislation, court rulings, and administrative decisions in defining the privileges, protections, and reduction of rights of the elderly. Yet there is relevant literature that identifies these critically important issues.

Our dependence on chronological age in the law remains dominant, despite mounting evidence that age is not an exact proxy for need. In the Faris chapter, I even suggested that legal age may be replacing rites of passage in industrial societies as the primary means of effecting a clearly recognized transition from one age status to another. Public rites may no longer proclaim a shift in status, but birthdays and the ensuing alteration of legal status have taken on great significance. But while legal age provisions are evident in many and diverse laws, neither the legal profession nor sociology has addressed the function of legal ages or their impact on individuals, families, or the entire social structure.

A decade later, with increasing recognition of the pervasiveness of chronological age in determining the status of the elderly in American society, I pointed to a number of challenges and invitations this brought—and continues to bring—to gerontology (Cain, 1974a). Some of these tasks are rather conventional: gerontologists need to conduct or consume historical research to determine the circumstances in which chronological age and age spans have been adopted by legislators and administrators and confirmed by judicial authorities to distinguish between adulthood and old age; and they surely need to keep close inventory on the gamut of laws and rules that grant or deny privileges because of achievement of a specified older age. A vast reservoir of untapped information, which focuses on age-related phenomena, is to be found in court decisions, legislative hearings, and administratively designed rules and regulations (see Cain, 1979, 1982b).

Yet additional tasks pose even greater complexities. The first task is to understand more fully the link between research discoveries and subsequent legislation related to aging. The second task is to monitor the impact of laws that define and modify the status of the elderly as a means not only of examining actual changes in the conditions of the elderly, but also of checking on the soundness of theories of aging.

It is also relevant to note that social scientists have been increasingly recruited as consultants to policy-makers, but it is not clear that their theories are taken very seriously. As we attempt to link theory and policy, the situation changes. It carries the possibility that one theory of aging may become dominant in law (and vice versa). For example, if, through legislation, we force the elderly to behave as though they are disengaging so that they can obtain certain services, we end up promoting disengagement and the theory becomes a self-fulfilling prophecy.

Two additional themes in my work related to the law continue to pose challenges for contemporary gerontological scholarship. The first concerns the equal and equitable treatment of the elderly. The second concerns an alternative to relying so heavily on chronological age in the law—counting backward from projected death.

The Equal and Equitable Treatment of the Elderly

In reviewing recommendations of the White House Conference on Aging in 1971, I identified a paradox of two recommendations for legislation: 1) "Public expenditures for education for older persons must be increased and directly related to the proportion of older persons within the population"; and 2) "Since older persons have special needs we recommend that public programs specifically designed for the elderly should receive categorical support" (Cain, 1974a, p. 172). The paradox is that older persons should be treated equally regarding allocation of funds for education; but that they should also be treated unequally regarding their special needs. Here was a basis for critiquing Riley's age stratification model for its focus on equality/inequality rather than equitability/inequitability (for elaboration, see Cain, 1987).

The same piece also served as a reminder of Aristotle's assertion that "injustice arises when equals are treated unequally, and also when unequals are treated equally." In a later article on legal age, I speculated about the implications of Aristotle's statement for policies related to aging (Cain, 1974b). In that article, I suggested that Aristotle's observation identifies the contemporary dilemma of providing both equality and equity for the elderly through law (p. 71):

> If the elderly are indeed equal to adults, but are treated unequally, injustice prevails. . . . If the elderly are both equal and treated equally, there appears to be no basis for the establishment of any separate age status in law for the elderly at all, except possibly to protect the maintenance of equal treatment. . . . If the elderly are unequal to adults, but are treated equally, injustice may also prevail. Support of legislation which provides social services or economic support differentially to the elderly also provides a means for the promotion of justice. Current national policy centers upon the providing of justice by accepting the elderly as unequals and by enacting laws which are designed to overcome the negative consequences of that inequality. Thus, a separate legal status for the elderly takes form.

Counting Backward from Projected Death

Another theme of my work related to the law concerns my proposal to use strategies related to "counting backward from projected death" as an alternative to chronological age. Indeed, in proposing a gerontology of legal age, Bernstein (1969, p. 276) stated that "Lawyers, as architects of the law . . . must try to design new legal arrangements, possibly whole institutions, to ease the burdens of aging and to maximize the opportunities of the elderly."

It was a brief paragraph by Kraus (1971, p. 1) that helped me identify a new way of approaching old age in the law, for which Bernstein had called. Kraus proposed that all jurisdictions provide rules whereby the elderly, as plaintiffs and defendants, can under certain circumstances, receive trial preference by being moved to the top of the docket:

> The candid policy of many attorneys is to take advantage of court delay and elderly plaintiffs by postponing trials as long as possible knowing that the pressure for settlement intensifies in proportion to the plaintiff's age, health, and resultant diminishing likelihood of remaining alive to enjoy his financial recovery.

Here was a vivid example of a new legal arrangement. That is, if a plaintiff's life expectancy is short enough to cast doubt on opportunity to obtain and enjoy adjudication before death, unless the trial is conducted more speedily than the policy of "waiting your turn" would permit, then the case should be before the court sooner than routine practice would provide. Thus, a new status of preferential treatment would be established, regardless of the chronological age of the plaintiff.

Another interesting idea raised by Jackson (1970) was already in my "mental file drawer" on legal age. In the late 1960s, Jackson had begun to testify before Congressional committees and elsewhere that, since African-Americans had a life expectancy several years less than Whites, African-Americans must become eligible for various benefits at an earlier chronological age than Whites.[2] When I placed Jackson alongside Kraus, I became aware of an emerging and distinctive legal basis for defining old age. That is, differential life expectancy had been proposed as a means of determining onset of old age. Thus, predicted time-remaining-to-live, rather than time-already-lived (chronological age), began to assume status as an alternative means for defining old age. Actually, this line of reasoning, which I began to call "counting backward from projected death," had long been applied in providing differential pensions for men and women (discussed below).

Since adding "years yet to live" as an alternative to "years already lived," and Aristotle's statement about equality and inequality as sensitizing concepts in my conceptual tool kit, I have discovered the practice of "counting backward" to be quite widespread. My first effort to introduce this idea to gerontologists came in my chapter on "Aging and the Law" (Cain, 1976a) in the *Handbook of Aging and the Social Sciences* (Binstock & Shanas, 1976). There, I argued:

> All the materials reviewed for this chapter have counted age from birth (or, in the case of abortion, from conception). But the farther an individual moves from the year of his [or her] birth, the less significant is that fact for the purposes of gauging functional capacity. A major breakthrough is likely to come as indicators of the length of time until death become perfected. . . . We know a bit about the significance of longevity of parents; we know that cigarette smoking shortens life; we predict how long a cancer patient is likely to live. The practice of retiring everyone at an age counted from birth results in some workers' receiving only a few months' return from many years of contribution to pension funds; others will receive payments for decades. If age could be counted backward from death . . . more equitable opportunity . . . could be accomplished (p. 366).

---

[2] It should be noted that demographers challenged Jackson by pointing out that African-Americans who have survived into their sixties, many of whom have overcome poverty, unequal access to medical services, and other aspects of racial discrimination, actually have a longer life expectancy than Whites of the same chronological age. Under these circumstances, Jackson's proposal assumes new dimensions. Actually, Jackson recast her quest for justice by turning to efforts to keep young minorities alive long enough to enjoy old age—to work to reduce infant mortality and death of children from malnutrition and neglect and violence, and to reduce despair and sense of fatalism in the young.

After submitting my manuscript for the *Handbook of Aging and the Social Sciences*, I discovered that Ryder (1975, p. 16) had also hit upon much of what I was suggesting about "counting backward":

> We measure age in terms of the number of years lapsed since birth. This seems to be a useful and meaningful index of the stages of development from birth to maturity. Beyond maturity, however, such an index becomes progressively less useful. . . . To the extent that our concern with age is what it signifies about the degree of deterioration and dependence, it would seem sensible to consider the measurement of age not in terms of years elapsed since birth [chronological age], but rather in terms of the number of years remaining until death. Such a suggestion is inapplicable in the individual case. . . . We propose that some arbitrary length of time, such as 10 years, be selected and that we determine at what age the expectation of life is 10 years, and that that age be considered the point of entry into old age.

After publication of that chapter (Cain, 1976a), Siegel and I conversed about the feasibility of "counting backward." He published a critique of the concept (Siegel, 1980). After stating that both "progress in longevity" and the definition of onset of old age have been determined by "years from birth," he introduced "counting backward," calling it "average number of years from death." Like Ryder, he insisted the term applies only to "population groups." He doubted the applicability of the concept at the individual-level because of inadequacies in current data and methodology.

As demographers, both Ryder and Siegel asserted that counting backward can apply only to population groups. Yet, much of the use of the concept is found in court decisions in which reduced life expectancy of a single plaintiff is at issue. Let me illustrate with two examples (for further discussion, see Cain, 1981). The first case deals with a settlement of a wrongful death suit filed by survivors of a worker who died in an industrial accident (Weeks vs. Alonzo Cothron, Inc., 1974). The fascination of this case is even greater because it involves counting backward from projected death of a person already dead. The court documents state:

> Decedent [Mr. Weeks] was age 50 at the time of death in August 1968. . . . He died [in an industrial accident]. His life expectancy under standard tables was 23 years. Plaintiff's [Mr. Weeks' wife's] expert computed the future value of decedent's earnings on an expectancy of his working 15 years to age 65, assuming that he would be able to perform heavy work until age 65. The expert admitted on cross-examination that his ultimate monetary average would be altered or modified depending on specific case history as to decedent's previous earning ability and capacity, his ability to perform the work required of him and his ability to hold a job by reason of health. He acknowledged that a previous existing infirmity that would have very much impaired decedent's ability to work at the same pace and at the same labor [as at age 50] would alter his opinion and could be a "pertinent factor" (p. 543).

The trial court, after hearing testimony from attorneys for the defense about "previous existing infirmity" and possibly deleterious habits of the deceased, concluded:

> In fact, there is a very serious question as to whether or not [Mr. Weeks] would have lived to age 65 with his heart condition and drinking problem. The greater weight of the credible evidence indicates, and I so find, that the deceased would not have worked past 60, or a total of ten years, if, in fact, he lived that long from the date of his [actual] death (pp. 543-544).

The Supreme Court then reviewed the (apparently) genetic factors, personal medical history, and deleterious personal habits of the decedent to support the trial court's conclusion that the decedent would not have lived to the projected age (73), or at least would not have been able to continue in the labor force to age 65. The Court considered not only work expectancy, but life expectancy as well:

> In reducing the award for decedent's future earnings to the 10 year life expectancy (age 60) figure, the District Judge appears to have taken two-thirds of the expert's figure for a 15 year life expectancy (age 65) period (p. 544).

As a second example, consider the following, which is possibly the first encounter of the United States Supreme Court with the practice of counting backward, and which led to the decision to rule illegal a practice that had been institutionalized over many years. The case is that of City of Los Angeles vs. Manhart (1978) (for further discussion, see Cain, 1979). The legal issue arose after the adoption of the Civil Rights Act of 1964, which mandated equal rights to men and women as individuals. As early as the 1840s, demographers began to confirm that women collectively had a greater life expectancy than men. Over time, public agencies, in administering employee pension programs, took cognizance of this differential life expectancy. The City of Los Angeles chose to call upon female employees to contribute a larger percentage of their paychecks than their male counterparts, under the logic that, if male and female employees with equal earning capacity were to receive equal monthly pension payments upon retiring, then there needed to be a larger number of dollars on reserve for each female, because many more monthly checks would be distributed to the average female retiree. States such as Arizona and Oregon adopted a different logic: call upon men and women of comparable earning capacity to contribute the same percentage of their salaries to the pension fund; then, upon retirement, the female would receive a smaller monthly check, since the funds for her would be distributed over many more months than would be the funds for the male counterpart.

The issue is that these public agencies used differential life expectancy of retiring men and women to produce differential economic statuses. Equal treatment was presumed because women received pension payments for many months more than men. The Court ruled that both schemes were unfair, because they used class-based statistics, whereas Congress passed legislation that declared equal treatment of individuals as individuals. Justice Stevens' majority decision included:

> This case . . . involves a generalization that the parties accept as unquestionably true. Women, as a class, do live longer than men. The Department [in Los Angeles] treated its women employees differently from its men employees because the two classes are in fact different. It is equally true, however, that all individuals in the respective classes do not share the characteristics which differentiate the average class representatives. Many women do not live as long as the average man, and many men outlive the average woman. The question, therefore, is whether the existence or nonexistence of "discrimination" is to be determined by comparison of class characteristics or individual characteristics (City of Los Angeles vs. Manhart, 1978, pp. 707-708).

Thus, the Court rejected a longstanding application of "counting backward" based on narrowly constructed life tables, thereby rejecting the use of differential life expectancy to determine legal rights of the elderly.

There is mounting evidence that the reasoning in the cases above is approaching acceptability. Among the numerous examples that might be cited, let me draw attention to various reports found in a single issue of the *New York Times* (June 24, 1997). Surely by coincidence rather than design, at least 11 articles deal with reduced life expectancy. For example, one article reports that, although 40 percent of all male middle-age deaths in Eastern Europe and the former Soviet Union are related to tobacco, the long-term goal of an executive of a major American tobacco company stationed in Poland is to get more Polish smokers to consume the company's brands ("Fenced in at Home, Marlboro Man Looks Ahead"). Another article suggests that health-care costs for smokers are not much larger than for non-smokers, given that "smokers die earlier, [and therefore] collect less from Social Security and pensions" ("Who Will Pay for the Tobacco Industry's Huge Bills? Smokers"). Two articles tap similar issues related to premature death related to asbestos exposure. Other articles deal with heart disease; new discoveries about the role of estrogen in promoting health; genetic causes of human obesity; research use of the worm C. elegans in isolating human genes linked to diseases; premature deaths related to diabetes; and physician-assisted suicide. At base in most of these stories is that when research confirms that various factors can be associated with reduced life expectancy, legal actions are often undertaken to promote justice.

These examples create a theoretical dilemma: Do those differential life expectancy variables—genetic factors, behavioral factors, medical-condition factors—represent an institutional modification? Or, in avoiding demographers' life tables and turning to individual biographies, do they represent the emergence of de-institutionalization? Despite these complexities, legal actions routinely rely on that which cannot be done (computations for individual cases) and that for which there are no adequate data (specialized life tables).

This results in several ironies, if not paradoxes. First, as life expectancy becomes increasingly standardized, society is able to focus on individuals and types of individuals whose life expectancies are at variance with the norm. Second, as chronological age has been increasingly adopted for determining legal age status variations, scientific evidence about functionality suggests that this usage is inadequate to deal with the needs of those who age "off time," especially prematurely. Third, what demographers declare is not feasible, that is, prediction of the life expectancy of individuals, is precisely what courts and legislated policies are increasingly calling upon specialists, especially in medicine, to do. And fourth, there are some categories of people, including African-Americans, who have had a shorter life expectancy at birth than the total population, but have greater age-specific life expectancy than the general population once they manage to reach old age.

There is intrigue and challenge ahead for life-course sociologists in encountering the prospect of counting backward. As we gain more knowledge about the consequences for life expectancy of behaviors such as smoking, diet and exercise, stress, exposure to toxic substances, poverty, genetic variations, and the like, the question must be raised: What does society do with such information, especially in the quest for fairness?

Recent accomplishments of the Genome Project provide insights into both the opportunities and challenges on the horizon. The charting of life expectancy, by categories as well as among individuals, may become routine. Awesome ethical issues appear to be immanent. Whose lives will be lengthened first? How will differential life expectancy information be shared and used? What new diagnostic information should be kept from employers, insurance agents, spouses, or individuals? There is increasing confidence that justice calls for factoring counting backward from projected death into financial and other arrangements for those with predictably shorter lives than the average. These examples and others suggest that this is indeed new basis for determining the onset of "old age."

THE FAMILY: FOCUS ON ITS RETAINING VIABILITY

A final theme pertains to aging and the family, though this theme remains less developed in my work than those discussed above. Historically, behaviors related to marriage and the family—dating; courtship; engagement; marriage; child bearing, rearing, and launching; empty nest; and widowhood—have been benchmarks for ordering the life course. Not all behaviors are, of course, "on time," but a pattern nonetheless has been identifiable.

My early work in the "trend report" (Cain, 1959, pp. 59-60) included efforts both sociological and gerontological to ascertain trends in the composition and function of the family:

> Social gerontology . . . has generally accepted the thesis that industrialization has spelled the doom of the kinship family, that the aged in a sense have no status within the emerging family system. . . . [Y]et there has developed in the 1950s a challenge to this position. . . . Welfare and pension programmes, recommendations for housing the aged, and proposed roles for the aged frequently delete the multi-generation family from consideration. Not only do some recent empirical data indicate a resuscitation of the three- and four-generation family, but changes in other segments of the social system—e.g., the expansion of bureaucratic careers with their postponement of "success" to later stages in the career, the early stage of marriage and completion of the reproductive period, the return to the work force of the middle-aged female, general improvement in living standards, the decline of immigration (in the United States) and therefore the lessening of conflict between familial generations in process of assimilation—give feasibility to the re-establishment of the three-generation family.

By the time I was writing the Faris chapter, this two-generation model had begun to erode, especially through rising divorce rates. At that time, I was comfortable in accepting the standard model family—the two-generation family—but nonetheless held out the prospect of the re-emergence of a viable three-generation family (Cain, 1964, p. 288):

> The family structure provides one of the more convenient ways to trace the life course. . . . From courtship to marriage, through parental statuses to grandparenthood, and possibly to the status of family ancestor, most individuals' life courses may readily be followed.

Yet I was reluctant to accept the predictions about age-related statuses within the family made by sociologists by the early 1960s (Cain, 1964, pp. 289-290):

> Most interpretations of the dynamics of American family structure have concluded that a shift from an extended, three-generation kinship structure to a compact, two-generation conjugal structure has taken place as urbanization and industrialization have proceeded. . . . [However,] a series of superficially unrelated trends . . . combine to give plausibility to the emergence of new forms of the three-generation family. Bureaucratization...postpones peak earning power to the later years of the work span, places highest income in the hands of workers when their conjugal family responsibilities may have already ended. Likewise, the trend to increased employment of middle-aged women provides capital, which may be used to subsidize married children and grandchildren. Furthermore, the institutionalization of seniority patterns . . . helps protect the security and earning power of older workers. Additional fringe benefits, such as non-transferable sick leave and pension schemes, and longer vacations based on years of employment, may encourage workers to forego temptations to migrate; permanence of residence increases the prospects of strong kinship ties. Finally, the postponement of entry into the labor force for educational reasons, combined with trends in earlier marriages,

provides an open invitation for older parents, with peak incomes, to subsidize their married children.

Later, I also suggested that, with an earlier and more compact period for child-bearing, with increased life expectancy, and with easier means of communicating at a distance, entry into great-grandparenthood would become "normal" (Cain, 1975). Although there is surely a continuing growth of four, even five surviving kinship generations in the United States, close social linkages among the generations hardly seem typical.

The reader, cognizant of recent trends in family roles and in roles linked to family life mentioned in the paragraphs above, is quickly aware that most of the anticipations and predictions have not materialized. Indeed, it is clear that over the past 30 years, the family has undergone profound changes in both its structure and values (see Smith, 1999). These include dramatic increases in the proportion of those who have divorced, remarried, never married, cohabited; delays in marriage; declines and delays in childbearing; and increases in the percentage of infants born to unmarried mothers. Each of these transformations has brought significant implications for the nature and experience of aging.

For both sociologists and gerontologists, a new challenge presents itself. If the kinship ("familistic"?) model of the family is under threat, what are the prospects for a family-like ("familial"?) model to emerge? There is the presumption that both children and older persons will continue to need dedicated attention and services from others. If family identity and loyalties become muddled by divorce, out-of-wedlock childbearing, and other schisms, from whence will come caregivers to serve children and elderly in family-like devotion?

One possibility might be to develop policy meant to revitalize the kinship role in supporting the elderly. For example, we might find ways to socialize the young to respect their parents and grandparents, to provide material and other incentives for relatives supporting their older kin, to emphasize maintenance of ethnic and sectarian identities so that covenant-type relationships may be preserved through the generations. Another alternative may be to avoid cultivation of the kinship-based model altogether: to develop a familial relationship without family. Perhaps it is in our best interest to accept reality: a large percentage of women will be widows, divorce will be high, rapid change and frequent mobility will strain intergenerational relations, and individuals will enter old age with widely different potentials for kinship support. Once accepted, we can perhaps find innovative ways to cultivate bonds between young and old, not be disturbed by homosexual liaisons, modify inheritance laws so that biological kin are not automatically the recipients of the estate, and redefine zoning laws and single family dwellings. In short, I have argued that we find ways to encourage young and old of all types to "live together, share their resources, their hurts, their yearnings" (Cain, 1982c, p. 84). This also serves as an important reminder that planners need to consider the role of their current decisions in affecting the future alternatives for individuals; for example, the ways in which their decisions strengthen or weaken kinship systems (Cain, 1971).

THE FUTURE:
NOTES ON OPPORTUNITIES AND CHALLENGES

Some "Intemperate" Remarks

From the standpoint of an "ameliorative gerontology" (rather than "antici-patory gerontology"), I have argued from early on that two major weaknesses characterize sociological scholarship on aging (Cain, 1959). The relevant point is that these continue to characterize contemporary scholarship. First, many research efforts unduly restrict themselves to study the aged in isolation. A vast literature has been built upon a foundation of poorly constructed life-course antecedents. While this has changed in recent decades, we still have much to learn about the connections between the earlier and later periods of life. Second, many research efforts had a narrow institutional scope and limited time perspective. The emphasis on amelioration led scholars to seek immediate answers to current problems. Insufficient attention to historical perspectives, comparative sociology, and dynamic social systems produced inadequacies and possibly inconsistencies in social gerontology. While these issues have been handled more systematically in the time since my comment at the end of the 1950s, they nonetheless warrant attention in future research. These are clearly issues that each of the contributors to this book hope to advance, both now and in the years ahead.

In 1982, I delivered an invited paper to the Association of Gerontologists in Higher Education, labeled "Intemperate Remarks from an Intrepid Observer of the Heretofore Inviolable Gerontology Movement" (Cain, 1982a). I thought I was performing then as a sociologist, but upon re-examination I realize my purpose was clearly to be a dedicated supporter for gerontology. My suggestions were, and are, intended to strengthen the Gerontology Movement, not destroy it. A few points from that early paper are worth reiterating, for they are as relevant now as then to scholarship on aging.

First, a critical posture toward the Gerontology Movement itself is needed to enrich the field. There is a persisting tendency among gerontologists to study the already old and to utilize findings to promote policy. An "anticipatory geron-tology" based on cohort analysis and a life-course perspective is called for, as I noted above.

Second, cohort analyses and other methods that can generate insights from an historical perspective are needed as well. Both contemporary and emergent gerontology need enrichment from the contributions of historians, but both need the insights and cautions that come from the skills of debunking selected memories of the past. In recent years, there have been bold strides in distinguishing among cohort, period, and age effects. Yet many gerontologists appear to be so preoccupied with these complex methodologies that the moods and the colorations emanating from the twists and turns of history are overlooked. This serves as a reminder that an informed and sensitive life-course and intergenerational perspective is needed to invigorate gerontology. Unless those who identify as gerontologists turn to cohort analysis and historical enrichment, turn to the reconstruction of the life courses of ordinary citizens (including minority representatives) through oral histories and similar innovative research methods, and break away from excessive dependence upon survey research and the like, gerontology will continue to suffer from data malnutrition as well as lack of heart.

Third, the perspective of jurisprudence as well as of politics is needed to enrich gerontology. As emphasized earlier, one of the greatest oversights has been a failure to focus on the law as it pertains to aging and age status. The Gerontology Movement has proceeded to promote legislation, unmindful of the inadequacy of chronological age in establishing capabilities and needs of older persons.

Fourth, an open, unencumbered exploration of alternatives to chronological age is needed to determine the onset of old age. This is reflected in the discussion of "counting backward from projected death." We must monitor what is happening to energy levels with age, to mobility, motivation, self-images, health, among those who are approaching old age as well as among those already designated as old. Using age 65 as a legal determinant of old age is no longer an acceptable convenience.

Fifth, gerontology must develop greater compassion and concern for the rights of people of all ages. The proper and vital task of theorists and practitioners concerned with aging phenomena is to confront issues of equitability—what resources do children need for education or older people for medical care, not whether young and old have equal resources for education and health.

Sixth, gerontologists must consider imaginative, equity-motivated policies for allocating resources among the elderly themselves. One of my concerns about the future is that our society is turning once again to a two-tiered structure, with the beneficiaries from the Gerontology Movement retaining and expanding their gains while those elderly who have not yet benefited become poorer. For example, one must have the capacity to own real property in order to benefit from tax exemptions at resale. Benefits from increasingly complex tax laws come to those who can afford attorneys. The poor elderly still get taxed. Ways must be devised to route increasingly scarce resources to the elderly on the basis of need.

Other Thoughts for the Future

As traditional institutions—especially family, economic, and religious institutions—change, almost dissolve, before us, strong lures to ask sociologically informed questions emerge. I cannot list, much less elaborate, these wide-ranging issues. Rather, let me end this essay with a report of my own unfinished business and some invitations to those early in their careers. There are themes in the Faris chapter that I have not commented upon, primarily because my scholarship nurtured since 1964 has not led me to exploit those themes. Here I mention but three themes: First, the "conditions"—namely biological and demographic conditions—with which I began that chapter. Advances in medicine and risks associated with pollutants and new bacterial and viral strains contribute to ever changing contexts for building upon biological conditions to establish an age status system. Spin-offs from genome research have almost unlimited possibilities for modification of age-related institutions. Ethical questions about who will survive, and for how long, already abound. Emerging shapes of population pyramids imply substantial threats and opportunity. Second, the changing nature of religious, educational, and political institutions. The quests for meaning in life, for socialization that facilitates adaptation to life's successive stages, and for responsible use of power, continue unbounded. And third, an awareness of, and celebration of, social change. Rites of passage await further exploration and linkage of generational phenomena to social change awaits penetrating study.

Two other tasks remain. The first is to seek to answer this chapter's original question: What are the prospects for a merger of gerontology and a sociology of age and the life course? The review of my own work above may seem to give a resounding, albeit wobbly, affirmative answer. Yet I have doubts that a merger, even a significant collaboration, will occur within the next few decades. Several forces continue to pose obstacles to this merger. These include the power in the hands of those with vested interests in gerontological organizations, research, programs, and business enterprises; demographic trends that predict increasing percentages of those in older age categories; and the success of the Gerontology Movement in gaining resources and services for the elderly and encouraging self-interested lobbying and voting.

I surmise that many who concern themselves with age-related issues as "pure scientists" or "theorists" likely see little advantage in joining forces with ameliorists and those tied to policy-making or social services. Recent sociological theory on the so-called "late modern," or "post-modern," age has given dramatically new interpretations of work and careers, and in so doing has appropriated the age status and life-course frames of reference in exciting ways (e.g., Giddens, 1991; Sennett, 1998; Wallulis, 1998). While these theorists give virtually no indication of awareness of the vast scholarship of gerontologists, they herald the coming of age of a sociology of age status and the life course. They offer a much-deserved validation of the field and an awesome challenge. Collaboration between, if not merger of, social gerontology and age-related sociology becomes more compelling even as it appears less likely.

It may be that theoretical considerations of the need for equitable allocation of resources to meet the needs of old and young, combined with emphasis on long-range futures, are needed to promote merger. Let me suggest that curiosity about age-related phenomena by sociologists remained minimal in the United States until the eruption of youth protest movements in the 1960s. At least this is a means by which I have made sense out of the hasty acceptance of the age stratification model, compatible with conflict theory, in the early 1970s. Regardless, there is need for theorists today to seek to understand the significance of youth movements and political activity of the young within oppressive nations world wide as the 21st century unfolds.

There are also specific issues that may be more likely than others to produce collaboration, particularly if there are significant interests in an issue on both the sociological and gerontological sides. For example, recent policies in criminal justice call for long-term sentences for increased numbers of those convicted of crimes. Prison facilities and services have been designed for a young inmate population—exercise yards for vigorous activity; several tiers of cell blocks, and no elevators; meager facilities for dealing with illness or frailty; vocational training. Issues related to aging in total institutions such as prisons have generally been overlooked.

There are two final appeals to be set forth. Whereas most works of social science and literature seem to focus on the adult as person—on the citizen, worker, believer, parent—it is imperative that equitability rather than equality or "sameness" be operative in dealing with the rights and needs of the young, old, poor or disabled. Whereas most research and most programs to provide services focus on residents within nation-states, both the emerging presence and the widespread promotion of globalization call for incorporation of all the world's people into scholarship and policy formation related to age. To date, globalization has focused on trade, on finding markets and workers and consumers abroad. Citizens of the poorer countries, especially the old and the young of those countries, are vulnerable to additional victimization and denial of their human rights unless imaginative programs are established. Those skilled in study of age-related issues are faced with awesome opportunities and obligations.

I conclude this essay by sharing a brief parable written by a beloved friend, Polish sociologist Adam Podgorecki. He called it, simply, "A Lesson" (1985, p. 21):

> "Master, I would like to acquire the most difficult skill of all: to be able to read the complicated currents of life," the student Xing said to [the wise sage] Si-Tien. "Could you help me in this?"
>
> Si-Tien gave no reply but took Xing to the beach. There he entered the deep water and told Xing to do the same. "Look at this wave," said Si-Tien. "It is making a horrible noise and is seething with foam. But do not worry; it has already spent its force. Look at the next one now; it has quietly and unexpectedly surfaced out of nowhere; beware of it. Watch this one; it is approaching us rapidly and seems harmless with its few bubbles on the top, but it will tumble down and crush us like a stone wall. It is dangerous indeed." After it had passed Si-Tien continued, "Now this one which looks like a flat giant is really almost laughable; it is weak because of infighting with all its neighbors; we only need to jump and it has passed. But look at the next one;

another huge wave is perched on its small, cobra-like crest; I hope we can survive its anger." No sooner had he spoken than they were both thrown onto the beach like sacks of sand.

As he groggily got back onto his feet, Xing turned to Si-Tien and said, "Master, I am not interested in waves! I asked you to teach me how to read the contradictory currents of life; will you?"

"Let's go back into the water then," said Si-Tien, already on his feet.

REFERENCES

Bernstein, M. C. (1969). Aging and the law. In M. W. Riley, J. W. Riley, Jr., & M. E. Johnson (Eds.), *Aging and society: Vol. II, Aging and the professions* (pp. 274-292). New York: Russell Sage.

Binstock, R., & Shanas, E. (Eds.) (1976). *The handbook of aging and the social sciences.* New York: Van Nostrand Reinhold.

Cain, L. D. (1955). *The role of myth-designation in social movements.* Unpublished doctoral dissertation, The University of Texas, Austin.

Cain, L. D. (1959). The sociology of ageing: A trend report and bibliography. *Current Sociology, 8* (2), 57-133.

Cain, L. D. (1964). Life course and social structure. In R. E. L Faris (Ed.), *Handbook of modern sociology* (pp. 272-309). Chicago, IL: Rand-McNally.

Cain, L. D. (1967). Age status and generational phenomena: The new old people in contemporary America. *The Gerontologist, 7* (2), 83-92.

Cain, L. D. (1968a). Aging and the character of our times. *The Gerontologist, 8* (4), 250-258.

Cain, L. D. (1968b). Commentary on "Student activists: Result, not revolt" by Richard Flacks. *Teachers Voice, 1* (2), 35-37.

Cain, L. D. (1970). *The 1916-1925 cohort of Americans: Its contribution to the generation gap.* Paper presented at the annual meeting of the American Sociological Association, Washington, D.C.

Cain, L. D. (1971). Planning for the elderly of the future. *Planning and the urban elderly—Today and tomorrow: Summary of proceedings of a two-day workshop* (pp. 14-24). Los Angeles: The Gerontology Center, University of Southern California.

Cain, L. D. (1973). *The contribution of cohort analysis to socialization strategies at various stages of the life course.* Paper presented at a meeting of the International Society for the Study of Behavioral Development, Ann Arbor, MI.

Cain, L. D. (1974a). The growing importance of legal age in determining the status of the elderly. *The Gerontologist, 14* (2), 167-174.

Cain, L. D. (1974b). Political factors in the emerging legal status of the elderly. *Annals of the American Academy of Political and Social Science, 415,* 70-79.

Cain, L. D. (1975). *Prospects for the four-generation family.* Paper presented at the regional meeting of the National Council of the Aging, Seattle, WA.

Cain, L. D. (1976a). Aging and the law. In R. H. Binstock & E. Shanas (Eds.), *The handbook of aging and the social sciences* (pp. 342-368). New York: Van Nostrand Reinhold.

Cain, L. D. (1976b). Letter to the Editor. *It's about time!: A search for radical perspectives on aging* [Brandeis University student publication], *1* (4), 8.

Cain, L. D. (1979). The impact of Manhart on pension payments and the legal status of the elderly. *Aging and Work, 2* (3) 147-159.

Cain, L. D. (1981, April). *An emerging alternative to chronological age in determining the legal status of the elderly.* Paper presented at the annual meeting of the American Association for the Advancement of Science, Pacific Division, Eugene, OR.

Cain, L. D. (1982a). Intemperate remarks from an intrepid observer of the heretofore inviolable gerontology movement. *Gerontology and Geriatrics Education, 3* (2), 111-119.

Cain, L. D. (1982b, August). *The sociology of aging: Age status vs. age stratification.* Paper presented at the meeting of the International Sociological Association, Mexico City, Mexico.

Cain, L. D. (1982c). Population aging and family life. In G. M. Gutman (Ed.), *Canada's changing age structure: Implications for the future* (pp. 67-88). Burnaby, British Columbia: Simon Fraser University Publications.

Cain, L. D. (1986). The Townsend Movement. In G. Maddox (Ed.), *The encyclopedia of aging* (pp. 671-672). New York: Springer.

Cain, L. D. (1987). Alternative perspectives on the phenomenon of human aging: Age stratification and age status. *Journal of Applied Behavioral Science, 23* (2), 277-294.

Cain, L. D. (1995) Age status. In G. L. Maddox (Ed.), *The encyclopedia of aging* (2nd ed., pp. 39-41). New York: Springer.

City of Los Angeles vs. Manhart (1978). 435 U.S. 702.

Davis, K. (1940). The child and the social structure. *Journal of Educational Sociology, 14,* 217-229.

Davis, K. (1944). Adolescence and the social structure. *Annals of the American Academy of Political and Social Science, 236,* 31-47.

Davis, K. (1948). *Human society.* New York: Macmillan.

Davis, K., & Combs, J. (1950). The sociology of an aging population. In D. B. Armstrong (Ed.), *The social and biological challenge of an aging population* (pp. 146-170). New York: Columbia University Press.

Faris, R. E. L. (Ed.) (1964). *The handbook of modern sociology.* Chicago: Rand-McNally.

Flacks, R. (1967). Student activists: Result, not revolt. *Psychology Today, 1* (2), 18-23.

Giddens, A. (1991). *Modernity and self-identity: Self and society in the late modern age.* Stanford, CA: Stanford University Press.

Jackson, J. (1970). Aged Negroes: Their cultural departures from statistical stereotypes and rural-urban differences. *The Gerontologist, 10* (2), 140-145.

Klain vs. The Pennsylvania State University (1977). 434 F. Supp. 571 M.D. Pennsylvania.

Kraus, J. (1971). The legal problems of the elderly poor. *New York Law Journal, 165,* 1.

Linton, R. (1942). Age and sex categories. *American Sociological Review, 7,* 589-603.

Mannheim, K. (1952[1928]). The problem of generations. In K. Mannheim, *Essays on the sociology of knowledge* (pp. 276-322). London: Routledge & Kegan Paul.

Mills, C. W. (1959). *The sociological imagination.* New York: Oxford University Press.

Neugarten, B. (1975). The future of the young-old. *The Gerontologist, 15,* 4-9.

Parsons, T. (1942). Age and sex in the social structure of the United States. *American Sociological Review, 7,* 604-616.

Podgorecki, A. (1985). *The ellipses of Si-Tien.* London: Poets and Painters Press.

Porterfield, A.L. (1957). *Mirror, mirror: On seeing yourself in books.* Fort Worth, TX: Leo Potishman Foundation.

Ryder, N. (1965). The cohort as a concept in the study of social change. *American Sociological Review, 30,* 843-861.

Ryder, N. (1975). Notes on stationary populations. *Population Index, 41* (1), 3-26.

Sennett, R. (1998). *The corrosion of character: The personal consequences of work in the new capitalism.* New York: Norton.

Siegel, J. (1980) On the demography of aging. *Demography, 17* (4), 345-364.

Sjoberg, G., & Cain, L. (1971). Negative values, counter-system models, and analysis of social systems. In H. Turk & R. L. Simpson (Eds.), *Institutions and social exchange: The sociologies of Talcott Parsons and George C. Homans* (pp. 212-229). Indianapolis, IN: Bobbs-Merrill.

Smith, T. W. (1999). *The emerging 21st century American family* (General Social Survey, Report No. 42), University of Chicago: National Opinion Research Center.

Strauss, A. (1959). *Mirrors and masks.* Glencoe, IL: The Free Press.

Strauss, W., & Howe, N. (1991). *Generations: The history of America's future, 1584 to 2069.* New York: William Morrow.

Wallulis, G. (1998). *The new insecurity: The end of the standard job and family.* Albany, NY: State University of New York Press.

Weeks vs. Cothron, Inc. (1974). 493 F. 2nd 538.

Contributors

LEONARD D. CAIN, Ph.D., is Professor of Sociology and Urban Studies, Emeritus, at Portland State University, and a Fellow of the Gerontological Society of America. He began his professorial career at Sacramento State College in 1952, where he soon developed a course, Sociology of Age Status. In 1969 he transferred to Portland State University, with assignment to help establish their Institute on Aging. Throughout his career, Cain has maintained major interest in social gerontology and the sociology of age status. His other interests have included sociology of minority groups, of religion, and of urbanization, as well as special concern for ethics and human rights. He is currently writing a biography of his mentor, Professor Austin L. Porterfield, with whom he studied at Texas Christian University, 1946-1949.

STEPHEN J. CUTLER, Ph.D., is Professor of Sociology and the Bishop Robert F. Joyce Distinguished University Professor of Gerontology at the University of Vermont. Prior to joining the UVM faculty in 1984, he taught at Oberlin College from 1969-1984. He received his Ph.D. from the University of Michigan. Cutler has served as Editor of the *Journal of Gerontology: Social Sciences,* as Chair of the Sociology of Aging Section of the American Sociological Association, and as President of the Gerontological Society of America. He is co-editor of *Promoting Successful and Productive Aging* (Sage, 1995), and his current gerontological research interests are in the areas of social and political attitude change, voluntary association participation, social aspects of cognition, and ethics.

DALE DANNEFER, Ph.D., is Professor of Education and Sociology at the Warner Graduate School of Education, University of Rochester, and Co-Director of the International Center for the Study of Social Change. He received his doctorate from Rutgers University, and has been a visiting scholar at the Max Planck Institute for Human Development and Education in Berlin and a research fellow at the Andrus Gerontology Center at the University of Southern California and at Yale University. He is the author of more than 50 articles on age, the life course and related topics. His current research centers on the potentials for organizational change to survive, and to redirect the life course trajectories of individuals, especially as related to reform efforts in the arena of long-term care institutions.

GLEN H. ELDER, JR., Ph.D., is the Howard Odum Distinguished Professor of Sociology and Research Professor of Psychology at the University of North Carolina at Chapel Hill. He has also served on the faculties of Cornell University and the University of California at Berkeley where, in 1962, he launched his research on the life course and social change using data from pioneering longitudinal studies in the United States. At the University of North Carolina, he directs the Carolina Consortium on Human Development at the Center for Developmental Science and an NIA training grant on population and aging at the Carolina Population Center. Among other works, he is author, co-author, or co-editor of *Children of the Great Depression, Children in Time and Place,* and *Children of the Land.*

CHRISTINE L. FRY, Ph.D., is Professor of Anthropology at Loyola University of Chicago. She earned her doctorate in anthropology at the University of Arizona in Tucson. She has investigated the culture of retirement communities, age grading in American society, health and well-being, and comparative issues in the study of life courses. She is co-director with Jennie Keith of Project A.G.E., a comparative study of age in seven communities around the world. She is co-author of *The Aging Experience* (Sage, 1994), which was given the Kalish Award in 1995 by the Gerontological Society of America. She is also the author of numerous articles and chapters on the life course and comparative research on the meaning of age.

LINDA K. GEORGE, Ph.D., is Professor of Sociology and Associate Director of the Center for the Study of Aging and Human Development at Duke University. She is the author/editor of seven books, more than 200 journal articles, and more than 80 book chapters. She is Past President of the Gerontological Society of America and former editor of the Social Sciences section of the *Journal of Gerontology.* She is currently Chair-elect of the Aging and the Life Course Section of the American Sociological Association. She is co-editor of the *Handbook on Aging in the Social Sciences.* Her major research interests include social factors and depression; the effects of stress and coping; the relationship between religion and health; and the effects of beliefs and expectancies on health.

GUNHILD O. HAGESTAD, Ph.D, is a sociologist educated both in Norway and the United States. She is currently a Professor at Northwestern University (in the Graduate Program in Human Development and Social Policy and the Department of Sociology) and at Agder University College in Norway. Her research has focused on intergenerational relations and life-course patterns in aging societies. She delivered the keynote address for the United Nations' International Year of Older Persons and served on a panel of experts who developed a research agenda in connection with the International Year of Older Persons. She also prepared a background paper for the Gender and Generation Programme of the United Nations' Economic Commission for Europe. Her current projects include a book on *Gender, Social Policy and the Life Course* (with Deborah Puntenney) and a monograph on time and illness.

JON HENDRICKS, Ph.D., is Dean, University Honors College, and Professor of Sociology, Oregon State University. Hendricks is a past-president of the Association for Gerontology in Higher Education and has served as chair of both the Sociology of Aging and the Life Course section, American Sociological Association, and Behavioral and Social Sciences, Gerontological Society of America. He has received the Distinguished Career Contribution Award as well as the Kalish Innovative Publication Award from the latter. Hendricks is author or editor of a dozen books, series editor for *Society and Aging* series, Baywood Publishing Co., and has published extensively in gerontology. He is Co-Editor-in-Chief of the *Hallym International Journal of Aging* and has served on the editorial boards of various gerontological journals.

JOHN C. HENRETTA, Ph.D., is Professor of Sociology at the University of Florida. His research focuses on retirement, life course institutionalization, intra-family transfers, and comparative family structure. With Angela O'Rand, he recently co-authored *Age and Inequality: Diverse Pathways Through Later Life* (Westview, 1999).

MONICA KIRKPATRICK JOHNSON, Ph.D., recently completed her graduate studies at the University of Minnesota and currently holds a postdoctoral research position through the Carolina Population Center at the University of North Carolina at Chapel Hill. Johnson's research interests include family and work, social stratification, and personal norms and values. She is particularly interested in the social psychological antecedents and consequences of work experiences, family formation processes, and adult attainment. Her recent work has focused on change in job values during the transition to adulthood, and she is currently collaborating with Glen Elder on the role of economic stress in the formation of adolescents' values.

BOAZ KAHANA, Ph.D., is Professor of Psychology at Cleveland State University. He received his Ph.D. from the University of Chicago in Human Development and Psychology. Kahana is a Fellow of the Gerontological Society of America (GSA), the American Psychological Society, and the American Orthopsychiatric Association. He is co-principal investigator of several NIA studies of retirees who have relocated to Florida. Kahana is author of numerous articles and chapters dealing with stress, coping, adaptation of the elderly, and late-life sequelae of extreme trauma.

EVA KAHANA, Ph.D., is Robson Professor of Humanities, Chair of the Sociology Department, and Director of the Elderly Care Research Center at Case Western Reserve University. She earned her doctorate in Human Development from the University of Chicago. She has received extensive scholarly recognition, including the Distinguished Mentorship Award of the Gerontological Society of America (GSA), the Polisher Award of the GSA, and the Distinguished Scholar

Award of the Section on Aging and the Life Course of the American Sociological Association (ASA). She is currently Chair of the ASA Section on Aging and the Life Course. She has published extensively in the area of stress, coping, and aging.

RICHARD A. SETTERSTEN, JR., Ph.D., is Associate Professor of Sociology at Case Western Reserve University, where he is also Co-Director of the Schubert Center for Child Development and a Faculty Associate of the University Center on Aging and Health. Settersten received his Ph.D. in Human Development and Social Policy from Northwestern University. Before moving to CWRU, he held fellowships at the Institute for Policy Research at Northwestern University and the Max Planck Institute for Human Development and Education in Berlin, Germany. His research relates to the ways in which the life course is conditioned by age, time, and social contexts. He is author of *Lives in Time and Place: The Problems and Promises of Developmental Science* (Baywood, 1999).

Author Index

Subject Index

Accelerated life course, 67
Accentuation dynamic, 64
Activities of daily living (ADLs), 171, 172
Acute stressors, 167
Adolescence and the principle of timing, 67–68
Africa, 260
African Americans, 67, 109, 111, 208, 210, 238
Age-classed life courses, 284–285
Age in the life course, the salience of
  cohort effects contrasted with age effects, 20
  cultural construct, the life course as a, 276–283
  diffuse status characteristic, age as a, 20
  expectations and goals, age-related, 19–20
  family, the, 19, 22, 144–145
  mental maps, age-linked, 19
  processes and mechanisms underlying age-related effects, 20
  social policy, 212–213
  status as an institution, age, 299–304
  stratified, the life course as age, 20–22
  variability in life-course experiences, 56
  work and retirement, 88–89
  See also Ameliorative and the scientific, interplay of the; Life-course concepts/principles/methods; *individual subject headings*
Ageism, 33–34

Agency, models of, 30–31, 60–62, 72, 123
"Age Status and Generational Phenomena" (Cain), 306
Age/time in status change, 277–278, 281, 291–292
Aggregated approach, 171, 172
Aging and Leisure (Kleemeier), 112
"Aging and the Law" (Cain), 313
Agoras, families as, 141–143
Agriculture, United States Department of (USDA), 203
AIDS (acquired immune deficiency syndrome), 174
Aleatory change template, 19
Alpha generation, 136
Amazonian Shamans, 265–266
Ameliorative and the scientific, interplay of the
  age status as an institution, 299–304
  backward counting from projected death, 312–317
  cohort and generation, differences between, 309–310
  equal and equitable treatment of the elderly, 311–312
  family, the, 317–320
  future: notes on opportunities and challenges, 320–324
  generational phenomena and cohort analysis, 304–310
  imagination, sociological, 297–298
  law, aging and the, 310–317
  overview, 8–9, 295–299
  static and the dynamic, the, 304–306

SPECIAL RESEARCH
METHODS FOR GERONTOLOGY
*edited by M. Powell Lawton
and A. Regula Herzog*

DEFINING ACTS
Aging as Drama
by Robert Kastenbaum

DORIAN GRAYING
Is Youth the Only Thing Worth Having?
by Robert Kastenbaum

THE OLD AGE CHALLENGE TO THE
BIOMEDICAL MODEL
Paradigm Strain and Health Policy
by Charles F. Longino, Jr., and John W. Murphy

SURVIVING DEPENDENCE
Voices of African American Elders
by Mary M. Ball and Frank J. Whittington

STAYING PUT
Adapting the Places Instead of the People
edited by Susan C. Lanspery and Joan Hyde

RURAL HEALTH AND AGING RESEARCH
Theory, Methods and Practical Applications
*edited by Wilbert M. Gesler,
Donna J. Rabiner, and Gordon H. DeFriese*

OLDER ADULTS WITH
DEVELOPMENTAL DISABILITIES
by Claire M. Lavin and Kenneth J. Doka